THE
HISTORICAL ATLAS
OF
NORTH
AMERICAN
RAILROADS

A CARTOGRAPHICA PRESS BOOK

This edition published in 2007 by
Chartwell Books, Inc.
A division of Book Sales, Inc.
114 Northfield Avenue
Edison, New Jersey 08837
USA

ISBN-13: 978-0-7858-2301-8
ISBN-10: 0-7858-2301-8

QUMHAO7

This book is produced by
Cartographica Press
6 Blundell Street
London N7 9BH

Managing Editor: Richard Wiles
Editor: Ian Penberthy
Designer: Mik Gates

Cartography:
Malcolm Swanston
Jeanne Radford
Jonathan Young

Printed in Singapore by
Star Standard Industries Pte Ltd.

The Historical Atlas

of

North American Railroads

JOHN WESTWOOD
AND
IAN WOOD

CHARTWELL
BOOKS, INC.

CONTENTS

Contents

Map List

INTRODUCTION

"LET THE COUNTRY BUT MAKE THE RAILWAYS, AND THE RAILWAYS WILL MAKE THE COUNTRY."

Across wide rivers, over the rolling Great Plains, and through jagged mountain ranges, the "tea-kettle" locomotives of the early railroads opened up the lands of the United States, helping to build a mighty nation.

Those words referred to the first public railroad. It may have been built in Britain, but it is difficult to think of any country that would benefit more from its railroads than the United States of America. The 50 years following the end of the Civil War in 1865 saw a nationwide transformation made possible by the railroads. Before the railroad, America's economic growth was limited to the slow pace of canals and other water transport for freight; horses and coaches for passengers and mail. The coming of the faster, more reliable trains was one of the most important factors that helped to create a modern industrialized nation.

Canal companies laid the first tracks, and early passenger trains used stage-coach-type bodies on railroad wheels and locomotives imported from Britain. But it soon became clear that British construction methods were too expensive and unsuited to the needs of a vast, rapidly developing country. The all-American railroads that followed were laid cheaply and quickly, while locomotives were manufactured locally to suit specific requirements. Railroads spread rapidly, opening up a host of new opportunities for the development of abundant natural resources. Many more tracks, both great and small, were laid to carry passengers and freight to previously undeveloped territories. Locomotives developed along well-defined lines, increasing in size and power while retaining the characteristics of earlier years—simplicity, reliability, and ease of maintenance. Passenger amenities improved, and safety features such as continuous automatic brakes were introduced and perfected.

By the early part of the 20th century, the railroad network had reached its maximum length, bringing a large part of the country within easy reach of a station. Locomotives had grown in size, weight, and sophistication, allowing increased train speeds and train weights—particularly freight. Locomotive and car builders were not only able to satisfy the needs of the United States, but were also healthy exporters.

Technology was keeping pace. The abundant coal in the eastern part of the United States, lumber, and the large natural deposits of oil had all been staple fuels for steam locomotives. But the mighty steam locomotive had reached its zenith. The increasing reliability of oil-fueled diesel engines, and their ability to run vast distances without attention soon saw their rapid introduction— even to the detriment of electrified lines, the other form of modernization instaled where traffic density made it viable. Meanwhile, other forms of transport were developing rapidly, particularly air

CSX Transportation is one of the two Class I railroads in the United States that serve most of the East Coast. Formed in 1986, and owned by the CSX Corporation, it is the product of mergers of some of the oldest railroad companies in the US, including the Baltimore & Ohio, the Chesapeake & Ohio, and the Seaboard Air Line.

travel, which became economic when it offered faster journeys between large centers of population.

The availability of the automobile had already reduced the pressure on commuting, and modern roads were being built at a fast pace. Rail travel became less popular until the war in Europe and the Far East found railroads hard-pressed to keep up with the nation's new mobility. It was a temporary respite. Postwar, many formerly profitable railroads had to retract their operation, shed some traffic, and combine with others to survive. The light construction of the original lines cost the companies dearly later, as practically every main line built had to be expensively rebuilt.

But America's railroads and the industry that supported them had served the country well. Today's railroads still have their place, and environmental pressures may yet see a change back to a new form of modern train travel.

Amtrak was created in the early 1970s to relieve the nation's railroads of the responsibility of running loss making passenger services. It operates services throughout the country.

Birth of a Nation

THE STEAM RAILROAD WAS A BRITISH INVENTION, BUT IT WAS THE FORMER AMERICAN COLONIES' REBELLION AGAINST BRITISH RULE—AND THEIR NEED TO UNITE A YOUNG NATION ACROSS EVER-GROWING DISTANCES—THAT WOULD PROVIDE THE INCENTIVE FOR RAPID EXPANSION OF THE COUNTRY'S TRANSPORT NETWORK.

The earliest explorers arrived by sea, and they—and the first settlers that followed—clung to the coasts, where they established forts and trading posts. But by the first half of the 18th century, colonial settlers had pushed inland from all sides, dividing North America along national lines. Spain controlled Mexico, Central America, and Florida, as well as most of South America. Russian colonists had edged into Alaska and the western seaboard of Canada. New France and other French settlements extended throughout eastern Canada and on down to Louisiana, with a large area of the surrounding land coming under French influence.

The British were relatively late arrivals, but between 1607 and 1732, British immigrants had founded what became known as the Thirteen Colonies running from New Hampshire down to Georgia—many of those in the South and East being dependent on slave labor. Together, the British colonies controlled much of the Atlantic coast east of the Appalachians—a natural barrier to east-west travel—and disputed an even larger area with the French. The Hudson Bay Company had also spread British settlements and control across a wide area of central Canada.

The center of the continent, the Great Plains and the Rockies, was largely unexplored. Numerous wars

The Pilgrims meet Samoset, leader of the Wampanoag people, in 1620. The Europeans' settlement near Plymouth later became part of the Province of Massachusetts Bay—one of Britain's Thirteen Colonies east of the Appalachians.

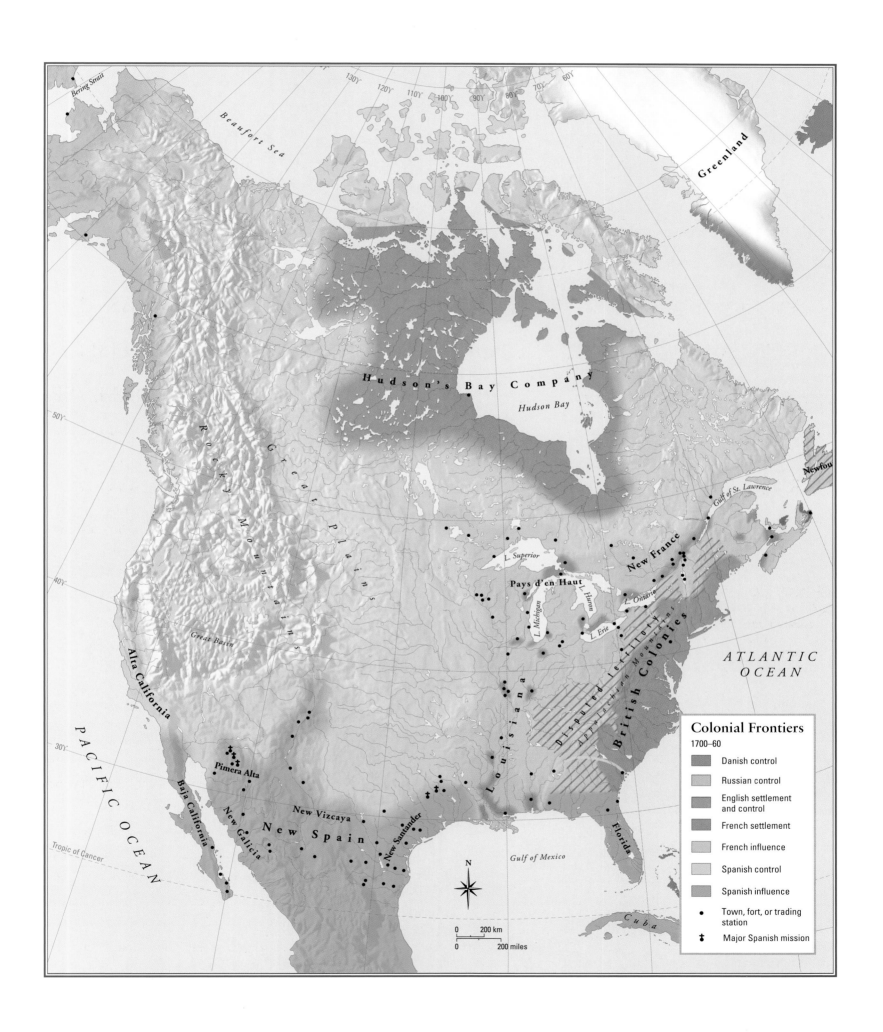

Bering Strait

Beaufort Sea

130°Y 120°Y 110°Y 100°Y 90°Y 80°Y 70°Y 60°Y

Greenland

50°Y

Hudson's Bay Company

Hudson Bay

Rocky Mountains

Great Plains

40°Y

L. Superior

New France

Pays d'en Haut

L. Huron

L. Michigan

L. Ontario

L. Erie

Newfou

Gulf of St. Lawrence

Great Basin

Appalachian Mountains

Disputed territory

British Colonies

ATLANTIC
OCEAN

Alta California

30°Y

PACIFIC
OCEAN

Baja California

Pimera Alta

New Vizcaya

New Galicia

New Spain

New Santander

Louisiana

Florida

Tropic of Cancer

Gulf of Mexico

N

Cuba

0   200 km
0   200 miles

Colonial Frontiers

1700–60

Danish control

Russian control

English settlement
and control

French settlement

French influence

Spanish control

Spanish influence

•   Town, fort, or trading
station

✝   Major Spanish mission

between the colonial powers and the Native Americans (who were also decimated by the introduction of European diseases) led to unsettled territorial boundaries between the colonists and the nomadic tribes who roamed the heart of the continent in pursuit of the buffalo and other game. The reintroduction of the horse into the south of the continent by early Spanish settlers, and the extra speed and mobility it brought, had a profound impact on the lives of the Native Americans. During the 1600s and early 1700s, the northward and eastward spread of the horse allowed the tribes to expand their territories greatly. By 1600, horses that had escaped captivity and bred in the wild had reached New Mexico and the territory of the Eastern Apache. By the end of the century, the use of horses had spread east and south through Texas, and north to the Cheyenne and Arapaho of Colorado. By 1720, riders were ranging right across Oklahoma, Nebraska, and South Dakota, and along the Missouri River. Spreading up through Montana and North Dakota, the more northerly ranges of the buffalo, the horse was in use in southern Canada by the middle of the century.

After the Thirteen Colonies declared their independence from Great Britain in 1776, the United States of America came into being. Naval superiority gave the British control of the sea and easy victories over coastal towns, but the difficulty of travel inland, where most of the population lived spread across a wide area, made control of the country impossible. This was in spite of the aid that the British frequently received from some of the Native American nations east of the Mississippi, who preferred the British policy of maintaining peace to the expansionism of the colonies.

Britain finally conceded victory to the Americans and their allies, France, Spain, and the

Below: The American buffalo, or bison, shaped the ecology of the Great Plains' grassland; its meat and pelt were central to the lives of the Native Americans of the region. The speed and mobility provided by the horse made it easier to follow the herds and improved the efficiency of the hunt.

In the 1870s and 1880s, following the westward expansion of the United States, the buffalo were hunted almost to extinction. The government subsidized hunt was intimately connected to the arrival of the railroad in the regions where they roamed.

Range of the Buffalo

- Maximum extent, c. 1600
- Extent in 1825
- Extent in 1870
- Surviving small herds, c. 1889, with number of animals

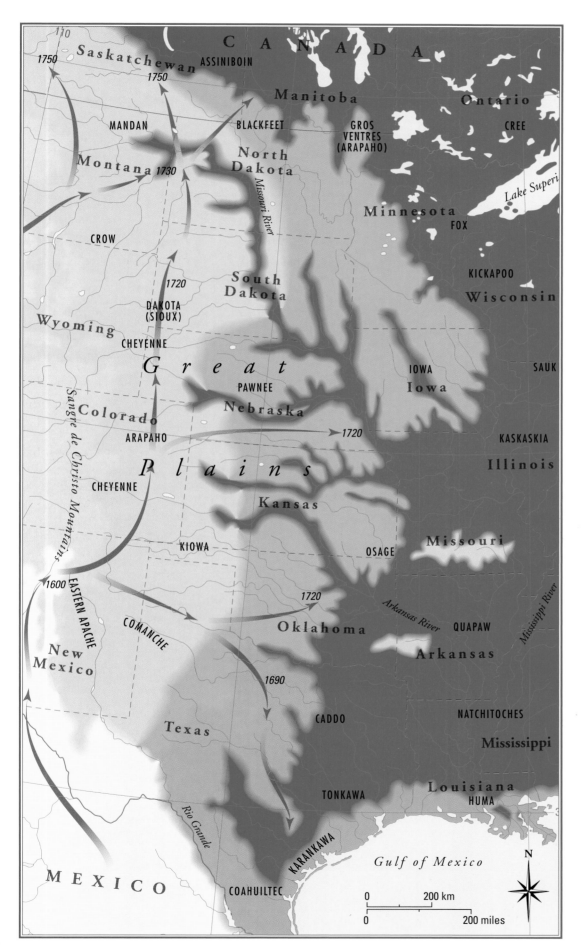

The horse was hunted to extinction in prehistoric times, but was reintroduced to the North American continent by the Spanish. From around 1600, those horses that escaped into the wild were captured and ridden by the Native Americans. The use of the horse gradually spread north and east across the Great Plains.

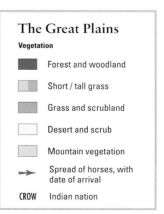

The Great Plains

Vegetation

Forest and woodland

Short / tall grass

Grass and scrubland

Desert and scrub

Mountain vegetation

Spread of horses, with date of arrival

CROW   Indian nation

Netherlands. In 1783, the Treaty of Paris formally ended the war and recognized the sovereignty of the United States over the territory bounded by the Mississippi River to the west, Florida in the south, and Canada to the north. In effect, the British had ceded a large amount of land that was occupied by their one-time allies among the Native American tribes. As the United States established its new republic, it faced the difficult challenge of incorporating a vast expanse of new land into the Union. The Articles of Confederation, adopted in 1781 as the country's first constitution, are often considered a failure. However, as well as settling land disputes with the Native Americans, they also established a far-reaching policy for the settlement and incorporation of western territory.

The horse transformed the lives of many Native Americans, turning them into nomadic people and allowing them to follow the buffalo on their seasonal migrations.

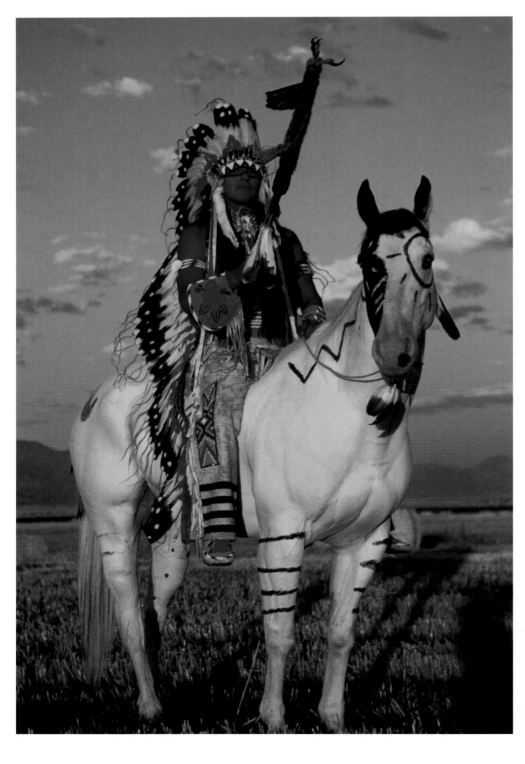

After providing for a survey of the land west of the Appalachians, between the Ohio River, Mississippi River, and the Great Lakes, known as the "Northwest Territory", Congress passed the Northwest Ordinance of 1787. This is often said to be the single most important piece of legislation under the Articles of Confederation. The Ordinance guaranteed that settlers in the new territories would be treated as equal citizens of the United States and enjoy all the rights of citizenship. This effectively was the legal basis that led to development of the Midwest, and settlers began pouring into the area.

Immediately after the war, the government claimed that, in conquering the British, it had also conquered the Native Americans, many of whom had allied themselves with the British. As compensation, the United States demanded land from the Indian tribes. However, many Native Americans in Ohio refused to recognize the validity of the treaties that ceded parts of the Northwest Territory, and the Northwest Ordinance itself acknowledged their rights to property and liberty. However, land grabs continued across the Great Plains as civilization spread west— and in the South, as more land was needed for cotton. Defeat for the Native Americans at the Battle of Fallen Timbers in 1794 led to the Treaty of Greenville, which granted Ohio and parts of Indiana to the United States.

Arctic Ocean

The South 1778–81
→ Galvez movements with dates

CHOCTAWS

Savannah

Fort Panmure (Natchez)

WEST FLORIDA

CREEKS

GEORGIA

Mississippi River

Alabama River

Chattahoochee River

St. Marys River

Baton Rouge
Fort Bute (Manchar)
Mobile
Fort Charlotte
Pensacola

St. Marks

SEMINOLES

Galvez 1779

New Orleans

Galvez 1779

Galvez from Havana 1781

St. Augustus

EAST FLORIDA

N

0   50 km
0   50 miles

RUSSIAN EMPIRE

Bering Strait

Alaska

Northwest Territories

Vancouver Island

Hudson Bay

Arctic Circle

Greenland
to Denmark

Rupert's Land
(Hudson Bay Company)

Newfoundland

New

Louisiana

Québec
Montréal
York
Detroit
Fort St Joseph

Nova Scotia

San Francisco

St. Louis

Boston
New York
Philadelphia

New Madrid
Louisville

THIRTEEN COLONIES

Los Angeles
San Diego

Santa Fe

Williamsburg

Tucson

Nashville

New Bern

ATLANTIC OCEAN

El Paso

Charleston

PACIFIC OCEAN

Nacogdoches

Savannah

Pensacola
New Orleans

St. Augustine

see inset above

S p a i n

Monterey

Gulf of Mexico

Bahama Islands

N

Tropic of Cancer

Léon
Guadalajara

Havana

Cuba

North America c. 1780

British territory

Spanish territory

Disputed Spain–Great Britain

Russian Empire

French possesions

Spanish attacks

Mexico City

Veracruz

Puerto Rico

British Honduras

Jamaica

Saint Domingue

Santo Domingo

0   400 km
0   400 miles

Mosquito Coast

OPENING THE TRADE ROUTES

FOR EARLY PIONEERS VENTURING ALONG RIVERS OR OVERLAND
TRAILS, JOURNEYS COULD BE MEASURED IN DAYS OR EVEN WEEKS.
DESPITE DIFFICULTIES, A STREAM OF EMIGRANTS AND GOODS
MOVED WESTWARD, WHILE RAW MATERIALS AND AGRICULTURAL
PRODUCE WERE SENT BACK TO MARKET IN THE EAST.

Daniel Boone was one of many
trappers and mountain men
who roamed throughout the
unsettled parts of the United
States, blazing trails that in later
years would be followed by the
great wagon trains of migrants
and, later still, the railroads.

By 1800, the spreading frontiers of the United States were still a long way from the Eastern Seaboard, in terms of both distance and journey time. The cities of the East were the main markets for the abundant agricultural produce and raw materials that lay inland, but transporting the goods to them was a considerable problem. To understand the vital role that the railroads eventually played in opening up the movement of people and goods, it is instructive to appreciate how they were transported before the arrival of the "iron horse".

For anything heavier than a man could physically carry or haul, the first American settlers employed draft animals—mules, oxen, and horses. Small farm carts used for local transport were an important part of any rural economy, but around 1720, the distinctive Conestoga wagon first appeared, taking its name from the region where it was introduced by German settlers. A heavy freight carrier with broad wheels and hauled by as many as eight draft animals, a Conestoga wagon was much larger than the "covered wagons" used by later settlers on the Oregon Trail to the new territories in the West. Long and rugged enough to carry a load of around 8 tons, the Conestogas often formed part of lengthy wagon trains. These slow-moving trains provided a vital link in the economies of the Thirteen Colonies and, after the American Revolution, were used to open up routes for inland commerce with Ohio.

There were few long-distance paved roads in the country. The first,

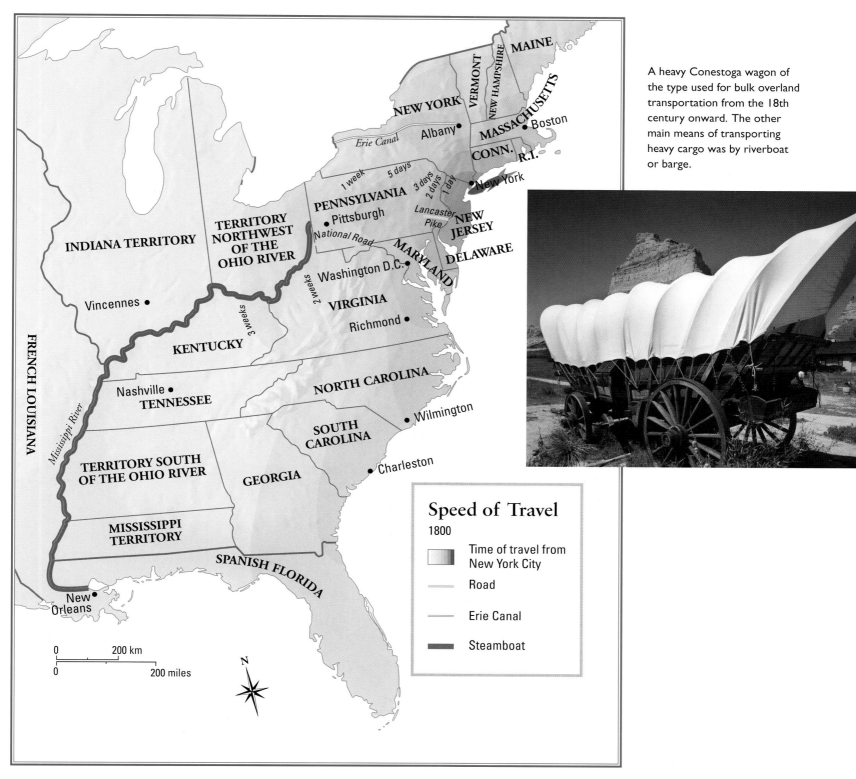

A heavy Conestoga wagon of the type used for bulk overland transportation from the 18th century onward. The other main means of transporting heavy cargo was by riverboat or barge.

Speed of Travel

1800

Time of travel from New York City

——— Road

——— Erie Canal

━━━ Steamboat

the Lancaster Pike, built privately during 1792–5, ran for some 60 miles (97km) between Lancaster and Philadelphia. The National Road, otherwise known as the Cumberland Road, was a government construction begun in 1811, providing an important overland route between the Potomac and the Ohio Rivers. It was gradually extended to 620 miles (998km), finally linking Baltimore, Maryland, to Vandalia, Missouri, in 1839. It had been intended to go all the way through to the Missouri and Mississippi, but funds ran out.

The most heavily traveled route led southwest through the Great Appalachian Valley, stretching

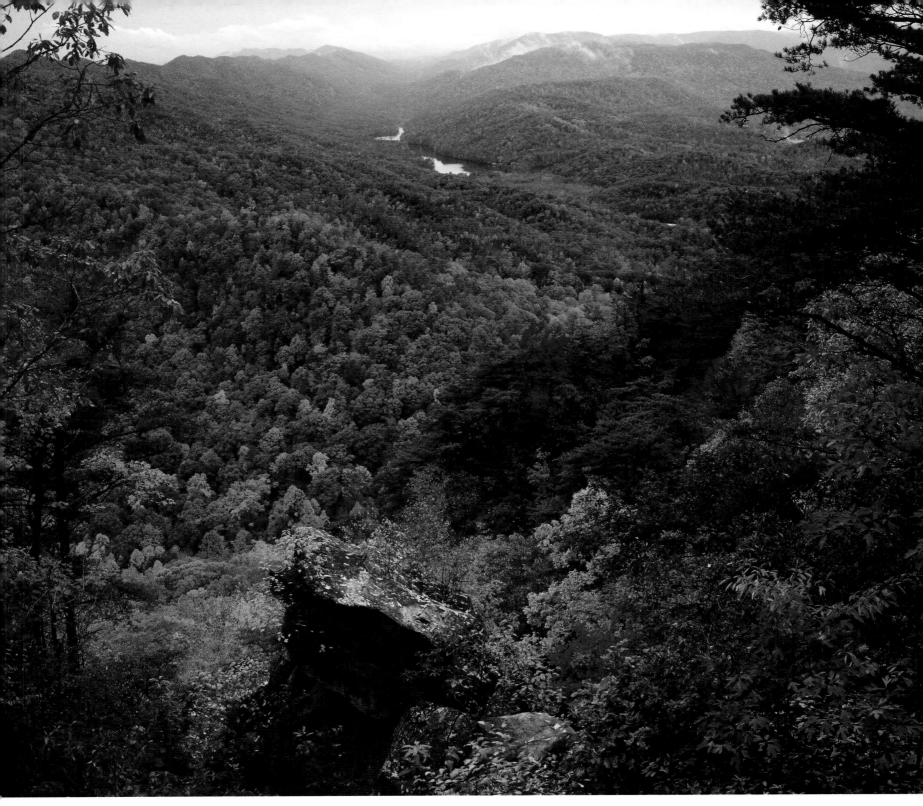

The Cumberland Gap in the Blue Ridge Mountains. The old Wilderness Road ran through here on its way to Tennessee and Kentucky, following a route pioneered by Daniel Boone.

some 700 miles (1,127km) from Canada to Alabama, which had been an important part of north–south communications since the first Native Americans settled in the area. The Great Wagon Road ran from Philadelphia to Augusta, Georgia. The route went inland through Lancaster and York, crossing the Blue Ridge Mountains to Cumberland Valley, over the Potomac, and down the Shenandoah Valley to Roanoke, Virginia. From there, a section also called the Carolina Road led past Winston-Salem, Salisbury, and Charlotte, to Augusta.

A branch at Roanoke led on to Tennessee and Kentucky, taking the Wilderness Road along the trail blazed through the Cumberland Gap by Daniel Boone in 1775. Despite the constant danger of attack by tribes of Native Americans, a flood of pioneers had established numerous frontier settlements, and the route became an important drover's way over which hogs and cattle were driven to market in the East. In the 1790s, the Governor of Kentucky commissioned a road to be laid over what had previously been a steep, rocky trail only passable on foot or horseback.

Wagon trains were slow, covering only around 15 miles (24km) a day, and were relatively expensive. Much of the earliest bulk transportation network in the country relied on the navigation of natural waterways, especially the great rivers that ran through the center of the continent—the Mississippi, the Missouri, and, first of all, the Ohio. The westward flow of the Ohio River meant that it was the most convenient route to take from western Pennsylvania. Upon reaching the junction of the Ohio and the Mississippi rivers, the pioneers would travel north on the Mississippi to St. Louis, from where they could continue on up the Mississippi, and join the Missouri or alternatively follow a land route to the West.

Most traders would head south on the Mississippi. The mountain ranges to the east and west ensured that the great river's only outlet to the oceans was where the Mississippi led to the port of New Orleans. From there, the traders were able to take larger boats to sail beyond the mouth of the river, on to the Gulf of Mexico, and to other ports in the Americas and Europe. This was an important route for the export of goods from the center of the continent, since the overland route east over the Appalachian Mountains was extremely difficult and dangerous. One of the main reasons for the Louisiana Purchase of territory from France in 1803 was the need of the settlers in the Ohio valley to ensure secure access to New Orleans.

With the Louisiana Purchase of 1803, under President Jefferson, the United States acquired some 828,000 square miles (2,144,520sq km) of territory from France. This is equivalent to almost one quarter of the modern United States. Part of the reason for the Purchase was the government's desire to secure New Orleans and the Mississippi, an important route for shipping goods to and from the new states west of the Appalachians.

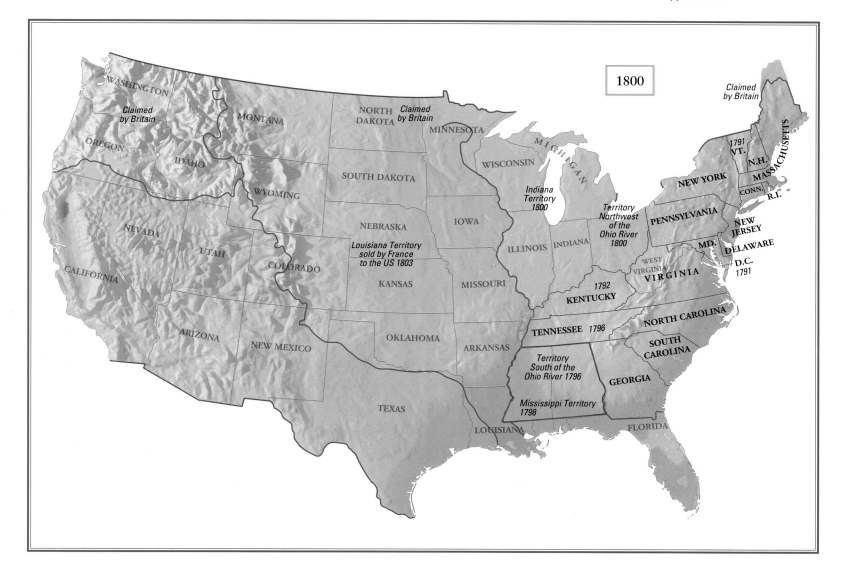

By Water to the West

Linking the inland waterways to the east was a great challenge. Driving the Erie Canal across hundreds of miles of tough terrain revolutionized bulk transportation and the fortunes of New York. America was ready for civil engineering on a huge scale.

Thomas Jefferson, who, like his presidential predecessor, George Washington, understood the importance of the river network. Both men wanted to build a canal that would develop the Potomac into a navigable route to the West.

The importance of water transport was taken for granted by Benjamin Franklin when he wrote of "the vast convenience of inland navigation or water-carriage by the lakes and great rivers, many hundred of leagues around" and noted the importance of ensuring the protection of trade routes "by means of the lakes, the Ohio, and the Mississippi." Thomas Jefferson, writing his *Notes on the State of Virginia* (1785) imagined the Mississippi becoming "one of the principal channels of future commerce" west of the Alleghenies. However, until the early 19th century, traffic to the east still relied on wagon trails or a long sea voyage from New Orleans.

Two natural waterways running into the Atlantic, the Hudson and the Potomac, both offered routes by which the wealth of the interior could flow to the sea, although waterfalls and treacherous rapids formed barriers to the free movement of water transport, and neither river linked up with the great rivers in the center of the continent. Solutions to these problems were proposed by George Washington, whose experience gained during his early work as a surveyor led to him favoring the Potomac River through his home state of Virginia. He championed the construction of a canal system to bypass the falls, together with the use of steamboats to accelerate upstream navigation, and sank a lot of his own money in the venture until his death in 1799.

Jefferson also favored developing the Potomac, pointing out that the Hudson froze over in winter and that its outlet at New York City was farther from the traffic that flowed along the Ohio and Mississippi rivers than the Potomac's outlet at Alexandria.

Keelboats (background) and flatboats (foreground) were the early solution to transporting cargo on the inland waterways. These craft were pictured on the Ohio River near Pittsburgh in the late 18th century. Moving a laden keelboat upriver was hard and slow work.

He also thought that the number of locks required for lifting boats up and down over the 600ft (183m) rise that lay between Albany on the Hudson and Lake Erie made it impossibly uneconomic.

In spite of the merits of Washington and Jefferson's case—which ensured that the Potomac route was eventually developed—it was the opening of the Erie Canal in 1819, and its completion in 1825, that ensured the future of the Hudson, and New York, as the primary shipping route. The Erie Canal, and the other feeder canals that soon followed to link it to the lumber forests and coal mines, would

The North River Steamboat (sometimes known as the *Clermont*) of Robert Fulton, a pioneer of steam power. From 1807, this began a successful, regular passenger service on the Hudson River between New York City and Albany. It was the first commercial steamboat service in the world. Steamboats began operations along the length of the Mississippi five years later, slashing journey times from four months to a little over a month. This was gradually reduced to well under a week.

The 363-mile course of the Erie Canal, running westward from Albany. This survey map of 1858 shows later feeder canals branching out to the side of the main watercourse.

have a profound effect on the development of the eastern cities and of the railroad network. Canal traffic boosted the importance and wealth of New York City and State, and increased the markets for the farmers of the Midwest. It encouraged the western migration of immigrants and made boom towns out of such places as Syracuse, Rochester, and Schenectady, which lay along the route. It also took trade from other eastern ports such as Philadelphia, Pennsylvania, and Baltimore, Maryland.

The natural result was that many early railroads linked canal towns, providing passengers with a faster alternative to the leisurely water traffic. Canal traffic was limited to around walking pace, partly by the speed of draft animals, partly because anything faster created a wash that risked eroding the clay bottom, undercutting the banks, and causing the channel to silt up. The building of railroads on other routes was encouraged by the cities and towns that had lost trade to the Erie Canal, and now wanted to be able to offer a transport network of their own.

This elevation shows the scale of the project. A complex network of locks was needed to handle the drop of 600ft (183m) between Albany and Lake Erie.

Building the Erie Canal had another benefit for any railroad entrepreneur. At 363 miles (584km) long, with 83 locks, its construction had shown that Jefferson had been wrong about the logistics. By cutting transport costs between the Eastern Seaboard and the wilderness of the western interior to around five percent of what they had been, it also made economic sense. The plan had been to carry 1.5 million tons of freight a year, but this was immediately exceeded.

A great deal was learned during the construction, on which the first civil engineers in the country were forced to learn their trade the hard way. All the work was carried out by manual laborers, and the first 15-mile (24km) stretch took two years to build, suggesting it would take half a century to finish the job. But solutions were found to the main problems of clearing the trees and shifting the dirt. Stump pullers were designed and built, and mule carts were brought in to haul away the spoil. The rate of progress increased enormously and more workers were brought in.

To follow the route chosen, the designers had to construct embankments and carve or blast cuttings through solid rock. They had to build an enormous aqueduct and cross the swamps of Montezuma Marsh. This proved one of the most difficult sections, with many workers succumbing to the swamp fevers carried by the mosquitoes. The cut was finally completed in winter when the insects were dormant, but the ground froze hard. Similar problems would face anyone trying to build a railroad over any significant distance.

Five locks cut through hard rock carried the Erie Canal up the 80ft (24m) Niagara Escarpment. Now without gates and used as a runoff for excess water, the structure shows the scale of the engineering work.

SURVEYING THE WEST, 1804-6

AN EXPEDITION COMMISSIONED BY PRESIDENT JEFFERSON SENT
THE EXPLORERS LEWIS AND CLARK TO CHART THE TERRAIN
OF THE NORTHWEST, SEARCHING FOR A RIVER ROUTE TO THE
PACIFIC, WHILE AND GATHERING INFORMATION ON THE PLANT
LIFE, GEOLOGY AND INDIGENOUS PEOPLES OF THE REGION.

Lewis and Clark on the Lower Columbia, a painting by C.M. Russell, which depicts the type of Native American craft that the expedition used to navigate the rivers they followed for much of the journey.

The first European to cross North America farther north than Mexico was Alexander MacKenzie, whose expedition crossed Canada to the Pacific in 1792–3. But it was the United States' Lewis and Clark Expedition of 1804-06 that first properly explored the overland route to America's Pacific Northwest, and bringing a new understanding of the geography of the Rocky Mountains, and the sources of the Missouri and Columbia rivers.

The driving force behind the expedition was President Jefferson, who, mindful of the important role that rivers played in commercial transportation, expressed his view that the government needed a better understanding of the upper reaches of the Missouri and the land beyond it. In 1803, claiming that a small expedition led by intelligent officers could easily undertake the work, Jefferson had Congress appropriate the funds and chose his capable private secretary, Captain Meriwether Lewis, to lead a search for the most direct route across the country by river.

The Louisiana Purchase, earlier the same year, had increased interest in western expansion of the

United States into the region that had nominally been under French control. It was politically sensitive, particularly because of opposition from the Spanish, who wanted a clear divide between their interests in what was then northern Mexico and the territory controlled by the United States.

For this reason, Jefferson instructed Lewis to cross in more northerly latitudes and avoid the Spanish region. As well as mapping the terrain and looking for an all-water route to the Pacific, Jefferson's brief to Lewis included instructions to study the plant life and geology. He was also charged with making an assessment of the human population the party encountered, whether they were Native Americans, or some of the British or French Canadian fur trappers in the area.

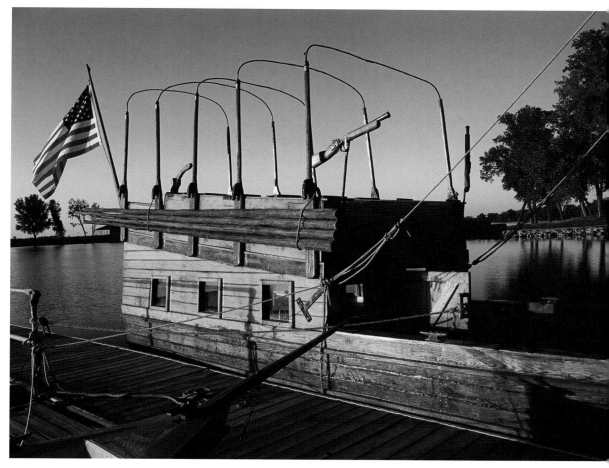

Lewis and Clark left St. Louis in the spring of 1804 in a long keelboat, such as this modern full-scale replica, now kept on Blue Lake at the Lewis & Clark State Park. When the way became less navigable, the explorers eventually had to abandon the boat in favor of more maneuverable canoes.

Lewis appointed his friend, William Clark, of the U.S. Army as his partner in the expedition, to be known as the Corps of Discovery. There were 33 in the group led by Clark who made preparations over the winter of 1803–4 at Camp Dubois in Illinois, finally setting out on May 14. Lewis joined them at St. Charles, Missouri, from where they followed the Missouri upriver to the west through Missouri, Nebraska, and Iowa. They reached the edge of the Great Plains and Sioux territory in late August. A skirmish with the Tetron Sioux was narrowly avoided, and they continued until they had reached what is now Washburn, North Dakota, at the onset of winter. There, they built Fort Mandan, named after the local tribe.

Next spring, some of the party returned to take back specimens and report to President Jefferson, while the rest of the expedition continued to the source of the Missouri. From there, they went overland, across the Continental Divide, descending into Oregon using canoes to follow the Clearwater River, Snake River, and Columbia River. As winter closed in for the second time, they built a new base, Fort Clatsop, at the mouth of the Columbia River, near present-day Astoria.

Lewis and Clark set out homeward on March 23, 1806, separating after crossing the Continental Divide so that Lewis could follow the Marias River. After reuniting where the Yellowstone and Missouri rivers met, they returned downstream on the Missouri, reaching St. Louis on September 23. They had achieved much, identifying hundreds of new species and opening up trade and diplomatic relationships across the West, as well as strengthening the United States' claim to the Oregon Territory. The map of their track across the Western Portion of America from the Mississippi to the Pacific Ocean had brought the first understanding of the terrain that transcontinental transport would have to cross.

The map of the expedition, which provided the first accurate information on the sources of the Mississippi and Columbia rivers and the path over the Rockies into Oregon.

The distinctive Haystack Rock and attendant seastacks, located off Cannon Beach, was at the terminus of Lewis & Clark's expedition across Oregon.

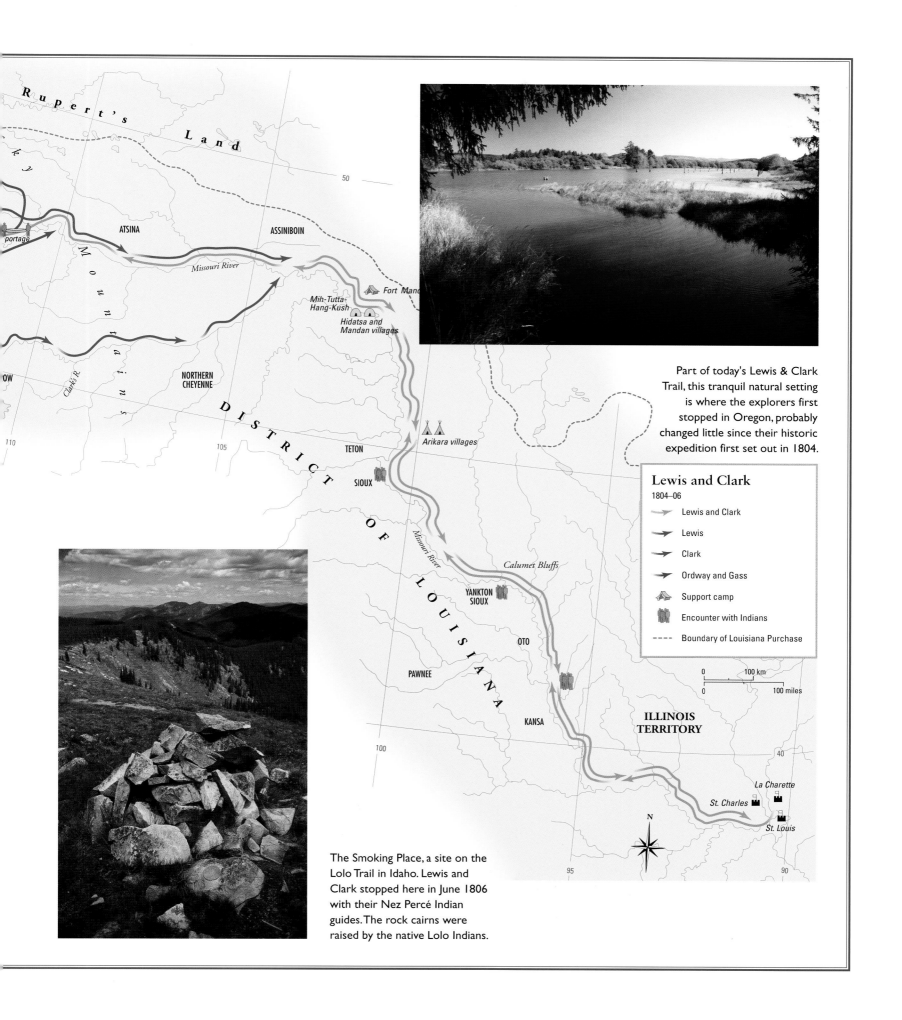

Part of today's Lewis & Clark Trail, this tranquil natural setting is where the explorers first stopped in Oregon, probably changed little since their historic expedition first set out in 1804.

Lewis and Clark

1804–06

→ Lewis and Clark

→ Lewis

→ Clark

→ Ordway and Gass

⌂ Support camp

Encounter with Indians

---- Boundary of Louisiana Purchase

0 ___ 100 km
0 ___ 100 miles

The Smoking Place, a site on the Lolo Trail in Idaho. Lewis and Clark stopped here in June 1806 with their Nez Percé Indian guides. The rock cairns were raised by the native Lolo Indians.

FIRST RAILROADS, 1700-1830

THERE WERE RAILROADS IN NORTH AMERICA LONG BEFORE THERE
WERE STEAM ENGINES TO RUN ON THEM. AS IN EUROPE, WHERE
THEY WERE INVENTED, THE EARLIEST TRACKS—MAINLY MADE OF
WOOD—WERE LAID TO EASE THE PATH OF WAGONS RUNNING
FROM QUARRIES AND CONSTRUCTION PROJECTS.

Waggonways similar to this
one were used for centuries
as a means of reducing friction
and guiding loaded cars. The
first railroads in the USA were
probably of this type, or the
even simpler "gravity road,"
down which wagons rolled
under their own weight.

The origin of railroads as a means of transporting goods and minerals using vehicles with flanged wheels can be traced back to mining in the Ruhr coalfields of medieval Germany, when wooden rails were used. Toward the end of the 17th century, bulky carts were made with four "rowlets" fitting the rails, suggesting a type of flanged wheel, which made movement so easy that one horse could draw four or five bulky carts laden with coal. The author Daniel Defoe wrote of coal being loaded "into a great machine called a Waggon," and run on an artificial road called a "waggonway."

The Incline on the Granite Railway, photographed in 1934, after modernization that included adding metal guide channels and motorized cable operation.

The development of railroads as a "public" means of transportation took place in Great Britain in the 18th century, when a coalition of colliery owners linked their mines by waggonways, in some cases using a double track so that loaded and empty "trains" would not interfere with one another. Because the railroads ran from inland regions to the banks of navigable rivers, their routes were arranged on a falling grade so it would be easier for a horse to pull a loaded wagon. It was thought necessary to keep a load horizontal when descending a grade, so the leading wheels of the wagon were of larger diameter than the trailing ones. On some wagons, the leading wheels were spoked, while the trailing ones were solid wood. Flanges 1in (2.5cm) or 1.5in (4cm) deep were fixed to the inner faces of the wheels to provide a guide. Wagons had a primitive lever brake acting upon the rear pair of wheels; on tracks running down to the rivers, there was usually one horse to a wagon, and trains of wagons were not run.

On some stretches of early colliery waggonways, the loaded vehicles would run by gravity, when the horseman would transfer from front to rear, hitch a ride on the wagon, and control the speed with the handbrake while the horse trotted behind. Later, where horses pulled a train of three or more wagons, a "dandy car" was provided for the horse to ride in during the downhill gravity run.

In America and Canada, by the time the Erie Canal opened, a number of short railroads had already been built. The earliest of these were temporary trackways along which men or draft animals could haul loaded wagons, or gravity railroads. The earliest recorded "gravity road" in North America was built in 1764. It was constructed at the Niagara portage in Lewiston, New York, for military purposes by Captain John Montressor, a British engineer and cartographer.

Thomas Leiper built the first commercial trackway between Ridley Creek and Crum Creek in Pennsylvania. He used it to move stone from his quarry to the nearest navigable waterway.

The earliest record of a trackway intended to be a permanent commercial carrier is of the Leiper Railroad connecting Ridley Creek to Crum Creek in Pennsylvania. Thomas Leiper was a wealthy tobacconist, and friend of Thomas Jefferson, who owned a stone quarry near Chester. Leiper had already made successful experiments with a short length of track before he built his line in 1810, which linked his quarry with the nearest waterway. The route was laid out by the engineer John Thomson and the mapmaker Reading Howell. The railroad closed 19 years later and was replaced by the Leiper Canal until the railroad was reopened in 1852, eventually becoming the Crum Creek Branch of the Baltimore & Philadelphia Railroad. Several similar wooden railroads were built in the next decade. However, a charter granted to the New Jersey Railroad Company in 1815 for an ambitious plan to link the Delaware near Trenton to the Raritan near New Brunswick came to nothing because it failed to attract investors.

The Granite Railway, constructed in 1826 to carry stone down to a loading dock. It has the distinction of being the first commercial U.S. railroad to evolve into a common carrier without a break in operations.

Photographed in April, 1934 by Arthur C. Haskell for the Historic American Buildings Survey, this view shows ties and metal guide channels halfway up the Granite Railway Incline.

The Granite Railway
1825
- - - - County boundaries

The Leiper Railroad may claim to be the first commercial railroad in the U.S., but the first to evolve into a common carrier without an intervening closure was the Granite Railway at Quincy, Massachusetts. Construction began in April 1826 and it went into operation in October that year. In 1871, it became a branch of the Old Colony & Newport Railroad, which was later incorporated into the New York, New Haven & Hartford Railroad.

The Granite Railway was built to carry granite three miles from quarries in Quincy to a dock on the Neponset River at Milton, Massachusetts, from where it was ferried to Charlestown. An extra section called the Incline was added in 1830 to convey stone from a higher level. It fell 84ft (26m) along the 315ft (96m) of the Incline.

The president of the Granite Railway Company was businessman and state politician Thomas Handasyd Perkins, who organized its finances and its charter. The railroad's designer and architect, Gridley Bryant, modeled it on similar systems in use in Britain, but incorporated ideas of his own. Trains of three wagons were drawn by teams of horses, and were equipped with 6ft (1.8m) diameter wheels that ran on wooden rails faced with iron and laid 5ft (1.5m) apart. Bryant's innovations included railroad switches or frogs, and a turntable, which he never patented. The Incline had rails of granite, and the wagons ran on an endless conveyor.

As well as being the first commercial railroad to go into continuous operation in America, the Granite Railway also made history as the site of the first fatal railroad accident in the United States, on July

The Granite Railway provided a more efficient means of moving stone from the quarry to the dock on the Neponset River. After 50 years in use, stone began to be hauled directly to Boston and the road closed.

Above: One of Gridley Bryant's historic switch frogs, with a plate recording the date of its exhibition at the World's Fair. *Above right:* Drawing showing the working details of a frog.

25, 1832, when passengers taking a tour of the Incline were thrown off after a cable broke, resulting in one fatality and causing severe injuries to three other visitors.

The railroad operated as Bryant had designed it for almost 50 years. After it was made part of the Old Colony & Newport Railroad, wagons were drawn directly to Boston, bypassing the dock. The Incline was given metal guide channels and converted to motorized cable haulage in the early 20th century. After the branch closed, the Incline and the Granite Railway itself were added to the National Register of Historic Places in 1973—and artifacts from the original structure, including the switch frog displayed at the Chicago World's Fair in 1893, are on display at the site.

The early railroads and canals were built to haul freight, not to carry people. For the mass of the population, personal transport outside of towns meant walking, or a horse or cart. The horsedrawn buggy was not introduced until the middle of the century, and in the early 1800s, even the stagecoach, icon of the "old west" had not yet appeared. Stagecoaches or mail coaches existed for centuries in Europe, but in the U.S. the Butterfield Overland Stage service was not inaugurated until the late 1850s.

An engineering drawing showing the details of the first car used on the Granite Railway.

By 1830, the nation was ready for the railroad. The building of the Erie Canal and the Granite Railway showed that driving tracks overland would pose no insurmountable difficulty, while the abundance of passengers and freight promised rich rewards to entrepreneurs. All that was needed was the steam-engine technology already developed in England.

A replica of the first granite car used on the Granite Railway. Quarried stone was loaded on to the wooden platform slung beneath the car; the platform could be raised and lowered by means of a hand winch on top of the car.

The remains of a braking device lying abandoned by the track at the top of the Incline.

ORIGINS OF THE STREETCAR

EARLY IN THE 19TH CENTURY, INCREASING INDUSTRIALIZATION AND POPULATION GROWTH LED TO A NEED FOR IMPROVED PUBLIC TRANSPORTATION IN THE CITIES OF NORTH AMERICA. THIS NEED WAS MET FIRST BY HORSEDRAWN VEHICLES, THE FORERUNNERS OF THE MODERN-DAY STREETCAR.

The horsedrawn streetcar was descended from the street omnibus or coach. The first horsedrawn streetcars resembled steel-wheeled stagecoaches running on iron straps or tracks that were fastened to wooden strips or stone blocks fixed to the street surface. The early horsecars built by the John Stephenson Car Company, of New York City, in the 1830s and 1840s, had the driver sitting on top, overlooking the team of horses. The passengers crouched below, handing their fares up through a trap door in the ceiling, and those travelers who were slow to pay could expect to hear the driver's whip rapping sharply on the roof. The horsecar's iron wheels were smaller than the spoked, wooden wheels of the typical carriage, because smooth iron rails had less rolling resistance than the unpaved or cobblestoned streets of the day, but the lower bodies of these first horsecars still had the inswept curve built into most carriages for wheel clearance. In fact, many early streetcar bodies retained this same "ogee" body section, which allowed wagons and carts to pass by on crowded streets. The cabin above swelled outward to provide hip room.

The earliest incantation of the horsecar was little more than a wooden box mounted on wheels, which ran along wooden strips or stones set in the surface of the street.

Later horsecars began to resemble their glamorous steam-powered cousins, and they became, in effect, miniature railroad cars, with straight-sided cabins and clerestory roof designs. The driver descended to a platform in front of the passengers, where he drove the horses or mules from a standing position, and a conductor was added to collect the fares. Wheels shrank to rail-car proportions.

A late example of a horsecar in New York. Such vehicles resembled scaled-down railroad cars, with end platforms and clerestory roofs.

These design trends were not incompatible, and features were freely mixed. The overriding consideration was that the horsecars should be as light as possible, and their evolution culminated in a combination of the carriage-maker's elegance and the mechanical directness of the rail car.

With the example of the steam locomotive before them, companies operating horsecars came to realize that draft animals were really not the perfect motive power for urban transportation. They were, after all, living in the industrial age and drawing closer to the unimaginable wonders of the 20th century. A modern city had little use for thousands of manure producing animals, which could work for only four hours a day and consumed grain by the bushel basket whether they were working or not. That this system was not only archaic, but also fragile was underscored by a calamity in 1872. In that year began the "great epizootic," a virulent and lethal flu-like disease that killed thousands of horses throughout Canada and the United States, and halted horsecar services in many cities for weeks. Almost 20,000 horses sickened in New York City alone, and the death rate in Philadelphia approached 200 a day. Desperate cities tried oxen as replacements; some even used teams of men to pull the cars, but with little success.

Although the disease had run its course by 1873, the lesson was plain: find a mechanical substitute for horse power. So began decade-long search for a powered alternative to transport the growing numbers of urban workers to and from their jobs. After fruitless experiments with steam, compressed air, naphtha, and even methane gas, the electric streetcar was developed. In the process, those city workers gained tremendous freedom to travel unprecedented distances for a nominal fare. A ring of "streetcar suburbs" grew up around most cities, and in the United States only the greater freedom granted by the automobile and the motor bus could turn people away from the rail-bound electric streetcar, or trolley.

RAIL TRACK DEVELOPMENTS

PROPONENTS OF THE EARLY AMERICAN RAILROADS TURNED TO BRITAIN FOR THEIR ADVANCED TECHNOLOGY. DURING THE LATE 1820s, SEVERAL DELEGATIONS OF U.S. ENGINEERS VISITED THE PIONEER BRITISH LINES AND QUITE OFTEN PLACED ORDERS WITH MANUFACTURERS FOR ROLLING STOCK.

The Delaware & Hudson line brought back some Stephenson locomotives to try out. Its wooden track, laid on wooden trestles after the fashion of some British tramways, proved too frail for the locomotives, which had to be discarded. John Bloomfield Jervis, an engineer who had worked on the Erie Canal, and then the Delaware & Hudson and Mohawk & Hudson railroads, was among those who were very aware that iron rails, necessarily imported from Britain at that time, were too expensive for American circumstances. It seemed far more sensible to exploit that rich local resource, lumber. The result was bar rail, which used iron for the running surface only. This type was later known as strap rail, a term that wrongly suggested that the metal surface was just a thin belt. In fact, it was a genuine bar, 1in (2.5cm) thick and 2in (5cm) wide. It was laid on a strip of hardwood, usually maple or walnut, which in turn rested on the wooden rails, which were 12in (30cm) deep and perhaps 8in (20cm) wide. The bars were attached by spikes located in countersunk holes. Ideally, this construction, with its

Various methods were used to anchor rails; the Baltimore & Ohio RR opted for stone blocks, but when the supply was interrupted temporarily, it switched to wooden ties, which proved much more resilient.

crossways ties, should have rested on an embankment, but some railroads found it cheaper to lay supporting trestles instead, or to sink piles. On the New York & Erie line, the trestle idea came to a bad end when it caught fire. The Mohawk & Hudson RR half buried the underlying frame, while the Baltimore & Ohio RR, which always liked to be different, thought stone blocks would be the best support. But a strike in the local quarry cut off supplies of blocks, and the B&O turned temporarily to wooden crossties instead; to its surprise, it found they were better than stone blocks, thanks to their resilience.

This kind of rail was used for several decades, even though as trains became heavier and faster, it became a handicap. However, in the early years, the main problem was not the rail, but the curves. Lines laid along city streets, as they often were, frequently turned corners and, as demolishing buildings was out of the question, could only negotiate those corners by using very sharp curves. Jervis chose the flexible 4-2-0 wheel arrangement for his locomotives for that reason, and the type became almost a standard layout before being superseded by the 4-4-0, by which time, most sharp curves had been bypassed.

An example of strap rail. Thick steel straps, or bars, were attached to a strip of hardwood with metal spikes. This assembly was fixed to wooden rails or crossties of thicker section.

One problem with strap rail was that the spike holes were weakened by rot, loosening the bar. Lateral pressure from wheel flanges tended to push the rails apart, and some roads widened the gauge by 0.5in (12mm) or sometimes more, for easement; wheels were wide enough to allow this. After some years, a few railroads replaced the bars with iron bridge rail, as used on the Great Western Railway of England. This had a bridge-form cross-section and was quite successful; bridge rails seem to have been the first iron rails to be produced in America.

The American press, even at that early stage eager to campaign against the railroads, agitated for the abolition of strap rail. It pointed out the perils of what it called "snakeheads," when dislodged iron bars might be forced through the floors of moving trains and cause horrific injuries. Such occurrences seem to have been far rarer than the journalists claimed, but because of the need to use heavier locomotives and the increasing maintenance cost of this type of rail, it ceased to be laid around mid-century. But in the South especially, where capital was short, it remained in use into the 1860s.

The long-term replacement for strap rail had existed in the United States since 1831, when the president of the Camden & Amboy RR, Colonel Robert L. Stevens, visited Britain and ordered 500 15ft (4.6m) iron rails of the so-called flanged T-rail cross-section (later known as flatbottom rail). This married the bullhead design used in Britain (which had a railhead that bulged to give a broader running surface) to a base consisting of a horizontal flange that could be spiked directly to the crossties rather than laid, as in Britain, in a chair that itself was bolted or spiked to the tie. This kind of rail became the world's standard type; even the British railways moved from bullhead to flatbottom in the 1950s. Long before then metallurgy had produced the steel rail, far more resilient and less likely to fracture than iron rails, although the chemistry of steel and the techniques of rail rolling would continue to be researched up to the present day. Rail weight would grow from the 36lb/yd (17.8kg/m) of the Camden & Amboy to 140lb/yd (69kg/m) by the mid-20th century.

Cross-section of flatbottomed rail. The top was bulbous to provide a running surface for train wheels, while the base was wider, allowing the rail to be spiked directly to the ties.

Harnessing the power of Steam, 1800-34

It is no exaggeration to assert that the invention of the steam locomotive changed the face of the world. By paving the way toward unprecedented speed in transport, it put the finishing touch upon the developments of the industrial revolution.

It was the indirect, and highly competitive, association of two men, both ingenious mechanics, that first blazed the trail. In 1765, James Watt, mathematical instrument maker at Glasgow University, Scotland, had to repair an instructional model of a Newcomen Cornish beam engine, and hit upon the idea of using a separate condenser as a means for effecting great economy in the use of steam. His innovation created such interest that eventually he went into partnership with Matthew Boulton, an industrialist in the West Midlands of England. The firm of Boulton and Watt prospered in the building of stationary steam engines, but it was when they began to receive orders for pumping engines in the Cornish tin mines in the West of England, that the practice developed by Watt had its first and only influence on the future of rail transport. One of the young men who saw the Watt engines installed in Cornwall was Richard Trevithick, and while Watt was timorous and self-effacing, albeit a superb mechanic, Trevithick was bold and confident to the point of rashness. Watt used steam at comparatively low pressure, Trevithick at once began to build engines using much higher pressure, and instead of condensing the steam after use, he exhausted it into the atmosphere; his first engine was nicknamed *"Capt. Dick's Puffer."*

From stationary engines used in the Cornish tin mines, Trevithick turned to rail traction, but not before he had made experiments with a locomotive on the roads in Cornwall, to the alarm of the populace. In 1803, a demonstration in London led to the "road carriage" getting out of control and tearing down the

Built by English father and son George and Robert Stephenson, the Rocket embodied all the basic features of successful steam locomotive design.

Richard Trevithick, from Cornwall in the Southwest of England, was the first in the world to build a steam railroad locomotive. His design would inspire many other engineers.

railings outside a private house. He became associated with industrial activities in South Wales, and then there came the famous wager that led to the building of the first steam railroad locomotive. The bet, between two prominent ironmasters, challenged Trevithick's "tram wagon" as it was called, to haul a load of 10 tons over the 9.75 miles (15.6km) from Pen-y-Darren to Abercynon Basin on the Glamorganshire Canal. That Trevithick won the bet for his sponsor is a matter of history, and now interest centers on the design of the locomotive. It had but one cylinder, and to carry the drive over dead center, there was an enormous flywheel. The piston, through the conventional crank/connecting-rod mechanism, rotated a small pinion wheel, which drove a large gearwheel. This engaged with gears mounted on the same axles as the road wheels of the locomotive. It was a triumph, but had shortcomings.

Although Trevithick himself took very little part in the development of his locomotive after this first experiment, those who followed profited by its failures. It frequently broke down, and its relatively great weight compared with horsedrawn wagons broke many rails. Matthew Murray, of Leeds, for example, suggested having two cylinders working cranks at right angles to each other. This eliminated the "dead center" position and dispensed with the huge flywheel. This suggestion was incorporated in Blenkinsop's locomotives put to work on the Middleton Colliery railway near Leeds, in 1812. It had been thought that the contact between a smooth rail and a smooth wheel tire would not provide a good enough grip to enable a locomotive to haul a heavy load, and, in 1811, Blenkinsop had taken out a patent for a toothed rail laid to one side of the running rail, in which a gear mounted on the axle of the locomotive worked as a pinion in a rack. Locomotives of this type, hauling trains of coal cars, achieved a certain degree of reliability, though progress was slow and the geared arrangement expensive. One of the Blenkinsop engines was purchased by Blackett, for trial at Wylam Colliery, Northumberland, and the outcome was that the toothed-rail arrangement was considered unnecessary. By the time this engine was at work, a man named George Stephenson was beginning to come into the picture.

With financial backing from Lord Ravensworth, he built his first locomotive for the Killingworth Colliery in 1814. It had many shortcomings, and the second Killingworth locomotive, in which Isaac Dodds was the joint patentee with Stephenson, was a vast improvement. The noise of the exhaust, about which many complaints were made, was practically silenced by turning the exhaust steam into the chimney, where it performed a second function, that of sharpening the draft of the fire and increasing the rate of steam production. Then the complicated gear drive was superseded by connecting the crosshead directly to the driving wheels through the connecting-rod. In this locomotive, Stephenson and Dodds together had reached nearly all the fundamental points of the orthodox, classic, steam locomotive,

Trevithick's steam locomotive had a massive flywheel to carry the cranks over dead center. Drive was passed to both axles through a large gearwheel.

in 1815: two cylinders, simple direct drive, exhaust turned from cylinders into chimney to increase draft on the fire. The partners had, in the second Killingworth locomotive, incorporated a synthesis of all the best features of the pioneer work of Trevithick, Blenkinsop, Matthew Murray, and Blackett, and the way was clear to introduce steam locomotive power on the projected Stockton and Darlington Railway.

The celebrated *Locomotion*, engine No. 1 of the first public railway in the world, incorporated all the best features of the Killingworth Colliery locomotives, but the working conditions on what was virtually a main line, by comparison, were much more severe. The *Locomotion* was found incapable of steaming continuously for any length of time, and stops had to be made to raise steam. In the meantime, George Stephenson was away and engaged with the surveys and estimates for the Liverpool and Manchester Railway. He had left his faithful assistant Timothy Hackworth in charge on the Stockton and Darlington, and to that painstaking and able man fell the task of making the pioneer locomotives reliable work units. In 1827, he built the *Royal George* locomotive at Shildon Works. It was much larger than any of the previous engines built by Stephenson, and had six coupled wheels. In it, Hackworth increased the steaming capacity by arranging the flue from the firebox to the chimney in the form of a U, instead of a single large pipe, and so presented an increased area of flue tube in contact with the water. Hackworth was also the inventor of the blast pipe, a narrowing cone, through the nozzle of which the exhaust steam passes at high velocity and creates an intense draft on the fire. The *Royal George* steamed very freely, but it was a curious thing to look at. Because of that return flue, the firedoor was at the chimney end of the boiler, and the fireman rode on a separate tender propelled in front of the engine, while the engineer was at the rear end, where there was a second tender carrying the water supply tank. The greatly improved performance of the *Royal George* was in many ways a turning point in railway history, because until then, in the later 1820s, there were many who felt that locomotives could not be made sufficiently reliable, and that cable traction would be the only preferable alternative.

Top The Stephensons' *Rocket* came out on top at the Rainhill trials to find the best type of locomotive for England's Liverpool & Manchester Railway. *Above* Robert Stephenson, son of George, was one of the most noted pioneers of steam locomotive design.

On the Liverpool and Manchester Railway, construction of which was nearing completion the directors decided to stage a competition, the Rainhill trials, for the best type of locomotive to work the line. Although Hackworth had done so much to pull the Stockton and Darlington Railway around from failure, George Stephenson and his son, Robert, felt that his *Royal George* type of locomotive was rather clumsy and slow, and in entering a locomotive for the competition they introduced some further novel features, particularly in the boiler. To promote rapid evaporation by increasing the surfaces in contact with the water, the flue from the firebox to the chimney was split up so that instead of passing through

Another competitor in the Rainhill trials was the *Sans Pareil* locomotive built by Timothy Hackworth. Although it performed well, poorly made components let it down.

one large tube, the hot combustion gases passed through a nest of much smaller ones. This feature was suggested not by a fellow engineer, but by the secretary of the company, Henry Booth. As the first of its kind, it gave much trouble in the constructional stage, because great difficulty was experienced in fitting the tubes to the boiler ends without leakage occurring. But Robert Stephenson persevered and eventually turned out a first-class job. The engine was the ever-famous *Rocket*, which steamed very freely.

Hackworth also entered the competition, and at his own expense built a four-wheeled engine. the *Sans Pareil*, having the return-flue type of boiler. But the conditions of the competition staged at Rainhill did not require such a massive engine as the *Royal George*, and the *Sans Pareil* had only one tender, propelled in front. The engineer stood on a small platform jutting out at the rear. Hackworth's engine was sound enough in concept but he was rather let down by some of the suppliers of parts. One of the cylinders was badly cast and burst at one point, then the feed pump supplying water to the boiler failed, and that of course put an end to the engine's participation.

The third competitor, the *Novelty* of Braithwaite and Ericsson, made some spectacular runs, but broke down frequently, and eventually the *Rocket* of George and Robert Stephenson was the only one of the three to stay the course. Not only did it win the competition, and ensure that the *Rocket* became the first standard engine type on the Liverpool and Manchester Railway, but also it became a world prototype, incorporating all those basic features of design that were perpetuated for more than 100 years in locomotives of increasing size all over the world, culminating in the gigantic "Big Boys" of America's Union Pacific Railroad, which were built in 1941.

When it came to day-to-day working on the Liverpool and Manchester Railway, the *Rocket* type did not prove entirely satisfactory, and Robert Stephenson overcame the trouble of jerky and rough riding by introducing the *Planet* type in 1830, which had the cylinders between the frames, situated beneath the smokebox. All the machinery became largely concealed; but while this produced a much smoother riding engine, a problem of another type was introduced, that of a driving axle that had to incorporate two cranks between the frames. The problems were, however, of manufacture rather than of principle, and locomotives with inside cylinders became very popular in Britain. The *Planet* type followed the *Rocket* type in having only a single pair of driving wheels, though situated at the rear instead of at the leading end of the locomotive. A single pair of driving wheels was favored for passenger trains, because it afforded a greater freedom in running; but the four-wheel coupled type, as in the *Locomotion* and the

Sans Pareil, was more suitable for freight trains, providing greater adhesion in hauling a heavy load, and locomotives of this latter type were among the first exported from Great Britain to North America. They were, however, not to have any lasting influence on the continent.

In the United States, the first ever railroad, the Baltimore & Ohio, had relied upon horse power from its inception in 1827; but in 1830, a New York industrialist and inventor, Peter Cooper, had made a large investment in Baltimore & Ohio land, and in his determination to see the railway succeed, he set to work to produce a steam locomotive.

To improve on some of the deficiencies of the *Rocket*, Robert Stephenson developed the *Planet*. This had its cylinders mounted between the frames, which provided a much smoother ride.

Coming of the Iron Horse

THE FIRST COMMERCIAL RAILROADS WERE LAID DOWN IN BRITAIN
IN THE EARLY 1820s, BUT THEIR POTENTIAL DID NOT ESCAPE THE
NOTICE OF U.S. CITIZENS. VARIOUS ENVOYS WERE SENT TO STUDY
THE PIONEER BRITISH LINES AND THEIR REPORTS INFLUENCED
THE PLANNING AND CONSTRUCTION OF RAILROADS IN AMERICA.

To prove the ability of his new steam locomotive, *Tom Thumb*, Peter Cooper organized a race against a horse, each pulling a carload of people. Sadly, mechanical failure let the horse win, but Cooper had demonstrated the potential of his machine.

In 1825 William Strickland made a study for the Pennsylvania Society for the "Promotion of Internal Improvement." Others sent to study pioneer British lines in the latter part of the decade were Horatio Allen of the Delaware & Hudson Canal Company, and George W. Whistler, Jonathan Knight, and Ross Winans for the Baltimore & Ohio Railroad. Horatio Allen and Ross Winans both attended the Rainhill trials near Liverpool, England, in 1829 when, on October 26, George Stephenson's *Rocket* was awarded the first prize. The reports compiles by these men were to exert a strong influence on those responsible for the planning and construction of the early United States railroads.

February 28, 1827, is one of the most important dates in the history of railroads in the United States. It was the day on which the State of Maryland granted a charter to the promoters of what was to become the Baltimore & Ohio Railroad. The aim was to reach the Ohio River and funnel commerce into Baltimore. The original route, which was surveyed with the help of the U.S. Army, included the splendid Carrollton Viaduct.

Some historians hold that the Granite Railway in Quincy, Massachusetts, a horse worked, iron-faced wooden track, which received its charter on April 3, 1826, and opened later the same year, was the first railroad in the United States. Be that as it may, the Baltimore & Ohio RR was the very first common carrier, and also the first to offer scheduled freight and passenger services to the general public.

August 28, 1830, was another red-letter day. Peter Cooper, an industrialist and inventor, had constructed a small, experimental, steam driven locomotive at his Canton Iron Works in Baltimore. Working with scrap iron and borrowed wheels, and using gun barrels for boiler tubes, he built America's first homemade railroad steam locomotive, the *Tom Thumb*. The first part of the Baltimore & Ohio Railroad had a 14 mile

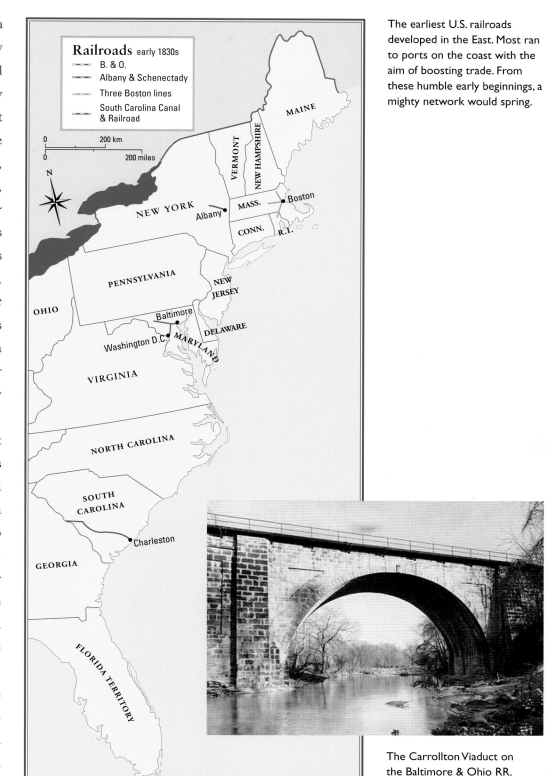

The earliest U.S. railroads developed in the East. Most ran to ports on the coast with the aim of boosting trade. From these humble early beginnings, a mighty network would spring.

The Carrollton Viaduct on the Baltimore & Ohio RR. Charles Carroll laid the first foundation stone for this bridge on July 4, 1828. The 92-year-old—sole surviving signatory of America's Declaration of Independence—lived to see the railroad completed as far as Point of Rocks, 73 miles (117km) southwest of Baltimore.

Map legend:

Railroads early 1830s
- B. & O.
- Albany & Schenectady
- Three Boston lines
- South Carolina Canal & Railroad

Cooper's Tom Thumb was the first steam locomotive built in the United States. He had assembled it from a variety of materials, including gun barrels, which he used as boiler tubes.

PETER COOPER'S "TOM THUMB" 1829-30 BALTIMORE & OHIO R.R.

Peter Cooper was an industrialist and inventor who was determined that the Baltimore & Ohio RR should succeed. That determination led him to design and build his own steam locomotive.

(23km) stretch of double-track, iron-faced wood road between Baltimore and Ellicott's Mills worked by horses. Cooper staged a race between *Tom Thumb*, drawing a carload of directors, and a horsedrawn car. The draft for the boiler of his little steam locomotive was provided by a belt driven fan, and in course of the race, the belt would not stay in place, and so steam pressure was lost. On this occasion, the horse won, but the contest certainly served to convince a lot of people of the potential practicability of steam as motive power.

Cooper's locomotive had a vertical boiler with the stack extending directly from the boiler end, and although having many defects arising from the primitive methods used in its construction, it paved the way to success and was followed by locomotives of the same general type, built by the firm of Davis and Gartner. The *Atlantic*, made by the same partners in 1832, was the first of the so-called "grasshopper" type, again with a vertical boiler, and the cylinders acting through large, rocking shafts mounted on the top of the boiler.

Motive power was at first imported from Britain, and the firm of Foster, Rastrick & Company of Stourbridge, England, built the first steam locomotive, the *Stourbridge Lion* costing $2,914, to the order of Horatio Allen for the Delaware & Hudson Canal Company. This was delivered in August 1829 for use on a coal line being built over the 11 miles (18km) from Carbondale to Honesdale, Pennsylvania. Even at 7 tons, it was too heavy for the lightly laid wood and iron road, and in particular was deemed unsuitable for a wooden trestle over Lackawaxen Creek. Although Allen himself drove over the trestle and back at 10mph (16km/h), many people thought it too dangerous.

Improvements were made to the track, and *Stourbridge Lion* was given a second try, but its 7 tons of unsprung weight led to derailments, and it was laid aside at Honesdale. In 1849, its boiler and cylinders were removed for use in a foundry in Carbondale. Many years later, the owners shipped the parts to the Smithsonian Institution in Washington, D.C.; a full-size, working replica of the *Stourbridge Lion* is now on permanent display at Honesdale.

On October 9, 1829, the Delaware & Hudson inclines and levels were opened, but these were worked by cable and gravity. January 15, 1831, saw the inauguration of 6 miles (19km) of track out of Charleston, South Carolina, the first railroad in the United States to provide a regular service for passengers, and freight hauled by steam. In 1833, the line was extended to Hamburg, just across the Savannah River, to make a total length of 136 miles (219km), the longest railroad in the world at that time. Its role as a public railroad and common carrier is notable, as up to then most lines had been built for specific purposes, such as coal, lumber or freight transportation, and were used almost exclusively by their owners.

While Peter Cooper's *Tom Thumb* was going through its teething troubles on the Baltimore & Ohio Railroad, a much larger engine of the vertical-boiler type was put to work in December, 1830, on the Charleston & Hamburg Railroad (later to become the South Carolina Rail Road Company), which took delivery of the first operational locomotive to have been built in America, from West Point Foundry of New York City. The *Best Friend of Charleston* goes down in history as the first locomotive to operate a regularly scheduled passenger run in the United States. It was, unfortunately, destroyed by a boiler explosion on June 17, 1831, after the fireman, irritated by the noise of escaping steam, had foolishly held the safety valve down!

The Delaware & Hudson Canal Company imported an English locomotive, the Stourbridge Lion, to work a coal line between Carbondale and Honesdale, Pennsylvania. This photo shows a coal train on the line in later days.

Horatio Allen drives the Stourbridge Lion over the trestle at Lackawaxen Creek to prove it capable of taking the locomotive's weight.

THE BOOM BEGINS, 1830-37

THE 1830S SAW A RAPID EXPANSION IN RAILROAD BUILDING IN THE UNITED STATES, AND WITH THE BULK OF THE 13 MILLION POPULATION CONCENTRATED IN THE STATES TO THE EAST OF THE MISSISSIPPI AND MISSOURI RIVERS, RAILROAD DEVELOPMENT WAS CONCENTRATED THERE.

The first train to run in New York State was hauled by the locomotive De Witt Clinton, in August 1831. It reached a speed of 15mph (24km/h), hauling a train of passenger cars modeled on the stagecoach.

During this first boom, such railroads as the Baltimore & Susquehanna (built 1828-32), Camden & Amboy (built 1830-1), Boston & Providence, Philadelphia & Reading, Newcastle & Frenchtown (1831), Paterson & Hudson River, Morris & Essex, Mohawk & Hudson, Saratoga & Schenectady, Western of Massachusetts, South Carolina, and others soon became familiar names. The B & O opened to Frederick, Maryland, 60 miles (97km) west of Baltimore, on December 12, 1831. The Elizabethtown & Somerville RR was incorporated the same year; later it formed part of the Central RR of New Jersey. The Main Line of Public Works, a canal built by the Commonwealth of Pennsylvania, was chartered to build a line from Philadelphia, westward to Columbia on the Susquehanna River. This later became part of the Pennsylvania RR.

One of the earliest railroads owed its existence to the Erie Canal. This had been profitable from its inception, unlike the Main Line in Pennsylvania or the C&O Canal in Maryland. However, the Erie

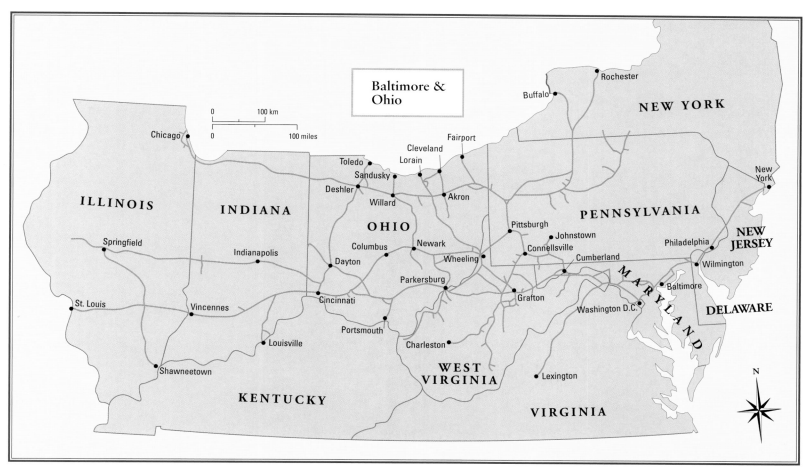

Baltimore &
Ohio

From its early, humble
beginnings, the Baltimore &
Ohio Railroad eventually spread
throughout the Northeast.

Canal merged with the Mohawk River in Schenectady, beginning a widening route with several locks downriver to the Hudson & Albany. By water, the 40-mile (64km) route took more than a day—so rather than stay with the barges, passengers would disembark to take the 17-mile (27km) land route by coach, passable in a quarter of the time and at half the expense. Seeing the potential for an expanded land transportation system between Schenectady and Albany, George Featherstonhaugh (pronounced fanshaw), of Duanesburgh, ran a newspaper notice on December 28, 1825, announcing the formation of the Mohawk & Hudson Rail Road Company, which was chartered in 1826. The road's original right of way from the historic marker northwest to Schenectady was opened for service on August 9, 1831.

Another notable American locomotive of early days, more in the contemporary British style, was the *De Witt Clinton* of 1831, which began work between Albany & Schenectady. This was an 0-4-0 with a horizontal boiler and a stack at the leading end after the style of the *Locomotion* on the Stockton & Darlington Railway. While American manufacturers were making their first attempts at locomotive building, the Stephenson inside-cylinder, 0-4-0 type, developed on the Liverpool & Manchester, had a limited phase of popularity, and in 1831 the firm of Robert Stephenson & Company of Newcastle supplied some locomotives of characteristic appearance, including the *John Bull*, to the United States' Camden & Amboy Railroad.

The *DeWitt Clinton* locomotive, named after the governor of New York State mainly responsible for the Erie Canal, made its first run on the 17 miles (27km) of the Mohawk & Hudson Rail Road on July 2, 1831 before going on show at the New York World's Fair later that year. It was the first steam locomotive to operate in the state and only the second to be built in the United States—also by West Point Foundry.

This excerpt from the 1833 South Carolina transportation map shows the 136 mile route of the railroad from Charleston to Hamburg, which was built and operated by the South Carolina Canal & Rail Road Company. The railroad was, at the time, the longest in the world.

May 1831 also saw an important technical advance with the introduction of iron rails, which were an improvement on lumber with iron straps. The first flanged T-rail, imported from Britain, was laid in Pennsylvania for the Camden & Amboy RR. However, such rails were made of cast iron, which broke easily and could only be laid in short lengths, so that they soon became uneven. At this time, there was no general agreement on rail gauges. In April 1832, the 6ft (1,829mm) gauge New York & Erie RR was chartered. Many other railroads were chartered the same year, such as the Portsmouth & Roanoke RR, which later formed part of the Seaboard Air Line Railroad.

In 1833, the New York & Harlem RR opened; the Paterson & Hudson River RR was chartered between Patersoll, New Jersey, and Jersey City; and also the Paterson & Ramapo RR north to Suffern, just across the New York state line. The South Carolina Canal & Railroad Company at this time had the world's longest line in service. The Philadelphia & Reading RR was chartered, and the Central Railroad & Canal Company of Georgia was organized. Also that year, the Petersburg RR opened between Petersburg, Virginia, and Roanoke River opposite Weldon, North Carolina.

The following year, 1834, the Philadelphia & Columbia RR opened 81 miles (130km) of line in Pennsylvania. This was the first state owned track. During this boom period, the Cayuga & Susquehanna RR was completed between Owego and Ithaca, New York State, and later renamed the Lackawanna & Western RR.

In 1835, Senator Chase of Ohio introduced a bill to Congress to provide for survey of four possible routes for a coast-to-coast railroad. Much interest, research, and speculation was raised, but no positive action was taken. Elsewhere, however, ground was broken for the New York & Erie RR near Deposit on November 7; the Morris & Essex RR was chartered to run from Morristown, New Jersey, to New York; the Boston & Lowell RR opened on June 24, followed by the Boston & Worcester RR on July 4. By this time, the Baltimore & Ohio RR had reached Washington, D.C. from Relay, Maryland.

The first combined steam railroad and steamboat service came into effect on the route from Boston, Massachusetts, to New York City. The journey took 16 hours, but was eventually reduced to 14 hours.

The Andover & Wilding RR opened in August 1836, the Elizabethport to Elizabeth, New Jersey, opened with horse traction, and the Louisa RR was chartered to run from Taylorsville (Doswell) westward to points in Louisa County, Virginia. The completion of the Erie Canal had shown the potential for unlocking the vast natural resources of the interior, and for 12 years from 1825, the building of canals and railroads captured a large part of American public attention, occupying endless debates in Congress and state legislatures, and speeches from governors and presidents. In 1831, President Andrew Jackson spoke with pride at the high wages earned by laborers constructing these works, which he said were "extending with unprecedented rapidity." There was much debate about constitutional power of the government to promote such projects on a federal level, because the work was on such a vast and accelerating scale. Railroads had proved themselves successful, and there was a seemingly exponential growth in what was planned. In 1830, only 23 miles (37km) had been constructed; the following year, it had gone up to 94 miles (151km); and by 1836, the total construction had risen to 1,273 miles (2,049km).

The Norfolk & Western RR could trace its roots back to 1838 and three small railroads that ran from the hinterlands to the port of Norfolk, Virginia. Over the years, it grew and spread westward, up into Ohio. Eventually, it became part of the mighty Norfolk Southern Corp.

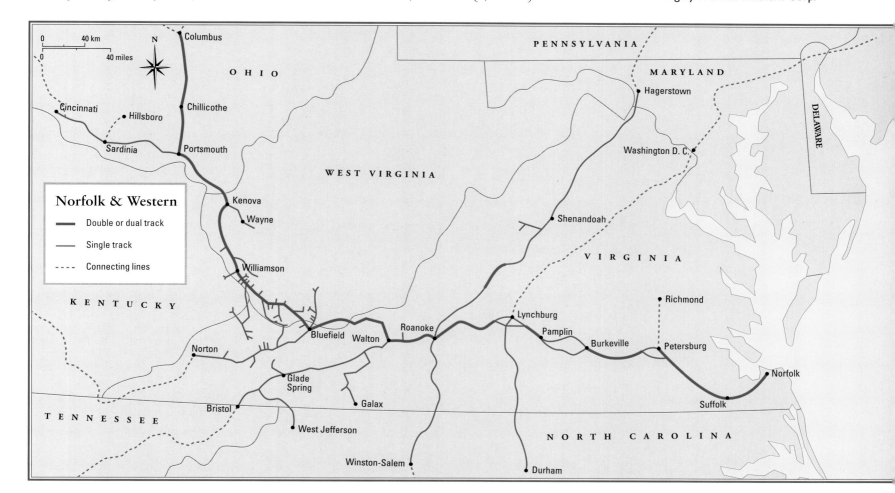

TECHNICAL IMPROVEMENTS, 1830-40

THE 1830s SAW A NUMBER OF IMPORTS OF BRITISH LOCOMOTIVES, BUT THE EARLY DEVELOPMENT OF THE NORTH AMERICAN RAILROAD INDUSTRY WAS AIDED BY A DUTY ON IMPORTED IRON PRODUCTS AND THE DESIRE TO "BUY AT HOME."

The Camden & Amboy RR in Pennsylvania imported the locomotive *John Bull* from England. Of the *Planet* type, the locomotive was built by Robert Stephenson and supplied as a kit of parts. During its long life it went through numerous adaptations and modifications.

At the same time it was laying the United States' first flanged T-rail, imported from Britain, the Camden & Amboy RR also imported a locomotive. *John Bull*, a four-coupled-wheel *"Planet"* type was shipped over as a kit of parts from Robert Stephenson & Company, England, and was assembled by Isaac Dripps, who added his own modifications (including the earliest cowcatcher). This historic engine is now at the Smithsonian Institution, Washington, D.C.

Despite the willingness of British builders to work to United States specifications, British locomotives were designed for well-aligned tracks and were soon found unsuitable for the lightly laid American railroads, so the fast growing nation quickly launched its own locomotive manufacturing facilities. Britain had by now established the basic fundamentals of locomotive design that were to remain to the end of the steam era, but from the late 19th century onward most of the major technological advances in steam locomotion were well established in the United States, decades before they were introduced in Britain. Despite the very poor quality of some of the products of the emerging builders, 1841 would see the last British locomotive imported—*Gem* of the Philadelphia & Reading RR. By this time, there were about 120 imported steam locomotives, but these accounted for only about 25 percent of those in service in the United States at that time.

What would become one of the most famous builders of steam locomotives in the world began in 1831, when Matthias Baldwin of Philadelphia established his works. Baldwin's first experimental locomotive was built that year. Unusually, it burned coal, widely available in the area, rather than wood, which was a more common fuel. Baldwin's first commercial locomotive (made in 1832) was called *Old Ironsides*. A 2-2-0 design, it was built to the order of the Philadelphia, Germantown & Norristown Railroad, which tried to renege on the last $500 payment. The Baldwin Locomotive Works would go on to build more than 1,500 engines

by the time its founder died in 1866, although most were of more conventional 4-2-0 design.

This was a fertile period for experimentation. The first "leading truck" incorporated in a locomotive, to make a 4-2-0 layout, was designed by John B. Jervis of West Point Foundry. Known as *Locomotive Experiment*, the prototype was supplied to the Mohawk & Hudson RR. Later known as *Brother Jonathan*, it was claimed to have reached a speed of 80mph (129km/h).

Iron-bar frames were introduced into the United States with the delivery of the 0-4-0 *Liverpool*, designed by the British engineer Edward Bury in 1833. Until this time, frames had been of reinforced lumber but within two years, iron frames were in general use. The last locomotives to use wooden frames were built by Baldwin in 1839. The first 4-4-0 type locomotive was developed by Henry R. Campbell of the Philadelphia, Germantown & Norristown RR, and built by James Brook of Philadelphia. Campbell was granted a patent on February 5, and the eight-wheeler was later to become a classic design, known as the "American" type. However, that same year, Isaac Dripps produced a strange 8-coupled-wheel machine,

the *Monster*, for the Camden & Amboy RR, combining both rod and gear coupling of wheels. In 1834, Imlay built a new passenger car, "Victory," for the Philadelphia & Columbia RR. This was an innovation, as it ran on two four-wheel trucks. Although it was not quite the world's first (one had been built for the St. Étienne-Lyon railroad in France), it was the first car of its type built in America. In 1836, the Cumberland Valley RR introduced "bunk" cars, enabling passengers to lie down, even though journeys were short. In 1840, passenger cars of two distinct types were introduced: those charging higher fares were called "Best Cars"; the more common type "Accommodation Cars."

Built by Baldwin Locomotive Works, *Old Ironsides* was the company's first commercial locomotive, and supplied to the Philadelphia, Germantown & Norristown RR. This illustration, by P. F. Goist and Frederick Gutekunst, marks the first run of a train in Pennsylvania, on November 23, 1832.

The first locomotive to have a leading truck was the work of West Point Foundry. It was supplied to the Mohawk & Hudson RR, where it was known as *Brother Jonathan*.

SAFETY ON THE TRACKS

WITH THE BURGEONING GROWTH OF RAILROADS—AND THE
NUMEROUS ACCIDENTS THAT HAD OCCURRED—SAFETY MEASURES
WERE BEGINNING TO BE CONSIDERED DURING THE 1830s. THESE
SERVED TO WARN OF THE APPROACH OF A TRAIN, OR EVEN TO
THROW OBSTRUCTIONS CLEAR OF THE TRACK.

Above Charles Babbage was an English mathematician and mechanical engineer. He designed the first cowcatcher, subsequently a common feature of U.S. locomotives. *Right* The headlight was an important train safety feature; this type comprises a square case containing an oil lamp in front of a parabolic reflector.

A steam locomotive hurtling down a railroad track was not only a danger to anyone—or anything—that should happen to get in its way but also was susceptible to damage or even derailment. In 1833 the first pilot wheels, or "cowcatcher," were fitted to *John Bull* by the Camden & Amboy RR. The pilot was mounted at the front of a locomotive to deflect obstacles from the track. It was invented by the English mathematician and mechanical engineer Charles Babbage in the 19th century, when he was working for the Liverpool & Manchester Railway. Pilots were not used on European locomotives, since their railroad systems were generally fenced off, while the North American tracks were not.

The pilot deflected an obstacle hit at speed, pushing it upward and sideways out of the way; it had a blunt wedge shape and shallow V appearance in plan. The earliest pilots consisted of bars mounted on a frame; later types were of smoother

Many locomotives were fitted with a bell and a steam whistle to warn of their approach. The whistle was also used to signal the train crew when the engineer wanted to apply the train's brakes.

sheetmetal. Cowcatchers were adopted by many other railroads, and became used universally from about 1855. A well-made cowcatcher could throw a buffalo weighing 2,000lb (907kg) some 30ft (9m).

The following year, a grade-crossing accident on the Boston & Worcester RR prompted a demand for all locomotives to carry warning bells. The State of Massachusetts enacted a law requiring warning bells for locomotives and other states followed. By 1839, bells had become commonplace on locomotives. Made of brass, they weighed between 60 and 215lb (27 and 98kg), were operated by a cord from the engineer's cab, and could be heard from a quarter of a mile (0.4km) away.

Other safety systems were also employed: semaphores were used to control trains between Newcastle and Frenchtown, Pennsylvania, while in 1836, there was the first reported use in the United States of a locomotive steam whistle. The whistle comprised a thin, circular bell, closed at the top and sharp at the lower edge; steam was vented from a narrow, circular orifice directly beneath the edge of the bell and entered the interior, setting up vibrations inside. The more rapid the vibrations, the higher the tone of

John Bull was fitted with Babbage's first cowcatcher, also known as pilot wheels. The wedge-shaped device could throw obstacles clear of the locomotive's path.

the whistle. Tone was influenced by the size of the bell and the pressure of the steam: the larger the bell, the lower the tone; the higher the steam pressure, the higher the tone. To avoid the shrill noise of a common whistle, chime whistles were used so tones harmonized to give an agreeable chord.

Locomotive headlights were introduced in 1840. Nighttime operation could be hazardous over twisting single tracks, and a lookout had to be kept for broken rails, misaligned switches, damaged trestles, and animals on the track. At first, a square case fitted ahead of the stack housed an oil lamp. Later, a parabolic reflector incorporating a central wick gave a beam for 1,000yd (914m).

AFTER THE PANIC OF 1837

THE SPECULATIVE BOOM IN CANAL AND RAILROAD BUILDING HAD LED TO RAMPANT INFLATION, UNDERPINNED BY PAPER MONEY ISSUED BY NUMEROUS LOCAL BANKS. THE BUBBLE FINALLY BURST IN 1837, THE RESULT OF A DISASTER TWO YEARS EARLIER THAT HAD BEFALLEN NEW YORK CITY.

A contemporary illustration of the conflagration that destroyed the commercial heart of New York in 1835. Many Erie RR investors suffered as a result, which delayed construction of the railroad.

Fires raged through New York City in December, 1835, consuming the Stock Exchange and most buildings on the southeast tip of Manhattan and around Wall Street. The disaster wiped out the fortunes of many Erie RR shareholders, delaying construction work. A great financial and commercial crisis began in March 1837 and reached its height in May, with what became known as the Panic of 1837—one of the worst economic disasters in United States history. The banks stopped payment in gold and silver, and many closed their doors forever.

Despite the financial problems of 1837, the railroads continued to grow apace. At the beginning of the 1840s, there were more than 345 locomotives running along the tracks of the United States. In 1837, the Northern Cross RR was chartered to connect Quincy, Illinois to a point on the Indiana state line; later it was renamed the Wabash RR. Also during this year, the Baltimore & Ohio RR opened a branch to Washington, D.C. from Relay (Washington Junction). The line included a stone viaduct across

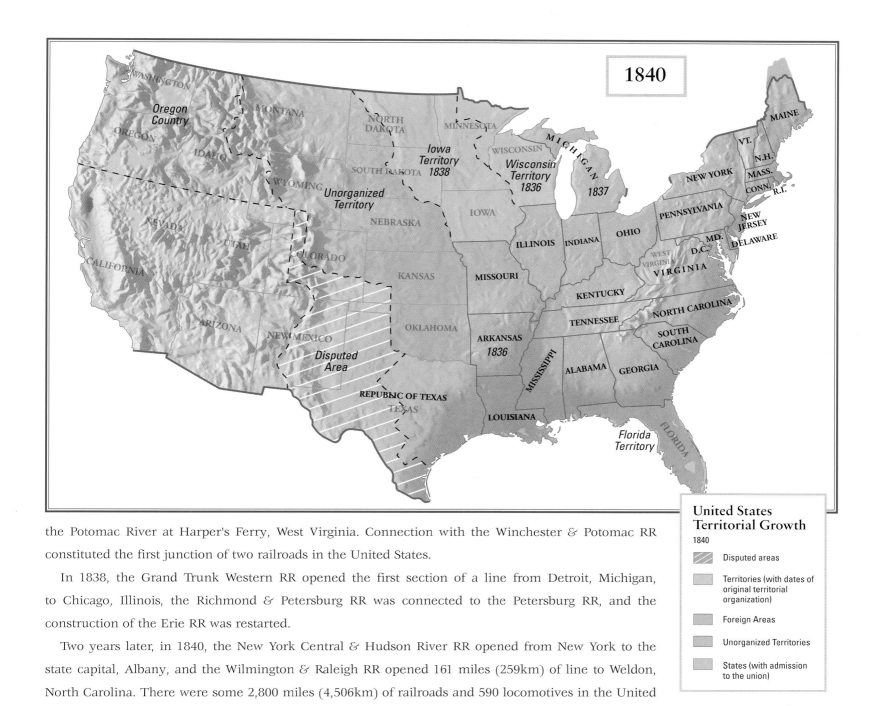

1840

the Potomac River at Harper's Ferry, West Virginia. Connection with the Winchester & Potomac RR constituted the first junction of two railroads in the United States.

In 1838, the Grand Trunk Western RR opened the first section of a line from Detroit, Michigan, to Chicago, Illinois, the Richmond & Petersburg RR was connected to the Petersburg RR, and the construction of the Erie RR was restarted.

Two years later, in 1840, the New York Central & Hudson River RR opened from New York to the state capital, Albany, and the Wilmington & Raleigh RR opened 161 miles (259km) of line to Weldon, North Carolina. There were some 2,800 miles (4,506km) of railroads and 590 locomotives in the United States. Greatest mileage, 754 (1,213km) was in Pennsylvania. The majority of railroads were built to what would become the standard gauge of 4ft 8½in (1,435mm); but others varied between 3ft (914mm) and 5ft (1,524mm), while the Erie RR adopted 6ft (1,829mm). In 1841, the first train ran on the New York & Erie RR. Construction costs of low trestle bridges drove the company into bankruptcy soon after opening. Construction continued regardless.

After the financial panic, the depression that lasted until 1843 dealt the fledgling railroad industry a hard blow. It resulted in near-failure to locomotive builder Matthias Baldwin, but owing to leniency on the part of his creditors and his decision to take on several partners, he was able to weather the storm and recovered in six years. Baldwin's plant in Philadelphia, Pennsylvania, went on to become the largest locomotive factory in the world. However, many other locomotive builders went under, among them George and Charles Sellers, and the Cardington plant, which had produced the locomotives *America* and *Sampson*

United States Territorial Growth
1840

▨	Disputed areas
▩	Territories (with dates of original territorial organization)
▦	Foreign Areas
▧	Unorganized Territories
▤	States (with admission to the union)

By 1840 the United States comprised the Union States in the East with territories in Florida, Winsconsin and Iowa. A central unorganized territory existed, while Texas was an independent republic, with Mexico a foreign area and New Mexico disputed. In the north west Oregon was an area claimed by the U.S. As the railroads spread, this picture changed radically as boundaries were disputed and changed.

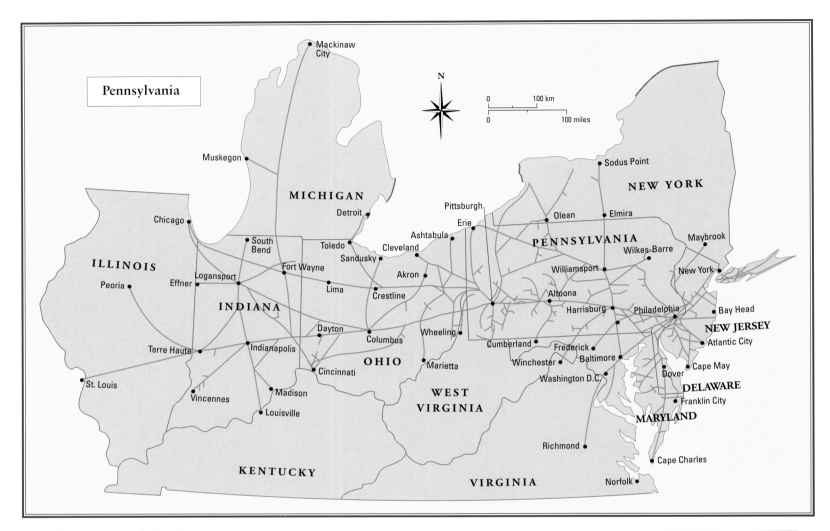

Pennsylvania

Above The Pennsylvania Railroad was begun in 1846 with a line from Harrisburg to Pittsburgh. In time, it grew to become one of the major railroads in the United States, with a 10,500-mile (16,900km) system serving 13 states.

Right The financial panic of 1837 brought many families to destitution, as depicted in this contemporary illustration, in which a beleaguered father, unemployed and penniless, finds himself under pressure from his starving family and the rent collectors at his door.

Champlain & St. Lawrence
Railroad

- - - Champlain & St Lawrence

- - - Montréal & Lachine

for the Philadelphia & Columbus RR. That same year, the Champlain & Connecticut River RR was incorporated to build between Bellows Falls and Burlington, Vermont, as part of a route from Boston, Massachusetts to Ogdensburg, New York.

Left The Champlain & St. Lawrence was Canada's first railroad, forming an important part of the route from Montreal to New York, accomplished mainly by steamers on Lake Champlain and the Hudson River. It was extended to New York in 1851 and became part of the Grand Trunk RR in 1872. *Above* the *John Molson* is a replica of a locomotive built in 1849 by Kinmonds, Hutton, & Steel of Dundee, Scotland, which ran on Canada's Champlain & St. Lawrence Railroad.

The Central RR of Georgia reached Macon from Savannah in October 1843, and its expansion continued in 1846 when it opened 171 miles (275km) from Augusta to Atlanta. Also that year, the Nashville, Chattanooga & St. Louis RR was incorporated. The Old Colony RR opened between Boston and Plymouth, Massachusetts, and consolidated with the Fall River RR. This was the earliest constituent of what became the New York, New Haven & Hudson River RR.

In 1846, an early example of trade-in was acceptance by Baldwin of his first locomotive, *Old Ironsides*, as part payment on a new locomotive. The construction of the Atlantic & St. Lawrence RR commenced, and the following year, the Alton & Sangamon RR was chartered to run from Springfield, Illinois to Alton, 20 miles (32km) north of St. Louis, Missouri. The Atlanta & La Grange (Atlanta & West Point) RR was chartered; the Galena & Chicago Union railroad was under construction. The New Albany & Salem RR was organized to build from New Albany, Indiana, on the north bank of the Ohio River, opposite Louisville, Kentucky, to the shore of Lake Michigan.

Also in 1847, the Milwaukee & Waukesha RR was chartered, as was the Rock Island & La Salle RR, which was to build between Rock Island, Illinois, and La Salle, connecting with the Illinois & Michigan Canal; later, it was renamed the Chicago & Rock Island RR. The New York & Erie RR had reached Port Jervis, New York, on the Delaware River, 74 miles (119km) from Piermont by December 31. In October of 1848, the Galena & Chicago Union RR opened its tracks between Chicago and Maywood, Illinois, a forerunner of the Chicago & North Western RR. At the end of the 1840s, the Evansville & Eastern Illinois RR was chartered to build north from Evansville, Indiana, and the Ligget's Gap RR combined with other lines in eastern Pennsylvania to form a corporate structure of the future Lackawanna & Western RR. The Aurora Branch RR was built from Aurora, Illinois, to Turner Junction to connect with the new Galena & Chicago Union RR, with train services to Chicago chartered. Later, this railroad became the Chicago, Burlington & Quincy RR.

The famous Chicago, Burlington & Quincy RR grew out of the Galena & Chicago Union and Aurora Branch railroads.

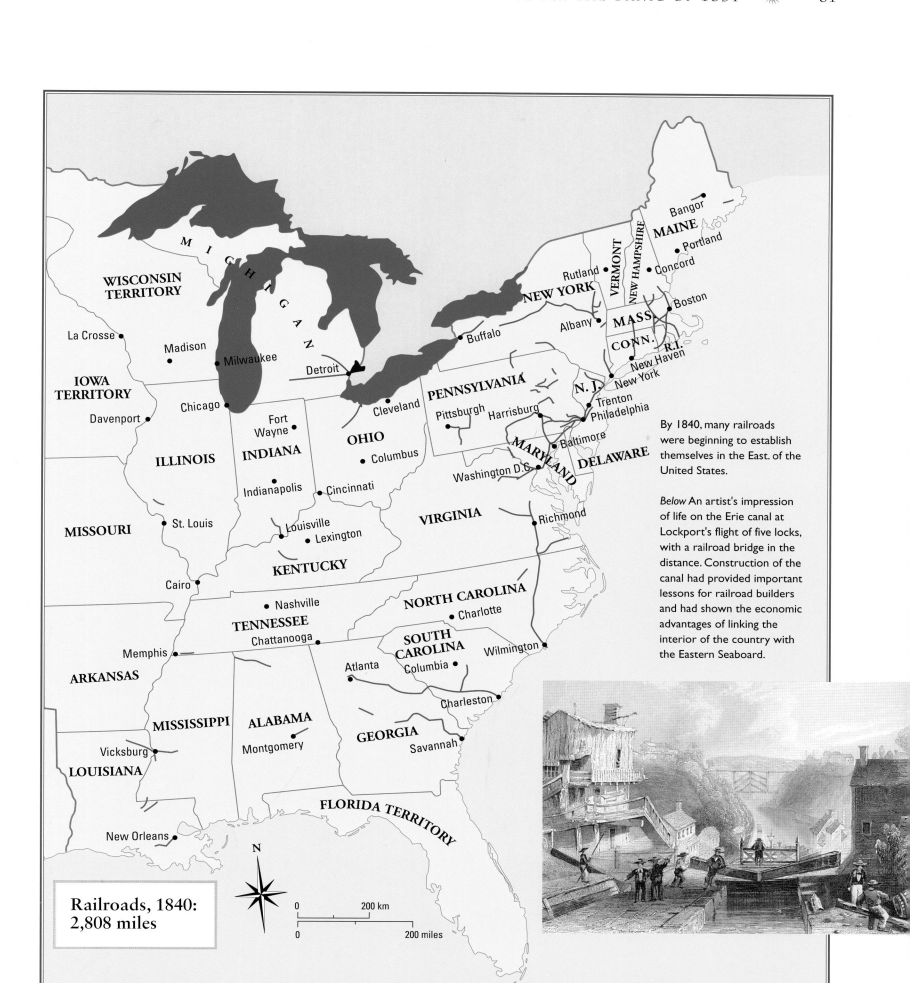

WISCONSIN
TERRITORY

MICHIGAN

IOWA
TERRITORY

La Crosse

Madison
Milwaukee
Detroit

Chicago

Davenport

ILLINOIS

Fort
Wayne

INDIANA

OHIO

Cleveland

Columbus

MISSOURI

St. Louis

Indianapolis

Cincinnati

Louisville
Lexington

KENTUCKY

Cairo

Nashville

TENNESSEE

Chattanooga

Memphis

ARKANSAS

MISSISSIPPI

ALABAMA

GEORGIA

Vicksburg

Montgomery

LOUISIANA

New Orleans

FLORIDA TERRITORY

NEW YORK

Rutland

VERMONT

NEW HAMPSHIRE

MAINE

Bangor

Portland

Concord

Buffalo

Albany

MASS.

Boston

CONN.

R.I.

New Haven

New York

N. J.

PENNSYLVANIA

Pittsburgh

Harrisburg

Trenton

Philadelphia

Baltimore

MARYLAND

DELAWARE

Washington D.C.

VIRGINIA

Richmond

NORTH CAROLINA

Charlotte

SOUTH
CAROLINA

Wilmington

Atlanta

Columbia

Charleston

Savannah

By 1840, many railroads
were beginning to establish
themselves in the East. of the
United States.

Below An artist's impression
of life on the Erie canal at
Lockport's flight of five locks,
with a railroad bridge in the
distance. Construction of the
canal had provided important
lessons for railroad builders
and had shown the economic
advantages of linking the
interior of the country with
the Eastern Seaboard.

N

0   200 km

0   200 miles

Railroads, 1840:
2,808 miles

ABE LINCOLN'S WHISTLE-STOP TOURS 1849 AND 1861

THE HISTORY OF THE U.S. ABOUNDS WITH MEMORABLE RAILROAD TRIPS, BUT THE TOURS OF PRESIDENTIAL CANDIDATES, AND THE FINAL JOURNEYS OF DECEASED PRESIDENTS, REVEALS THE IMPORTANCE OF THE RAILROADS. ONE OF THE FIRST POLITICIANS TO MAKE USE OF THE TRAIN WAS ABRAHAM LINCOLN.

Abraham Lincoln was President of the United States from March 4, 1861 to April 15, 1865. He was an outspoken opponent to the expansion of slavery and also a respected railroad and transportation lawyer.

Trains were the primary form of overland transportation for almost a century, and became symbols of America's movement and progression. It was hardly surprising that political campaigners used the railroads as a means of meeting the electorate face to face. Abraham Lincoln (1809-1865), a young lawyer, had worked as a railroad lobbyist and attorney in Illinois, where one of his clients was the Illinois Central RR, which the young lawyer defended in tax litigation. He also represented the Alton & Sangamon RR in an 1851 dispute with one of its shareholders. In a landmark case he defended the Rock Island RR in a suit that confirmed the railroads' right to build bridges over navigable rivers. He also defended the Chicago & Alton, and the Ohio & Mississippi railroads in other litigation. So great was Lincoln's reputation that the New York Central RR attempted to hire him—for the huge salary of $10,000 dollars—on the eve of his presidential election, which he of course declined.

During his election campaigning, Lincoln had traveled widely throughout the States seeking support from the electorate. In 1849 his travels had been at times slow and arduous. Traveling by stagecoach, steamboat and rail, he had journeyed from Illinois to Washington. In 1861, when president-elect, his travels had been more rapid, exclusively using the railroads in a lengthy whistle-stop tour. After being elected president, Lincoln undertook another landmark whistle-stop tour by rail from his home in Illinois to Washington. When his train arrived in Harrisburg, Pennsylvania, the rumor of an assassination attempt was circulated and the new president left town by an alternative route.

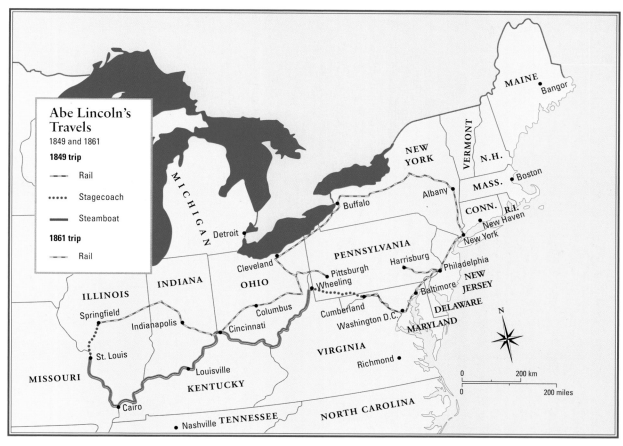

Abe Lincoln's Travels
1849 and 1861

1849 trip

- - - Rail

• • • • Stagecoach

—— Steamboat

1861 trip

- - - Rail

Abraham Lincoln was well traveled in his political campaigning, making use of the stagecoach, steamboat and above recognizing the speed with which the railroads could put him in the heartland of his presidential electorate.

During his presidency, Lincoln signed into law the Pacific Railroad Act on July 1, 1862, which authorized and subsidized the Union Pacific and Central Pacific railroads, which eventually completed the first transcontinental railroad in 1869. On November 18, 1863, Lincoln and his party traveled on

a special, brightly decorated, four-car, Baltimore & Ohio RR train from Washington, D.C. At Baltimore's Camden Station the train was pulled through the city streets by a team of horses to access Bolton Station, the depot of the North Central RR. The train then steamed north to Hanover Junction, switched tracks to the Hanover Branch and Gettysburg lines and continued on to Gettysburg.

At the public dedication of the new National Cemetery—founded in honor of the 51,000 casualties resulting from the three-day Battle of Gettysburg five months earlier—Lincoln delivered one of the most significant Presidential addresses of all time, marking a key point in America's history while reinforcing the president's continuing association with railroading.

The next time Abraham Lincoln would pass this way, April 1865, he would be lying in state in his funeral train, killed by an assassin's bullet.

Hanover Junction, Gettysburg, Pennsylvania, and the arrival of President Abraham Lincoln's official train in route to Gettysburg for dedication of National Cemetery. The man in front of the center window, wearing a stovepipe hat, is believed to be President Lincoln.

THE CLASSIC AMERICAN LOCOMOTIVE, 1840-60s

BY THE 1840s, THE 4-4-0 WHEEL CONFIGURATION WAS THE MOST WIDELY USED IN THE UNITED STATES, ON WHAT WAS TO BECOME KNOWN AS THE CLASSIC "AMERICAN" EIGHT-WHEELER: A FLEXIBLE LOCOMOTIVE WITH AN INITIAL LOW COST, WHICH WAS SIMPLE TO MAINTAIN AND REPAIR.

Constructed in 1861, the locomotive *William Crooks* is a classic 4-4-0, and one of the few Civil War veterans still surviving. The first locomotive to operate in the U.S. state of Minnesota, it was first placed in service on the St. Paul & Pacific RR, which later became part of the Great Northern RR. Railroad executive J.J. Hill used the locomotive to pull his personal train, and he later saved it from being scrapped when faster, more powerful engines were being introduced.

Early locomotives burned coal or anthracite, but wood soon became widely used. Production of live embers and sparks from wood-burners proved a constant hazard and a continuing expense in compensation payments. Many different designs of stack of varying efficacy were used. Probably most widely used was a design by French & Baird. It became a favorite on southern railroads, where pine forests and cotton fields made spark arresting a vital consideration.

Robert Stephenson's link-motion valve gear was first fitted to locomotives in England. While it was soon adopted in the United States, it was not accepted there so quickly as in Britain, although it was later to become standard in the American eight-wheeler.

Introduced in February 1836 with a patent taken out by Henry R. Campbell, chief engineer for the Philadelphia, Germantown & Norristown RR, by 1842 the 4-4-0 eight-wheeler had become the most widely used

2-2-2
1-1-1

4-4-0
2-2-0

0-6-0
0-3-0

0-6-2
0-3-0

4-6-0
2-3-0

4-6-2
2-3-1

2-8-2
1-4-2

● Power transmission
Continental European notation in italics

2-10-0
1-5-0

Steam locomotive wheel notation, although perhaps a mystery to the uninitiated, in fact is a simple system. A distinction is made between driving and trailing wheels.

locomotive in North America. In the Whyte notation, 4-4-0 signifies that the locomotive had a two-axle truck that helped to guide it into curves, and two driving axles coupled by a connecting-rod. The eight-wheeler was a flexible locomotive, rode uneven tracks well, was suited to all classes of service, including switching, and was simple to maintain and repair. Low in first cost and relatively powerful, it was a truly national locomotive. Campbell's prototype 4-4-0 weighed 12 short tons (11 metric tons), had 14in (365.5cm) diameter cylinders, with a 16in (40cm) piston stroke; its driving wheels were a huge 54in (1.37m) diameter, and it could maintain 90lbf/sq in (620kPa) of steam presssure. It was estimated that the locomotive would be able to pull a 450 short ton (410 metric ton) train at 15mph (24km/h) on level track, which would beat the strongest of Baldwin's 4-2-0s in tractive effort by about 63 percent.

Despite the success of Campbell's prototype, its frame and driving gear were to prove too rigid for the railroads of the day, making it prone to derailments. In 1837, the company of Eastwick & Harrison had built *Hercules*, a version of the 4-4-0 for the Beaver Meadow RR; this refinement of the type had a leading truck that was separate from the locomotive frame, meaning that it would be more suitable for the tight curves and quick grade changes of the railroads. There was a number of other designers, such as William Norris, but the name most firmly associated with the outside-cylinder 4-4-0 is that of Thomas Rogers. Campbell successfully sued other manufacturers and railroads for infringing his patent, and Matthias Baldwin settled with Campbell in 1845 by purchasing a license to build 4-4-0s.

Eugène Bourdon of Paris, France, perfected a practical steam-pressure gauge in 1849, which is still in use today. The gauge registered pressure on a dial as high as 100,000lb/sq in. Since steam engines had become bigger and operated at higher pressures, there were numerous accidents and failures. The device consisted of a tube that would straighten at higher pressure, moving a gear that rotated a needle. Although highly accurate, it could be damaged by rapidly changing pressures. The gauge was introduced into the United States by E.H. Ascent and readily accepted.

Although the 4-4-0 became known as the "American" type, due to the large number that were produced and used in the United States, the term would not be used until 1872, when *Railroad Gazette* published an article about the locomotive; prior to the article, the type was known simply as the "Standard" or "Eight-wheeler." So successful was the type that many of the earlier 4-2-0 and 2-4-0 locomotives had been rebuilt as 4-4-0s by the middle of the 19th century. During the 1840s, the dimensions of the type increased, with a longer boiler and a connecting-rod attached to the front driving axle, larger-diameter drive wheels, and a fire grate of a larger area. In the 1850s, the wheelbase of the leading truck and the driving axles was extended, and the boiler increased in width, giving more steam power and tractive effort. In 1852, the "Most modern 4-4-0" was introduced in the United States. This was the *New Jersey*, which and epitomized the type built in increasing numbers over the next three decades as the classic "American" eight-wheeler. Its chief characteristics were two outside cylinders; a spread (long) wheelbase leading truck; Stephenson link-motion; and a wagon-top boiler.

By 1855, the typical eight-wheeler had the following characteristics: 4-4-0 with 15 x 20in (38 x

Fig. 64. Standard Stephenson Valve Gear.

51cm) outside cylinders; 60in (1.5m) wheels; 100lb (45kg) steam pressure; weight 20 tons; tractive effort 6,375lb (2,892kg). This type was represented by the *General*, a product of Rogers Locomotive Works, Paterson, New Jersey, which was preserved and is today exhibited in the Smithsonian Institution, Washington D.C. The *General* is slightly larger than other eight-wheelers, with 15 x 22in (38 x56cm) outside cylinders; 60in (1.5m) wheels; 140lb (64kg) steam pressure; weight 22½ tons; tractive effort 9,820lb (4,454kg).

Robert Stephenson's link-motion valve gear was eventually adopted in the United States, becoming standard on the American eight-wheeler.

The first United States coal burning locomotive, *Daniel Webster*, completed trials on the Illinois Central RR in 1855. By this time, there were about 6,000 locomotives in the United States, most burning wood rather than coal. Two years later, with the 1,000th locomotive built by Norris, there were about 9,000 locomotives in service.

In 1858, Levi Bissell patented a swiveling, two-wheel leading truck, known as a "pony truck." From this time, the smaller-wheeled 2-6-0 began to supersede the 4-4-0 for freight work.

The 4-4-0 was not universally adopted, however. In 1847, the world's first 4-6-0, *Chesapeake*, was built by Norris for the Philadelphia & Reading RR. The ten-wheeler had small driving wheels and was intended primarily for freight work.

NORRIS BROTHERS *10 Wheel Freight Engine. Manufactured at their Works in* PHILADELPHIA. PA.

The world's first 4-6-0 locomotive was built by Norris Brothers of Philadelphia for the Philadelphia & Reading RR. Named *Chesapeake*, it was used mainly for freight work.

THE TELEGRAPH REVOLUTION

BEFORE THE ARRIVAL OF THE TELEGRAPH, MESSENGERS HAD
BEEN THE MOST RELIABLE MEANS OF COMMUNICATING OVER
DISTANCE. BY THE LATE 1800s, TELEGRAPHS WERE IN WIDESPREAD
USE IN THE UNITED STATES, OPERATED BY PRIVATE BUSINESSES,
NEWSPAPERS—AND PARTICULARLY BY THE RAILROADS.

Samuel Finley Breese Morse
invented a telegraphic
communication system using
electrical pulses sent along a
wire. Known as Morse Code,
the system proved invaluable for
sending messages quickly over
long distances. It became a vital
part of railroad equipment.

The telegraph greatly speeded up man's ability to communicate, especially over long distance, and it proved invaluable across the vast expanses of the United States. Numerous types of telegraph had been developed in England, but it was the American Samuel Finley Breese Morse (1791–1872) who invented the system that was eventually adopted in the United States. Morse, from Charlestown just outside Boston, Massachusetts, was the son of a pastor, Jedidiah Morse, a well-known geographer. After studying at Yale College, the young Morse became an enthusiastic painter of miniature portraits. He studied art in England, and on settling in New York City at the age of 34 soon became established as a respected portraitist.

In 1832, while returning from a period of art study in England, Morse—who had long been interested in the newly developing field of electricity—was further enthused by a discussion about the newly discovered electromagnet. He began to conceive the notion of an electric telegraph, wrongly believing this to be unique, and later acquired partners to help in the development of the system. In 1837, two Englishmen, Cooke and Wheatstone, had patented the "five needle" telegraph system, whereby needles were used to translate the electric signal into words; the system had its drawbacks, since the needles would quickly wear out. Morse developed a method that would become known as Morse Code—a series of dots and dashes sent by electrical impulses along a wire to a receiving point, where they were deciphered into a message. Working to perfect the system, he developed a suitable insulation for the wires consisting of hemp soaked in tar. Convinced of the telegraph's widespread potential, Morse began to demonstrate the system to businessmen during the late 1830s and met with comittees of Congress seeking funds for a large-scale test. Many people were skeptical about Morse's assertion that messages could be sent from city to city over a wire, but he patented the idea in 1840, and in 1843, his Magnetic Telegraph Company received the sum of $30,000 from Congress for the construction of the first telegraph line in the United States from Baltimore, Ohio to Washington, D.C.

The development of the railroads and that of the telegraph were inextricably linked from the outset: in 1827, the Baltimore & Ohio Railroad—the country's first common carrier to be chartered—had begun construction of its line into the West. The B&O's Mount Clare Shops had designed and built a machine that would simultaneously plow a trench and bury a lead pipe containing the telegraph wires. It was discovered, however, that the wires contained in the pipes were improperly insulated. The entire line was dug up and restrung overhead on wooden poles.

By 1844, the first inter-city electromagnet telegraph in the world was completed. On May 24, Samuel Morse sent the first test message from the Capitol building in Washington to Baltimore. The biblical quotation, "What Hath God Wrought!" was written by Anne Ellesworth, the daughter of the Commissioner of Patents. The following day, a telegram was sent back to Morse, marking the establishment of the first commercial use of telegraph on the railroad's right-of-way.

Even so, the B&O was dubious about the system's worth, and many other railroad companies simply refused to allow the electric wires to be strung along their roadbeds. By the late 1800s, however,

Morse Code relied on short electrical pulses (dots) and long pulses (dashes) to pass messages. Each letter of the alphabet and numerals were given specific combinations of dots and dashes so that messages could easily be coded and deciphered. A simple key device was used to make and break the circuit to transmit the electrical pulses.

Telegraph wires were strung on poles alongside railroad tracks; many roads not only used the system for sending their own messages, but also offered a commercial telegraph service for anyone who needed it.

A written message could be passed to a moving train by means of a length of bamboo called a Train Order Hoop, which was easily retrieved by a member of the train crew inserting his outstretched arm through the loop.

various private companies, leasing Morse's patent, had constructed telegraph lines from Washington to as far afield as Boston and Buffalo.

Telegraph had been used in Europe as a means of train dispatching since 1839, and this had resulted in a laudable record free from accidents caused by locomotives running into each other on the largely single track lines. In the United States, railroad companies were initially distrustful of the system. Hurried and somewhat poor-quality construction of the first telegraph lines meant that the network was not wholly dependable, and there were accidents on an almost daily basis on the railroads, which caused extensive damage to rolling stock and track, and in some cases resulted in loss of life.

Telegraph rapidly became an intrinsic part of the railroad structure, with offices consisting of small residences built close to the track with a small board platform between. Colored flags mounted on a pole would signal instructions to a train: a green pennant allowed the train to proceed without stopping; a red one demanded that it stop; a white one revealed that there was another train close by in front or behind, requiring caution from the crew. Eventually, semaphore was used to advise train crews. Bamboo hoops were used to pass telegraph messages to trainmen, either as the train passed by or when it stopped at the station. On the operator's desk were two sending keys and receiving relays, and, as improvements were introduced, a switchboard that linked the numerous telegraph wires to leads, which enabled the operator to plug into specific circuits, such as the "dispatcher's wire."

The broader adoption of telegraph as a vital part of the railroads occurred in 1849, when Charles Minot, superintendant of the New York & Erie Railroad, persuaded his board of directors to grant the telegraph company that was running a commercial line through Erie territory a right-of-way along the track from New York to the Great Lakes. His arrangement, later to become standard practice on most railroads, would give clerks and depot managers double duty as telegraph operators. This meant that the railroads would incur no other charges for unlimited use of the telegraph.

In 1850, the first transatlantic telegraph cable was laid beneath the Atlantic Ocean, between London and Halifax, Nova Scotia, and by 1858, direct telegraphic communication was established between the United States and England. The system worked for only one month before it failed after attempts were made to increase the speed of communication. The transatlantic link would not be reestablished until after the American Civil War.

On June 16, 1860, Congress authorized the Pacific Telegraph Act, a bill instructing the Secretary of the Treasury to subsidize the construction of a transcontinental telegraph line from the Missouri River to the Pacific coast. The following year the Overland Telegraph Company of California and the Pacific Telegraph Company of Nebraksa were formed. Poles were set for the Nebraska company's line westward from Julesburg, Colorado, to Salt Lake City, and The Overland Telegraph Company's line from Fort Churchill, Nevada, was begun. On October 26, 1861, the lines

A typical railroad telegraph key. The device made and broke the electrical circuit, sending pulses along the wire that were heard as short and long tones (dots and dashes).

were joined at Salt Lake City, allowing San Francisco to be in direct telegraphic contact with New York City. The line was soon upgraded with a multiwire line along the length of the transcontinental railroad's right-of-way.

Between the 1860s and 1880s, contracts were taken out between the railroad companies and the telegraph companies. The latter would be charged with supplying the poles, wire, and telegraphic instruments required for new lines, for both their use and that of the railroads, while the railroad companies would transport all this equipment along the track at a cost of $30 per mile (1.6km). The railroad companies' employees would be responsible for maintaining the telegraph lines. The telegraph companies would own receipts for all messages, by either party, at offices set up along the line. Western Union began to dominate the network by buying up smaller telegraph companies. By 1866, it had acquired more than 300 companies, and by the 1880s, it operated such agreements with more than four-fifths of U.S. railroad companies. Western Union sent 80 percent of the country's messages along its wires, which linked more than 12,000 offices. Many of the company's telegraph offices on small branch lines doubled as railroad stations, and also provided commercial telegraph facilities for the general public.

The use of telegraphy began to diminish during the 1900s with the improvement of technology and other sources of communication, such as the telephone and teletype, although it remained a mainstay with the railroads for many years.

Eventually, telegraph lines were laid around the world, including across the Atlantic Ocean. These permitted rapid intercontinental communication.

RAILROAD EXPANSION, 1850S

BY 1850, THE MILEAGE OF UNITED STATES RAILROADS EXCEEDED 9,000 (14,483KM). NEW YORK STATE LED THIS GROWTH WITH 1,361 MILES (2,190KM) OF TRACKS, SOME 121 MILES (195KM) AHEAD OF PENNSYLVANIA. THE RAILROADS, HOWEVER, HAD NOT YET PENETRATED WEST OF THE MISSISSIPPI RIVER.

In 1850, the Louisa RR reached westward to Charlottesville, Virginia, and became the Virginia Central. The Louisville & Nashville RR was chartered, and the Milwaukee & Waukesha became the Milwaukee & Mississippi Railroad. The Mobile & Ohio Railroad launch was aided by Congress' Land Grant Bill. The Norfolk & Petersburg Railroad was chartered to build a line connecting those two Virginia cities, and was the earliest constituent of the Norfolk & Western. On April 22 the following year, the New York, Erie & Western Railroad completed a line to Lake Erie, which was officially opened in May. The Alton & Sangamon RR opened a line from Springfield, Illinois, to Alton, 20 miles (32km) north of St. Louis, Missouri.

By the year 1850, Wisconsin, Iowa, Florida, Texas, and California had all been granted statehood.

The Montgomery & West Point RR opened 88 miles (142km) of standard gauge track in Georgia to add to 32 miles (51km) of railroad built earlier, while the Virginia Central RR built a line from Taylorsville to Richmond. The New Albany & Salem RR opened to Salem, Indiana.

The year 1851 saw much growth, since the Illinois Central RR was chartered to

1850

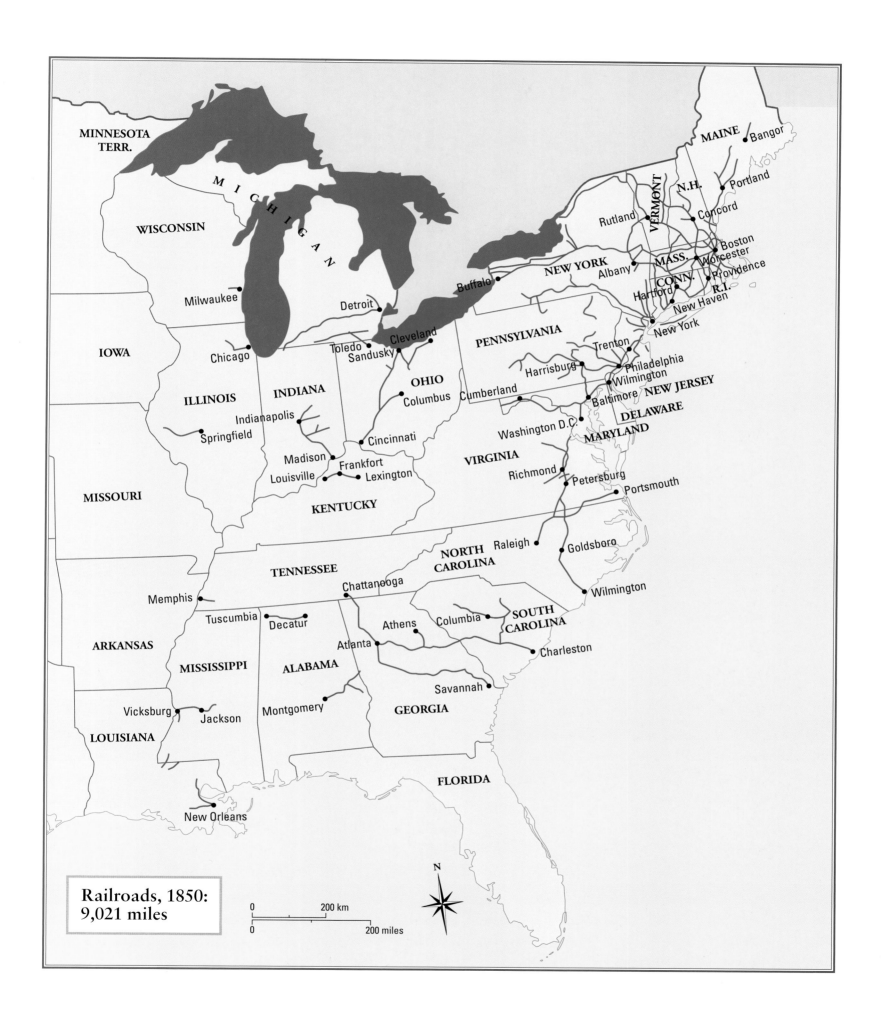

MINNESOTA TERR.

WISCONSIN

M I C H I G A N

MAINE • Bangor

VERMONT N.H. • Portland

Rutland • Concord

NEW YORK MASS. Boston

Albany • Worcester

CONN. Providence

Buffalo Hartford R.I.

New Haven

Milwaukee

Detroit

IOWA

Chicago Toledo Cleveland New York

Sandusky PENNSYLVANIA Trenton

ILLINOIS INDIANA OHIO Harrisburg Philadelphia

Columbus Cumberland Wilmington

Indianapolis Baltimore NEW JERSEY

Springfield Cincinnati Washington D.C. DELAWARE

MARYLAND

Madison Frankfort VIRGINIA

Louisville Lexington Richmond

MISSOURI Petersburg

KENTUCKY Portsmouth

NORTH Raleigh

CAROLINA Goldsboro

TENNESSEE

Chattanooga Wilmington

Memphis Columbia SOUTH

Tuscumbia Decatur Athens CAROLINA

ARKANSAS Atlanta Charleston

MISSISSIPPI ALABAMA

Savannah

Vicksburg Montgomery GEORGIA

Jackson

LOUISIANA

FLORIDA

New Orleans

N

**Railroads, 1850:
9,021 miles**

0   200 km

0   200 miles

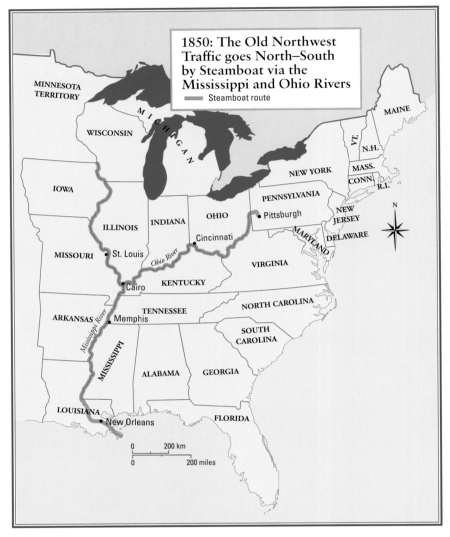

1850: The Old Northwest Traffic goes North–South by Steamboat via the Mississippi and Ohio Rivers

▬ Steamboat route

Water transport played a vital role in moving passenger and freight traffic in the U.S. hinterland before the coming of the railroads. In the 1850s, the best route for Northwest traffic to reach the sea was north–south via the steamboats that operated on the Mississippi and Ohio rivers.

build from Cairo, Illinois, at the confluence of the Ohio and Mississippi rivers, as far as Galena, with a branch from Centralia to Chicago. The construction of these lines was aided by the inceptionn of the first ever land grant act.

The Milwaukee & Mississippi RR reached Waukesha, Wisconsin, a distance of some 20 miles (32km), while the Nashville, Chattanooga & St. Louis RR opened its first 9m (14km). Ground was broken for the 5ft 6in (1,676mm) gauge Pacific RR at St. Louis, Missouri on July 4, 1851. This year also saw the first rail tunnel in the United States started—the Hoosac Tunnel, located in the Berkshires.

By December 1852, there was a through road from Philadelphia to Pittsburgh, Pennsylvania. Construction of the first rail suspension bridge was commenced over Niagara River, New York. The Chicago & Aurora RR (formerly the Aurora Branch RR) was authorized to build a line to Mendota, Illinois. On October 10, the first train to run between Chicago & Joliet, Illinois—the Rock Island RR—was hauled by a 4-4-0 *Rocket*-type locomotive. The New York & Erie RR leased the Paterson & Hudson River RR and the Paterson & Ramapo RR, and built a connection at Suffern, New York. The Mobile & Ohio RR opened its line running from Mobile to Citronelle, Alabama, a distance of 30 miles (48km). The New York City–Albany through-rail route was also established.

The first 4m (6km) of the Pacific RR were opened in 1852, which enabled the first train to operate west of the Mississippi River. On January 1 the next year, the B & O reached the Ohio River at Wheeling, West Virginia, 379 miles (610km) from Baltimore, almost 25 years from commencement of the railroad.

The Niagara Falls suspension bridge was opened on March 8. On August 1, the Pennsylvania RR reached the Ohio River at Pittsburgh, Pennsylvania, and the New York Central & Hudson River RR was opened throughout as far as Buffalo, New York. The Evansville & Eastern Illinois RR opened from Evansville to Vincennes, Indiana, and the Delaware, Lackawanna & Western RR was established. The Nashville, Chattanooga & St. Louis opened to Bridgeport, Alabama, and the Atlantic & St. Lawrence RR completed its tracks between Portland, Maine, and Montreal, Canada. The line was leased by the Grand Trunk Railway of Canada. By the end of this year, 13 railroads between Albany and Buffalo were consolidated as the New York Central.

In 1854, rails reached the Mississippi at Rock Island, Illinois, the Evansville & Eastern Illinois RR opened to Terre Haute, Indiana, and the Chicago & Rock Island line opened to Rock Island on February 22. Chattanooga, Tennessee, was reached by the Nashville, Chattanooga & St. Louis RR, with a connection to Atlanta, Georgia, provided by the Western & Atlantic RR. The Atlanta & La Grange RR opened with 5ft (1,524mm) gauge.

The mighty Illinois Central RR was born in 1851, when it was chartered to build a line from Cairo to Galena, with a branch from Centralia to Chicago. Eventually, it had a network that stretched from Sioux Falls, South Dakota in the North to New Orleans in the South.

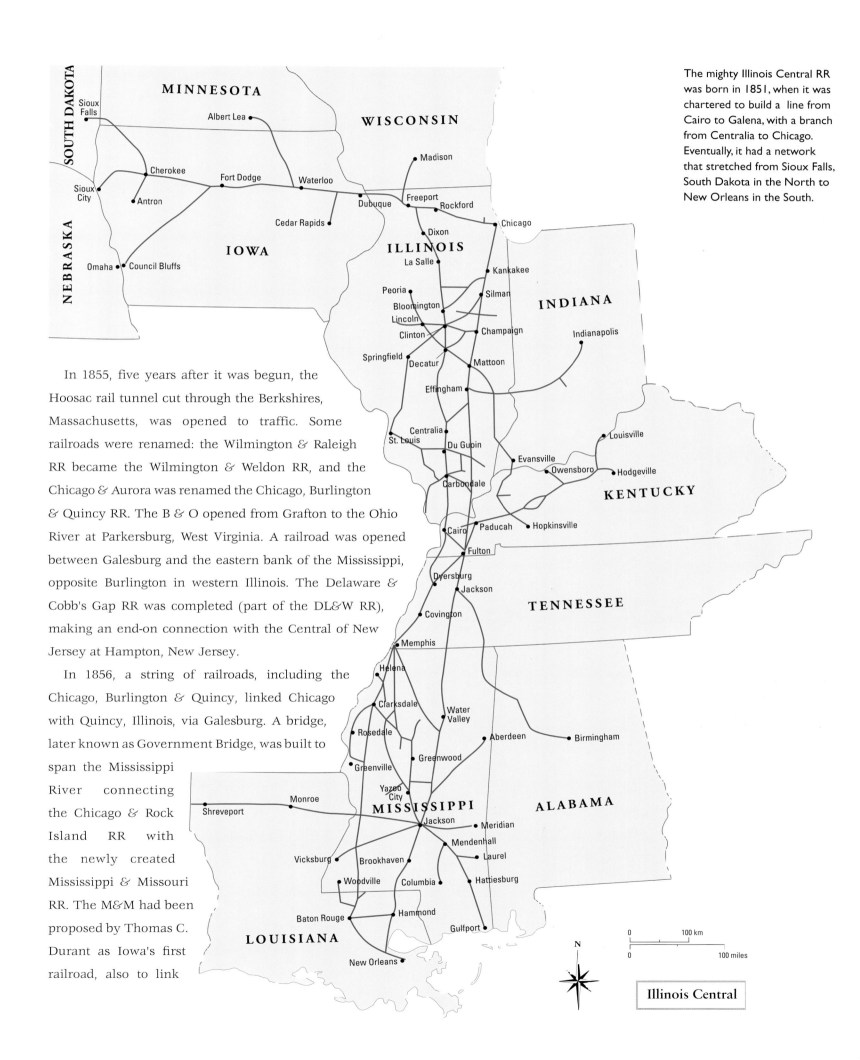

In 1855, five years after it was begun, the Hoosac rail tunnel cut through the Berkshires, Massachusetts, was opened to traffic. Some railroads were renamed: the Wilmington & Raleigh RR became the Wilmington & Weldon RR, and the Chicago & Aurora was renamed the Chicago, Burlington & Quincy RR. The B & O opened from Grafton to the Ohio River at Parkersburg, West Virginia. A railroad was opened between Galesburg and the eastern bank of the Mississippi, opposite Burlington in western Illinois. The Delaware & Cobb's Gap RR was completed (part of the DL&W RR), making an end-on connection with the Central of New Jersey at Hampton, New Jersey.

In 1856, a string of railroads, including the Chicago, Burlington & Quincy, linked Chicago with Quincy, Illinois, via Galesburg. A bridge, later known as Government Bridge, was built to span the Mississippi River connecting the Chicago & Rock Island RR with the newly created Mississippi & Missouri RR. The M&M had been proposed by Thomas C. Durant as Iowa's first railroad, also to link

Illinois Central

Established in 1851, the Chicago & Rock Island RR became the Chicago, Rock Island & Pacific in 1866 when it acquired the Mississippi & Missouri RR. The road eventually spread into Colorado and New Mexico, but ran its last train in 1980, having become bankrupt.

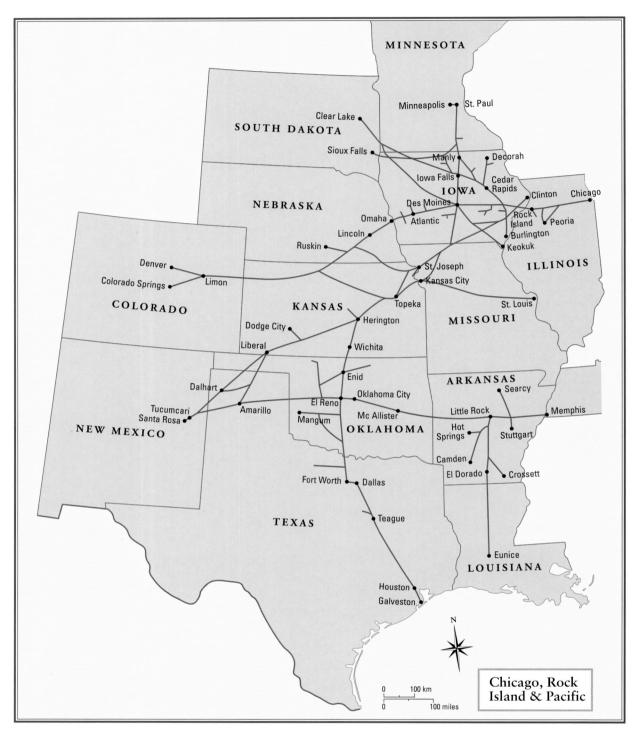

Chicago, Rock
Island & Pacific

Davenport, Iowa and Council Bluffs, Iowa.

Companies operating steam ships on the Mississippi opposed the bridge, complaining that it would pose a navigation hazard and alter their trade monopoly. The bridge crossed an island that was formerly the home of Fort Armstrong, so the Department of War influenced in its construction. Future Confederate President Jefferson Davis, Secretary of War under President Franklin Pierce, initially approved the bridge, considering that the first transcontinental railroad was going to pass through the South to Los Angeles, California. Davis eventually opposed the bridge, believing that it would result in the transcontinental railroad passing through the north. He ordered construction halted but the courts would not agree; the bridge opened on April 22, 1856. On May 6, 1856, the steamer *Effie Afton* hit the

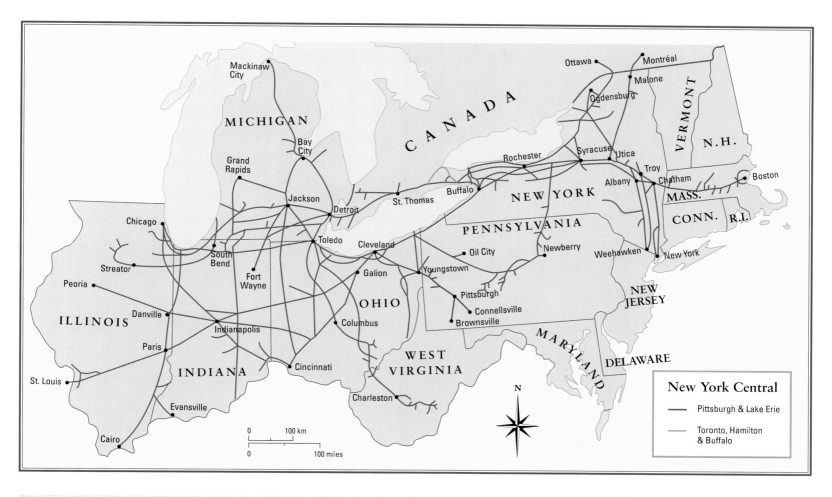

New York Central
— Pittsburgh & Lake Erie
— Toronto, Hamilton
& Buffalo

The famous New York Central RR opened its first line between Albany and Buffalo in 1853. It would go on to become one of the greatest U.S. railroads of the 20th century, operating in the Northeast and around the Great Lakes, where its Water Level Route ran to Chicago. As with many great railroads, it encountered financial difficulties in the 1970s and became part of the Conrail experiment. Eventually, it merged with its major rival, the Pennsylvania, to form the Penn Central.

The current Government Bridge—built in 1896 on the piers of the 1872 structure and 1,500ft (457m) from the original—is the fourth crossing of the Mississippi in this vicinity. It is a twin deck structure carrying rail and road traffic, but with two tracks to ease the rail traffic bottleneck.

One of the first railroads west of the Mississippi, the Missouri Pacific had its beginnings in St. Louis, Missouri, in 1851. By 1980, it had over 11,400 miles (18,300km) of route running through 11 states. In 1982, it merged with the Union Pacific and Western Pacific to form the Union Pacific System.

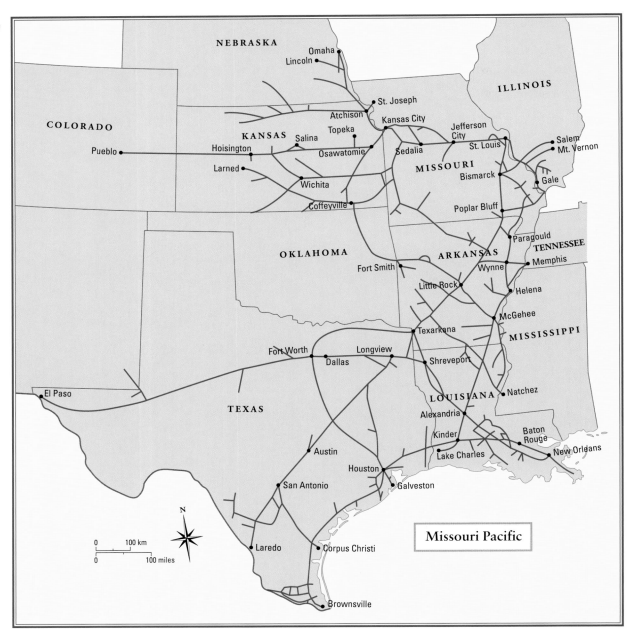

bridge, destroying the steamer, and one of the spans. It was rebuilt and reopened on September 8. This year saw the start of 10-year "war" between railroad and steamboat interests, during which no new bridges were built. Steamboat companies sued to have the bridge dismantled. The M&M and the Rock Island RR hired Abraham Lincoln to defend the bridge. The case was heard in the Supreme Court and decided in the bridge's favor in 1862. Meanwhile, the M&M and Rock Island railroads had merged to become the Chicago, Rock Island & Pacific RR. Durant formed a new company called the Union Pacific. In 1866, the bridge was considered inadequate for the increasing loads caried by the railroad and replaced with a heavier wooden structure that reused the original piers. This structure was replaced by an iron, twin deck bridge in 1872, carrying a single rail line and a separate roadway, at a new location on the western tip of Arsenal Island. The original bridge was abandonned.

By the year 1857, the rail network had extended from Charleston, South Carolina, to Memphis, Tennessee, although gauges varied from 2ft (610mm) to 6ft (1,829mm). The Milwaukee & Mississippi RR reached Prairie du Chien, the Atlanta & La Grange RR was re-named the Atlanta & West Point, and the

New York & Erie RR entered receivership and reorganized as the Erie RR with Jay Gould as president.

A financial crisis during 1857 caused the closure of many small lines and railroad construction companies, many of which had unwisely extended credit to potential purchasers. For example, Seth Wilmarth was under contract to build a large number of locomotives for the Erie RR, which had promised payment in cash. Financial flurry caused the railroad to renege on the deal, and payment was offered in stocks instead. Wilmarth's creditors demanded cash. He was forced to suspend production. Typical was Breeze, Kneeland & Company of New Jersey, which was forced to close by "the iniquitous conduct of certain western railroad managers who were buying engines on credit while they knew their companies were hopelessly insolvent."

During 1859 the first major railroad to abandon wood for coal burning was the Reading RR.

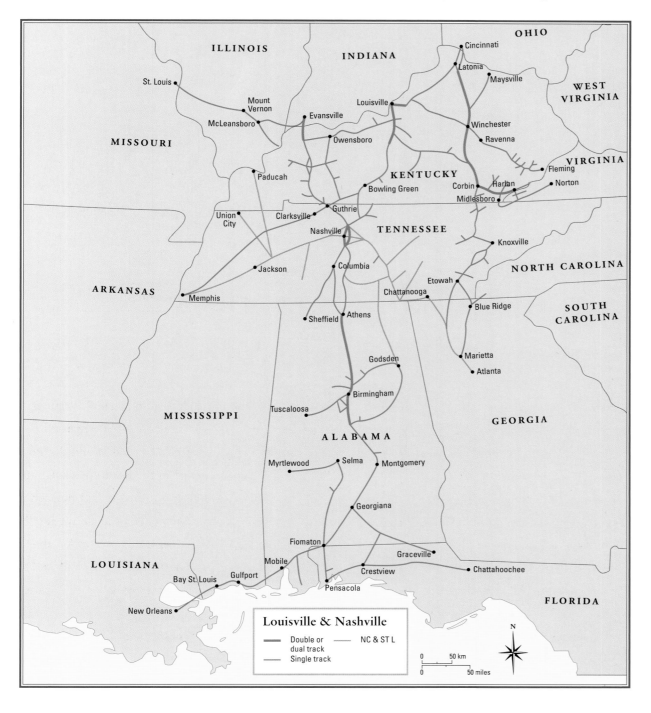

The first train on the Louisville & Nashville RR ran in 1855, between Louisville, Kentucky, and Nashville, Tennessee. During the Civil War, the railroad was in the center of the action, ending up working for first one side, then the other as the armies seized and lost ground. The network eventually ran down through the Southern states to the Gulf. In 1957, the L & N acquired the Nashville, Chattanooga & St. Louis RR. In 1971, it was taken over by the Seaboard Coastline RR, losing its separate identity in 1982.

The Drive Westward, 1843-69

SETTLERS HAD TRAVELED ACROSS THE NORTH AMERICAN CONTINENT SINCE LEWIS AND CLARK HAD FIRST BLAZED THEIR TRAILS, BUT 1843 SAW THE START OF THE LARGEST PEACETIME MIGRATION IN HISTORY, THE PIONEERS' STEADY PROGRESS ONLY ECLIPSED BY THE INEXORABLE SPREAD OF THE RAILROADS.

One thousand pioneers with more than 100 wagons and 5,000 head of livestock assembled at Independence, Missouri, at the start of what was to become known as the "Great Migration of 1843." Their goal was the promise of a better life out West, part of the concept that the United States of America regarded as its cultural goal of "Manifest Destiny" to expand the nation from the Atlantic to the Pacific Ocean. The settlers' route spanned more than half the continent, over some 2,710 miles (3,500km), terminating at what was to become Oregon City, the proposed capital of Oregon Territory. From there, they spread northward to what became the Washington area, or deeper south into Oregon.

The lure of free land had attracted pioneers to make the arduous journey, with some states setting up a process of land claims. In the Willamette Valley, for example, married couples were allowed to claim up to 640 acres (259ha), or a "section" consisting of a square mile (2.59sq km), while single people could claim up to 320 acres (130ha). Oregon Country was declared part of the United States in 1848, and the Donation Land Act of 1850, while recognizing earlier claims, granted settlers half a section if married, and a quarter-section if single.

The locomotive William Crooks was the first locomotive to operate in the U.S. state of Minnesota. Constructed in 1861, it first provided service a year later in 1862 for the St. Paul and Pacific Railroad, a company that eventually became part of the Great Northern Railway. James J. Hill had the locomotive

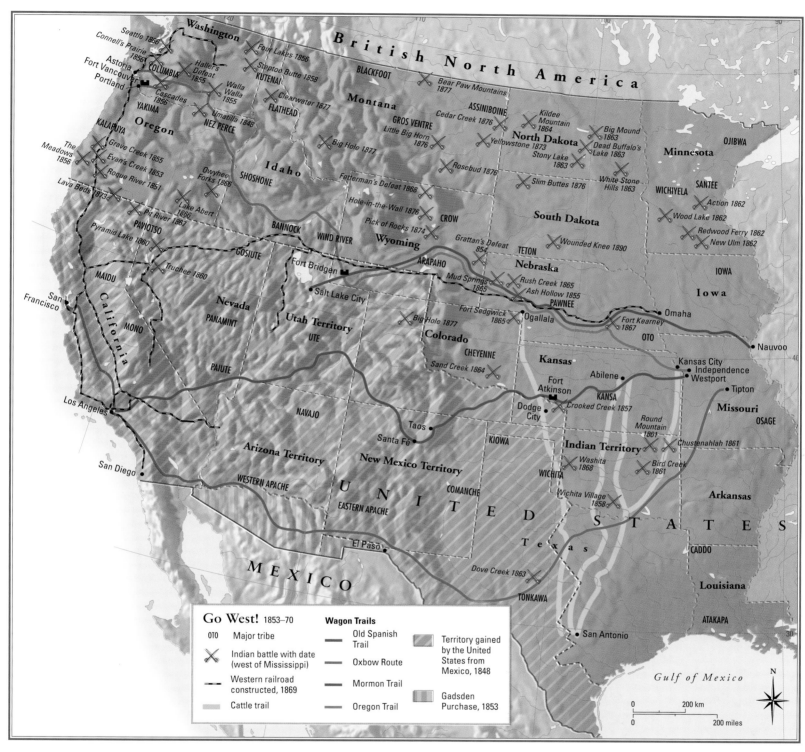

Go West! 1853–70

OTO   Major tribe

✕   Indian battle with date
     (west of Mississippi)

- - -   Western railroad
        constructed, 1869

        Cattle trail

Wagon Trails

         Old Spanish
         Trail

         Oxbow Route

         Mormon Trail

         Oregon Trail

         Territory gained
         by the United
         States from
         Mexico, 1848

         Gadsden
         Purchase, 1853

pull his personal train. It is reported that he was responsible for saving it from the scrap heap when engines of its vintage were being replaced by faster and more powerful vehicles. The classic 4-4-0 is one of the only locomotives from the age of the American Civil War to survive to the present day.

William Crooks was displayed at the 1939 New York World's Fair and again at the Chicago Railroad Fair in 1948 where it was operated as part of the "Wheels A-Rolling" pageant. It was displayed for some time at the Saint Paul Union Depot, but currently resides at the Lake Superior Railroad Museum in Duluth, Minnesota. Numerous other groups left the vicinity of the Missouri River and headed for the northwest territories, following the Oregon Trail, which had been first scouted by fur traders and

The middle of the 19th century saw a major westward migration as many settlers headed toward the setting sun in the hope of finding a new life, lured on by the promise of free land. The journey was not easy, however, and travelers faced many hardships, including a hostile indigenous population, before they reached their goal.

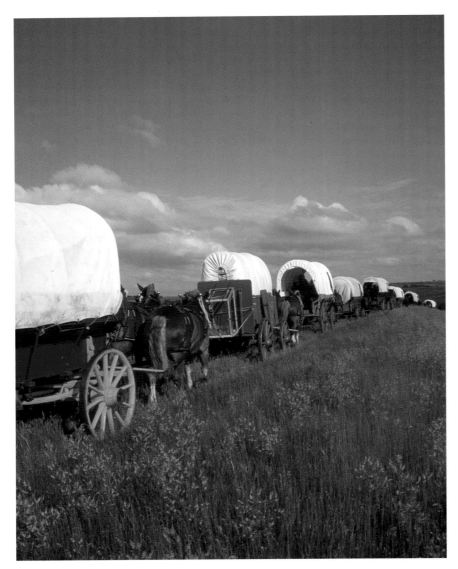

Until the first transcontinental railroad was built, the only way west for most was on horseback or by wagon train. Long lines of the "prairie schooners" would follow one of several established trails from Missouri, heading for California or Oregon. This photograph shows a modern day tour simulating the pioneers' experience on the trail.

explorers in the 1820s. Subsequently, it had been used regularly by missionaries and military expeditions since the 1830s. U.S. Highway 26 now follows the Oregon Trail for much of its length. In those early days, many pioneers branched off or stopped along the route, establishing settlements that thrived from the commerce of pioneers who continued to flood along the route for the next 70 years. The journey along the Oregon Trail was arduous in the extreme. The big, lumbering Conestoga wagons, hauled by oxen, were replaced by wagons about half their size pulled by teams of horses. Over 30 years 300,000 people traveled the Oregon Trail, while many more opted to stop off in Utah or California. Migration continued even as the railroads pushed westward, but it was not until 1869 and the establishment of the first transcontinental railroad that the use of the trail diminished, to be replaced by a more comfortable and quicker route to the new lands.

The Old Spanish Trail was a historic trade route stretching for 1,200 miles (2,000km) between the northern New Mexican settlement of Santa Fe and Los Angeles, California. Although it had been explored by European travelers since 1776, the trail was used extensively by pack trains from about 1829, which ferried Native American slaves and woolen goods from New Mexico to trade for horses in California. By the 1850s, the widespread use of freight wagons had begun to make the route obsolete. After the Mexican-American War of 1846-48, New Mexico and California had become U.S. territories, the presence of Mormon immigrants, and later the arival of railheads, badly affected the trade of produce and slaves.

The settlement of Mormons had begun in 1847 along the Mormon Trail. Led by Brigham Young and The Church of Jesus Christ of Latter-day Saints, about 13,000 Mormons—having been driven out of their communities by other settlers or because of rifts among themselves—set out from Nauvoo, Illinois, to find a new home in the West. Organized into military companies, a militia, and a night guard, Young's Mormons began the trek with a train of 73 wagons, draft animals, livestock, and supplies, eventually settling on the shore of the Great Salt Lake, which was then in Mexican territory. Over the next two years, most emigrants left Iowa, after the church created a fund known as the Perpetual Emigration Fund to help their poor followers, who could not afford wagons, oxen, and supplies. Intending to find land that no one else wanted, they were brought within the United States at the end of the war with Mexico in 1848. Emigration continued, and in 1856 a series of handcart companies were formed to ferry poor European emigrants to their new home. On completion of the transcontinental railroad in 1869, future emigrants were able to travel by rail, and the Mormon pioneer trail became redundant.

In 1853, the United States purchased from Mexico an area of 29,640 square miles (76,770sq km), a region that is now Southern Arizona and New Mexico. The purpose of the purchase had been to secure land for an envisioned southern route for a transcontinental railroad, and to compensate Mexico for lands taken by the United States. James Gadsden was sent by President Franklin Pierce to negotiate with Mexican President Antonio López de Santa Anna. The sum of $10 million was agreed upon, although only $7 million had been agreed by Congress. When the money finally arrived, $1 million had been lost. Gadsden had ulterior motives for the success of the purchase, since he was a supporter of a southern railroad and a shareholder in the railroad company that would build the line to unite Texas with California. In 1861, during the Civil War, the Confederacy created the Confederate Territory of Arizona, which included the land acquired by the Gadsden Purchase. Two years later, the Union formed its own Arizona Territory from the western half of the New Mexico Territory, which was later admitted to the Union as the State of Arizona in 1912.

Another passage west that operated between 1857 and 1861 was known as the Oxbow Route, or the Butterfield Overland Mail. This stagecoach route—an early operation of American Express and Wells Fargo—was used to transport U.S. mail and passengers between St. Louis, Missouri. and San Francisco, California, in 22 days, for a one-way fare of $200. Although 600 miles (966km) longer than central and northern routes, the Oxbow had the benefit of being free of snow to hinder progress. At its peak, the Butterfield operation used 250 Concord stagecoaches and 1,800 head of stock (horses and mules). It had 139 relay stations and employed more than 800 people. On the outbreak of the Civil War on March 21, 1861, the final Oxbow Route was run. The Butterfield enterprise continued until 1862 under the Confederate States of America, while Wells Fargo operated stagecoach routes in the north until 1869.

The threat of Civil War prompted the formation of the Pony Express in 1860 to deliver mail at a faster pace—just 10 days—on a central-northern route avodiing the volatile southern Oxbow. On the

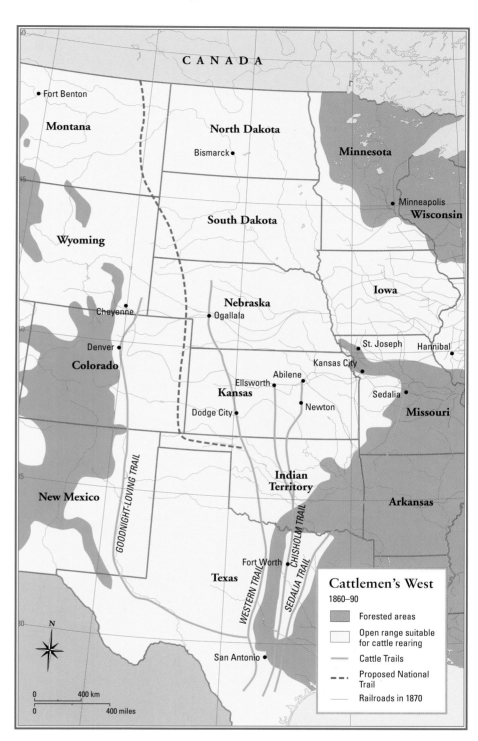

The West was cattle country, and the arrival of the railroads prompted cattlemen to drive their herds to the railheads so that they could be shipped to markets in the East. Several trails were established, running north from Texas to Colorado, Nebraska, Kansas, and Missouri.

THE PACIFIC RAILROAD SURVEYS, 1853-55

VAST NUMBERS OF THE POPULATION HEADED WEST WITH THE RAILROADS ON THEIR HEELS. IN 1853, JEFFERSON DAVIS ORDERED SURVEYS FOR THE RAILROADS, REPORTING ON THE GEOLOGY, ZOOLOGY, BOTANY, AND PALEONTOLOGY OF THE LAND, WITH ETHNOGRAPHIC STUDIES OF THE NATIVE AMERICANS.

B y the year 1848, the United States encompassed a vast expanse of territory stretching across the continent from the Atlantic to the Pacific oceans, but the only ways to get from one coast to the other were by a difficult and dangerous journey by horse or wagon, crossing mountain ranges, or a long voyage by ship. Gold had been discovered in California, and it became a priority to establish a faster and more convenient way to cross the continent with passengers and freight. The obvious answer was the construction of a transcontinental railroad.

Various government sponsored expeditions had already been undertaken during the early 1840s, and numerous routes put forward. No single route could be decided upon, however, since rival groups were determined that the railroad would pass through their state or town, with the promise of the economic riches that would result. In 1853, Congress authorized the Secretary of War, Jefferson Davis, to commission a number of surveys, and appropriated $150,000 for the Army's Topographic Bureau to finance the project. There followed four main expeditions across the West during 1853, with three supplemental surveys over the next two years.

In addition to determining the most favorable route for the transcontinental railroad, the survey teams were directed to compile reports on the general nature of the country, such as its flora and fauna, its geology, and climate. They were also required to compile ethnographic descriptions of the

Opposite Several survey expeditions were mounted in the mid-19th century to look for suitable railroad routes to the Pacific. They were also charged with recording everything of interest about the lands through which they traveled and the indigenous peoples they met.

native peoples they would encounter along the way.

The Northern Pacific survey set off between the 47th and 49th parallels, from St. Paul, Minnesota, to the Puget Sound. It was led by Isaac I. Stevens, who, having resigned his army commission, became governor of the Washington Territory. Stevens was accompanied by Captain George B. McClellan and Lt. Rufus Saxton. Also attendant were the natural scientists J.G. Cooper, G. Gibbs, and George Suckley, and the artists John Mix Stanley and Gustavus Sohon. During this most comprehensive survey photography was used for the first time west of the Mississippi.

The Central Pacific survey set off from St. Louis, Missouri, to San Francisco, California, between the 37th and 39th parallels. The

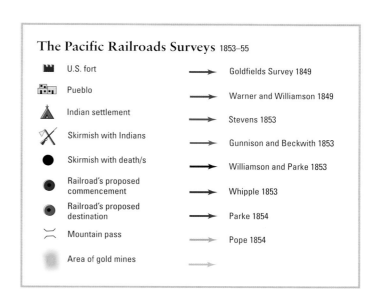

The Pacific Railroads Surveys 1853–55

🏰	U.S. fort	→	Goldfields Survey 1849
🏘	Pueblo	→	Warner and Williamson 1849
⛺	Indian settlement	→	Stevens 1853
✗	Skirmish with Indians	→	Gunnison and Beckwith 1853
●	Skirmish with death/s	→	Williamson and Parke 1853
◉	Railroad's proposed commencement	→	Whipple 1853
◉	Railroad's proposed destination	→	Parke 1854
⌣	Mountain pass	→	Pope 1854
	Area of gold mines	→	

CAÑON OF PSUC-SEE-QUE CREEK NEAR CAMP 41 A

MARIA'S RIVER

On this page and opposite are lithographic prints of contemporary illustrations produced by members of the transcontinental railroad survey teams, showing scenes from their journeys.
Top the Canyon of Psuc-see-que Creek, Oregon.
Above Negotiating a difficult incline above Marias River, a tributary of the Missouri River, Montana.

expedition was led by Lt. John W. Gunnison, assisted by Lt. Edward G. Beckwith and the artist Richard H. Kern. Other members of this survey team were George Stoneman and Lt. Gouverneur K. Warren. The team left Westport, Kansas, in June 1853, traveling up the Arkansas River and arriving in the Great Basin in the fall. After a skirmish with the Ute indians on October 26, Gunnison, Kern, and several other members of the expedition were killed. Beckwith took over command and continued the survey. He and Gunnison had considered that a route between the 38th and 39th parallels was unrealistic; evdentually, he concluded that the 41st parallel was the most practical. Although his suggestion was not considered at the time, ultimately this became the route on which the transcontinental railroad was built.

An expedition led by Lt. Ameil Weeks Whipple surveyed the route along the 35th parallel, from Little Rock, Arkansas, through Oklahoma, New Mexico, and Arizona. It then passed through the Mojave Desert to Los Angeles. Accompanying Whipple were a number of geologists, naturalists, botanists, and astronomers. In addition, the German artist Heinrich Balduin Mollhausen was recruited.

Another survey, led by Lt. Robert S. Williamson, accompanied by Lt. John Parke, traveled along the Californian coast from San Diego to Los Angeles and on to San Francisco, returning via an inland route. A further southern survey in 1854, led by Parke, traveled between San Diego, California, and El Paso, Texas, while Pope led a team from El Paso through Texas in an easterly direction. In 1855, Lts. Williamson and Henry L. Abbot carried out a north-south survey to search for the best route for a railroad between the Sacramento Valley and the Columbia River.

The extensive results of the surveys were published by the United States War Department between 1855 and 1860 in a 12-volume document, *Reports of Explorations and Surveys, to ascertain the most practicable and economic route for a railroad from the Mississippi River to the Pacific Ocean.* The surveys included hundreds of maps and prints, and many hand-colored illustrations of reptiles, amphibians, birds, and mammals. Each of the survey leaders believed that his route was the most advantageous for the railroad. but a final decision by Congress did not occur until after the Civil War, when the route along the 38th parallel, from Kansas City to the Pacific, was commissioned. The railroad, however, was not to be completed until 1869.

APPROACH TO CADOTTE'S PASS.

The exploration party moves up the Sun River valley "in the direction of the pass between the Crown Butte and the Rattlers, prominent landmarks west of Sun River and visible at a great distance."

DISTRIBUTION OF GOODS TO THE ASSINIBOINES.

Having set up their own camp close to the encampment of the Assiniboine Indians, the expedition members distribrute goods to the curious members of the tribe.

Railroads and the Indian Wars, 1850-90

THE WESTWARD EXPANSION OF THE RAILROAD AND THE FLOOD OF SETTLERS IT BROUGHT RIPPED THROUGH THE HOMELANDS, HUNTING GROUNDS, AND VERY CULTURE OF THE INDIGENOUS PEOPLE, TIPPING THE BALANCE OF THEIR COEXISTENCE WITH NATURE AND SPARKING VICIOUS CONFLICTS.

Communities of Native Americans had existed on the plains and in other areas of North America for centuries, their cultures and ways of thinking sculpted by the natural environment, and by their relationship with the vast herds of buffalo that were their livelihood. The tribes of Plains Indians had learned how to exploit the buffalo in many ways. The animal provided not only their food, war, and hunting implements, but also its hide as a covering for the teepees in which they lived.

To the settlers the railroad was a symbol of progress, but to the native Americans it heralded an erosion of their lifestyle. This illustration, from *Leslie's Illustrated News*, July 9, 1870, accompanied the report of an attack by Indians on a Union Pacific train east of Cheyenne. The train was able to escape unscathed, but General Dodge wrote to General Sherman "We've got to clean the Indian out, or give up. The government may take its choice."

The coming of European settlers and missionaries from England, Spain, France, Russia, Sweden, and the Netherlands in the 1500s, with their starkly different values, religions, technology, and diseases, gradually began to change the Native Americans' way of life. The tribes did not merely acquiesce to the onslaught of the foreigners, however, and numerous battles were fought with the colonists during the late 1600s. The 1700s also witnessed much strife as the settlers sought to relocate the Native Americans. As early as 1815, the U.S. government had a policy of removing the indigenous population to reservations. Wars continued to be waged throughout the 1800s, but it was not until the arrival of the railroad that the most dramatic and lasting changes occurred. The plains warfare between the Native Americans and the U.S. Army, between 1854 and 1890, stemmed from the need to secure safe routes for the transcontinental migration of settlers and the establishment of the railroad.

In 1854, the government wished to secure a northerly route for the proposed transcontinental railroad, which would run through the Native American lands west of the Missouri River. This sparked confrontations with the Shosone Indians. The wars continued apace after 1860 west of the Mississippi, the Great Plains witnessing most

In 1886, after a long campaign in Arizona and New Mexico, the U.S. Army finally subdued the Chiricahua Apaches, led by Geronimo and Nachez. The entire band was shipped off to exile in Florida by train.

of the fighting, although conflicts were also fought in the Southwest and Northwest, mainly against the Sioux, Apache, Comanche, and Cheyenne. Other tribes also waged war against the white settlers, notably the Arapaho, the Kiowa, the Ute, the Blackfoot, the Shoshone, and the Nez Percé.

On the southern plains, between 1868 and 1869, a war erupted between the Army and the Cheyennes, Kiowas, and Comanches, who were being forced into reservations; its deciding conflict was the Battle of Washita on November 27, 1868, when Lt. Col. George Armstrong Custer and his company attacked the Cheyenne village of Chief Black Kettle. On the northern plains, the railroads struck toward Sioux country, while gold was discovered in the Black Hills, which was part of the Sioux reservation. This sparked the Great Sioux War of 1876, and pitched battles with Chiefs Sitting Bull and Crazy Horse, culminating in the Battle of the Little Bighorn, when Custer and more than 200 men under his command were overpowered and killed by Crazy Horse and his warriors. The major wars on the Great Plains ended with the Great Sioux War, although battles were still fought against the Apache Chief Geronimo, who eventually surrendered in 1886.

While the Native Americans skilfully hunted the buffalo with bow and arrow for the very survival of their communities, the settlers hired professional hunters armed with rifles to supply meat for the railroad crews, while others slaughtered the animals merely for sport. The landscape changed forever as the railroad gouged a permanent corridor through the traditional buffalo hunting grounds; trees were felled to make ties and construct bridges, and the wild game that had once proliferated decreased rapidly in numbers. The presence of the railroad helped to cause the depletion of the buffalo from its conservatively estimated 15–60 million at the arrival of the settlers to virtual extinction, with fewer than 1,000 animals in the West by the end of the 19th century.

The Native Americans fought more than 200 ferocious battles with the Army between 1869 and 1878, but the onward spread of the railroad and the unstoppable flood of settlers rendered their resistance futile.

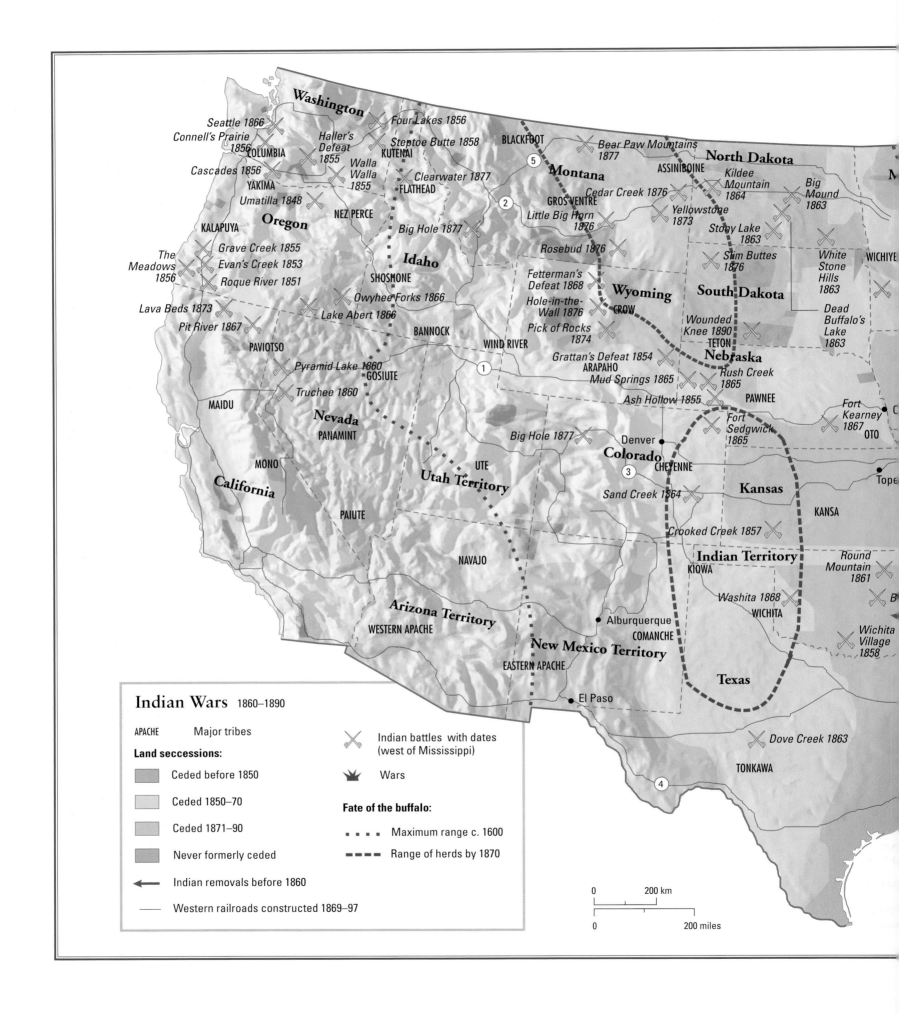

Washington

Seattle 1866
Connell's Prairie 1856
COLUMBIA
Cascades 1856
YAKIMA
Umatilla 1848
KALAPUYA
Oregon
The Meadows 1856
Grave Creek 1855
Evan's Creek 1853
Roque River 1851
Lava Beds 1873
Pit River 1867
PAVIOTSO
MAIDU
MONO
California

Haller's Defeat 1855
Walla Walla 1855
NEZ PERCE
SHOSHONE
Owyhee Forks 1866
Lake Abert 1866
Pyramid Lake 1860
GOSIUTE
Truchee 1860
Nevada
PANAMINT
PAIUTE

Four Lakes 1856
Steptoe Butte 1858
KUTENAI
Clearwater 1877
FLATHEAD
Big Hole 1877
Idaho
BANNOCK
WIND RIVER

BLACKFOOT
Montana
GROS VENTRE
Little Big Horn 1876
Rosebud 1876
Fetterman's Defeat 1868
Hole-in-the-Wall 1876
Pick of Rocks 1874
Wyoming
CROW
Grattan's Defeat 1854
ARAPAHO
Mud Springs 1865
Ash Hollow 1855
Big Hole 1877
Denver •
Colorado
CHEYENNE
Sand Creek 1864

Bear Paw Mountains 1877
ASSINIBOINE
North Dakota
Kildee Mountain 1864
Big Mound 1863
Cedar Creek 1876
Yellowstone 1873
Stony Lake 1863
Slim Buttes 1876
White Stone Hills 1863
WICHIYE
South Dakota
Wounded Knee 1890
Dead Buffalo's Lake 1863
TETON
Nebraska
Rush Creek 1865
PAWNEE
Fort Sedgwick 1865
Fort Kearney 1867
OTO
Kansas
KANSA
Crooked Creek 1857
Indian Territory
KIOWA
Washita 1868
WICHITA
Round Mountain 1861
Wichita Village 1858

Utah Territory
UTE
NAVAJO

Arizona Territory
WESTERN APACHE

New Mexico Territory
EASTERN APACHE
Alburquerque •
COMANCHE
El Paso •

Texas
Dove Creek 1863
TONKAWA

Topeka

Indian Wars 1860–1890

APACHE   Major tribes

Land seccessions:

▨ Ceded before 1850

▨ Ceded 1850–70

▨ Ceded 1871–90

▨ Never formerly ceded

← Indian removals before 1860

— Western railroads constructed 1869–97

⚔ Indian battles with dates (west of Mississippi)

♛ Wars

Fate of the buffalo:

· · · · Maximum range c. 1600

– – – Range of herds by 1870

0   200 km

0   200 miles

The relentless westward push of the white man, aided in no small part by the railroads, had steadily constricted the range of the buffalo herds and the indigenous population, leading, inevitably, to conflict. During the second half of the 19th century, battles with Native Americans raged throughout the Midwest and West, from Texas to the Canadian border.

OJIBWA

Michigan

ction 1862
e 1862
vood Ferry 1862
ew Ulm 1862

OWA

a

Wisconsin

Maine

V.T.

N.H.

New York

Mass.

Conn.

R.I.

Pennsylvania

New Jersey

Ohio

Illinois Indiana

Maryland

Delaware

West Virginia

Virginia

City

Missouri

OSAGE

Kentucky

North Carolina

enahlah 1861

861

Tennessee

Arkansas QUAPAW

South Carolina

Mississippi

Alabama Georgia

ODO

Louisiana

ATAKAPA

N

Florida

NTRAL PACIFIC RR–
NION PACIFIC RR 1869

RTHERN PACIFIC RR 1883

TCHISON, TOPEKA AND
ANTA FE RR 1883

④ SOUTHERN PACIFIC RR 1883

⑤ GREAT NORTHERN RR 1893

Sitting Bull (1831–90) foresaw Custer's defeat at the Battle of Little Big Horn. He surrendered in 1881 and eventually left the reservation to join Buffalo Bill Cody's Wild West Show.

Geronimo (1829–1909) leader of the Chiricahua Apache, warred against U.S. for more than 25 years, surrendering in 1885. In late life he converted to the Christian religion.

George Armstrong Custer (1839–76) was a flamboyant U.S. cavalry commander, defeated at the Battle of Little Bighorn by Indian tribes led by Sioux chiefs Sitting Bull and Crazy Horse.

Expansion of the Railroads, 1860-65

BY 1860 SOME 30,635 MILES OF RAILROAD HAD BEEN COMPLETED IN THE UNITED STATES. THE MAJOR STATES WERE OHIO WITH 2,946 MILES, ILLINOIS WITH 2,799 AND PENNSYLVANIA WITH 2,598. IN THE DECADE THAT FOLLOWED THERE WAS ALSO A GREAT EXPANSION OF RAILROAD BUILDING IN THE SOUTH.

Opposite The United States saw major urban expansion during the second half of the 19th century, the populations of many cities, particularly in the Northeast, growing rapidly. Industrialization was also on the rise in the Northeast and in the region around the Great Lakes, as well as farther south.

At the beginning of the decade, the 1,000th locomotive had been built by Norris, and by that time, there were about 9,000 locomotives in service in the United States. Also during this period, the modern practice of "remanufacture" had already been established, and the steam injector was introduced to replace the somewhat unreliable boiler feed pumps. Invented by the French balloonist Henry Giffard, the steam injector had been introduced to the United States by William Sellers of Philadelphia.

The railroads continued a steady expansion, and the Morris & Essex RR extended from Morristown, New Jersey, to New York, the Louisville & Nashville RR opened between Louisville, Kentucky, and Lebanon, Tennessee, in March; it was completed westward into Nashville in May, with a new bridge over the Cumberland River and another over the Green River at Munfordville, Kentucky.

In 1861, the outbreak of the Civil War far outshadowed any financial "panic" in its effect on rolling-stock prices. For example, the price of a standard eight-wheel locomotive rose 280 percent in little over three years. Many railroads benefited considerably from inflated wartime traffic. The demands of the United States military railroads enabled some commercial railroads to unload obsolete locomotives at a handsome profit. Other railroads, particularly in the Confederacy, were either halted, abandoned, or blown up. The Mobile & Ohio RR was completed to the port of Cairo, Illinois, on April 22; the Alton & Sangamon RR was extended and purchased by the St. Louis, Alton & Chicago RR, and the Virginia Central

Urban Expansion 1860–1900

Main industrial areas: 1860 | 1900 | 1920

Main industrial cities:

Population	1860	1900	1920
100,000–500,000			
500,000–1 million			
1–5 million			
Over 5 million			

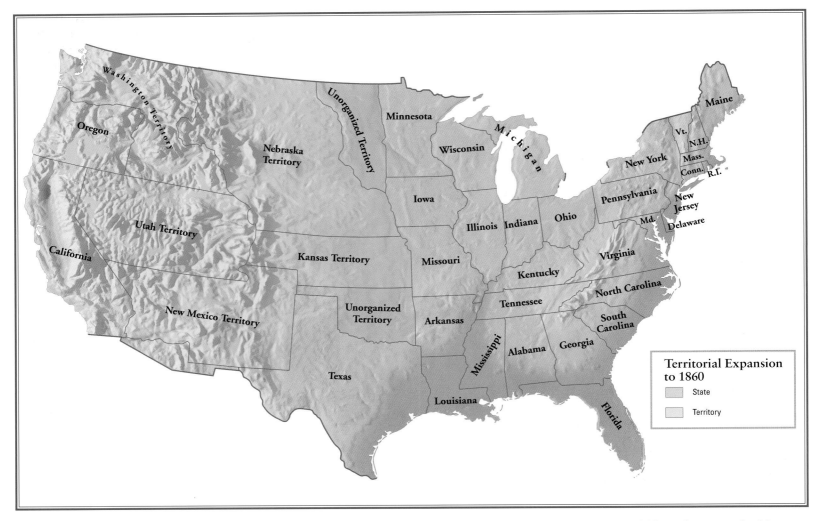

Territorial Expansion to 1860

☐ State

☐ Territory

By 1860, more states had been added to the Union, while little unorganized territory remained.

RR's westward expansion was halted by the war, despite the fact that it would have been a valuable asset to the Confederacy.

July 1, 1862, saw the signing of the Enabling Act by President Abraham Lincoln, which created the Union Pacific Railroad Company and authorizing it to "lay out, construct, furnish and maintain and enjoy a continuous railroad and telegraph line, with appurtenances, from a point on the 100th meridian of longitude west from Greenwich between the south margin of the valley of the Republican river and the north margin of the valley of the Platte in the Territory of Nebraska to the western boundary of Nevada Territory."

A system of hand signaling was brought into use on the Hudson River RR, the St. Paul & Pacific RR ran its first train between St. Paul and Anthony (now Minneapolis), Minnesota, and the Maine Central RR was incorporated. All four roads between Portland, Maine, Waterville, and Bangor,

In 1863, Levi Bissell's two-wheeled, swiveling pony truck was incorporated into the first "Mogul" class locomotive, built by Rogers for the New Jersey Railroad & Transportation Company; the truck was able to adjust to the curvature of the track than the normal types.

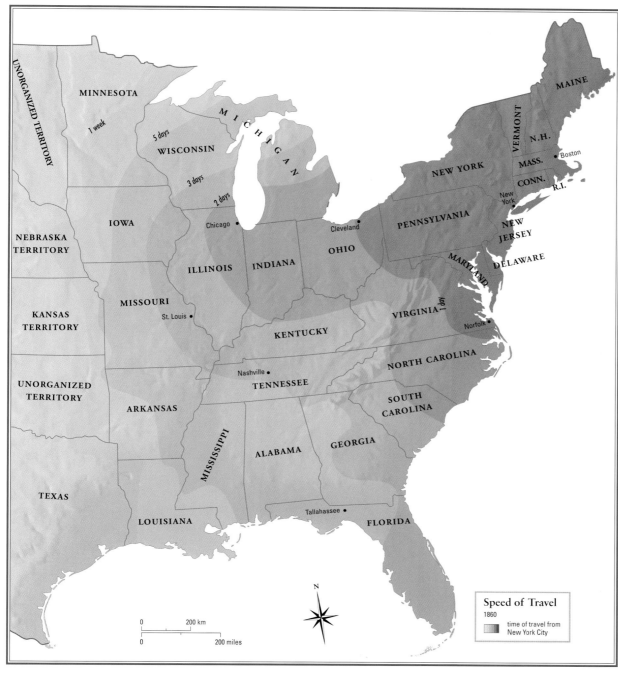

MINNESOTA

UNORGANIZED TERRITORY

1 week

5 days

MICHIGAN

WISCONSIN

3 days

2 days

NEBRASKA TERRITORY

IOWA

Chicago

Cleveland

PENNSYLVANIA

NEW JERSEY

DELAWARE

MARYLAND

NEW YORK

ILLINOIS

INDIANA

OHIO

KANSAS TERRITORY

MISSOURI

St. Louis

VIRGINIA

1 day

Norfolk

KENTUCKY

UNORGANIZED TERRITORY

ARKANSAS

NORTH CAROLINA

Nashville

TENNESSEE

SOUTH CAROLINA

MISSISSIPPI

TEXAS

ALABAMA

GEORGIA

LOUISIANA

Tallahassee

FLORIDA

MAINE

VERMONT

N.H.

MASS.

Boston

CONN.

New York

R.I.

N

0   200 km

0   200 miles

Speed of Travel
1860

time of travel from
New York City

By 1860, thanks to the railroads, the speed of travel from New York to many parts of the Northeast had increased considerably.

all broad gauge lines, were converted to standard gauge. The Nashville, Chattanooga & St. Louis roadway was damaged by floods in 1862.

Two years later, steel making was evolutionized by the Bessemer process, cutting the price of steel rails by half. Iron rails were gradually replaced, and steel rails were adopted on new projects. In this year, the design was perfected for the three-point suspension of the Hudson-Bissell swiveling, two-wheel leading truck for locomotives. This was also the landmark year that George Mortimer Pullman (1839–97) produced the first real sleeping car, the *Pioneer*, which boasted folding upper berths and extendable seat cushions for the lower berths. Further developments included the replacment of candle lighting in passenger cars with kerosene lamps. The "block" signaling system was first introduced on the New Brunswick, New Jersey and Philadelphia RR, on March 27.

As the Civil War progressed, on April 2, 1865, the Confederate government was evacuated by the

The Erie RR completed its first line, from the Hudson River to the shore of Lake Erie in 1851. It had been conceived as a trunk line from the very outset; eventually the network extended to southern New York State and around Lake Erie to Chicago. In 1960, it merged with the Delaware, Lackawanna & Western RR to become the Erie Lackawanna RR.

Richmond & Danville RR from Richmond to Danville, Virginia. The Chicago, Burlington & Quincy RR had a virtual railroad monopoly in western Illinois and the southern half of Iowa. The Milwaukee & St. Paul RR (Milwaukee Road) was formed by an amalgamation of the Milwaukee & Prairie du Chien and the La Crosse & Milwaukee railroad. The Montgomery RR was shut down following an attack by Union forces a few days after General Lee's surrender.

The Virginia Central RR was restored and was soon running again, while the Nashville, Chattanooga & St. Louis RR was rebuilt by the U.S. Government's Military Railroads Department and returned to its owners. Even as the war progressed, construction of the Union Pacific Railroad continued; it had reached Kansas City, Missouri, a distance of some 279 miles (449km).

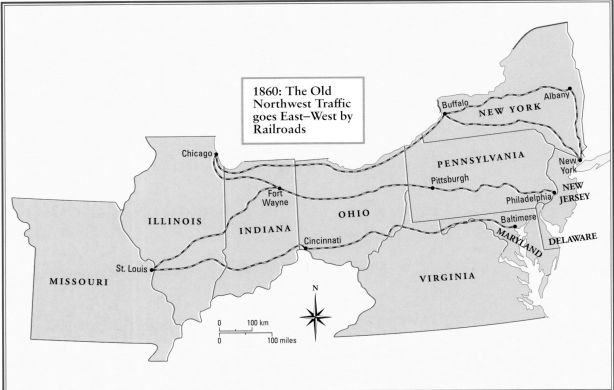

By 1860, thanks to the railroads, Northwest traffic could travel east–west to the Atlantic seaboard, rather than taking the long river trip to New Orleans.

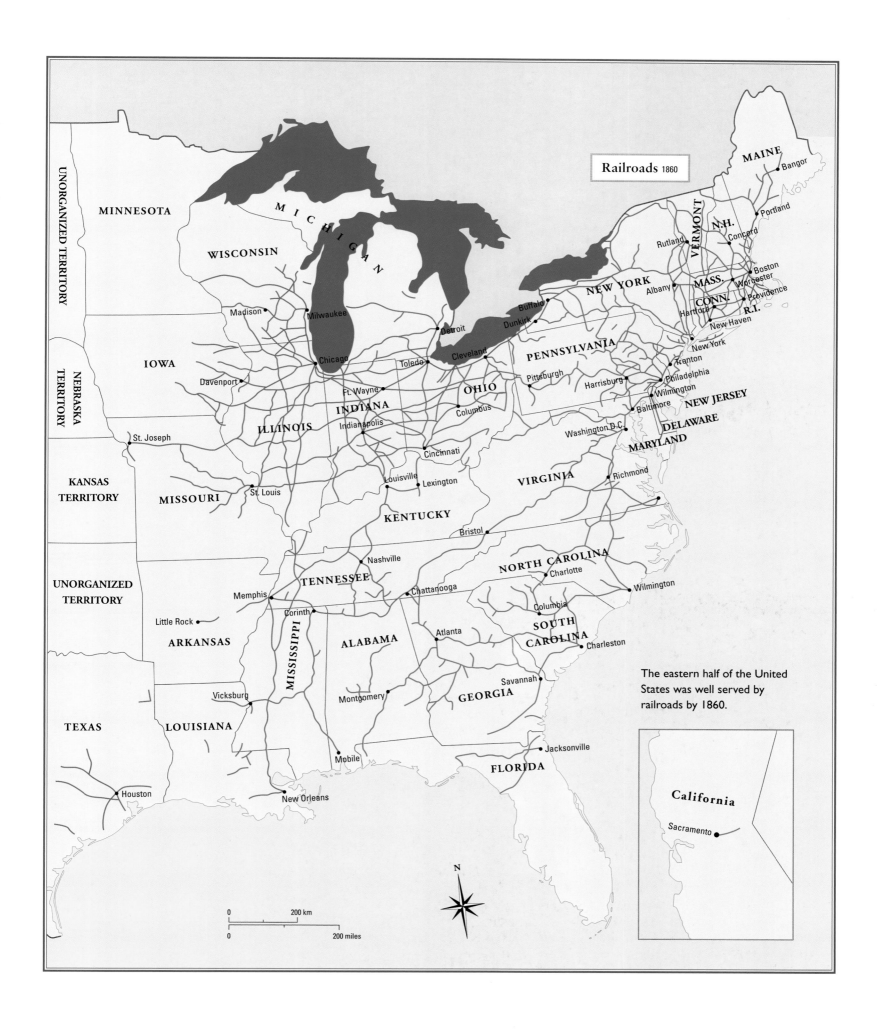

Railroads 1860

The eastern half of the United States was well served by railroads by 1860.

California

BACKGROUND TO WAR, 1861

THE CIVIL WAR TORE THE UNITED STATES IN HALF AND HAD A LASTING IMPACT ON THE COUNTRY'S DEVELOPMENT. APART FROM FIVE YEARS OF HOSTILITIES WITH DEVASTATING DESTRUCTION AND LOSS OF LIFE, RECONSTRUCTION LASTED FOR MORE THAN A DECADE AFTER THE END OF THE WAR IN 1865.

Perhaps surprisingly, one of the major effects on the railroads was to increase the rate of construction—partly because trains played a major role in warfare for the first time, and were second only to the waterways in providing logistical support and maintaining the economies of both sides. Tactically, trains were used to carry men and munitions to the battle zones, evacuate the wounded, and serve as makeshift hospitals. Some were even pressed into active service as platforms for mobile artillery. As a result, large amounts of track and rolling stock were damaged or destroyed, although most was rapidly rebuilt or replaced.

African American recruits to the Federal Army board railroad cars bound for Murfreesboro, Tennessee in 1863.

NEGRO RECRUITS TAKING THE CARS FOR MURFREESBORO, TENN., TO JOIN THE FEDERAL ARMY.—FROM A SKETCH BY C. E. F. HILLEN.

The American Civil War began on April 12, 1861, when Confederate forces attacked a federal military base at Fort Sumter, South Carolina, but its causes had been festering long before that. Much of the political strife of the 1850s had been concerned with the expansion of slavery into the new territories, with both pro- and anti-slavery factions convinced that this was the factor that would ensure its survival. The coexistence of a slave owning South and an increasingly anti-slavery North could lead to many anomalies, such as the one tested by the Dred Scott case of 1856. Scott was a slave who sued unsuccessfully for his freedom, on the grounds that while traveling with his master, an Army officer

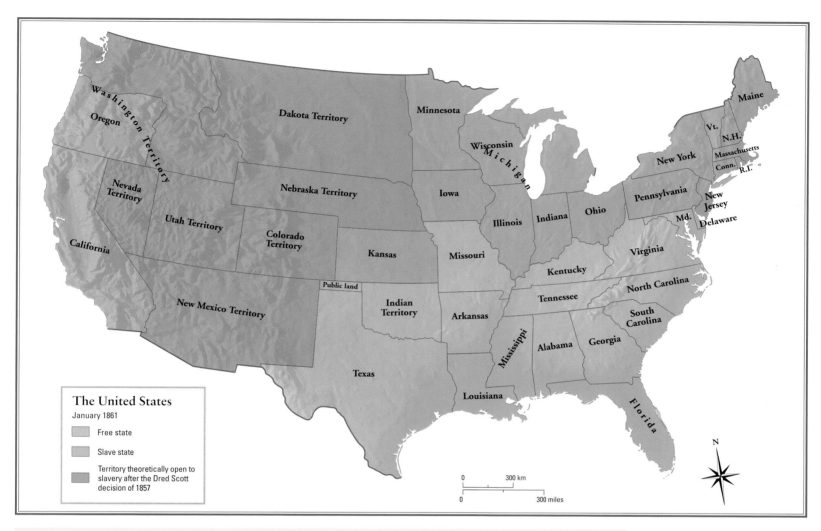

The United States

January 1861

☐ Free state

☐ Slave state

☐ Territory theoretically open to slavery after the Dred Scott decision of 1857

0   300 km

0   300 miles

N

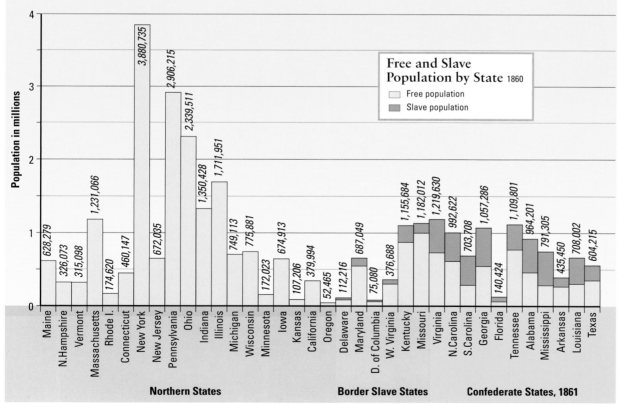

Free and Slave Population by State 1860

☐ Free population

☐ Slave population

Population in millions

Maine 628,279
N. Hampshire 326,073
Vermont 315,098
Massachusetts 1,231,066
Rhode I. 174,620
Connecticut 460,147
New York 3,880,735
New Jersey 672,035
Pennsylvania 2,906,215
Ohio 2,339,511
Indiana 1,350,428
Illinois 1,711,951
Michigan 749,113
Wisconsin 775,881
Minnesota 172,023
Iowa 674,913
Kansas 107,206
California 379,994
Oregon 52,465

Delaware 112,216
Maryland 687,049
D. of Columbia 75,080
W. Virginia 376,688
Kentucky 1,155,684
Missouri 1,182,012

Virginia 1,219,630
N. Carolina 992,622
S. Carolina 703,708
Georgia 1,057,286
Florida 140,424
Tennessee 1,109,801
Alabama 964,201
Mississippi 791,305
Arkansas 435,450
Louisiana 708,002
Texas 604,215

Northern States

Border Slave States

Confederate States, 1861

Following Lincoln's election in 1860, seven southern slave states seceded from the Union to form the Confederate States of America. After the attack on Fort Sumter in 1861, four more states joined the Confederacy.

A breakdown of the free and slave populations in the United States in 1860

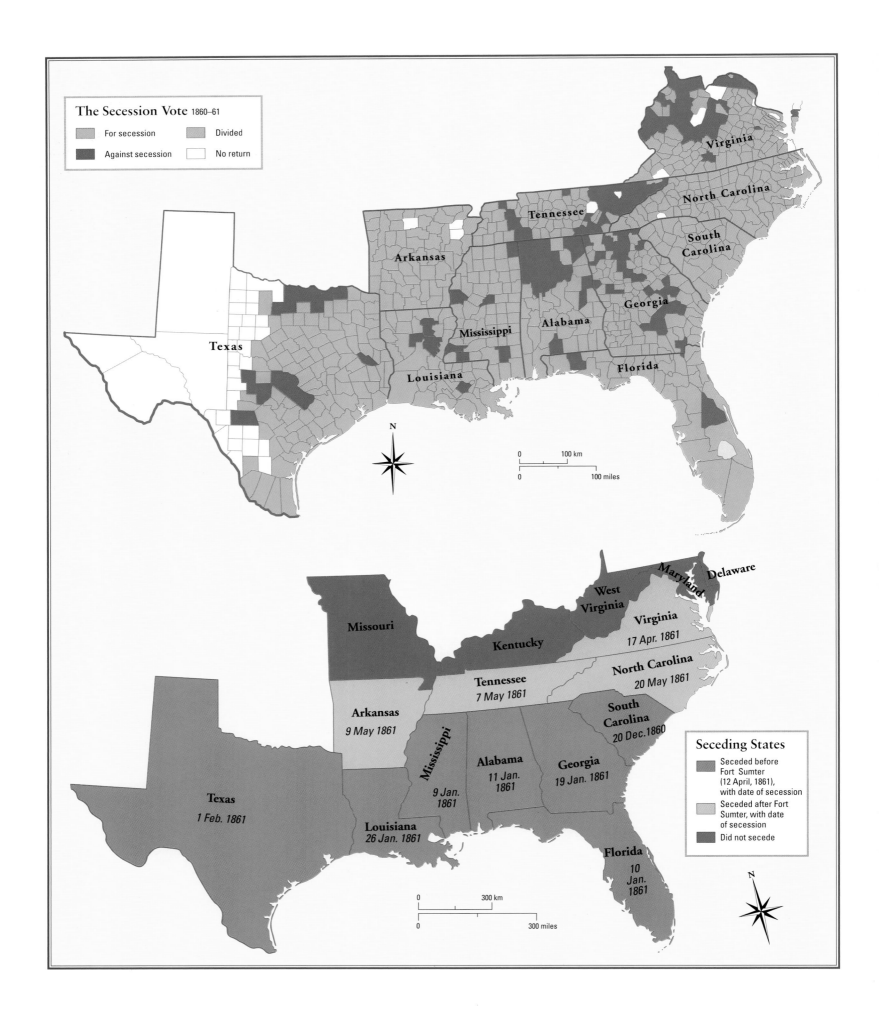

The Secession Vote 1860–61

- For secession
- Against secession
- Divided
- No return

Virginia

North Carolina

Tennessee

Arkansas

South Carolina

Georgia

Mississippi

Alabama

Texas

Louisiana

Florida

N

0   100 km

0   100 miles

Missouri

Maryland   Delaware

West Virginia

Kentucky

Virginia
17 Apr. 1861

Tennessee
7 May 1861

North Carolina
20 May 1861

Arkansas
9 May 1861

Mississippi
9 Jan. 1861

South Carolina
20 Dec. 1860

Alabama
11 Jan. 1861

Georgia
19 Jan. 1861

Texas
1 Feb. 1861

Louisiana
26 Jan. 1861

Florida
10 Jan. 1861

Seceding States

- Seceded before Fort Sumter (12 April, 1861), with date of secession
- Seceded after Fort Sumter, with date of secession
- Did not secede

0   300 km

0   300 miles

N

who was often transferred, Scott had lived in states where slavery was illegal. After almost a decade of legal action that went to the Supreme Court, it was ruled that any person of black African descent could not be considered a citizen of the United States, and that the free states could not confer freedom on black people.

Abraham Lincoln's presidential campaign platform was the promise to restrict or end slavery. While he had not proposed making slavery illegal where it already existed, he had made it clear that he was set on its "ultimate extinction." Following his election in 1860, seven southern slave states seceded from the United States on February 4, 1861, and formed the Confederate States of America, with Jefferson Davis as president. The Confederate constitution was similar to that of the United States, but contained several provisions to protect the institution of slavery. The first capital of the Confederacy was Montgomery, Alabama, but it was moved to Richmond in May 1861 after Virginia joined the Confederate States. It was one of four more states that joined the Confederacy that spring after Lincoln called on them to provide troops for the Union, while Missouri and later New Mexico allied themselves with the Confederacy without coming under its formal control. For a time, the border state of Kentucky had two governments, one of which supported the Confederacy, the other the Union. Fort Sumter became a Union stronghold within Confederate territory when federal troops of the United States retreated there after South Carolina declared its secession.

There were important economic differences between the South, the northeastern states, and the Midwest–and immediately before the secession, many businessmen and politicians had made the point that their trade with each other was vital to their joint prosperity. The Northeast was industrial (containing four-fifths of the country's manufacturing capacity) and urbanized, with an extensive transport network, including many railroads. The agrarian Midwest had historically been linked by road and rail to the ports and markets in the East, as well as the river network of the south.

On paper, the Union began the war with an enormous advantage over the South because it had over twice the railroad mileage—20,000 miles (23,186km) of track compared to the South's 9,000 miles (14,84km) of mostly lighter rail, while its two biggest railroads had more locomotives than the whole South. The South's system was also split into many separate small organizations, with crippling gaps in the network—and while most of the North's lines were at standard gauge 4ft 8½in (1,435mm), those in the South varied widely, forcing many more transfers. However, the North was not immune to the problem of a fragmented network, as would be shown when the war was barely a week old. In 1861, Baltimore's two rail stations were widely separated, and as soldiers arrived from the North on their way to join the Army of the Potomac, they had to cross the city. When the Sixth Massachusetts Regiment disembarked and tried to transfer to the other station, its troops were attacked by Confederate sympathizers, forcing the soldiers to fire on the crowds.

Jefferson Davis (1808–89), originally a Democratic senator for Mississippi, was chosen as president of the Confederate States. He continued to lead the Confederacy throughout the Civil War, but was captured at Irwinsville, Georgia, on May 10, 1865. Indicted for treason by a Grand Jury, he was never bought to trial and eventually was included in an amnesty granted to all members of the Confederacy in 1868. Subsequently, he became president of a life assurance company in Memphis, Tennessee.

Opposite Following Lincoln's election in 1860, seven southern slave states seceded from the Union to form the Confederate States of America. After the attack on Fort Sumter in 1861, four more states joined the Confederacy.

The Railroads at War

MILITARISTS HAVE CLAIMED THAT WARS ARE MORE OFTEN
DECIDED BY LOGISTICS THAN TACTICS. THIS WAS TRUE OF
NORTH AMERICA, WHICH WAS TOO LARGE A BATTLEGROUND FOR
ARMIES DEPENDENT ON MOVING ON FOOT OR HORSEBACK, AND
THE RAILROADS BECAME A CRUCIAL RESOURCE.

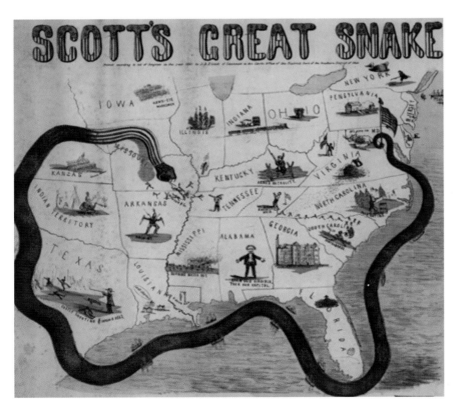

The Anaconda Plan was mooted by General Winfield Scott as a way of blockading the South's main ports.

I n the same way that the use of military airplanes in the wars of the 20th century vastly accelerated the development of aircraft technology, the Civil War had a similar impact on the railroads–particularly in the Southern states where the Confederate Army had a heavy dependence on trains to carry supplies to its battle lines.

As well as making it possible to wage war over a greater area than ever before, the railroads increased the scale of the conflict. For the equivalent weight of fuel compared to animal fodder, a railroad train of the era could carry 10 times the payload of a wagon pulled by draft animals. It could also deliver its payload at five times the speed. General Sherman's campaign of 1864 fielded 100,000 men and 35,000, animals whose supplies were all shipped by rail from Louisville to Atlanta. Sherman estimated that the single railroad track did the work of 220,000 mules and 36,800 wagons.

The area claimed by the Confederacy was almost all rural, and there were few large towns or cities. Prior to the Civil War, the extensive network of navigable rivers had provided cheap and easy transport for farm produce. What railroad systems there were had mainly been built to link the larger plantations

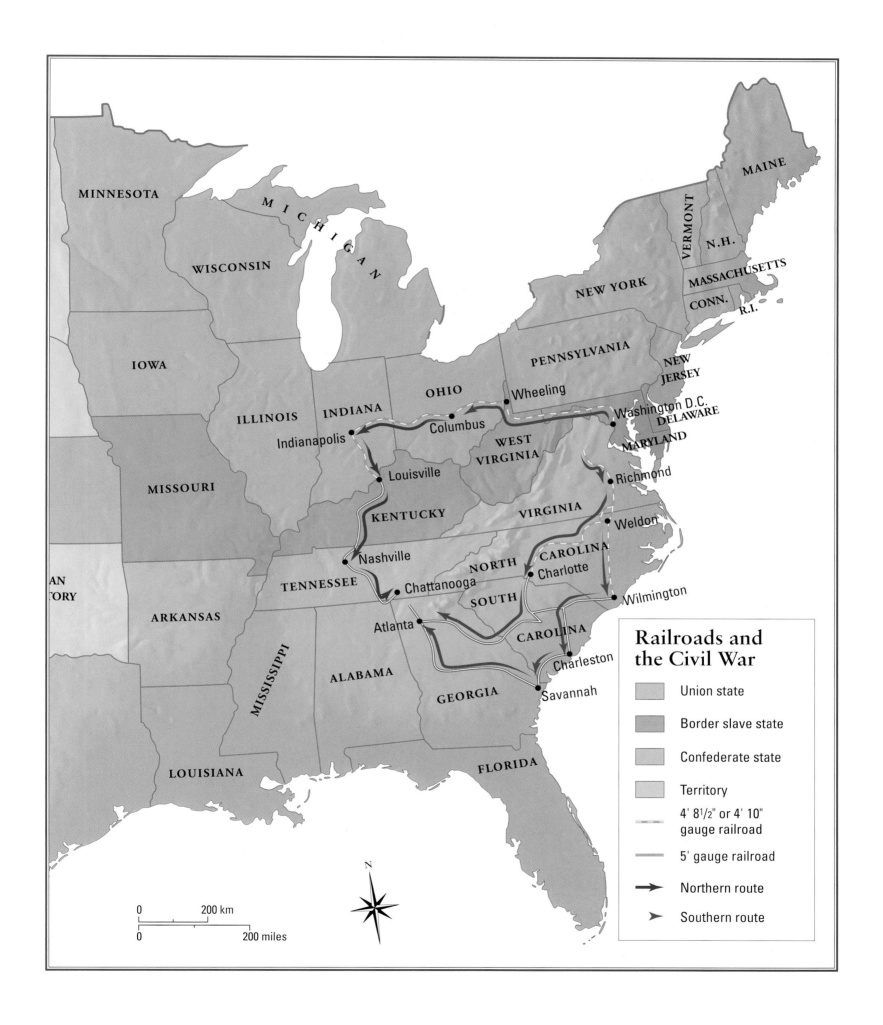

Railroads and
the Civil War

Union state

Border slave state

Confederate state

Territory

4' 8½" or 4' 10"
gauge railroad

5' gauge railroad

Northern route

Southern route

Cotton bolls, ripe for the picking, in a Tennessee field. The crop was a valuable resource to the Southern States, but its transportation to market was strangled by the Union Army's blockade of the Southern ports during the Civil War, while the rail network was patrolled by the Union's military trains.

The logging industry relied upon the railroads for the transportation of logs used in the construction of trestle bridges, and even the ties on which the rails themselves were laid. Narrow gauge trains were employed for their maneuverability on the winding tracks laid through the forests.

to the nearest river or port, and in some places rival railroads ran on parallel routes. Stations were sited irregularly and there were few through routes. The Southern states produced many of their own staple foodstuffs and raw materials—although the availability of these relied on good internal transportation, by waterways more often than rail—but their economy depended on cash crops of cotton, with some tobacco and sugarcane. Union General Winfield Scott's "Anaconda Plan" proposed a naval blockade of the South's main ports, followed by the capture of the Mississippi River, which would strangle and then split the South. As early as May 1861, world markets for the South's "King Cotton" were closed after the Union blockaded its ports.

Naval units of the Union had seized many of the main rivers by 1862, making it easy for the Union Army to move its troops and munitions, and pinning those of the Confederacy into small regions. After the siege of Vicksburg in 1863, the Union controlled the Mississippi, making it impossible for Confederate forces to cross, and cutting off the western Confederate states. Vicksburg, a fortress city on the Mississippi River, was typical of such Southern towns, in that it was a railhead for the Southern Railroad of Mississippi, down which General McClernand, one of the three Union leaders in the battle, had brought his troops. However, the defending forces were able to use the interior lines to move their own reinforcements, helping them to repulse the attackers.

All but two of the significant battles of the Civil War were fought in Confederate-controlled territory, almost half of them in Virginia and Tennessee. The first major land engagement, known as the First Battle of Bull Run, took place at Manassas, Virginia, on July 21, 1861, when inexperienced Union troops were routed by the Confederates, who advanced along the Manassas Gap Railroad from

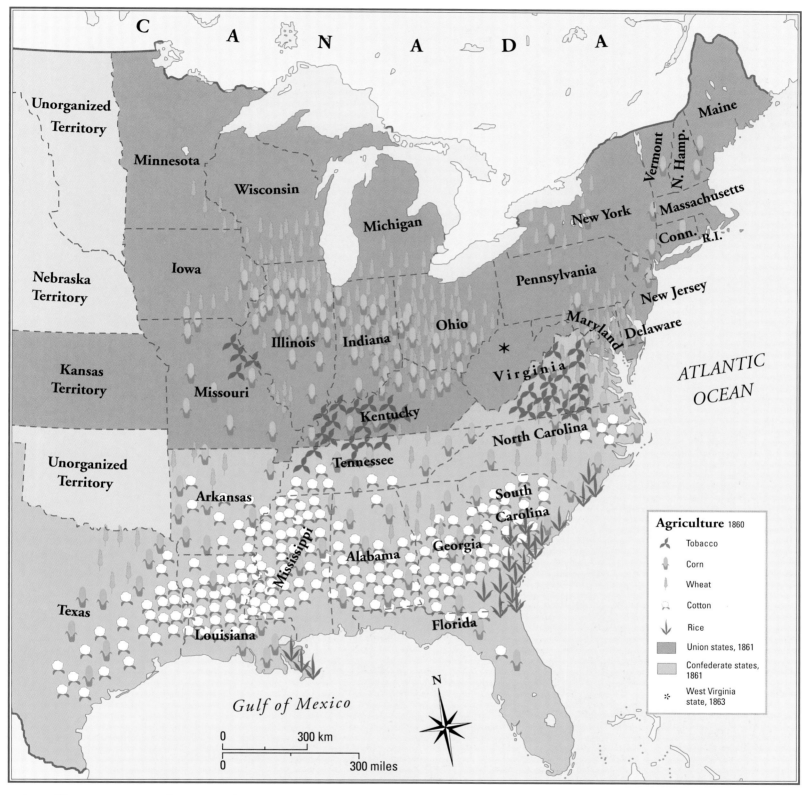

C A N A D A

Unorganized
Territory

Minnesota

Wisconsin

Michigan

Maine

Vermont

N. Hamp.

New York

Massachusetts

Conn. R.I.

Nebraska
Territory

Iowa

Pennsylvania

New Jersey

Kansas
Territory

Missouri

Illinois Indiana Ohio

Maryland Delaware

Virginia

ATLANTIC
OCEAN

Unorganized
Territory

Kentucky

Tennessee

North Carolina

Arkansas

South
Carolina

Texas

Mississippi

Alabama

Georgia

Louisiana

Florida

Gulf of Mexico

N

Agriculture 1860

Tobacco

Corn

Wheat

Cotton

Rice

Union states, 1861

Confederate states,
1861

West Virginia
state, 1863

0   300 km

0   300 miles

Gainesville to Manassas and encamped near Manassas Junction within 25 miles of the capital. Manassas Junction was little more than a railroad crossing, but it was strategically important, with tracks leading to both sides' capitals of Richmond, Virginia, and Washington, D.C., as well as the Shenandoah. Despite the Confederate Valley victory, the South's forces were soon repulsed, and Manassas Junction remained in Union hands for much of the war. However, it was also the site of General Robert E. Lee's resounding victory over the Union forces in August 1862 at the Second Battle of Bull Run, after the Confederates

The southern states were largely rural, and while capable of growing most of their own foodstuffs, their economies relied on cash crops such as cotton, tobacco, and sugarcane.

Professor Thaddeus Lowe's observation balloon *Intrepid* is inflated using the aeronaut's revolutionary portable gas generators, shown left of picture. Hydrogen was created by dropping iron filings into containers of sulfuric acid, and the gas was then piped into the balloon's envelope of varnished silk. This process could take two days to complete.

broke through the encirclement of Richmond and drove General McClellan's Army of the Potomac back into the Virginia Peninsula.

Important technological changes were taking place within the military bureaucracy, which sought new methods of gathering information about the enemy. One of these was the employment by the Union Army of manned, hydrogen–filled balloons, which up until then had been used chiefly for cartographic work. The balloons, made of varnished silk, were winched to altitudes of 2,000ft (610m) to observe enemy troop movements and those of trains on the railroads. The Union Army has formed a Balloon Corps of several gas balloons, under the command of the civilian aeronaut Professor Thaddeus Lowe. Lowe's balloons were inflated using his revolutionary, portable gas generators rather than by tapping a town's gas supply. Kept inflated for weeks, they were transported by rail, boat, or carried cross-country; trees obstructing their path were felled. Telegraph was used for the first time to communicate between balloons and the ground, enabling coordinated actions against the Confederate Army. Thus the Union Army was able to gain the upper hand in many battles. Experienced aeronauts were commissioned to join the Corps.

The First Battle of Bull Run demonstrated that the Confederates had been quick to realize the strategic advantage of rail transport as a means of moving fresh troops rapidly up to the front from an area that was not under threat. The North had been slower to make use of its rail network. This was partly because the war was being fought farther south, and partly because the Northern rail companies were often more concerned with ensuring they were properly recompensed rather than supporting the war. All that changed when the Railways and Telegraph Act, passed on January 31, 1862, formally authorized Union forces to commandeer any railroad necessary to support military operations. The chief reason that the

Opposite Throughout 1861 and 1862, the Union and Confederate forces clashed in a number of battles, while Union naval forces maintained a blockade of Confederate ports.

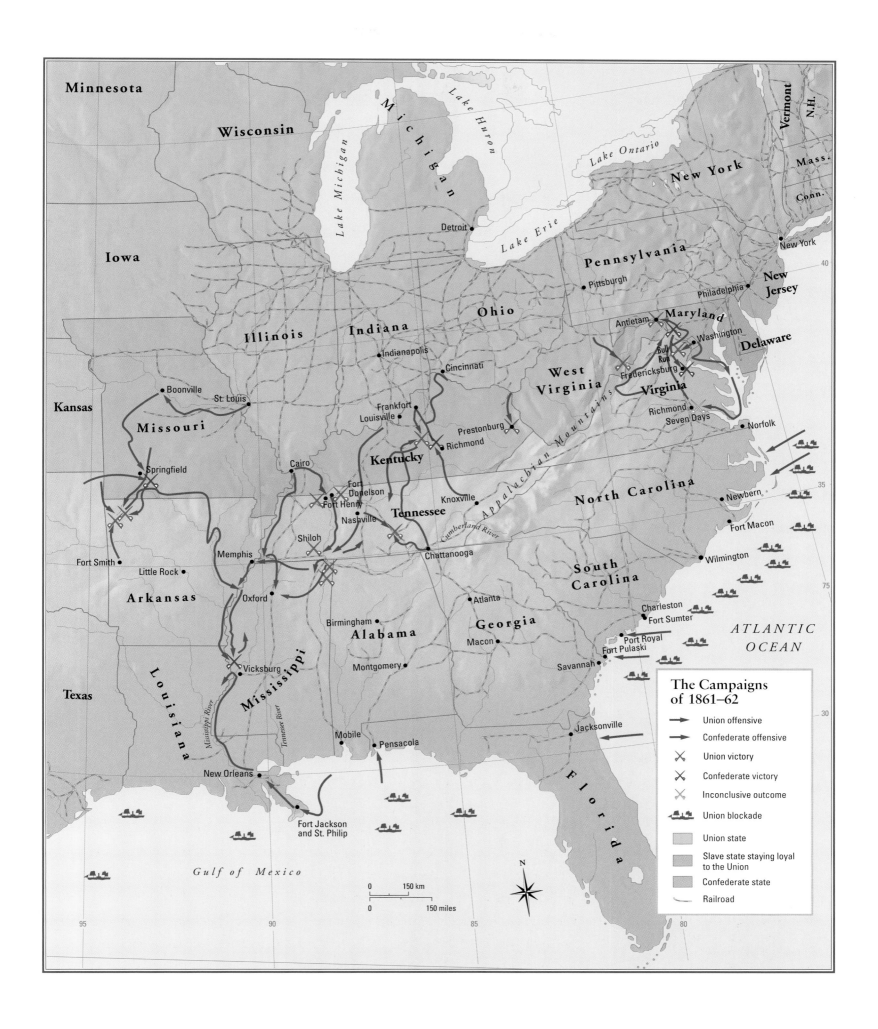

Minnesota

Wisconsin

Michigan

Lake Huron

Lake Michigan

Lake Ontario

New York

Vermont

N.H.

Mass.

Conn.

Detroit

Lake Erie

Iowa

Pennsylvania

New York

Pittsburgh

Philadelphia

New Jersey

Kansas

Illinois

Indiana

Ohio

Indianapolis

Cincinnati

West Virginia

Antietam

Maryland

Washington

Delaware

Boonville

St. Louis

Frankfort

Louisville

Bull Run

Fredericksburg

Virginia

Richmond

Missouri

Prestonburg

Richmond

Seven Days

Norfolk

Springfield

Cairo

Kentucky

Fort Donelson

Appalachian Mountains

North Carolina

Newbern

Fort Henry

Knoxville

Nashville

Tennessee

Cumberland River

Chattanooga

Fort Macon

Fort Smith

Memphis

Shiloh

Wilmington

Little Rock

Oxford

South Carolina

Arkansas

Atlanta

Charleston

Fort Sumter

Birmingham

Georgia

ATLANTIC OCEAN

Alabama

Macon

Port Royal

Fort Pulaski

Mississippi

Vicksburg

Savannah

Texas

Louisiana

Montgomery

Mississippi River

Tennessee River

Mobile

Pensacola

Jacksonville

New Orleans

Florida

Fort Jackson and St. Philip

Gulf of Mexico

The Campaigns of 1861–62

→ Union offensive

→ Confederate offensive

✕ Union victory

✕ Confederate victory

✕ Inconclusive outcome

🚢 Union blockade

◻ Union state

◻ Slave state staying loyal to the Union

◻ Confederate state

〜 Railroad

0 — 150 km
0 — 150 miles

N

Virginia
10 June–12 October 1861

← Union movement

← Confederate movement

1 Federal forces concentrate on Virginia's northern border.

2 **21 July:** McDowell's Federal forces, some 37,000-strong, meet the combined forces of Beauregard and Johnston at Manassas Junction. The Battle of Bull Run ensues. The Federals withdraw in confusion toward the Washington defenses.

3 **21 Oct.:** Reconnaissance by the Union into northern Virginia result in clash at Ball's Bluff in which Federals are surprised and defeated by a Confederate brigade.

The railroad crossing at Manassas Junction was strategically important to both sides, having lines leading to both Washington, D.C., and Richmond, Virgina. It was the site of the first major battle of the war, on July 21, 1861, known as the First Battle of Bull Run.

Where there was no access across rivers, or no railroad bridge, troops constructed pontoon bridges. Here a group of Union soldiers relaxes by a bridge over Bull Run, photographed in October 1862.

Act was passed was to pressurize the Northern railroads into cooperating. In practice, however, seizure was limited to enemy railroads captured during the conflict.

At first, such operations were run by the Army's Quartermaster Department, but in 1863, a new U.S. Military Railroads Department was formed to streamline the organization. As a measure of its importance and the scale of its operations, by the end of the war, in Tennessee alone, the U.S.M.R.R. was running two-thirds of the 15 private railroads that existed before the conflict. The existence of the U.S.M.R.R. set the precedent for government control of the railroads in World War I.

At the end of hostilities, several railroad lines that had either been destroyed or abandoned were rehabilitated by the U.S. Military Railroads Department, the most famous being the Nashville & Chattanooga RR, which was completely rebuilt in 1865–6 and returned to its former owners.

The Battle of Stones River (December 31, 1862–January 2, 1863), in Tennessee, had the highest percentage of casualties on both sides, although the Union Army, led by General William S. Rosecrans, repulsed the Confederates, led by General Braxton Bragg. The single track railroad running through the battlefield (center of illustration) was badly damaged and urgent repairs were needed before troop trains could run again.

RAILROAD SABOTAGE

BOTH SIDES USED THE RAILROADS TO TRANSPORT TROOPS AND
SUPPLIES. IN THE BATTLE OF CHATTANOOGA, THE UNION SENT
25,000 MEN AND 10 BATTERIES OF CANNON 1,200 MILES (1.931KM),
BY RAIL FROM VIRGINIA, TO REINFORCE ITS ARMY IN JUST 12 DAYS.

Men of the U.S. Army Railroad
Construction Corps at work
on the Orange & Alexandria
RR at Devereaux station, near
Manassas Junction, under the
watchful eye of General Haupt
(in the long black coat, right), in
whose honor the locomotive
was named.

The decisive impact of such troop movements was so great that commanders were known to shuttle empty trains back and forth in an attempt to deceive the enemy into thinking that reinforcements were being sent in. During the first week of the war, exactly this ruse was used to bluff the Union troops into abandoning the shipyards in Portsmouth by repeatedly running the same train into Norfolk along the Norfolk & Petersburg Railroad.

Railroad tracks soon became prime military targets for raiders from both the North and South, and one of the strategic goals of many campaigns was to capture rail centers. Such attacks destroyed bridges and rolling stock as well as the rails themselves. Snipers were also stationed to attack locomotives, either by shooting the engineer or attempting to puncture a boiler. As a result, some trains were armored, although full enclosure had a tendency to trap too much heat.

Because the early engines were relatively inefficient, they relied on stocks of wood and water being available at frequent intervals, as often as every 5 miles (8km). A surprising hazard was suggested by military orders that prohibited soldiers from washing in the railroad water tanks because of the risk that soapy water would cause air locks in an engine's boiler. General Herman Haupt, the Union Army's chief of construction, also arranged for stockpiles of railroad materials and prefabricated parts, including bridge sections, so that repairs could be made quickly. He pioneered a system of transporting loaded rail cars by

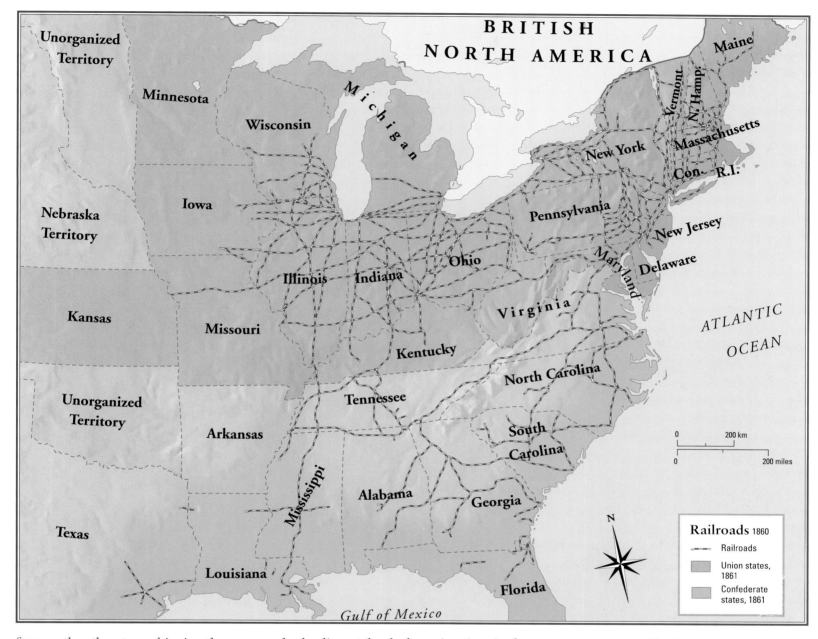

ferry, rather than transshipping the cargo and reloading at the dock, saving time in the process.

Both sides attacked the others' railroads. The Confederates twice raided the Baltimore & Ohio RR at Martinsburg, West Virginia. In 1861, "Stonewall" Jackson's troops attacked the B & O's workshops and engine house, where they destroyed 42 locomotives and removed another 14 partially dismantled units, using horses to drag locomotives and cars along dirt roads to the Confederate controlled Virginia Central Railroad at Staunton, Virginia for use in the South. The B & O was vulnerable because it had been built to the 5ft (1,524mm) gauge.

Even though it was ultimately of minor strategic significance, the most famous railroad action of the Civil War was the Great Locomotive Chase, featuring the *General*, the 4-4-0 steam locomotive built by Rogers, Ketchum & Grosvenor in Paterson, New Jersey, in 1855. In service on the Western & Atlantic Railroad between Georgia and Tennessee on April 12, 1862, the locomotive and a few railcars were hijacked by Northern spies, led by James J. Andrews, at Big Shanty (now Kennesaw, Georgia). Andrews and his men headed north, ripping up tracks and telegraph lines to sabotage the supply line

The United States had an integrated railroad network with over twice the mileage of that in the Confederacy, which was far less integrated. Moreover, southern railroads used a variety of gauges, while the northern lines were all of standard gauge. This gave the North a definite advantage.

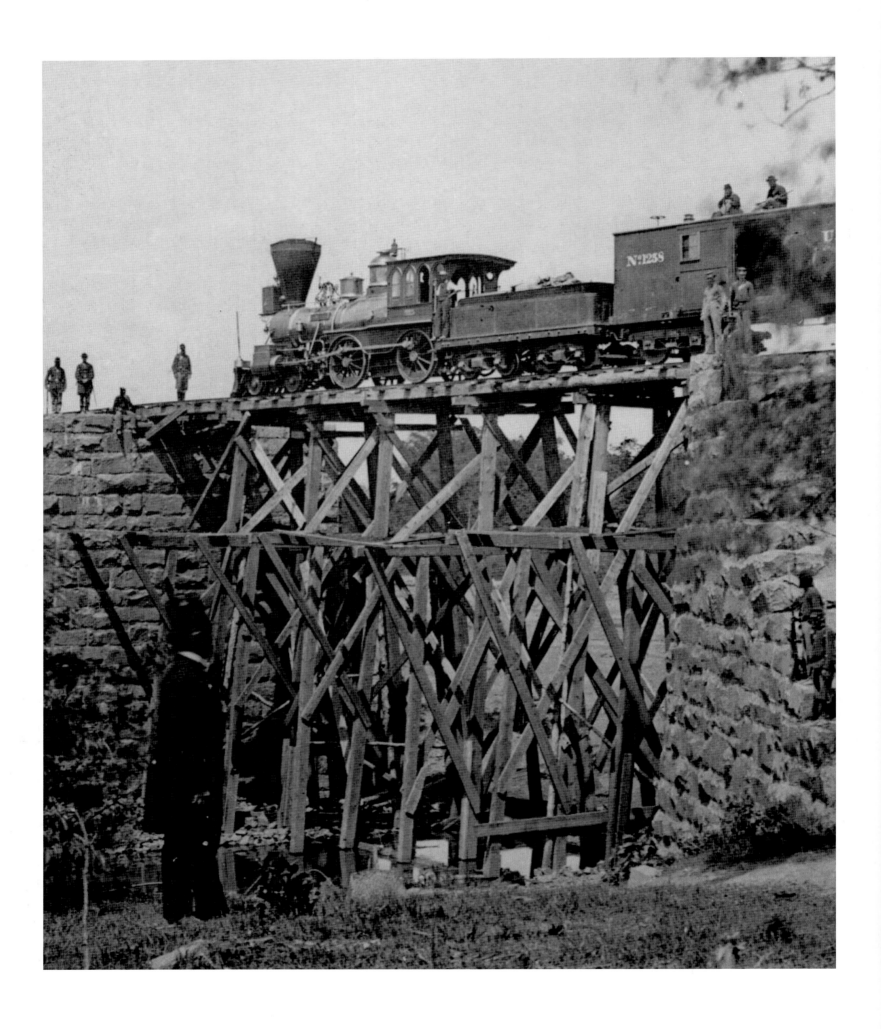

to Confederate troops in Tennessee. Their plan had been to dynamite tunnels and bridges, then escape north to Union lines. However, using a variety of other transport—most notably the *Texas*, which he drove for over 50 miles (80km) from Adairsville in reverse—the conductor of the *General*, William Allen Fuller, chased the raiders for 87 miles (140km), until the *General* ran short of water and wood, and lost steam pressure. The Union spies were forced to abandon the train near Ringgold, Georgia, south of Chattanooga, and tried to escape on foot. Had Andrews not been pursued by Fuller, there is little doubt that his plan could have

A ruined Confederate machine house at Atlanta, Georgia, in 1864. Several locomotives are being maneuvered with the aid of a turntable.

done significant damage to the Confederates. It was the second time that he had been unlucky. He had already tried to steal a train earlier that year, planning to destroy the strategically important bridge over the Tennessee River at Bridgeport, but that plan had been thwarted when his engineer failed to make a rendezvous. Captured soon after leaving the *General*, he was court-martialed and hanged as a spy, as were half his men, although eight escaped from captivity and returned home.

The *General* itself was almost blown up when the Atlanta depot was destroyed by General Hood in 1864, but the locomotive survived to become a museum piece on the National Register of Historic Places. The events were dramatized in Buster Keaton's classic silent film, *The General* (1927), and a later Disney film *The Great Locomotive Chase*.

The industrialized North had the advantage that damaged rails and rolling stock could easily be replaced, while the Confederacy's only locomotive works, in Richmond, had to be turned over to the manufacture of armaments. Advancing armies were forced to relay tracks that had been destroyed in action or sabotaged by the retreating soldiers. Some trains were converted for these engineering operations, but only one facility in the South was able to reclaim rails bent into "Sherman's bowties."

Typical damage to railroad tracks following enemy action. Each side tried to deny the other the use of this valuable form of transport.

Opposite Both sides used the railroads to move troops and supplies, so the trains and tracks became targets. Damaged by enemy action, this trestle bridge on the Orange & Alexandria RR in Virginia, was quickly repaired by Union Army engineers, allowing the locomotive *Firefly* to pass safely over.

The Railroad Campaigns, 1862-65

The strategic importance of the railroad network was clearly demonstrated in spring 1862, when Forts Donelson and Henry fell to the Union Army, and the Confederate General Albert S. Johnston decided to evacuate Nashville, Tennessee.

General Albert S. Johnston made great use of the railroads to move Confederate troops to meet Union threats.

Opposite As the war progressed, attack was followed by counterattack. The Confederacy used the railroads to move troops over 1,000 miles (1,610km) to attack Grant at Chattanooga.

General Albert S. Johnston was partly prevented from evacuating Nashville when panicking civilians overwhelmed all southbound trains. He was, however, able to use the railroads to concentrate troops from all over the Confederacy at Corinth, Mississippi, the junction of the Memphis & Charleston and Mobile & Ohio lines.

In April, Johnston's army battled General Grant's Union troops near Shiloh Church. When Johnston was killed and his men were defeated, the Union gained control of the only railroad north of Vicksburg and west of Chattanooga, giving them an easy route east to within striking distance of Chattanooga and southwards into Alabama. Grant defended the railroads around Corinth, Memphis, and Humboldt, but Confederate General Bragg launched raids against the Nashville & Chattanooga and Memphis & Charleston lines, as well as roads in Kentucky, with the effect of cutting Grant's supply line. This tactic delayed the Union Army and gave the Confederate forces time to move men by rail from Tupelo to Chattanooga.

Both sides in the war poured resources into the area using the railroads. The Union shipped in supplies to Murfreesboro, using the Nashville & Chattanooga RR, while the Confederacy brought in reinforcements from 1,000 miles (1,610km) away in Virginia to supplement those who marched from nearby Mississippi. By September, Union forces were under siege in Chattanooga, where General Bragg had seized control of the supply routes. To relieve the starving troops, the North devised a plan to move

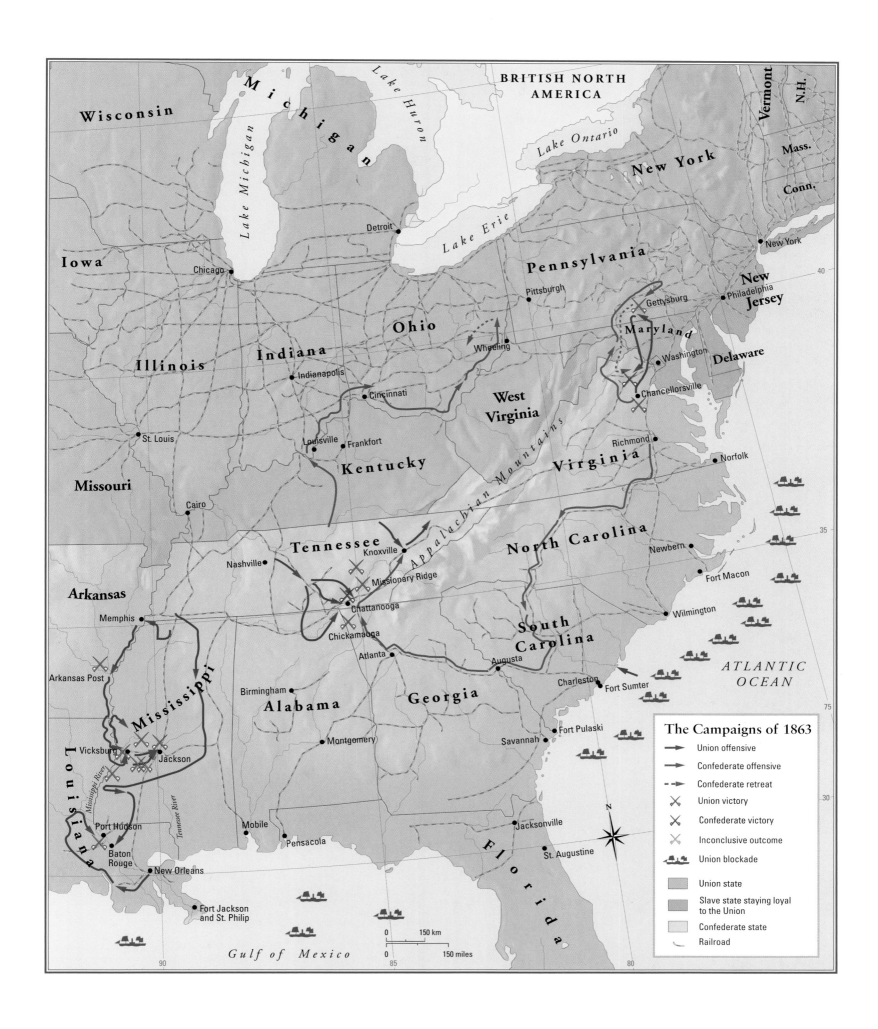

BRITISH NORTH AMERICA

Wisconsin

Michigan

Lake Huron

Lake Michigan

Lake Ontario

New York

Mass.

Conn.

Lake Erie

Detroit

Iowa

Chicago

Pennsylvania

Pittsburgh

New York

Ohio

Indiana

Wheeling

Gettysburg

Maryland

Philadelphia

New Jersey

Delaware

Indianapolis

Cincinnati

West Virginia

Washington

Illinois

Chancellorsville

St. Louis

Louisville

Frankfort

Kentucky

Richmond

Norfolk

Missouri

Appalachian Mountains

Virginia

Cairo

Tennessee

Knoxville

North Carolina

Newbern

Nashville

Missionary Ridge

Fort Macon

Arkansas

Chattanooga

Memphis

Chickamauga

Wilmington

Atlanta

South Carolina

Arkansas Post

Augusta

ATLANTIC OCEAN

Mississippi

Birmingham

Georgia

Charleston

Fort Sumter

Louisiana

Vicksburg

Jackson

Alabama

Mississippi River

Montgomery

Fort Pulaski

Savannah

Tennessee River

Port Hudson

Mobile

Baton Rouge

Pensacola

Jacksonville

New Orleans

Florida

St. Augustine

N

Fort Jackson and St. Philip

Gulf of Mexico

0   150 km

0   150 miles

The Campaigns of 1863

→ Union offensive

→ Confederate offensive

⇢ Confederate retreat

✕ Union victory

✕ Confederate victory

✕ Inconclusive outcome

⛴ Union blockade

◼ Union state

◼ Slave state staying loyal to the Union

◻ Confederate state

〜 Railroad

1. **21 Dec. 1864:** Sherman occupies Savannah.

2. **1 Feb. 1865:** Sherman begins march into South Carolina.

3. **17 Feb.:** Sherman occupies Columbia.

4. **18 Feb.:** Confederates evacuate Charleston, which is then occupied by the Union.

5. **22 Feb.:** Schofield occupies Wilmington, evacuated by the Confederates.

6. **1 March:** Major General Jacob D. Cox's "provisional corps" of Schofield's army heads west from New Bern toward Goldsboro.

7. **5 March:** Sherman reaches Cheraw.

8. **8–10 March:** Bragg checks Schofield's corps at Kinston.

9. **9 March:** Hampton's and Wheeler's cavalry make surprise night attack on Kilpatrick's cavalry near Solemn Grove.

10. **11 March:** Sherman occupies Fayetteville.

11. **16 March:** Hardree's Confederates hold up Slocum, until they withdraw to avoid being flanked.

12. **19–21 March:** Available Confederate forces concentrate at Bentonville and again attack Slocum. In the ensuing battle the Confederate forces lose over 2,600 irreplaceable men.

13. **21 March:** Johnston orders retreat in the face of overwhelming odds.

14. **23 March:** Sherman and Schofield link up at Goldsboro.

15. **13 April:** Sherman occupies Raleigh.

16. **17–18 April:** Sherman and Johnston meet at Bennett House near Durham Station and sign agreement providing for disbandment of all Confederate forces.

17. **26 April:** His agreement with Johnston having been rejected by President Andrew Johnson, Sherman again meets at the Bennett House with Johnston, who surrenders his army.

Sherman's March
16 November 1864–26 April 1865

⊔⊓ Confederate fortification line

�→ Union advance

●-➤ Confederate retreat

✗ Battle (Union victory)

General William Tecumseh Sherman (1820–91) was credited with creating the most destruction during the Civil War. His "March to the Sea," from Atlanta to Savannah, cut a 60-mile (97km) swath through the country that split the Confederacy in two. Nothing of any use to the Confederate Army was left intact, and the railroads were systematically disabled (*far left*). After the war, Sherman rose to command the entire U.S. Army.

in thousands of men from Virginia, finally succeeding in delivering Chattanooga and the rest of Tennessee into Union hands.

This experience helped to prepare General Sherman for his "March to the Sea," the campaign on Atlanta and Savannah. Realizing that his lines of supply would be under threat from Confederate saboteurs, he trained 10,000 troops in the art of railroad repair before he left Chattanooga. The troops became so skilled that damaged lines would commonly be returned to use within a day or two at most.

After the fall of Atlanta, when Sherman abandoned his supply line and continued the march to Savannah, his men turned their attention to the systematic destruction of the railroads as they progressed. A section of track would be ripped up, and all the ties piled into a heap

General Ulysses S. Grant (1822–85) was admired by President Lincoln for his fighting spirit. His troops had taken Vicksburg, seized Forts Henry and Donelson, and broken havoc in the South. Their combined actions brought about the Confederate surrender. Grant served two terms as President of the United States, from 1869 to 1877.

to make an enormous fire under the rails. When the rails had become red-hot, the troops would bend them around a convenient tree, and also put a twist in them to ensure that they could not easily be straightened. This gave birth to the term "Sherman's Bow Ties." This process made it virtually impossible for the Confederate forces to send men in pursuit of General Sherman and his troops, as he marched onward from the Georgia State Capital and on through the Carolinas. General Grant was well aware that the South's shrinking industrial base would have enormous difficulty in reclaiming the damaged rails or producing new ones.

Opposite After attacking Atlanta and Savannah, Sherman turned his men northward and continued through the Carolinas, destroying railroads as they went to prevent pursuit.

TECHNOLOGICAL AND ECONOMIC DEVELOPMENT

ALTHOUGH THE CIVIL WAR HAD CRIPPLED THE SOUTHERN
ECONOMY AND DIVERTED MANY OF ITS MOST ABLE MEN INTO
MILITARY SERVICE, THE RAIL NETWORK REMAINED VITAL TO ITS
SURVIVAL, TO THE EXTENT THAT NEW RAILROADS THATWERE
BEING CONSTRUCTED EVEN WHILE THE CONFLICT RAGED.

A large artillery piece mounted on a flatcar, with a wooden shield to protect the gun crew. While such arrangements provided mobility, they restricted the direction in which:the cannon could be fired.

The South's existing railroads had been built because they made economic good sense. Now, new connections were being made because they made strategic sense. A good example was Florida, where before the war, the railroad network in the peninsula had no connection to other tracks in the South.

Farther north, work on the Atlantic & Gulf Railroad, running from Screven south of Albany, was halted by the war, and in 1863, the Atlantic & Gulf Railroad merged with the Savannah & Albany, which ran east to Savannah. Late in the war, the Confederate government wanted to connect the Florida railroads with the rest of the network, so a spur was built from Dupont south to the Florida state line to link up with another spur running from Live Oak on the Pensacola & Georgia Railroad. Although this came too late to be of military importance, it usefully extended the Atlantic & Gulf's network when it acquired the extra track after the war. Pensacola, the first European settlement in what would become the United States, had weathered many changes of allegiance during its long history. It was evacuated early in 1862, leading to the seizure of the Alabama & Florida Railroad, part of which was replaced by the Mobile & Great Northern Railroad.

Other lines that were extended in 1862 included sections of the Alabama & Mississippi Rivers Railroad and the Northeast & Southwest Railroad. The following year, the Piedmont Railroad connected the North Carolina Railroad to the southern section of the Richmond & Danville Railroad, at Danville, Virginia. In 1864, this would prove strategically important after the Petersburg Railroad—previously the only line connecting Richmond to the South was cut off. Construction of other lines was abandoned owing to a shortage of money, even though some, like the Covington & Ohio RR, might have been valuable to the Confederacy.

The more industrialized North already had better rail connections that assisted in the movement of supplies, arms, and munitions, but the Union Army also extended railroads, building a new section of the Nashville & Northwestern to bypass a stretch of the Tennessee River. More importantly, the Civil War

Because the railroads were of such strategic importance to both armies, they were major targets. Bridges were particularly vulnerable; their loss could deny the use of a road for a long time. This bridge, over the Cumberland River, Nashville, Tennessee in 1864, has been fortified with gates, towers, and lumber siding, all furnished with firing slits.

was a major factor behind plans to build the Union Pacific Railroad to the west.

Closer to the battle zone, trains were widely used to transport artillery to the front, and also as mobile gun platforms. Field guns were conventionally moved by horses, which had to be unhitched before the weapons could be deployed. Mounting a battery on flatcars meant that it could be fired without such a pause, or even while on the move. Guns were mounted so that they would recoil down the length of the car against restraining ropes. Some carried angled shields made of wood or metal to protect the gun crews, in which case, the guns were arranged so that they fired through gaps in the shields.

Whole trains were often made up with the locomotive in the center, where it was less vulnerable to attack. Passenger cars or boxcars would be coupled to the locomotive, with flatcars at the ends. These carried troops or artillery where they would command the widest field of fire. Such armed cars could protect supply trains or even be used as attack vehicles.

Following the naval action between the ironclad vessels *Monitor* and *Merrimack*, armored railroad cars were built. These looked like iron boxcars, the infantrymen inside being given apertures through which to fire, but their armor was only protection against small-arms fire. A later development had an artillery piece mounted on top to give it a field of fire all around the train. The final development of the "railroad monitor" had thick, angled armor and artillery resembling a modern tank, although turrets were not fitted until well after the Civil War. Armor could protect a train from bullets and artillery shells, but the easiest target was the track or roadbed. A damaged track would prevent forward progress until it was repaired, but would not wreck the train if the engineer were vigilant enough to stop in time. Far more deadly was a mine rigged to detonate when a train passed over it. Such devices, then known as "torpedos" included specially constructed mines filled with gunpowder and provided with a pressure-sensitive firing

This giant mortar, known as *The Dictator*, was used in the Union seige of Petersburg. Weighing 17,120lb (7,766kg), it could throw a 13in (33cm), 200lb (91kg) shell over a distance of 2.5 miles (4km). It was mounted on a special flatcar and operated on a branchline of the City Point & Petersburg RR

U.S. Military Railroad engineers point out damage sustained by the locomotive *Fred Leach* during operations in Virginia. It received hits on the smokestack and tender.

device, but artillery shells with percussion caps were sometimes used in this way. Where such hazards were expected, it was common practice to send a loaded flatcar ahead to detonate any hidden torpedo instead of risking the whole train. Another way to sabotage tracks and installations such as bridges, or even an oncoming train, was to pack an empty car or locomotive with explosives or set it on fire, then to send it on a collision course.

A less obvious use for the railroads was for reconnaissance. While a locomotive did not possess the advantage of stealth, it could travel at 60mph (97kmph), twice as fast as mounted cavalry, so commanders were willing to risk a dash into enemy territory, followed by reversing at speed out of the danger zone. Although they were much slower, handcars, which could move more quietly than a locomotive, as

A contemporary illustration of an armored boxcar.

well as being cheaper, were also used to reconnoiter or inspect tracks for damage. On occasion, they were used to transport supplies and evacuate personnel.

The war forced the development of other specialized rail vehicles. Hospital cars for transporting the wounded were often converted from passenger cars, being fitted with double rows of stretchers in place of the bench seats, although some were purpose built. Mobile medical cars were also made, providing surgical facilities on the move. Mobile field kitchens were developed as a way of efficiently feeding large numbers of soldiers.

END OF THE WAR, 1865

THE RAILROADS FORMED PART OF A STRATEGY THAT ENDED THE WAR AFTER LINCOLN MADE ULYSSES S. GRANT COMMANDER OF ALL UNION ARMIES. THEY BELIEVED THAT DEFEATING THE CONFEDERATES WOULD ONLY BE POSSIBLE BY STRIKING THEIR ECONOMIC BASE AND SUPPLY LINES AS WELL AS THEIR ARMIES.

Railroad equipment and infrastructure suffered considerable damage during the siege of Petersburg.

The campaigns of 1864 were decisive. Grant's siege of Petersburgh, plus Sherman's March to the Sea led to the Confederates' surrender.

While Lincoln had blockaded the Confederate ports since May 1861, Grant instructed Generals Crook and Averell to attack railroad supply lines in West Virginia. At the same time, other forces would destroy the agricultural bases in the Shenandoah Valley and Georgia. Toward the end of the war, the North was supplying its troops by the trainload, through its extensive rail network, while the Confederate Army, whose railroads had nearly been completely destroyed, was starved of both food and munitions.

The strategic importance of the railroads to both sides is particularly clear from one incident during the spring campaign of 1864. Crook, sent on a mission to destroy the salt works at Saltville, Virginia, met a sizable Confederate force near Dublin, Virginia. In what would become known as the Battle of Cloyd's Mountain, Crook's men routed the Confederate defenders, who were already on the run, until a train pulled into Dublin carrying 500 fresh Confederate cavalrymen from the force that had just defeated Averell. Although Crook won the pitched battle that followed, it cost the Union almost 700 dead.

Crook then marched on Dublin, where he destroyed the railroad buildings and stores. To prevent further railroad movement, his men tore up sections of the tracks and burned the ties. Next morning, they marched east to capture the New River Bridge, a strategic crossing. Although the Union troops were halted by Confederate artillery on the opposite bank, the bridge was blown up and collapsed into the river, after which the Confederates, cut off from their supplies, withdrew to the east.

The advantages were so great that when General Grant laid siege to the cities of Petersburg and

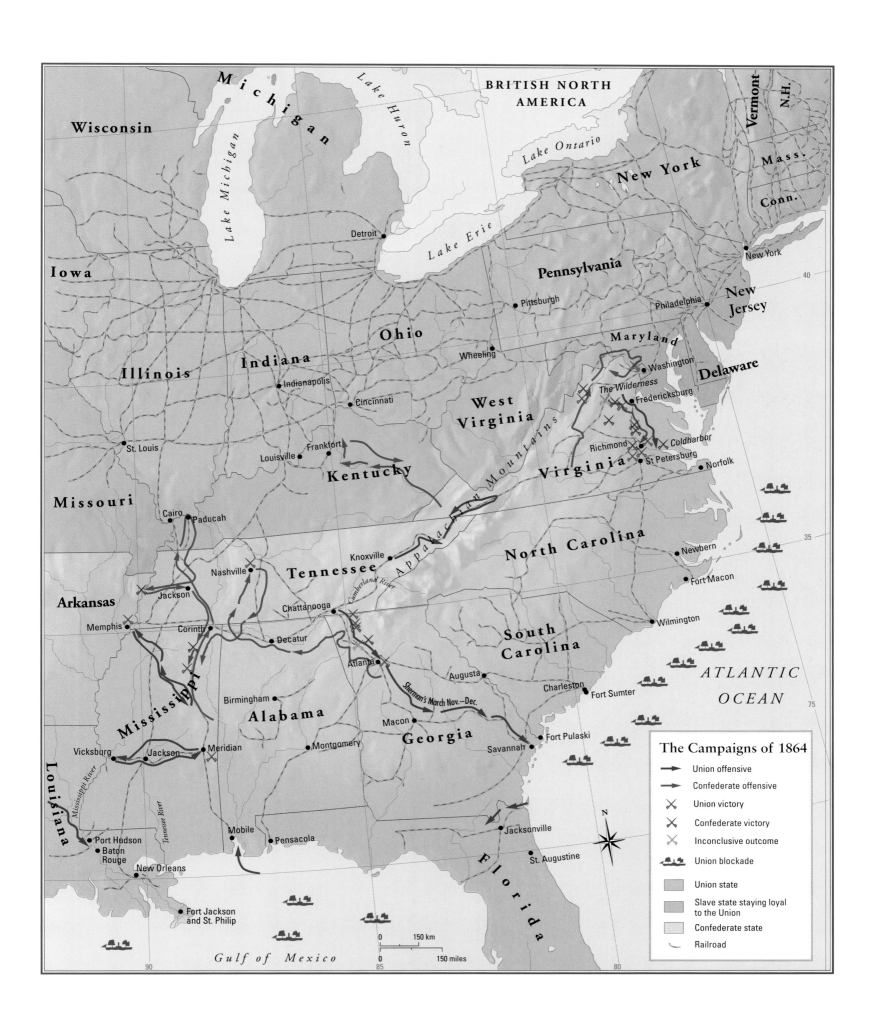

BRITISH NORTH
AMERICA

Wisconsin

Michigan

Lake Michigan

Lake Huron

Lake Ontario

Vermont

N.H.

Mass.

New York

Iowa

Detroit

Lake Erie

Conn.

New York

Pennsylvania

Pittsburgh

Philadelphia

New
Jersey

40

Illinois

Indiana

Ohio

Wheeling

Maryland

Washington

Delaware

Indianapolis

Cincinnati

West
Virginia

The Wilderness

Fredericksburg

St. Louis

Louisville

Frankfort

Kentucky

Richmond

Coldharbor

St Petersburg

Norfolk

Missouri

Appalachian Mountains

Virginia

Cairo

Paducah

Knoxville

North Carolina

Newbern

35

Nashville

Tennessee

Cumberland River

Fort Macon

Arkansas

Jackson

Chattanooga

Memphis

Corinth

Decatur

South
Carolina

Wilmington

Mississippi

Birmingham

Alabama

Atlanta

Augusta

Charleston

Fort Sumter

ATLANTIC
OCEAN

75

Louisiana

Vicksburg

Jackson

Meridian

Montgomery

Georgia

Macon

Sherman's March Nov.–Dec.

Savannah

Fort Pulaski

Mississippi River

Tennessee River

Mobile

Pensacola

N

Jacksonville

St. Augustine

Florida

Port Hudson
Baton
Rouge

New Orleans

Fort Jackson
and St. Philip

Gulf of Mexico

90

85

80

The Campaigns of 1864

→ Union offensive

→ Confederate offensive

✕ Union victory

✕ Confederate victory

✕ Inconclusive outcome

⛴ Union blockade

Union state

Slave state staying loyal
to the Union

Confederate state

〜 Railroad

0   150 km

0   150 miles

Richmond, he considered it worth building a vast rail depot to carry supplies from the harbor at City Point between the two cities.

General Grant's own overland campaign of 1864 was directed against Petersburg, Virginia. The port of Petersburg had been an important commercial center for transporting and processing cotton and raw materials. As railroad technology developed, Petersburg became established as the center linking Richmond to the North, Farmville and Lynchburg to the west, and Weldon, North Carolina, to the south. It had been connected to the East when the 85 miles (137km) of the Norfolk & Petersburg Railroad were completed in 1858.

On 15–16 December, 1864, General John B. Hood brought his reduced army before the defenses of Nashville, determined to force Sherman's Army out of Georgia, but was beaten by General George H. Thomas in the most complete victory of the war. In this photograph, believed to have been taken during the course of the battle, lines of U.S. Military Railroad locomotives stand ready for action.

Because of the port and the railroad, with its total of six locomotives, Petersburg became an important lifeline to the Confederate capital at Richmond, and General Grant decided that this link must be cut. On June 9, 1864, Generals Smith and Hancock began the siege of Petersburg, starting a 10-month campaign of trench warfare that ultimately led to General Robert E. Lee's surrender at Appomattox, and the end of the war itself in April the following year. The railroad was used to evacuate the entire Confederate Government staff from Richmond to Danville, Virginia, on April 2, 1865, less than a week before Robert E. Lee's surrender.

The locomotive *General J.C. Robinson*, and other locomotives of the U.S. Military Railroad, at City Point, Virginia, around 1864 after the seige of Petersburg. The important port blockaded by General Grant's troops can be seen in the background.

MAP
OF
UNITED STATES MILITARY RAIL ROADS,
Showing the Rail Roads operated during the War from 1862–1866,
as
MILITARY LINES,
UNDER THE DIRECTION OF
BVT. BRIG. GEN. D.C.Mc CALLUM,
DIRECTOR AND GENERAL MANAGER.
1866.

EXPLANATION.

Scale of Statute Miles

The U.S. Military Railroad played a major role in the Union campaigns, moving troops and supplies where needed. The U.S.M.R.R operated over many captured roads and carried out much repair work following enemy action.

STANDARDIZING THE RAILROAD GAUGE

THE START OF THE WAR IN 1861 EMPHASIZED THE VULNERABILITY

OF THE WEST COAST AND THE NEED FOR COMMUNICATION

BETWEEN EAST AND WEST. IT ALSO HIGHLIGHTED THE PROBLEMS

CAUSED BY THE DIFFERENT RAIL GAUGES USED IN THE NORTH

AND SOUTH, AND THE FRAGMENTED LINES OF THE LATTER.

Although standard gauge predominated among railroads of the North, in the South, 5ft (1,524mm) gauge was commonly used. A number of other gauges were employed throughout the East. The need for a nationwide standardization became imperitive.

It was national defense that led to the introduction of the Enabling Act in Congress, which was passed in the House of Representatives in May and approved by the Senate in June 1862. President Lincoln signed the Pacific Railroad Act on July 1, 1862. The Act empowered the Central Pacific Railroad Company to build a line from California eastward and appointed a new company, the Union Pacific Railroad Company, to provide a connection between a point on the western boundary of the State of Iowa and the 100th meridian (the exact point to be determined by the President) "...to the western boundary of the State of Nevada, there to meet and connect with the line of the Central Pacific Railroad Company of California." This was all to be completed by July 1, 1874. The Act also provided for land grants and bond issues to help finance the railroad, which was to receive a strip of land 130yd (119m) wide along its whole length. In addition, it was granted 3,000 acres (1,214ha) of land "to be freely selected by the railway authorities within ten miles of the tracks for every mile of line." There was still difficulty in raising money, so in July 1864, Lincoln doubled the land grants.

Although the president had signed the formal Enabling Act, there were disagreements and disputes from the start. The engineers wanted the new line to connect with the existing standard-gauge line east from Bellevue, Missouri, and started construction there, spending $100,000 before the president forced a stop. Lincoln specified Council Bluffs, Iowa, across the Missouri and opposite Omaha, Nebraska, as

Railroads in 1861:
Myth of an Integrated Network

— 6' railroad gauge

— 5' 6" railroad gauge

— 5' 4" railroad gauge

— 5' railroad gauge

— 4' 10" railroad gauge

— 4' 8 1/2" railroad gauge

the Union Pacific railhead, and he was not prepared to change his decision.

California already had a 5ft (1,524mm) gauge line cast from San Francisco to Sacramento, and Lincoln supported its demand for that gauge on the new line. But Congress prescribed standard gauge through an Act that declared, "the gauge of the Pacific Railroad and its branches throughout the whole extent, from the Pacific coast to the Missouri River, shall be, and hereby is, established at four feet eight and one half inches." This also established officially the standard gauge as the gauge for railroads throughout the United States, as it is today.

The rail gauge, as already noted, was standardized at 4ft 8½in (1,435mm), and this enabled former isolated systems to be joined and rolling-stock standards to be established, although the process took quite a long time. It was not until 1886 that railroads in the South, almost all built to 5ft (1,524mm) gauge, were converted to standard gauge.

While major existing railroads consolidated on the 4ft 8½ in (1,435mm) gauge, there developed strong support for narrow-gauge lines, particularly the 3ft (914mm) gauge. The Denver & Rio Grande RR is probably the best example. The D & RG was incorporated in 1870 and, with the mountainous terrain of Colorado and New Mexico to contend with, chose the narrow gauge because it was less costly to build than standard gauge. Locomotives and cars were smaller and cheaper, tracks could follow the contours and curves of mountainous terrain more easily, and the smaller rolling stock required smaller cuts and tunnels.

The original intention was to build from Denver, Colorado, south to Pueblo, west along the Arkansas River and over the Poncha Pass into the San Louis Valley, then south following the Rio Grande to El

While homesteaders received free land from the government, large tracts of land were granted to the railroads by the states and the federal government, with the goal of encouraging the railroads to construct their tracks where few people lived, and to help settle the country. Below is a portion of a map of Nebraska, showing the Union Pacific Railroad land grant, which was published by H. R. Parge, Omaha, in 1880.

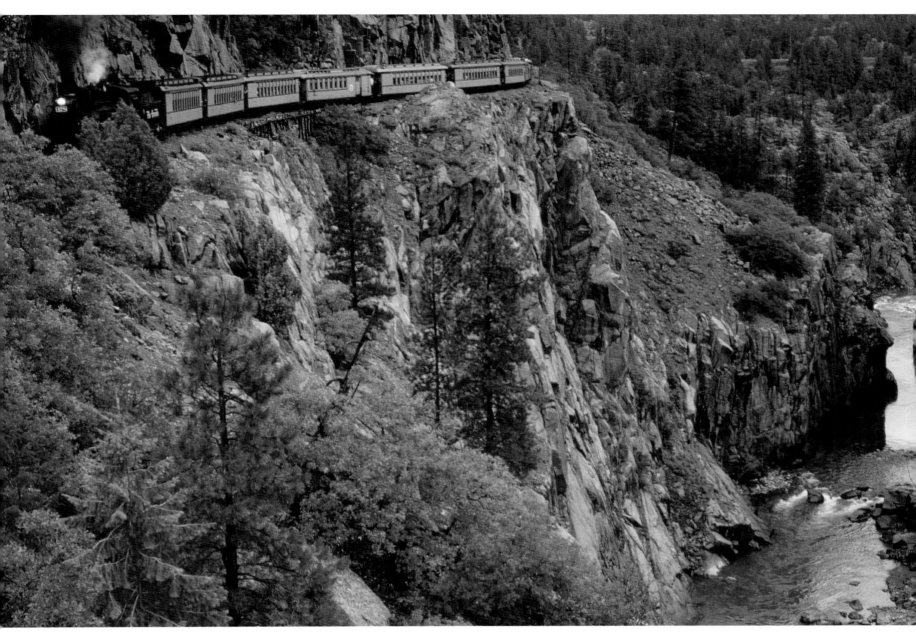

Paso, Texas. In 1877, there was the silver rush at Leadville, Colorado, and this resulted in skirmishes with the Santa Fe over the occupancy of Raton Pass and the Royal Gorge on the Arkansas River. The D & RG gave way and changed its ultimate goal to Salt Lake City.

In 10 years, the Denver & Rio Grande had built lines between Denver and Pueblo, Leadville, Walsenburg, Alamosa, and Antonito to Chama, New Mexico. A year later, there was a line from Chama to Durango, and another from Salida to Gunnison. Within 30 years, many of the narrow-gauge lines were converted to either mixed gauge or standard gauge, although narrow gauge remained on some routes well into the 20th century.

The period following the end of the Civil War saw expansion of the rail tracks westward and the uniform adoption of standard gauge. The few non-standard-gauge lines of the eastern states and the 5ft (1,524mm) gauge lines of the South were converted to standard gauge by 1886; but there remained many miles of narrower gauge, mainly 3ft (914mm), chosen because of economy or for reasons of the local terrain: the trains could negotiate sharper curves than those of standard or broad gauge lines.

The Durango & Silverton narrow gauge railroad was founded by the Denver & Rio Grande RR in 1879. By July, 1882, the track to Silverton, Colorado, was completed. Constructed to haul silver and gold ore from the San Juan Mountains, passengers loved the spectacular views along the Animas River in the San Juan Mountains between Durango and Silverton. This historic train has been in continuous operation for more than 126 years, carrying passengers behind vintage steam locomotives and rolling stock indigenous to the line.

BUILDING THE UNION PACIFIC RAILROAD

THE CENTRAL PACIFIC BEGAN CONSTRUCTION OF THE FIRST

TRANSCONTINENTAL RAILROAD AT SACRAMENTO, CALIFORNIA,

ON JANUARY 8, 1863; THE UNION PACIFIC SET OUT FROM COUNCIL

BLUFFS, IOWA, ON DECEMBER 2, THAT YEAR. BUT BECAUSE OF THE

CIVIL WAR, THE FIRST RAILS WERE NOT LAID UNTIL JULY 1865.

The task of providing raw materials for the construction of the Union Pacific Railroad was formidable. These included 6,250 ties and 50,000 tons of rails, which had to be carried over hundreds of miles by ox wagon or by steamers on the Missouri River. As construction progressed, 30 rails at a time were conveyed to the end of the line by open railcars hauled by two horses; the final move to the end of the line was by a team of 10 men, five at each side of the car, who unloaded each length of rail and placed it in position. An average length of 2 miles (3.2km) a day was constructed by these means. Construction westward to the Sierra Nevada was by Irish laborers, and eastward from California by Chinese coolies.

On the plains, there were frequent attacks by Indians, who made railroading a hazardous operation. The tribes saw the railroads as a threat. They opened up new territory

Chinese laborers working on the Central Pacific line high in the Sierra Nevada, where snow added to their difficulties.

and were responsible for the virtual extinction of the buffalo (on which the whole economy of many Indian nations depended), destroyed the Native American hunting grounds, and led ultimately to their confinement in reservations.

The construction gangs took everything they needed with them, and trains of special dormitory cars accompanied the construction teams. Every few miles, a new "end-of-track" construction town grew up, complete with saloons, gambling houses, and brothels operated by unscrupulous hangers-on, who saw a way of making easy money. Known as "Hell-on-Wheels," the traveling community would often revolt. On one occasion, an Army detachment from Fort Russell, Wyoming, had to be called in to restore order. The whole population was run out of the shantytown, and permitted to return only when a measure of law and order had been reestablished.

By 1867, the UP line over the Rockies was being constructed, reaching its maximum altitude of 8,247ft (13,272m), at Sherman Hill, between Cheyenne and Laramie, Wyoming. However, this was not all. The Central Pacific company was building its road along watercourses up the western slopes of the Sierra Nevada, performing incredible feats of engineering with Chinese labor and the crudest of tools—notably gunpowder. Instead of stopping at the Nevada state line, the Central Pacific pressed on across the flat plains of Nevada and into Utah, making for the Great Salt Lake.

Both companies pushed forward as fast as possible, eager to obtain grants for land. They met in

Working in the intentse heat, teams of workers lay down track in Nevada as the Central Pacific RR progresses eastward. A telegraph line kept pace with the track. The hand-picked gang of Irish rail-layers, backed by a small army of trackmen, set an all-time record of ten miles of track, working from sunrise to sunset on April Day in 1869.

The first transcontinental railroad was created by the meeting of two railroad companies. The Central Pacific RR set out from Sacramento, California, on January 8, 1863, while the Union Pacific RR struck out from Council Bluffs, Iowa, in December of that year. After a mammoth construction project, on May 10, 1869, both roads were joined at Promontory Summit, Utah, forming a 1,775-mile (2,856km) rail route across the country.

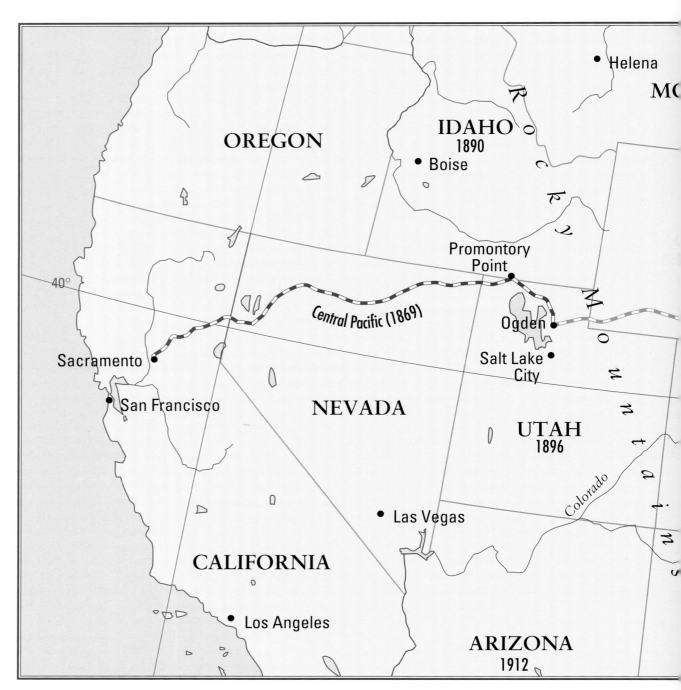

early 1869 in western Utah, but neither company would acknowledge the existence of the other. They continued to build parallel lines in opposite directions. It was on April 9 that a deputation representing both sides met in Washington D.C. and agreed that the meeting point of the two roads would be at Promontory Summit, a few miles north of the Great Salt Lake. (By now, the two competing railroads had a 225-mile/362km overlap!) Congress swiftly approved the meeting point.

The inauguration ceremony on May 10, 1869, at Promontory Summit in Utah, included the driving of two spikes of silver and two of gold into a specially polished California laurel tie by Governor Sandford of the State of California, President of the Central Pacific, and Dr. Thomas C. Durant, President of the Union Pacific. Two trains had been brought up face-to-face, the Central Pacific's train with *Jupiter*, a wood-burner, and the Union Pacific's locomotive *No. 119* from Omaha, a coal-burner, both being eight-wheelers. Both locomotives were detached from their cars and moved forward until their cowcatchers

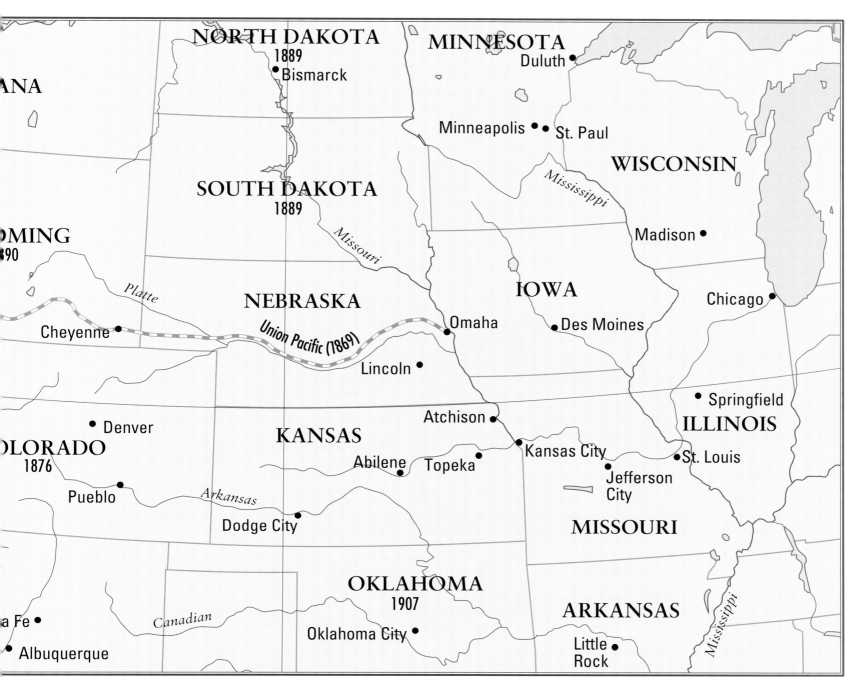

touched, at which point bottles of champagne were broken in celebration. The photographer A.J. Russell recorded the ceremony for posterity.

The locomotives were then recoupled to their respective cars and moved in turn over the ceremonial tie. Then conventional materials were used to replace the ceremonial spikes and tie, after souvenir hunters had torn the latter to pieces. Six more ties and two rails had to be replaced over the next six months.

The Union Pacific had built 1,086 miles (1,748km) from Omaha, and the Central Pacific 689 miles (1,109km) from Sacramento in five years under the Congress deadline. The "first total cost" was officially returned as $115,214,587 and 79 cents—a good price for opening up the West.

In just under three decades from the opening of the first-ever American railroad, the rails extended from the Atlantic to the Pacific. Passengers and freight could now travel from New York City to San

The inauguration ceremony at Promontory Point, Utah, May 10, 1869. With locomotives from both railroads nose to nose, silver and gold spikes were driven in to complete the first transcontinental railroad in the United States.

Opposite The Central Pacific's locomotive at the ceremony was named *Jupiter*. This fully working replica is on display at Promontory Point, long since bypassed by the railroad, which now takes a shorter route across the Great Salt Lake.

Francisco, although at first such through traffic was chiefly freight. The railroad now connected New York with Philadelphia, Pittsburgh, Chicago, Omaha, Cheyenne, Ogden, Salt Lake City, Sacramento, and San Francisco.

Track construction was rudimentary, by European standards, with rough-hewn wood ties laid either with minimal ballast or even directly on the soil or rock. Steel, flat-bottomed rails were laid directly on the ties and secured, for the most part, by spikes driven into the ties on each side of the rail. Tracks were normally unfenced, and undefended against cattle and other wild animals, as well as marauding Indians and the lawless. It made the use of powerful headlights and cowcatchers (not to mention armed guards at times) essential.

The electric telegraph was an essential feature of these early railroads; it was specified in the Enabling Act that the coast-to-coast operation was to be a continuous railroad and telegraph line. The telegraph was used as a crude signaling system, as the location of a train between depots had to be known before another train was dispatched. The telegraph was also a valuable asset to the many lonely townships along a route, providing contact with the outside world.

The Union Pacific had their locomotive *No. 119* at the ceremony. It is represented at present-day Promontory Point by this magnificently colored, gleaming replica.

Landmarks in Locomotive Design, 1860-80

To keep pace with the expansion of the railroads and their ever-increasing traffic, motive power had to develop. Technological innovations were introduced in the 1860s—along with the appearance of the world's first mountain-climbing cog railroad.

Financial panics and the civil war had reduced the number of locomotive constructors, but those who survived were in a strong position. Some railroads, like the Pennsylvania and the Reading, were building their own locomotives and had developed design teams to produce engines specifically suited to their needs. There were still a number of independent builders, however, the two best known being Baldwin and the American Locomotive Company (ALCO). Other well-known names were Long & Norris of Philadelphia, Pennsylvania, Norris Brothers of Schenectady, New York, Sellers Brothers of Cincinnati, Ohio, and Eastwick & Harrison of Philadelphia, PA (and later of Aleksandrovsk, Russia).

An example of a steam locomotive builders' plate, from Baldwin. These were carried on all locomotives, giving the builder's name, construction number, and the date the locomotive was completed.

The fundamentals of American steam locomotive design had been well established by 1870 and differed in some important respects from contemporary European practice. Simplicity and ease of maintenance were two important principles that characterized American practice with, as far as possible, the use of outside cylinders. Multi-cylinder designs were never popular if they involved inside as well as outside cylinders. In the 1860s and 1870s, many strange beasts were produced to satisfy the operators' needs for more powerful locomotives, but in the end, convention won the day. The eight-wheeler, or "American" type, was the standard passenger locomotive and was used, also on freight haulage, until loads and gradients made

The first official World's Fair in the United States, the International Exhibition of Arts, Manufactures and Products of the Soil and Mine opened in Philadelphia, Pennsylvania, in spring, 1876. The extravaganza celebrated the 100th anniversary of the signing of the Delcaration of Independence, the country's emergence from Reconstruction, and scientific, industrial and cultural successes. More than 10 million visitors attended—equivalent to about 20 percent of the population (although many were repeat visitors). On display in the Machinery Building were classic and new designs of locomotive, such as the new freight-hauling "Moguls" from Baldwin (whose stand is visible in the stereograph).

the provision of more specialized types necessary. The first compound-expansion locomotive was built in the United States for the Erie Railroad. It was a rebuild of No. 122, by Shepherd Iron Works of Buffalo, New York.

In 1866, the class name "Mogul" was probably applied for the first time to a 2-6-0 locomotive, fitted with a two-wheeled Bissell truck and constructed by the Taunton Locomotive Works, Massachusetts, for the Central RR of New Jersey. The Pennsylvania RR commenced building its own locomotives in their Juniata, Pennsylvania shops.

"Helpers" to assist trains over the steep gradients of the Alleghenies were built with more driving axles and, often, no carriers. Typical was James Millholland's 0-12-0 *Pennsylvania,* built in 1863 in the

FREIGHT LOCOMOTIVE, "MOGUL" TYPE.

A technical drawing of a Baldwin "Mogul" 2-6-0 freight-hauling locomotive, which became a standard type during the 1880s.

Reading's own shops. It was intended for pusher service for coal trains on the summit between the Delaware and Schuylkill rivers in eastern Pennsylvania, but it had to be rebuilt in 1870 as an 0-10-0 for better curving ability, and then was provided with a tender.

Interest was soon shown in coupled eight- and ten-wheelers of more conventional design, although the inferior tracks of the time often handicapped locomotives with long wheelbases, Alexander Mitchell, the master mechanic of the Lehigh Valley RR, drew up a design for a 2-8-0 freight locomotive fitted with a Hudson-Bissell truck. In 1865, Baldwin built it from Mitchell's drawings with some reluctance, predicting it would be a "colossal failure." Instead, the machine demonstrated its prowess by hauling a train of 100 empty coal cars weighing 340 tons, up a 1 in 67 (1.5 percent) gradient near Delano, Pennsylvania. To commemorate the railroad's merger with a number of feeder lines, which included the Beaver Meadow Railroad, the Lehigh Valley christened the locomotive *Consolidation*, which henceforward gave its name to the 2-8-0 configurations. More than 30,000 *Consolidation* workhorses were constructed in U.S. shops for many railroads over the following 45 years.

Mitchell's *Consolidation*, the first 2-8-0 wheel configuration, was built by the Baldwin Locomotive Company in 1866.

Encouraged by his success, in 1867, Mitchell designed a 2-10-0, of which two were built by James Norris's engine works at Lancaster, Pennsylvania. But the *Ant* and the *Bee*, as they were named, were handicapped by poor tracks and derailed so frequently that they were converted to 2-8-2s. Much later, in 1897, Baldwin christened some 2-8-2s for Japan's Nippon Railroad *Mikado*, and this was the name by which the type was known until World War II.

On the other side of the continent, big was also deemed to be beautiful. The Central Pacific Railroad in 1882 built a 4-8-0 locomotive, *Mastodon*, designed by the mechanical superintendent, A.J. Stevens, at its Sacramento, California, shops, to cope with the steep grades of the Sierra Nevada. It was capable of hoisting a 240-ton train up a 25-mile (40km) grade with a vertical rise of 3,900ft (1,189km)—an average gradient of 1 in 34, or 3 percent. Twenty more were built by Danforth-Cooke.

Encouraged by their success, in 1883, Stevens designed a 4-10-0, *El Gobernador*, which weighed 73 tons without a tender—by far the largest American locomotive at that time. But the Central Pacific's trestles had to be strengthened to accommodate it, and it stood idle for a year. It turned out to be an unreliable machine, often breaking down in the High Sierras.

The first "rack" rail roads were demonstrated by Sylvester Marsh in the United States and by Nicholas Riggenbach in Switzerland. On July 3, 1869, Marsh's Mount Washington Cog Railway opened in New Hampshire. It was recognized as the first cog (or rack-and-pinion) railway in the world by some six months. A cog railway has a special toothed rack

rail, usually between the running rails. The trains are fitted with one or more cog wheels or pinions that mesh with the rack rail. This enables the trains to climb steep gradients. Marsh's railway climbs Mount Washington in New Hampshire. The railway ascends the mountain from an elevation of about 2,700ft (823m) above sea level and ends at the summit of Mt. Washington, at an elevation of 6,288ft (1,916.6m). It is the second steepest rack railway in the world, with an average grade of over 25 percent and a maximum grade of 37.41 percent.

The 3 mile (4.8m) long railway has always used a team of vintage steam locomotives, apart from an experimental diesel that was introduced between 1976 and 1981. The train ascends at 2.8mph (4.5k/h) in about 65 minutes, and descends at 4.6mph (7.4k/h) in about 40 minutes.

Near the end of the decade, in 1869, other technical developments were coming to the fore. The first experiments with compressed--air brakes (non-automatic) were invented by George Westinghouse.

Few photographs exist of the muscular, 14-wheel, *El Gobernador*, the 73 ton locomotive built by Central Pacific RR at its Sacramento, California shops. It was the only locomotive of the 4-10-0 wheel arrangement to operate on U.S. rails. When built, it was the largest railroad locomotive in the world.

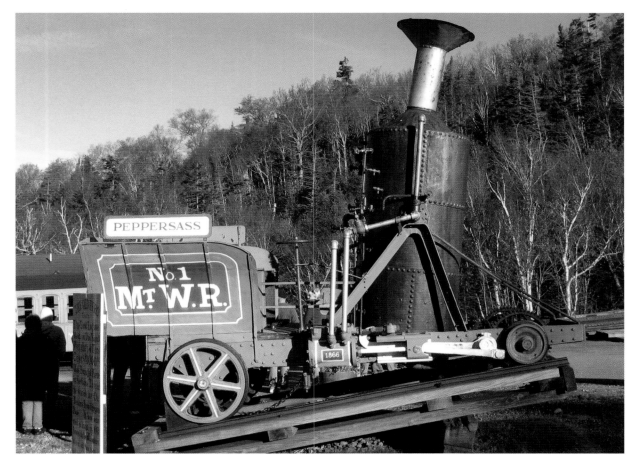

Peppersass, the vertical-boiler locomotive used to build Sylvester Marsh's Mount Washington Cog Railway in the 1860s, was wrecked in an accident in 1929, during which many passengers were injured and one—the photographer Daniel P. Rossiter—died when a cog tooth broke, causing an uncontrolled descent of the 25ft (7m) high trestle "Jacob's Ladder." *Peppersass'* boiler was not ruptured and, after being repaired, the historic old engine is now on permanent display at the cog railroad's base station.

The locomotive *Ammonoosuc*, named after the ravine that lies on the west side of Mt. Washington, belches steam as it nudges its railcar up the 37.41 percent gradient of the trestle "Jacob's Ladder". The locomotive burns one ton of coal and consumes 1,000 gallons (3.785 liters) of water on the 3 mile (4.8km) ride, which generates the necessary energy to climb the 6,288ft (1,916.6m) mountain. Engine and coach are pulled up the mountain by a cog with 19 teeth, which mesh into the track's central rail. Two sets of ratchets are engaged during ascents, which keep the trains from moving backward at stops or in the event of an emergency, causing a distinctive "clinking" sound when going uphill.

Spreading Railroad Networks, 1865-79

THE UNITED STATES RAILROADS CONTINUED TO EXPAND RAPIDLY AFTER THE END OF THE CIVIL WAR, WITH EXISTING LINES ADDING NETWORKS OF BRANCH LINES FOR THE TRANSPORTATION OF FREIGHT, WHILE CONNECTING TOWNS AND CITIES AND REVOLUTIONIZING COMMUNICATION.

Cities benefited vastly from the expansion of the railroad network. By 1865, Cincinatti, Ohio, for example, was served by four different railroads, all operating on the 4ft 10in (1,473mm) gauge, with the exception of the Ohio & Mobile, which used 6ft (1,829mm).

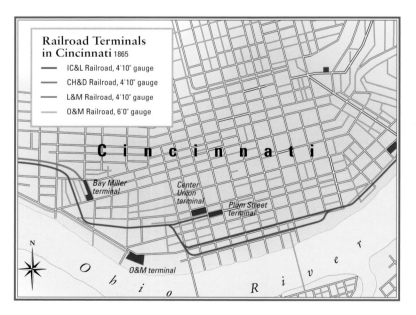

Railroad Terminals in Cincinnati 1865
— IC&L Railroad, 4'10" gauge
— CH&D Railroad, 4'10" gauge
— L&M Railroad, 4'10" gauge
— O&M Railroad, 6'0" gauge

Cincinnati

Bay Miller terminal
Center Union terminal
Plum Street terminal
O&M terminal

N

Ohio River

In terms of railroad expansion, the years between 1865 and 1879 witnessed considerable growth. In 1866, the Baltimore & Ohio RR leased the Central Ohio line from Bellaire, Ohio, through Newark to Columbus; and the New York & Oswego Midland RR was incorporated to build a line from Oswego, New York, on the shore of Lake Ontario, to the New Jersey state line, and thence to a terminal on the Hudson River. The Montgomery Railroad reconstruction began with a gauge conversion from standard to 5ft (1,524mm). In 1867, the Illinois Central reached Dubuque, Iowa (Sioux City, 1870), and Cornelius Vanderbilt gained control of the New York Central RR.

The next year, Col. Holliday turned the first shovelful of earth in Kansas City, Kansas, in construction

After its meeting with the Central Pacific at Promontory Point, the Union Pacific railroad spread northwest and southwest, laying tracks from Ogden, Utah, into Oregon and Washington, and across Nevada to Los Angeles, California.

Railroads published maps of their networks, expounding their benefits over rival roads. This map from 1876 proudly highlights the New York Central & Hudson River RR and its principal connections, with the claim that it is "The only four track railroad in the World, all laid with steel rails."

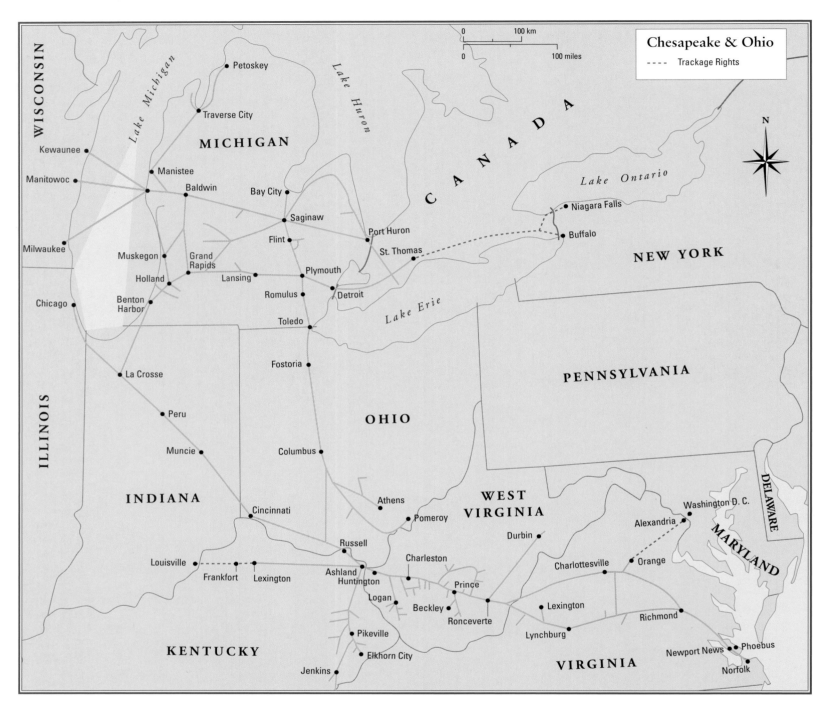

The Chesapeake & Ohio RR was formed in 1869, in Virginia, from many smaller railroads begun in the 19th century. Tapping the coal reserves of West Virginia, it formed the basis for the city of Newport News and the coal piers—transloading facilities for transfering coal between rail and ship—on Hampton Roads, and forged a rail link to the Midwest, eventually reaching Columbus, Cincinnati, and Toledo, Ohio, and Chicago, Illinois.

of the Santa Fe RR. The Lehigh & New England RR was inaugurated. This railroad had been constructed specifically for the haulage of cement, slate and anthracite from Hauto, Pennsylvania, to Campbell Hall, New York.

Also in 1868, the Virginia Central and Covington & Ohio RRs consolidated as the Chesapeake & Ohio RR. The very first dining car to appear on North American railroads, named *Delmonico's*, had its initial trip on the Chicago & Alton RR.

Existing tracks continued to grow by this time, notably the Baltimore & Ohio RR, which, in 1869, had penetrated westward by leasing a line from Newark to Sandusky, Ohio, on Lake Erie. The Central of Georgia RR leased the South Western RR, and in so doing gained access from Macon westward to Columbus and then southward into Alabama at Eufaula. The Evansville, Terre Haute & Chicago RR was

Grand Central Depot, seen here in 1880, was the forerunner of today's Grand Central Terminal, and was built between 1869-71. The train shed, north and east of the L-shaped headhouse, had two innovative facilities in U.S. railroads: the platforms were elevated to the height of the cars, and the roof was a balloon shed with a clear span over all the tracks. Cornelius Vanderbilt died on the same day a blizzard caused the glass roof to collapse.

Chartered in 1836, the Chicago & North Western RR grew to have one of the largest networks in the Midwest. Its tracks spread northward from Chicago into Michigan, west into Wyoming and south into Illinois.

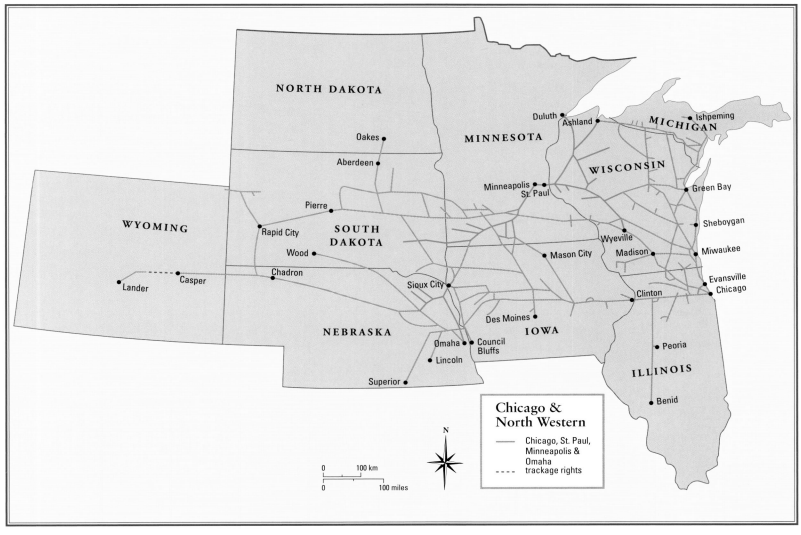

Chicago &
North Western

——— Chicago, St. Paul,
Minneapolis &
Omaha
----- trackage rights

Missouri, Kansas, Texas

Formed originally from the southern branch of the Union Pacific in 1852, the Missouri-Kansas-Texas RR was the first to operate west of the Mississippi. Never a major line, it merged with the Union Pacific in 1988.

chartered, the Lackawanna RR leased the Morris & Essex RR to avoid using the Central of New Jersey tracks, while the New York, Ontario & Western RR opened its tracks from Oswego, on lake Ontario, southward to Norwich, New York. The NYC RR and the Hudson River RR were consolidated by Cornelius Vanderbilt as the NYC & HR Railroad. On July 18, 1869, the Pacific Railroad conversion to standard gauge was completed.

As the decade drew to a close, in 1869, the construction of Grand Central Station Depot was commenced at the corner of 42nd Street and Fourth Avenue, New York City, when Cornelius Vanderbilt was in charge of the New York Central & Hudson River RR. The station was designed to bring the trains of the NYC & H RR, the New York & Harlem RR, and the New York & New Haven RR together in one large station.

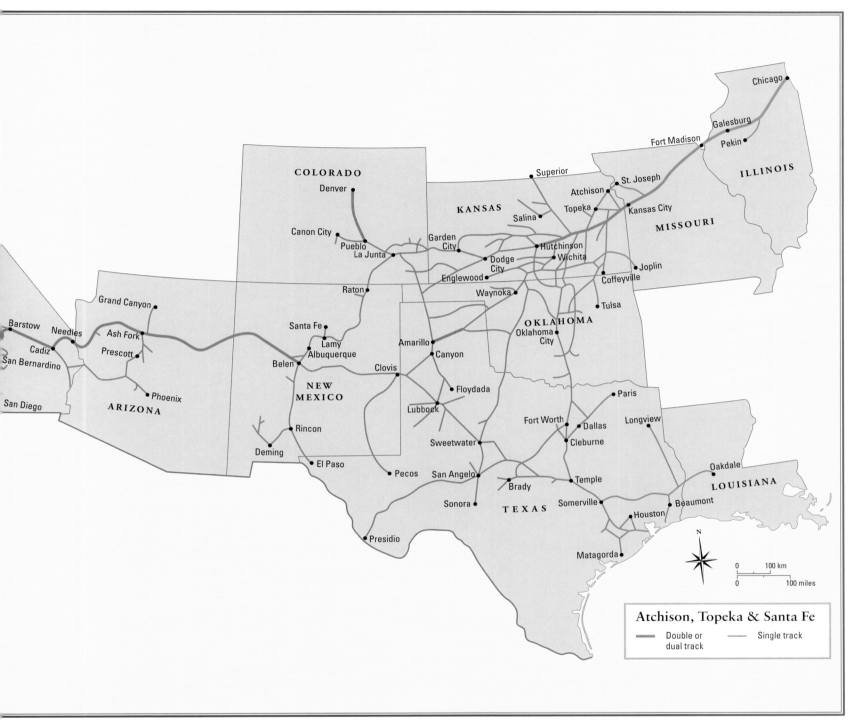

This building was the first to be built on the site now occupied by Grand Central Terminal. Grand Central Depot proved to be inadequate from the day it opened in 1871, until it was replaced by Grand Central Terminal in 1913. Three problems doomed the old station—congestion, and the suffocating smoke from the steam engines, and chaos in baggage transfer. Exacerbating the problems, work also commenced in 1869 on a new connecting railroad from Spuytn Duyvil—a subsection of the Riverdale section of the Bronx in New York City—to Mott Haven, the southernmost neighborhood in the South Bronx.

Over the decade that followed, competition between rival railroad companies and locomotive manufacturers began to become extremely intense, as the United States' transportation system continued to blossom.

The Atchison, Topeka & Santa Fe became one of the largest and most well-known railroads in the United States. It was chartered in 1863, and portions of its main line from Chicago, through Kansas, New Mexico, and Arizona to California ran over the route of the original Santa Fe Trail. In 1996, it merged with the Burlington Northern to form the Burlington Northern Santa Fe.

COMMERCIAL RIVALS

BY THE YEAR 1870, THE RAILROADS HAD BECOME FIRMLY ESTABLISHED AS THE OVERWHELMINGLY DOMINANT MEANS OF MEDIUM- AND LONG-DISTANCE TRANSPORT FOR PASSENGERS AND FREIGHT. NOW CAME AN INTENSE AND OFTEN BITTER RIVALRY BETWEEN RAILROAD COMPANIES.

From the commercial point of view, the die was cast and things did not change much in the running of the railroads until well into the 20th century. Wherever the rails advanced, the other carriers and coach firms retreated. Although the river steamboats were able to challenge the railroads on the big rivers, they could hold their own only on bulk carriage, not on speed. As time went on locomotives became even faster.

The bitter rivalry that existed between companies for the domination of territory continued, and although the physical battles between rival concerns that had occurred over the previous three decades abated, they were replaced by more subtle, and often equally vicious, commercial battles that were waged by the railroad barons. Many of the smaller railroads were consolidated into larger units; this was most pronounced in the New England states, where many railroads had grown up in the earlier years.

The first rail tunnel had been built through the Hoosac Range, part of the Western Massachusetts mountain range, in place of a canal tunnel that had been proposed some 50 years earlier. At the time of its completion, it was the second longest tunnel in the world (after the 8.5-mile/13.7km long Mont Cenis Tunnel through the French Alps). The previously proposed canal route became a railroad to connect Boston, Massachusetts, with the Great Lakes at Oswego or Buffalo, New York. Although begun in 1851 by the state of Massachusetts, the Hoosac (also called the Hoosic) Tunnel was not completed until 1875.

The project required the excavation of 2 million tons of rock. First, a tunnel boring machine was used, but it failed after excavating 10ft (3m). Builders resorted to hand digging, and later used the

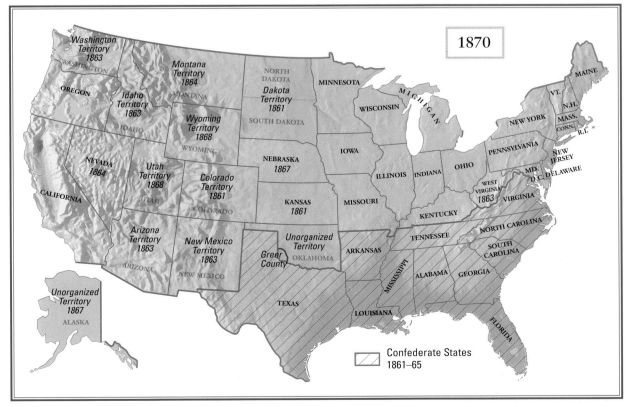

This 1870 engraving, *The Great Race for the Western States*, caricatures the intense rivalry that developed between Cornelius Vanderbilt and Jay Gould, as the former attempted to gain control of the Erie RR from the latter. Vanderbilt is pictured saying "Now Jim, no jockeying, you know!" while Gould replies "Let 'em rip, Commodore! But don't stop to water, or you'll be beat."

By 1870, there was very little unorganized territory left. The country was steadily forming into a cohesive nation.

Cyrus W. Field (1819–92) had made a fortune by the age of 33. He pioneered the transatlantic telegraph cable in 1858. In 1884, the Canadian Pacific RR named the community of Field, British Columbia, Canada in his honor. Bad investments left Field bankrupt at the end of his life.

Jay Gould (1836–92) was seen by many as a railroad "pirate." A reckless speculator, by 1880 he owned 10,000 miles (16,000km) of railroad route. He owned the Union Pacific RR and Western Union telegraph company.

Edward H. Harriman (1848–1909) was a successful stock broker who bought his first railroad in 1881. He took over the Union Pacific in 1890, the Southern Pacific in 1901, and the Erie RR in 1908.

Railroads, 1870:
52,922 miles

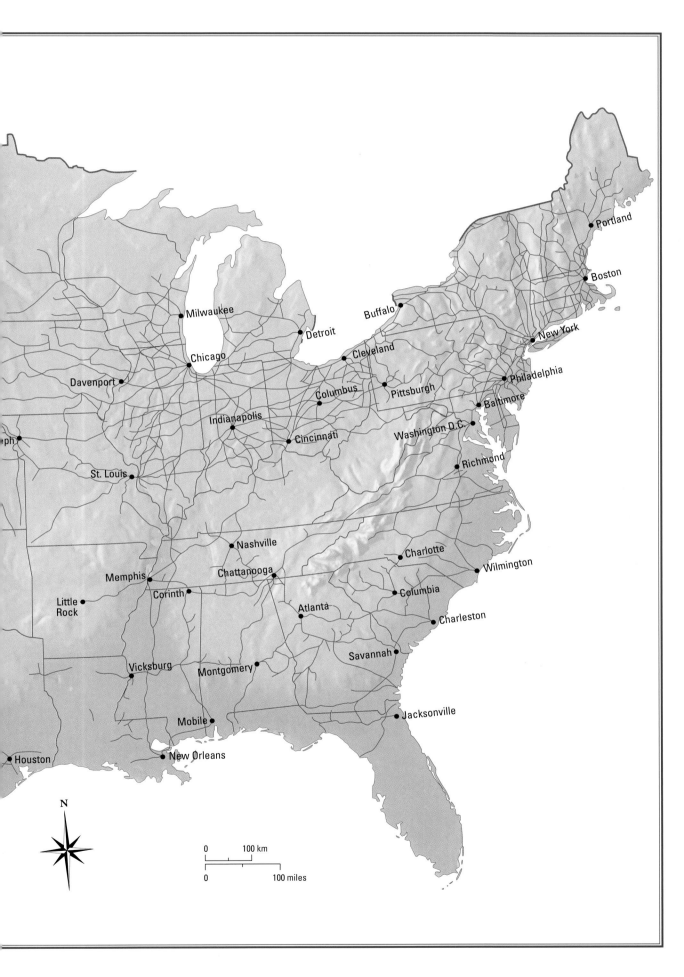

Portland

Boston

Buffalo

New York

Milwaukee

Detroit

Cleveland

Chicago

Philadelphia

Columbus

Pittsburgh

Davenport

Baltimore

Indianapolis

Washington D.C.

Cincinnati

ph

Richmond

St. Louis

Nashville

Charlotte

Memphis

Chattanooga

Wilmington

Little
Rock

Corinth

Columbia

Atlanta

Charleston

Savannah

Vicksburg

Montgomery

Jacksonville

Houston

Mobile

New Orleans

N

0   100 km

0   100 miles

By 1870, stimulated by the
first transcontinental lines, the
railroads were pushing out
toward the west.

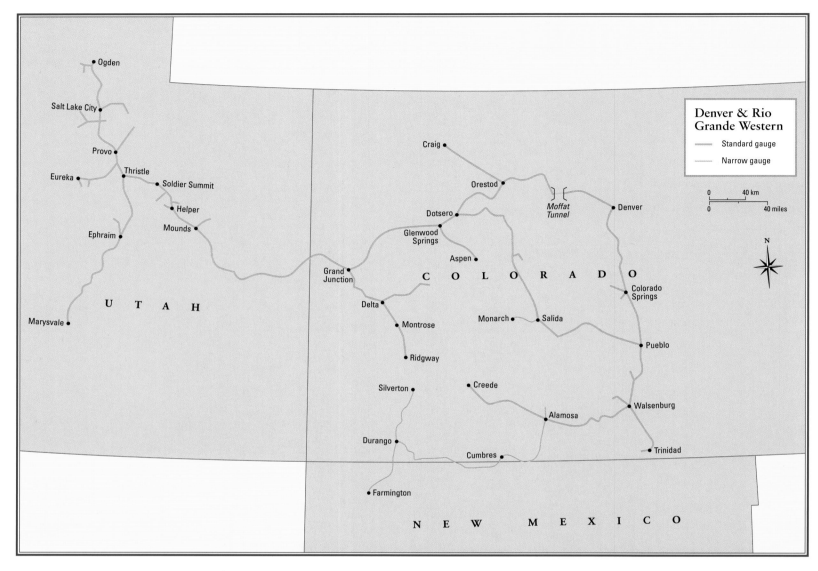

Denver & Rio
Grande Western

—— Standard gauge

—— Narrow gauge

Above The Denver & Rio Grande Western RR had its beginnings in the Denver & Rio Grand RR of 1870, chartered to build a narrow-gauge line from Denver, Colorado, to El Paso, Texas. This line had progressed as far as Pueblo in 1872, but never made it to Texas. Eventually, it built a network of narrow- and standard-gauge lines in Colorado and Utah. After financial problems in the 1920s–30s, it survived to merge with the Southern Pacific in 1988.

Right The New York, New Haven & Hartford RR operated between 1872 and 1969, serving New England and providing an essential link between Boston and New York. It finally became part of the Penn Central system.

New York,
New Haven &
Hartford

- - - Passengers and
freight

—— Freight only

Burleigh Rock Drill, one of the first pneumatic drills. Tunneling also saw the introduction of large-scale commercial use of nitroglycerine and electric blasting caps.

Digging a central vertical shaft down through the mountain allowed tunnelers to expose two additional faces to excavate: when the shaft was complete in 1870, workers dug outwards from the center to meet the tunnels being dug from the east and west portals. Engineers built a 1,000ft (305m) elevator to hoist the excavated rock from the shaft.

The Hoosac Tunnel earned itself the nickname the "Bloody Pit"—and was considered to be haunted—due to the unhappy fact that 195 lives had been lost during its construction. Many of these deaths had been caused by the unstable nature of nitroglycerine.

The Hoosac tunnel was the first railroad tunnel built in the United States. Its completion led to a battle between several railroads for control of it.

On its completion, the battle for control of the tunnel between six competing railroads resulted in a legislative committee proposal to consolidate all of them, which the roads all but turned down. The Fitchburg RR wanted to control the 4.7-mile (7.6km) long tunnel, but the State would permit this only if the Fitchburg had its own route to the Hudson River. In the 1880s, the Fitchburg acquired three other roads, including the Boston, Hoosac Tunnel & Western, and three branches. Ultimately, the Fitchburg became a part of the Boston & Maine RR.

The rapid growth of the United States into an industrial nation was crucially aided by the railroads, and by the late 1880s, vast industrial empires were being built. Famous names such as Daniel Drew, Cyrus Field, Jay Gould, Cornelius Vanderbilt, and Edward H. Harriman had become synonymous with railroading. They and others assembled railroad systems, bought connecting lines, and built empires, buying parallel lines in order to control competition. These titans of industry often gave the railroads more than their fair share of publicity. The railroads were larger than most other contemporary enterprises and, as today, industrial empires and tycoons preoccupied the newspapers and magazines.

Regulation, however, was just round the corner. In the Midwest and West, for example, farmers were more dependent on railroads than in the East to move their products to market; also railroads were fewer. The farmers complained that rates were unfair, with favored shippers receiving rebates.

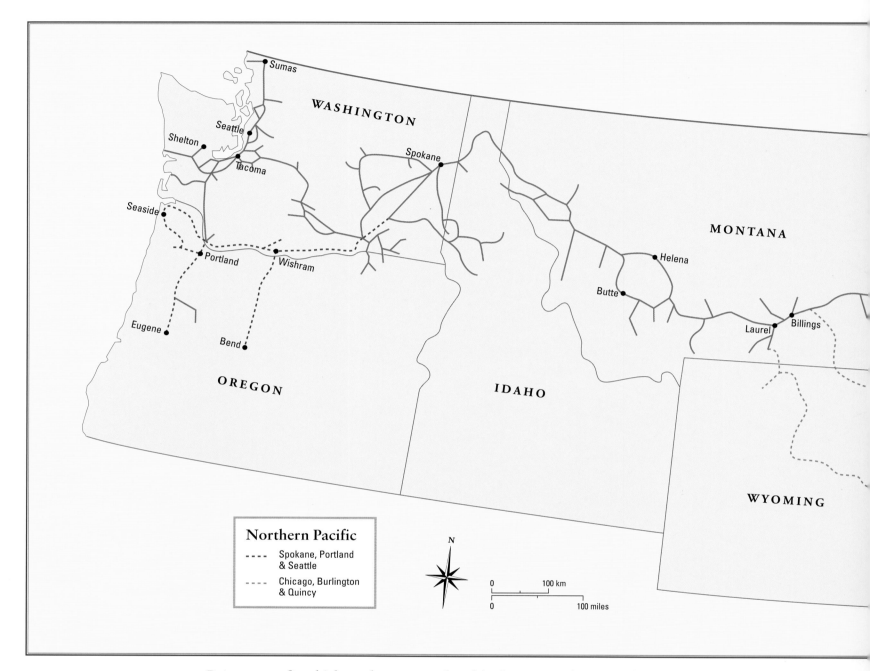

Northern Pacific

- - - - Spokane, Portland & Seattle

- - - - Chicago, Burlington & Quincy

N

0   100 km

0   100 miles

Rates were often higher where one railroad had a monopoly. As early as 1871, the state of Illinois passed legislation regulating freight rates and, in 1873, passenger fares. Minnesota did the same in 1874. By 1880, pressure for regulation had reached national level and resulted in the Interstate Commerce Act of February 1887, effective April 5, 1887.

The Interstate Commerce Commission (I.C.C.), the first president of which was Judge Thomas M. Cooley, was set up by the Act to regulate all railroads engaged in interstate commerce, even if they were located entirely within one state. Today, the Act also applies to motor carriers, water carriers (riverboats, barges, ferries, etc) that are owned or controlled by railroads, and freight forwarders operating in interstate commerce. The Act stated that rates charged by the railroads had to be "just and reasonable," but unfortunately the members of the commission were unable to agree amongst themselves as to what was meant by "reasonable."

In exchange for land grants, the government stipulated that the railroads had to provide reduced-

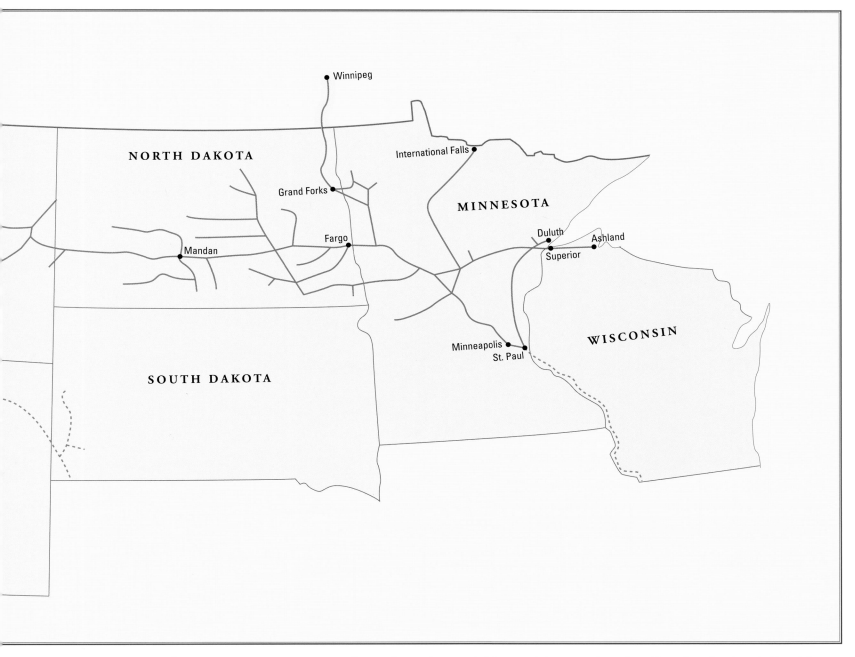

rate transportation for government property, mails. and employees. This provision continued well into the 20th century, by which time the government had received more than 10 times the value of the land it had granted.

Railroads were forbidden to give preference, advantage, special rates, or rebates to any person, company, location, or type of traffic. They were not allowed to charge more for a short haul than for a long haul, Pooling (that is, sharing of revenue or freight) was forbidden, and railroads were required to publish their rates and give advanced warning of any change. In general, this was accepted until, in 1897, the Supreme Court ruled that the I.C.C. had no power to fix rates; this took most of the bite out of the clause requiring that short haul should cost no more than long haul.

In time, other acts modified the terms of reference, and the I.C.C. became more powerful, with widespread responsibilities, with the effect that the railroads found themselves more and more inhibited commercially.

President Lincoln signed the Northern Pacific RR's charter in 1864, but it was not until 1883 that the first northern transcontinental line was completed. It had received substantial land grants and massive government subsidy. The line took a somewhat circuitous route from Duluth, Minnesota, to Seattle, Washington State. In the 1970s, the NP became part of the Burlington Northern.

Railroad Dispatch and Signaling, 1870-1900

THE INCREASED SPEED OF LOCOMOTIVES BROUGHT PROBLEMS OF SAFETY. FROM 1851, TRAIN DISPATCHING FROM A CENTRAL POINT HAD BEEN INSTITUTED, AND ALL RAILROADS SET ABOUT INSTALLING TELEGRAPH LINES. AS TRAFFIC GREW, TRAINS WERE DISPATCHED ON A TIME-INTERVAL SYSTEM.

The earliest U.S. railroad signal instalation was on the New Castle & Frenchtown RR in 1832, consisting of peach baskets suspended from masts and raised on lowered by pulleys. Their position (high, middle, or low) and color (black or white), conveyed information to trains and stations, whose staff observed them with telescopes. This ball signal became widely used, its aspect for "proceed" giving the term "Highball!"

There was a gradual change from locomotives burning wood in favor of coal or anthracite, both of which were plentiful. Geographical development led to mechanical improvement and more sophisticated operating methods. Locomotives and rolling stock grew in physical size, and train weights increased. Trackbeds were improved and tracks re-laid to stand up to the heavier rolling stock and higher speeds that commercial pressures demanded. Many of the earlier railroads had been built to convey coal, iron ore, and other minerals to meet the demands of growing industrial production, and much of this traffic was lost to the canal companies, which had the foresight to invest in their own railroads, particularly in the East and South. Where there were double tracks this system worked well enough. But after a disastrous accident between New York City and Philadelphia in 1863, when two trains met head-on—and there had been many such incidents—Ashbel Welch, president of the New Jersey Canal & Railroad Companies, instituted a system of block working.

On the line between New Brunswick, New Jersey and Philadelphia, Pennsylvania, Welch installed a system of signals. Each signal consisted of a red banner that was dropped into view by a signalman through a hole in a box the moment a train had passed. The track ahead was thus closed (blocked) until a message was received over the telegraph from the next station that the train had passed. The block was then cleared and the red banner was removed. Thus the railroad formally adopted the system on March 27, 1865.

There were a number of places where tracks of rival companies crossed on the level, at grade. One such point was on the prairie outside Chicago, Illinois, known as Grand Crossing, where the Illinois Central tracks crossed those of the rival Southern Michigan. This was a notorious place where trains of one road would race to get to the crossing before the trains of its rival, and in 1853, a serious collision left a wrecked locomotive and cars, 16 passengers dead, and many more injured. This caused the authorities to issue an edict that no train could enter a crossing with another road at grade until after it had stopped and the crossing was seen to be clear. This rule was made state law in Massachusetts in 1854, and most states followed suit; the law was soon extended to apply to most busy junctions.

This grade crossing rule led ultimately to the adoption of an invention of 1856 by the English engineer John Saxby, which eliminated this nuisance and led to the development of the modern signaling system. In Saxby's invention, levers from a central tower operated signals and switches, the

Ensuring safety at a multitrack railroad crossing like this would be impossible without an effective signaling system. Greater Grand Crossing is an official community area of Chicago, Illinois, located on the city's south side. The neighborhood's name is the result of an 1853 right of way feud between the Lake Shore & Michigan Southern RR and the Illinois Central RR, which led to a "frog war" and a crash that killed 18 people.

ONE ARM ELECTRIC SEMAPHORE GROUND SIGNALS
STYLE "S" 90 DEG. UPPER QUADRANT

For many years, semaphore signals were used as a means of informing train crews on whether the train was cleared to proceed. Semaphore signals became the most widely-used form of mechanical signal, although they are now decreasing in number.

levers being interlocked to eliminate incorrect movements. This system was first installed in the United States in 1870. The control of train movements came into the hands of one man instead of having several men operating switches, with the ever-present problem of communication. Now trains could run safely through such crossings and junctions without the need to "stop, look, and listen."

The trial of the system worked so well that the first permanent installation was made at East Newark, New Jersey, in February 1875, on what had become the Pennsylvania RR. It was refined in the light of experience, and soon trains were detected by electrical track circuits, invented by Dr. Andrews of New Jersey in 1871. An electric current was fed into sections of the rails so that the passage of a train over those sections caused an electrical relay to operate and either work a signal or release a lock to enable the signalman to operate a switch or signal. It was vital for the system to be fail-safe, and the presence of a train "shorted" the relay coil so that the relay was deenergized and its contacts completed an electrical lock. At the same time, a light was illuminated on a diagram to show the controller that the particular section of track was occupied.

In the early 1880s, compressed air was experimentally integrated with electric-circuit controls to operate switches and signals in complex switch interlocking arrangements. This meant that switches several miles away from any given control tower could be reliably operated in the correct sequence to establish a "safe route." By 1890, this all-American system was well established.

It took quite a long time for railroad chiefs to accept what many of them saw as obstructive: the costs of better signaling diverted funds from building new lines, or money from investors' pockets; it was not until after 1885 that safe signaling enabled the "full stop" at grade crossings and junctions to be finally abolished. Productivity was improved by the passage of more trains through busy junctions, and time schedules were shortened. Gradually, signal systems and rules were standardized. It was largely the action of the railroads, through the General Time Convention of 1874—the body responsible for the introduction of a standard time and four time zones throughout the United States and Canada, which was finally adopted by the railroads in 1883—that rules were formulated for harmonization of signaling, cars, train movements, and safety appliances. The rules were still only recommendations, rather than mandatory requirement—although non-observance was often not regarded favorably. The convention became the American Railroad Association in 1891.

Mechanical signals themselves were initially of the rising and falling "ball" type, superceded by semaphore. The semaphore arm consisted of two parts: a blade, vane, or arm, pivoting at different angles, and a spectacle holding colored lenses, which moved in front of a lamp for nighttime signaling. Vanes were combined, or "somersault" types, in which the blade pivoted in the center, the arm separate from the spectacle. The blade projected horizontally in its most restrictive aspect; other angles indicate less restrictive aspects.

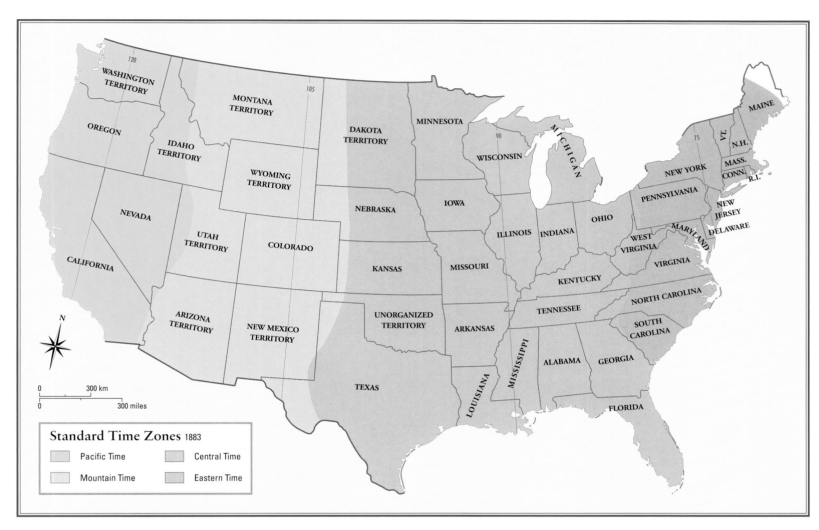

Standard Time Zones 1883
- Pacific Time
- Mountain Time
- Central Time
- Eastern Time

Semaphores are either "lower quadrant" or "upper quadrant" types. In the former, the blade pivots down for less restrictive aspects; in the latter, the blade pivots upward. it was common in the United States for train order signals to point the blade straight down to indicate "proceed". The color and shape of the blade was varied to show the type of signal and indication, such as red, square-ended blades for "home" signals and yellow fishtail blades for "distant" signals. A third type, with a pointed end extending outward, may indicate "proceed at restricted speed after stopping". Semaphores were controlled through mechanical linkages controled from the tower by levers to move switches and signals. Signals were later operated by electric motors or hydraulically. They were designed to be failsafe, so that if power is lost or a linkage broken, the blade moves by gravity into the horizontal position. Lower quadrant semaphores need counterweights to cause the blade to rise, one reason for a widespread switch to upper quadrant types.

The General Time Convention of 1874 standardized time throughout North America, introducing four time zones. These were adopted by the railroads in 1883, proving essential for the efficient operation of the roads.

In the early 20th Century, the "wigwag" was used at grade crossings. Its pendulum motion to signal the approach of a train—accompanied by a gong sound—was intended to mimic that of the crossing watchman swinging a red lantern from side to side, meaning, in railroad parlance, "stop".

ADVENT OF THE AIR BRAKE

THE DESIRE TO INCREASE TRAIN SPEEDS MEANT THAT THE MEANS
OF STOPPING THEM SAFELY HAD TO BE IMPROVED. FROM THE
EARLIEST TIMES, LOCOMOTIVES HAD BEEN FITTED WITH HAND
BRAKES. THESE HAD BEEN SUPERSEDED FIRST BY "SCREW-DOWN"
MECHANICAL BRAKES, THEN BY STEAM BRAKES.

Signaled by the engineer's whistle, the brakeman would walk the length of a train atop the cars—whatever the weather—to turn the brake wheel to apply the train's brakes. A brakeman's duties included ensuring the couplings between cars were correctly set, lining switches, and signalling to the train operators while performing switching operations.

Passenger and freight cars were fitted with screw-down brakes, and brakemen rode the trains to operate them. Train speeds had to be low enough to be able to stop in all conditions. To stop a train at a particular point needed good judgment. Each train carried an engine crew and a train crew of conductors and brakemen. When a train had to be stopped at a station, the engineer blew the steam whistle to alert the brakemen. The brakemen then ran along the tops of freight cars, jumping from car to car to apply the brakes and hope they had been given enough time to stop at the required point.

By the 1860s, a few applications of the European-style vacuum brake had been made on railroads on the eastern seaboard. The vacuum brake, which was dependent on atmospheric pressure, quickly lost effectiveness with increased altitude, so it had severe limitations on North American railroads. The most important improvement was the invention, in 1869, by George Westinghouse of the world's first continuous air brake. This was demonstrated between Pittsburgh and Steubenville, Ohio, on the Panhandle RR (the so-called Panhandle of West Virginia), later part of the Pennsylvania system. Compressed air, generated by a steam-driven compressor and stored in a reservoir on the locomotive, was fed by a valve operated by the driver into a pipe that ran the length of the train. Cylinders on each vehicle pressed "shoes" on to the wheel tires. At the end of each car, a flexible pipe took the air to the next car. The trial installation prevented an accident when a farm wagon and horses became stuck on a grade crossing. The driver yanked the steam whistle cord to call the brakemen, then the air brake was applied. The train was brought to a safe stop and no lives were lost.

The "straight" air brake had three undesirable features. If one of the flexible pipes developed a leak, air escaped and all braking was lost. If cars became uncoupled on upgrades only hand brakes could save them from rolling backward. Also, with long trains, it took a considerable time for the air pressure to build up on the most rearward cars. Two of these problems were solved in 1871 when Westinghouse invented the automatic brake with a fail-safe system. The air pipe was charged at a specific pressure all the time, and each car carried an auxiliary air tank and a triple valve, operated by a change in pressure in the main pipe. Any reduction of pressure in the pipe applied the brakes, while recharging the pipe to normal pressure released the car brakes.

The control handle and valve used by the engineer to apply the train brakes in the Westinghouse air-brake system.

With normal running conditions, all the auxiliary air tanks, air pipes, and flexible hoses were charged at the same pressure and formed a continuous system; the triple valves shut off the air to the brake cylinders. To stop the train, the engineer operated the control valve in his cab and reduced the air pressure in the train pipe. This caused the triple valve on each car to operate and allow air to flow from the auxiliary tanks to the brake cylinders and so slow down or stop the train. The brakes were released by recharging the train pipe to normal pressure. This allowed the triple valve to void the air from the brake cylinders, at the same time equalizing the auxiliary tank pressure with the train pipe. The system has now been refined, but the fail-safe remains. Anything that results in a reduction of the air pressure in the train pipe will cause the brakes to be applied. The rupture of a flexible pipe, such as might be caused by a coupling breakage, will activate the brakes on all cars, bringing both the separated sections of the train to a stand. The brakes can then be released only manually on each car of the broken-away section of the train or by replacing the faulty flexible hose.

An express out of Boston, Massachusetts, in August, 1871, crashed, killing 29 passengers and injuring 57 as it ploughed into the back of another train. Public and press denounced the directors of the railroad as murderers. The railroad reacted and the fitting of continuous brakes to passenger trains began. It took another 20 years before they were fitted to all freight cars. Many railroads were reluctant to spend money, and mixed braked/non-braked trains resulted, with the "fitted" vehicles at the head. Regulations compelled car owners to fit through-brake pipes if not air brakes, so "mixed" trains could be run. Such trains presented an operating hazard on mountainous lines; braking was accompanied by bunching and surging as trains slowed, and breakaways were not unknown.

George Westinghouse established a small works in Pittsburgh, Pennsylvania, in 1870 with a work force of 105. By 1872 the Westinghouse automatic brake was in full production. Even so, with the link and pin couplers then in vogue, train separations were a quite common occurrence and the new brake took this into account. Passenger-train separations were considerably reduced and by the late 1870s most passenger rolling stock was equipped with some form of air brake. By the early 1880s developments were in hand to enhance the braking of freight trains and a new device was being fitted to freight vehicles: the brake cylinder pressure-retaining valve. This allowed safe operation on long grades and permitted the system to be recharged without having to release and re-apply the brakes.

Electric Streetcars and Locomotives

COAL-FIRED, STEAM POWERED STREETCARS WERE EXPERIMENTED WITH IN MANY CITIES IN NORTH AMERICA, BUT THEY PROVED TO BE UNSUITABLE FOR LARGE, CROWDED AREAS. IN NORTH AMERICA AND OTHER CITIES OF THE WORLD, THE SEARCH FOR A CLEANER, QUIETER, AND SAFER SOURCE OF POWER BEGAN.

Between 1870 and 1900, advances in technology saw steam heat and electric light replacing stoves and oil or gas lamps—a welcome move since wooden rail car construction was vulnerable to fires caused by overheated stoves or spilled oil. Automatic block signaling and the first electric locomotives appeared in the last 10 years of the 19th century. The standard eight-wheeler steam locomotive gave way to the rapid development of larger and more sophisticated types, as train weights and speeds increased with the introduction of much better and stronger tracks.

Electrical pioneer Thomas Edison had produced a strange-looking electric locomotive in 1880 to demonstrate the practicality of electric traction, although the results were greeted with skepticism by exponents of steam. In 1888, however, the first practical electric streetcar appeared. In 1893, a four-wheeled electric locomotive was built and exhibited at the Columbian Exposition in Chicago, and by this time, a number of electric streetcar lines were already attracting attention of those with the foresight to see the development as the way forward.

Another unusual development was introduced by a partnership between two companies, Baldwin and Westinghouse. This was an electric locomotive that resembled a railcar without any visible means of driving it. The collaboration between the two companies was to continue until the second half

Opened in 1873, San Francisco's cable car system was an effective public transport system. Still in operation today, it is an icon of the city.

American inventor and businessman Thomas Alva Edison (1847–1931) developed many devices that influenced life around the world, including the phonograph and incandescent electric lamp. Applying the principles of mass production to the process of invention, he is credited with the establishment of the first industrial research laboratory, at Menlo Park, New Jersey. His company merged with a rival organization in 1892 to become General Electric.

The 1893 General Electrics boxcab, displayed at the Chicago Exposition, was a new breed of locomotive in which machinery and crew areas are enclosed in a box-like superstructure. This electric boxcab was used on the New Haven RR, and is now on display in the Museum of Transport, St. Louis, Missouri.

of the 20th century. From these humble beginnings evolved the electric interurban railroad (the equivalent of today's light rapid-transit). The rolling stock was smaller than standard, and the rails ran partly in the street, partly on private rights-of-way. The emphasis was on local service, which main-line railroads found difficult and expensive to provide. Some traditional railroads encouraged neighboring electric interurban roads, but in the main, they ignored or treated with open hostility.

The cable car, invented by Andrew Hallidie, seemed the ideal replacement for the horsecar. A remote powerplant, which could drive a loop of cable beneath the street, to which cars could grip and haul themselves around, had many advantages and excelled on hills. In 1873, San Francisco was the first city to install a practical system, and its cable cars are now a public icon. Cable cars, although expensive, were cheaper than horsecars to maintain, and every city wanted them. Systems were installed in the United States in Seattle, Chicago, New York, and Denver, in addition to Melbourne, Australia, and Wellington, New Zealand. For a few years, the "gripman," as the driver was called, ruled the streets.

A buzz of activity produced dozens of competing electric-car designs, including battery powered cars, but none was wholly practical. William Siemens had some success in Germany. His cars ran sporadically just outside Berlin in 1881, but he used dangerous high-voltage track for power. In the United States, experimenters such as Leo Daft, who used electric locomotives, and Charles Van Depoele, who pioneered the use of the trolley pole to collect power from overhead wires, built lines that were almost profitable. It was Van Depoele who built the first city-wide electric streetcar system in the United States—in Montgomery, Alabama—after electrifying the city's horsedrawn Court Street Line in 1886. Edison also experimented with electric streetcars. Baltimore and Cleveland installed lines—and paid the price of frustrating unreliability. The early systems created unforeseen side effects: hissing and static-ridden telephone lines, electrocuted cats and dogs, and burst water and gas pipes, caused by ground-circuit induced corrosion. Not one of the 10 lines running in 1887 had made any money for its host city or its investors.

All of the parts of the puzzle were put together by one man. In the spring of 1877, Richmond, Virginia, had given a contract to build a 12-mile (19km), 30-car streetcar line to a young ex-Navy officer and engineer, Frank Sprague. Although he was a successful builder of automobiles, he came fresh from a failed demonstration of electric-car technology to Jay Gould, a potential backer of a New York elevated trolley system. Sprague's naval experience and technical training prepared him for the type of trial and error needed to build a viable system. His motors, already good by the standards of the times, were combined with a "wheelbarrow" method of mounting to drive wheels that didn't shake them to pieces. He perfected a power regulator and controller that allowed up to 22 cars to start up at once, and a spring-mounted trolley pole topped the ensemble. Sprague's system worked. Although the line had to scramble to stay functional, it improved almost daily, until even people like Boston horsecar magnate Henry Whitney visited Richmond to investigate. They departed impressed, leaving Sprague with orders. Once Sprague set things in motion, the new system got under way as city after city rolled out its colorful new machines. Soon, foreign cities as distant as Florence in Italy had Sprague trolleys. His company was absorbed by General Electric, and although he stayed on for a while, his name was removed from all patents and from the trolleys he had worked on, so except for rail and trolley enthusiasts, few know of him today.

Once practical trolleys were running in a few cities, local authorities everywhere from Canada to Mexico rushed to install them. Windsor, Ontario, was the first Canadian city with an electric streetcar system in 1886, followed by Vancouver in 1890, Winnipeg (1891), Montreal, Hamilton, and Toronto (1892), Edmonton (1908), Calgary (1909), and Regina (1911). Mexico's first trolley service began in 1890, when a line was built from Laredo, Texas, to Nuevo Laredo in Tamaulipas State. It was the world's first international electric streetcar line, and the first electric railroad in Latin America.

As cities electrified and built powerplants, the extra infrastructure required to switch from horse-drawn cars to electric trolleys was minimal, for not only could existing track systems be used, but the horsedrawn cars themselves could have motors installed and be up and running on their old routes with minimum delay. This was hardly necessary, as new designs poured out of such firms as Stephenson and the Philadelphia-based J.G. Brill. The advances in motor design went on behind the scenes, and invisible—except to the technicians and mechanics—were new generations of motors and trucks that could be fitted to existing rolling stock.

Among the early trolleys, there were many different types of design for both interiors and exteriors. They ranged from luxurious heated Pullmans to open-sided cars. Most importantly, weight was no longer a drawback, but actually aided traction, so the bare-essential interiors of horsecars, with their wicker or pierced-plywood seats, took on a gilded-age splendor, and their beautiful steam-bent tulipwood or birchwood sides were replicated in stamped metal or cast iron on the new electric cars.

By the 1900s, many cities across the United States boasted electric streetcar lines. Traffic on the roads frequently became clogged, as the slower-moving horsedrawn vehicles jostled with the colorful cars. This photograph, taken in 1909, shows a traffic jam without automobiles at the corner of Dearborn and Randolph Streets in Chicago, Illinois.

Master Car Builders' Association

THE AMERICAN CIVIL WAR BROUGHT ABOUT A CONSIDERABLE INTERCHANGE OF ROLLING STOCK, PARTICULARLY OF FREIGHT CARS, WHERE TRACK GAUGES ALLOWED, AND IT SOON BECAME APPARENT TO CONSTRUCTORS THAT A DEGREE OF VEHICLE STANDARDIZATION WAS NEEDED.

Henry Bessemer (1813–98) was an English engineer and inventor. He was the first person in the world to develop a method of producing steel inexpensively.

The need for standardization brought about the founding of the Master Car Builders' Association in 1867. Its purpose was to simplify the interchange of cars among railroads. In 1876, it established rules for the prompt interchange of cars, and of repairs to damaged and defective cars, with billing and payment for the repairs. The association then went on to establish standards for other car parts that, for example, helped to reduce the enormous variety of axles and journal boxes at the time to five different types.

Another problem tackled by the Master Car Builders' Association was one that had arisen from the growth of the many unconnected railroads—that of the confusion of part-names. In 1871, a publication called *The Railroad Gazette* was produced, which served as a dictionary, defining by words and pictures everything from "adjustable globe-lamp" to "yoke."

A British invention of 1856 had far reaching effects in revolutionizing the process of rail manufacture. The introduction of Henry Bessemer's converter to steel making resulted in the quantity production of stronger, more durable, and less expensive steel rails. The widespread use of steel rails led to the development of bigger and heavier cars, longer trains, and more powerful locomotives. At the same time, with the interchange of rolling stock by the middle 1880s, the need was recognized for an acceptable, standard, continuous power brake system. From tests organized by the Master Car Builders' Association, a quick-action, automatic air-brake system was developed

Bessemer's steel making process relied on an egg-shaped device known as a converter. Molten pig iron was poured into this through the aperture in the top and air blasted through the base, which converted the iron into steel. The converter was then turned in its mounting so that the steel could be poured out. The process marked the beginning of mass steel production and provided the railroads with steel in large quantites for rails, etc.

Many variations of Janney's coupler were made, but the Master Car Builders' Association standardized the types in use, ensuring that all would intercouple.

in 1888 and subsequently adopted in 1889 as the American standard.

The Westinghouse system was modified to allow air to be voided to the atmosphere, not only at the engineer's control valve, but also at every triple valve in a train. Trials conducted in 1886 at Burlington, Iowa, by the Master Car Builders' Association with three different types of brake, applied to strings of 50 boxcars weighing a total of 1,000 tons, showed that the lag of 20 seconds or more in braking effect between the front and rear of the train gave unsatisfactory emergency stopping distances. The modified Westinghouse system improved this so much that there was only one-and-a-half to two seconds delay in actuation between the front and rear of the train. This was known as the quick-acting (QA) triple valve.

These tests also demonstrated the need for sweeping changes to car drawbars and couplings. Until that time, the standard coupling had been the combined drawbar, link, and pin coupling. As car and train weights increased, this type of coupling proved too weak, was dangerous to operate, and introduced a considerable amount of free slack in a long train. By the 1870s, passenger cars were already using some form of semi-automatic coupling—the Miller Hook was heralded as the greatest life-saving invention of the age—but even so, American draftgear was not designed generally to absorb energy, as was the case in Europe, where cushioned screw couplings and spring-loaded side buffers were the norm.

A typical automatic coupler. The air hose for the train brake system can also be seen.

In 1868, Major Eli Janney invented (and in 1873 patented) an automatic knuckle-coupler that operated in the vertical plane. In the next decade, many other coupler designs of the same general type emerged. By 1889, there were around 80,000 freight cars in the United States, and 39 different varieties of coupler, the majority of which would not intercouple. It is thought that this was the single greatest factor responsible for the formation of the Master Car Builders' Association. The association adopted automatic couplers in 1887. Due to its efforts, the number of designs was reduced to 16 and subsequently to 12, all able to intercouple.

The first truly automatic coupler was the Tower coupler, invented in 1892. It would couple and lock on impact (as indeed would many other designs), but it could also be unlocked and the knuckle thrown fully open by means of a lever at the side of the car.

Many railroads were slow to adopt automatic couplers and other safety devices until the Safety Appliances Act was passed by Congress in 1893. This made it mandatory, after January 1, 1898, that all cars used in interstate commerce be equipped with couplers that were capable of coupling automatically by impact, and uncoupling without the need of trainmen. Coupler development was stimulated as the result.

In the same period, the strength of freight cars was improved. Early freight cars had been made entirely of lumber. As early as 1829, the Delaware & Hudson Railroad had introduced anthracite coal traffic in New York State with wooden, open-top hopper cars, each running on two four-wheel trucks. This general type of car, updated, still appeared in the *Carbuilder's Dictionary* in 1878, having a carrying capacity of 40-50,000lb (18,150–22,680kg).

Boxcars of wooden construction averaged about 28ft (8.5m) in length and had a capacity of about 30,000lb (13,600kg). By 1888, the length had grown to about 35ft (10.6m), with a capacity of 50,000lb (22,680kg) and a tare weight of 24,800lb (11,250kg), giving an axle load, fully laden, of a little over 9 tons. About this time, wooden frames gave way to wrought iron.

Tankcars had been used for the carriage of water and oil from early times; the first purpose-built tankcar went into service in Pennsylvania in 1865. The tank was formed from riveted steel plates and was strapped to a wooden underframe with wooden crossmembers. It had a typical empty weight of 28,000lb (12,700kg) and a capacity of 3,700 gallons (14,000 liters).

Major Eli Janney invented this automatic knuckle-coupler in 1868., shown illustrated in the patent application of 1873.

Pullman and the New Passenger Cars

DEVELOPMENT OF THE PASSENGER CAR WAS PROCEEDING APACE. BETWEEN 1865 AND 1880 THERE WAS A TRANSITION FROM CARS THAT WERE LITTLE MORE THAN SMALL, UNCOMFORTABLE BOXES TO DELUXE VEHICLES COSTING 10 TIMES AS MUCH TO PRODUCE.

Railroad publicity made much of the luxury offered by their passenger cars for long journeys. This 1880s advertisement for the Chicago & Alton RR likens the dining car to an hotel, and offers the tempting delights of "Meals, 75 cents."

These luxury rail cars were intended to allow people to make long-distance journeys in comfort. Passage between adjoining cars when the train was in motion had been extremely hazardous in earlier types of car, since the end platforms were narrow and completely open to the elements, and there were no buffers or tread plates between the end sills of the cars. Some early cars were fitted with various types of semi-automatic coupler, such as the Miller hook, but there were no continuous brakes.

Car bodies were of lumber and were constructed like a simple bridge truss, with wrought-iron diagonal tension rods in the side framing. Support and control of vertical deflection was by wrought-iron truss rods under the floor. Brakes were primarily manual, and in the 1860s, some cars were equipped with elementary, non-automatic, vacuum brakes introduced from England. Westinghouse straight air brakes were fitted on some cars in the early 1870s. Speeds were relatively low and did not normally exceed 35–40mph (56–64km/h).

Passenger cars carried their own coal- or wood-burning stoves, although the luxury cars were equipped with circulating hot-air or hot-water systems from Spear & Baker heaters. As early as 1856, a heating and ventilating system had been developed that introduced fresh air from the top of the car. Forced in as the train moved, the air was passed through a plenum chamber, where it was heated by a stove, the warm air being distributed around the car through ducts in the ceiling. Cold air was removed through suction heads and returned to the stove for reheating. Steam heating from the locomotive was first introduced in 1883 on New York's Manhattan Railroad. Steam was passed through

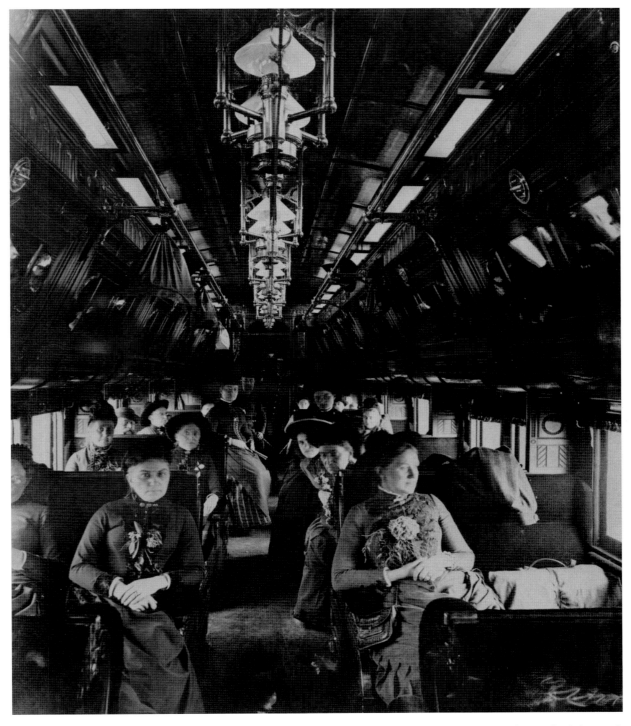

The Pullman Palace Company's "Holden" was, during the 1880s, an extremely plush and comfortable ride for its passengers. The ornate car was illuminated by oil lamps, and was heated in winter and ventilated in summer.

pipes running around each car. Wooden-truss construction continued to be used to the end of the 19th century, although it was developed so that the car sides, rather than the underframe, were used to support the weighty of the car. Elaborate wooden trusses or arch constructions were developed for use between the side sill and the belt rail, although truss rods continued to be used under the cars.

By the early 1890s, the automatic locking knuckle coupler with friction draftgear was developed to the point where knuckle contours could be standardized. Henceforward, cars could be interchanged between different railroads, making it no longer necessary to change trains between one system and another. In 1887, the enclosed-end vestibule was invented by a Mr. Sessions, for the first time permitting passengers to walk safely through a moving train and thereby encourage the use of dining, lounge, and

George M. Pullman (1831–97) trained originally as a cabinetmaker. After remodeling two cars for the Chicago, Alton & St. Louis RR, he went into the sleeping-car business, and developed it to such an extent that he had a virtual monopoly on the provision of sleeping and dining cars to U.S. railroads.

Pullman's cars were commonly named. This one bears the name of President Abraham Lincoln.

other special-purpose cars. At first, the vestibule was only between the step wells, but by 1893, it had been enlarged to cover the full width. In conjunction with the instalation of automatic couplers, the construction used a metal faceplate with a canvas curtain to aid moving between adjacent cars.

Although George M. Pullman did not invent the sleeping car, he developed its design and construction to the point where it became a national institution. Pullman was a cabinetmaker from Brocton, New York, and after successfully remodeling (with Benjamin Field) two Chicago, Alton & St. Louis cars in 1859, he decided to go into the sleeping-car business. In 1863, he set up his first works in Detroit, Michigan, and built a luxury car he named *Pioneer*, which was larger and more luxurious than other cars of the era. Legend has it that *Pioneer* was in the train that carried Abraham Lincoln's body home to Springfield, Illinois, in April 1865. The Pullman Palace Car Company was chartered in 1867, and the first build totaled 48 cars. The company grew, acquiring cars from other operators, which it leased out to railroads, and moved to a larger plant near Chicago, Illinois. It owned all the sleeping cars on the Chicago & Alton RR, the Burlington & Quincy RR, the Michigan Central RR, the Great Western RR of Canada, and the New York Central railroads. Pullman built the first "hotel car," a forerunner of the dining car, for the Great Western of Canada.

The entrepreneur entered into arrangements with railroads whereby he would provide the cars and staff, and the railroads would haul, light, and heat them. The railroad charged the regular coach fare for each passenger journey, and a supplement was charged for a single berth or seat occupancy, which went to Pullman. Pullman was not the only sleeping-car operator—there were some 40 others in the second

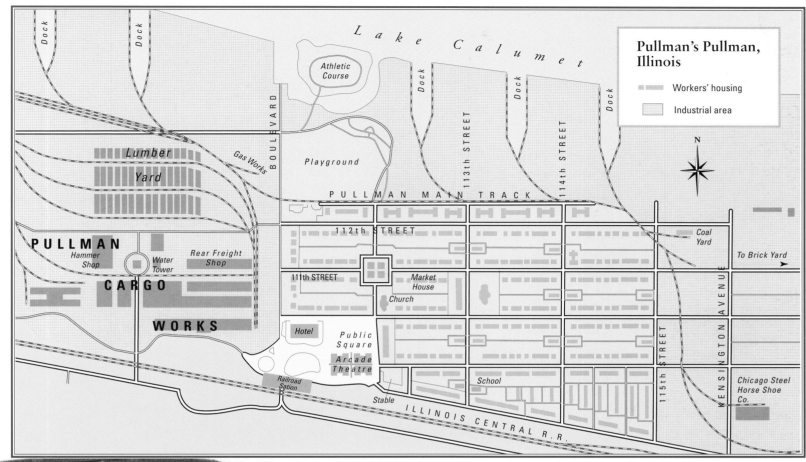

Pullman's Pullman,
Illinois

Workers' housing

Industrial area

half of the 19th century—but ultimately all the others failed or were absorbed into his empire. The Pullman Company was renowned for its standardization of both cars and service. Staff were trained from manuals that stipulated everything from the positioning of the pillows and the correct way to fold towels to the proper way in which to serve beer. The usual staff per car was one African-American porter and one Filipino lounge attendant.

By the time George M. Pullman died in 1897, his company enjoyed a virtual monopoly of the sleeping-car services in the United States and ran dining- and parlor car services as well. Its railroad car plant was the largest in the world and it was a pioneer in the building of steel cars. Later, it expanded into production of freight cars by buying other car builders.

George Pullman created Pullman, Illinois, the first model industrial town, in 1880, on 4,000 acres (1.6ha) of land he had bought, west of Lake Calumet, surrounding the Illinois Central RR. At the center of the town was was his car business. The housing boasted "modern" conveniences by 1880's standards, including indoor plumbing, sewage, and a gas works. During the Depression of 1893-94, Pullman reduced wages and hours, prompting a notorious strike. The company sold its non-industrial property, and all the housing had been bought by 1907.

SPREADING NETWORKS AND CANADA, 1885-90

IN THE 20 YEARS FROM 1870, U.S.
RAILROADS HAD SPREAD ACROSS
THE COUNTRY, AND A SECOND
LINK EXISTED TO THE PACIFIC.
IN CANADA, SIGHTS WERE
ALSO SET ON BUILDING A
TRANSCONTINENTAL RAILROAD TO
CONNECT BRITISH COLUMBIA IN THE
WEST WITH THE EASTERN PROVINCES.

Even today, much of Canada is uninhabited. In 1885, the majority of the population was spread thinly along the border with the United States. The Canadian Pacific RR provided a vital link with British Columbia in the West, helping to create a unified nation.

A look at a United States railroad map of 1870 shows a single transcontinental line and a burgeoning network of lines. The 1890 map shows four main transcontinental lines, plus other connecting lines and a very dense network of lines in the East and around the Great Lakes, with minor networks in Colorado and Utah. With the original transcontinental route from Omaha, Nebraska, to Sacramento, California, completed, thoughts were directed to the development of other routes on the basis of those proposed between 1853 and 1855. Several rail routes to the Pacific were constructed

As in the United States, building railroads in Canada often meant laying tracks through difficult, rugged country. Although part of the British Empire, Canada's railroads employed U.S.-style rolling stock.

Canada 1885

Area settled by Europeans, c. 1890

Canadian Pacific railroad, completed 1885

0   300 km
0   300 miles

N

Victoria Island

Baffin Island

Hudson Strait

T e r r i t o r i e s

Newfoundland

Hudson Bay

District of Keewatin created 1876

abasca

f Saskatchewan

Lake Winnipeg

Québec

St. Lawrence River

St. Pierre and Miquelon to France

Assiniboia
egina

Manitoba
Winnipeg

provisional border 1874

New Brunswick

Québec

Nova Scotia • Halifax

T A T E S

L. Superior

O n t a r i o

Montréal

L. Michigan

L. Huron

Toronto

L. Ontario

L. Erie

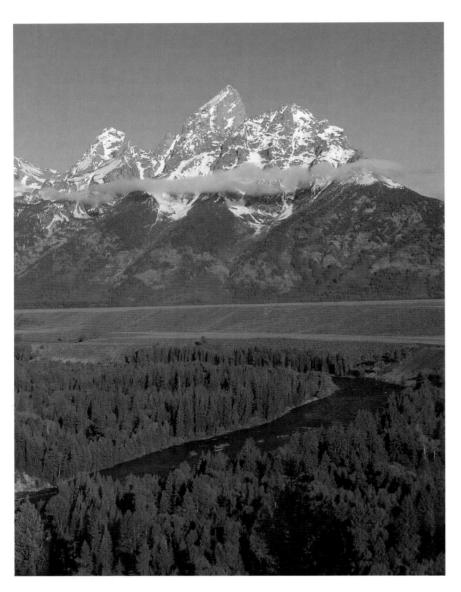

The Canadian Rockies were a formidable barrier to a Canadian transcontinental railroad. There were few routes by which they could be crossed.

during the 1880s. The Santa Fe RR and Southern Pacific RR met at Deming, in southwestern New Mexico, in 1881, and three more routes were completed in 1883. The Santa Fe now had its own route across northern New Mexico and Arizona, while the Southern Pacific completed its line from New Orleans, Louisiana, to Los Angeles, California. At the same time, the Northern Pacific opened its line through the Rockies from Duluth, Minnesota, to the Pacific at Portland, Oregon.

Competition was such that the Union Pacific RR also set its sights on the northwest, and in 1884, it opened a route from Ogden, Utah, through Idaho to Portland.

In Canada, also, the first trans-Canada route was opened by the Canadian Pacific in 1885. The Dominion of Canada was created on July 1, 1867, but British Columbia, in the west, did not join the other states until 1871. Canada's first railroad, the Champlain & St. Lawrence, opened in 1836, and ran between the St. Lawrence River and St. John's, Quebec, at the head of open-water navigation on the Richelieu River, which flows from Lake Champlain.

By the time British Columbia joined the Dominion in 1871, it had been promised a railroad by the Canadian government to link it with the rest of the country. Since other lines were not interested, the Canadian Pacific Railroad was incorporated in 1881 to build a western extension from Callander, Ontario, to the Pacific at what is now the capital of British Columbia, Vancouver.

The builders of the trans-Canada railroad had to cross 1,300 miles (2,090km) of wilderness, 1,000 miles (1,600km) of prairie, and 500 miles (800km) of difficult terrain in the Rockies. While construction of the line along the shores of Lake Superior was difficult enough, nationalistic sentiment prevented a detour through United States territory. Construction of the route over the Rockies was a formidable challenge, involving gradients of 1 in 22 (4.5 percent). The line was opened on November 7, 1885. The boring of two spiral tunnels later eased the grades.

Coincidentally with the line to the west, construction was also proceeding eastward to Ottawa and Montreal. By 1890, the eastern lines extended from Windsor, Ontario, through Montreal, over the national frontier into Maine, and onward to St. John, New Brunswick.

Today, the other major railroad system is the Canadian National, which was formed by merging five major components—Intercolonial, National Transcontinental, Canadian Northern, Grand Trunk Pacific, and Grand Trunk Railroad.

The Intercolonial began operations between Halifax, New Brunswick, and Rivière du Loup, Quebec province, in 1876, taking in the operation of the Grand Trunk's line from Rivière du Loup to the west of Levis, across the St. Lawrence from the city of Quebec, in 1879. The National Transcontinental was a product of the Canadian administration that took office in 1896. The Canadian Northern began in the 1890s, when William Mackenzie and Donald Mann merged a series of other projects. The Grand Trunk Railroad was incorporated in 1852 and included the former Champlain & St. Lawrence Railroad. By 1856, it was operating between Levis and Windsor, Ontario. Three years later, it opened the Victoria Bridge across the St. Lawrence at Montreal.

When Canada became a Dominion in 1867, it was proposed to extend the Grand Trunk west to the Pacific, and east to New Brunswick and Nova Scotia at public expense. Public opinion was against the proposal, and in the end the GTR built south to Chicago, Illinois, which it reached in 1880. It used the tracks of several short lines it purchased, then the Michigan lines were connected to the rest, first by ferry and in 1890 by the St. Clair Tunnel. By 1890, the GTR owned a majority interest in the Boston & Maine RR, and went on to expand in the first few years of the 20th century.

Victoria Bridge, spanning the St. Lawrence River at Montreal, under construction in the early 1850s. The structure was finally opened in 1859 but the cost of building it was so high that the Grand Trunk RR was obliged to ask the government to bear most of the cost.

Growth of the Mexican Railroads, 1873-83

AFTER A SLOW START, RAILROAD CONSTRUCTION GAINED MOMENTUM IN MEXICO, ONCE IT HAD OPENED THE NATION'S FIRST INTER-CITY LINE IN 1873. JUST OVER A DECADE LATER, THE COUNTRY HAD A GROWING NATIONAL NETWORK AND LINES CONNECTING IT TO THE UNITED STATES.

José de la Cruz Porfirio Díaz Mori (1830–1915) was a Mexican-American War volunteer, French Intervention hero, and president of Mexico from 1876 to 1880 and from 1884 to 1911, and actively encouraged the growth of the railroads in Mexico.

Mexico's railroad network began with a line linking the capital, Mexico City, with the port of Veracruz on the Gulf of Mexico. The first step toward building this line came in 1837, when the government awarded a concession for its construction to Francisco de Arrillaga, a trader from Veracruz.

Progress was painfully slow, however, so the government withdrew de Arrillaga's concession and in 1842, awarded one to the commission responsible for roadbuilding in the Veracruz region. But by 1850, the commission had completed just 7 miles (11.5km) of the line, from Veracruz to El Molino, so the government again withdrew the concession. Following several more failed concessions, the project was eventually handed over to the Mexican Imperial Railway Company (Compañia Limitada del Ferrocarril Imperial Mexicano, later Ferrocarril Mexicano), which had been established in 1864. The company completed the construction of the railroad in

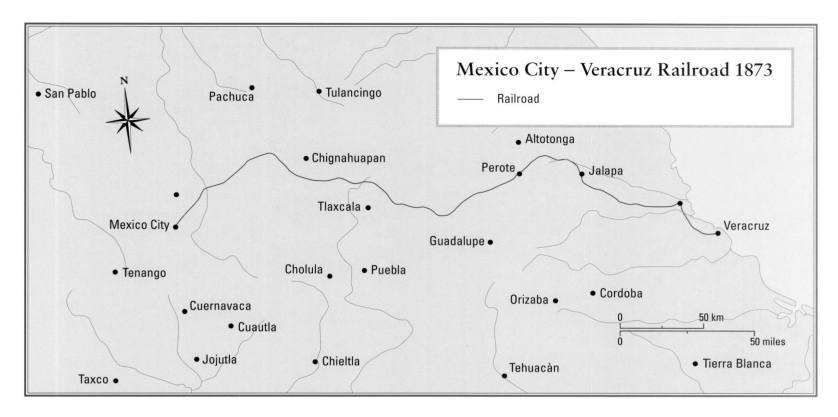

The first railroad in Mexico ran between Mexico City and the port of Veracruz on the Gulf of Mexico. After a number of false starts, it finally opened in 1873.

late 1872, and the 270-mile (433km) line was inaugurated on January 1, 1873.

Ferrocarril Mexicano built a number of branch lines to connect the line between Mexico City and Veracruz with nearby towns, but connections with United States railroads were discouraged by the Mexican government for a while, and as a counterpoise to the company's monopoly, concessions or subsidies were granted to railroads prepared to construct alternative lines between the Gulf and the interior. But Mexico could not afford to ignore the United States for long, so two lines connecting the border with Mexico City were built with the aid of concessions. The principal line, from El Paso, Texas, across the Rio Grande through Ciudad Juárez, was built by Santa Fe interests as the Mexican Central (Ferrocarril Central Mexicano) and completed in 1884. One of the cities along the line's route was Aguascalientes, and in 1897, the Mexican Central and the Mexican government chose this city as the site for the country's main railroad engineering depot. This depot, the General Workshops for the Construction and Repair of Machines and Rolling Stock, was completed in 1903. At its peak, it covered an area of about 200 acres (81ha) and employed more than 7,000 workers. It was also the center for training railroad workers, not just from Mexico, but from all over Central America, becoming known as the "Railroad University."

Work on the second international line to Mexico City, from Laredo, in eastern Texas, began in 1881. It was built to the narrow 3ft (914mm) gauge as the Mexican National (Ferrocarriles Nacionales de México) by General William Jackson Palmer, builder of the Denver & Rio Grande RR, and reached Mexico City in 1888.

Later, the line had branches in the North from Monterrey to Matamoros on the Gulf of Mexico, and, farther south, from Acámbaro to Uruapan. A third line, the Mexican International (Ferrocarril Internacional Mexicano), was completed in 1892 and ran from Durango in central Mexico to the border town of Piedras Negras, then across the Rio Grande to Eagle Pass, Texas.

Black smoke rises from a steam locomotive, hauling a train through the dramatic scenery of Mexico. This train is part of a the Cumbres and Toltec Scenic Railroad in the Carson National Foresst, Chama, New Mexico.

This antique print of the "Ferro Carril Mexicano", dated 1877, shows a map of the first railroad line from Mexico City to Vera Cruz, Mexico, with additional lines between Apizaco and Puebla and between Jalapa and Vera Cruz. Evocative of the type of terrain the railroad passed through, the map also includes the locations of five volcanoes in the region.

In the southeast of Mexico, the first line of the United Railroads of Yucatán (Ferrocarriles Unidos de Yucatán, or UdeY) was opened in 1881. UdeY developed into a system of narrow- and standard-gauge lines linking much of the state of Yucatán with its capital, Mérida, with a line into the neighboring state of Campeche. On the Pacific Coast, the grandly named Pan-American Railway (Ferrocarril Panamericano) linked the standard-gauge network south of Mexico City with the town of Tecún Umán just over the border in Guatemala.

By 1910, Mexico had most of its national railroad network in place, built with the active encouragement of President Porfirio Díaz, who had ruled the country from 1876 to 1880, and from 1884 to 1911. Díaz had embarked on a program of modernization in an attempt to bring Mexico up to the level of a modern state. He was keen to see steam machines and technological appliances used in industry, and the construction of factories in Mexico City, while actively inviting and encouraging foreign investment. This policy resulted in the rise of an urban proletariat in Mexico, and the influx of foreign capital (principally from the United States). Díaz' plans included the building of railroad and telegraph lines across the country. Under his presidency the amount of track in Mexico increased tenfold; many of these rails remain in operation today without remodelling. In less than 40 years, it had constructed some 12,000 miles (20,000km) of track, often over difficult terrain across deserts, through rainforests, and across hills and mountains that called for many high bridges and long tunnels.

Watched by one of the crewmen, Mexican locomotive No.124 emerges from the mouth of a tunnel in the Tamasopa Canon, and prepares to negotiate the tight curve around a giddyingly steep stonebuilt grade.

FARMERS VERSUS THE RAILROADS, 1866-90

AT FIRST, FARMERS WELCOMED THE ARRIVAL OF THE RAILROADS WITH OPEN ARMS, BUT SOON THEY BEGAN TO SUFFER DEMANDS FOR UNFAIR RATES AND OTHER DISCRIMINATORY PRACTICES AT THE HANDS OF THE BIG RAIL CORPORATIONS, WHICH WERE SWALLOWING UP THE SMALLER LOCAL LINES.

Oliver Hudson Kelley (1826–1913) was the "Father" of the Order of Patrons of Husbandry. Born in Boston, Massachusetts, he moved to the Minnesota frontier in 1849 and became a farmer. He felt the need to gather together farmers and their families in a fraternal organization, and in 1867 he formed the "Grange",

A t the end of the long and costly American Civil War, farmers faced a range of social and economic problems that made their rural lives dismal. The seller's grain market that had existed during the war had disappeared as supply began to outweigh demand. The price of crops fell, and farmers who had borrowed heavily during the prosperous war years to expand their businesses were unable to repay their debts. Carpetbagging was rife as the northerners took advantage of the southerners during postwar reconstruction. These problems were not limited solely to the devastated southern states; many farmers in the North had been left physically disabled as a result of combat and were unable to work on the land, or had lost family members who were vital to their farm's workload. Exacerbating matters, a national depression set in during 1873.

The root of the farmers' problems, as they saw it, lay with the devious and greedy railroad magnates. While the farmers had actually helped to fund the establishment of railroads during the 1850s, they had subsequently witnessed the smaller regional lines being bought out by the larger corporations based in distant places such as New York. The railroads set rates for haulage that were not prompted by a competitive market, but through agreements secured with other railroads, giving the farmers no choice: to transport their crops, they were obliged to pay the rates.

The Railroads: Getting Agricultural Products to Eastern Markets 1890

- Over 90 people per square mile
- Wheat growing
- Corn growing
- Railroad

Shipment of grain, 1890, in thousand tons:

- 3,450
- 1,500
- 380

- Wheat
- Corn

The railroads made it easy for farmers to send their produce to markets in the East. At the same time, the presence of railroads encouraged agriculture within reach of their tracks.

In 1866, Oliver Hudson Kelley, a Minnesota farmer, agricultural writer, and member of the Masonic Order, was commissioned by President Andrew Johnson to carry out a survey of agricultural conditions in the southern states. He was horrified to see the farmers so beleaguered, and determined to do something to alleviate their woes. On December 4, 1867, having foresaken farming for a job in the Post Office Department in Washington, DC, Kelley established the Order of Patrons of Husbandry, known simply as the "National Grange". Joining Kelley were six other founders: four Washington government officials, a banker, and a minister. Although some of the seven had an agricultural background, none was actively involved in farming. The Grange was set up as a fraternal, socio-economic organization that would act on behalf of the farmers, their families, and their interests, which Kelley envisioned as encompassing all the rural areas of the United States.

Grange members were able to meet in township halls to discuss their problems, many of which were centered on the railroads and their middlemen. The railroads, it was stated, deliberately withheld vital information from farmers, such as the amount of grain held in storage, and some were known to cheat when weighing crops. They would frequently levy transportation charges that were more per ton for short hauls than for longer ones. The fledgling Grange made a name for itself as a railroad reformer, although this was not its original intention. In 1870, for example, the Illinois Grange won a constitutional

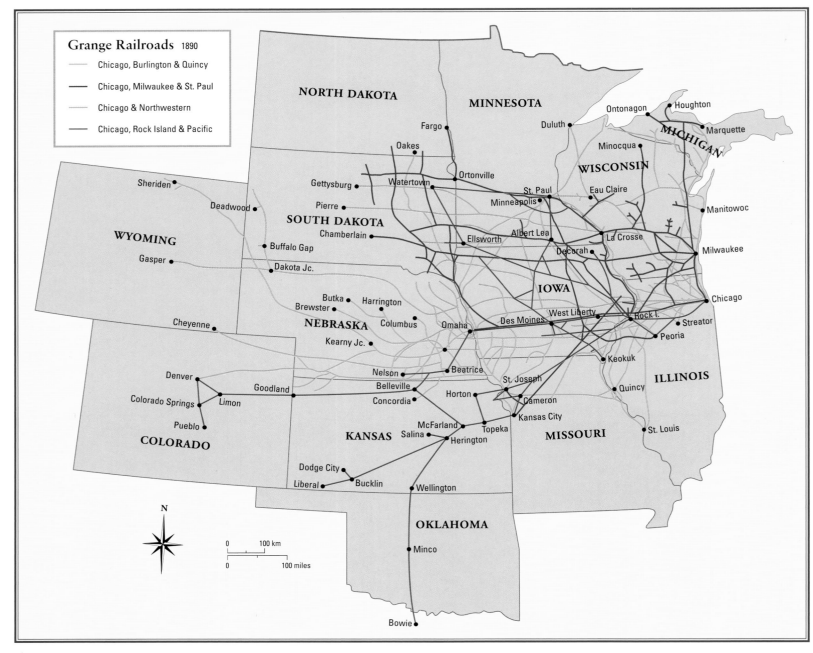

Grange Railroads 1890
— Chicago, Burlington & Quincy
— Chicago, Milwaukee & St. Paul
— Chicago & Northwestern
— Chicago, Rock Island & Pacific

Railroads that operated in the Midwest were most affected by the Granger Laws.

amendment that gave the state control over the railroads. The following year, the State Legislature fixed a constant rate for freight and passenger trains. The Granger Laws dictated rules the railroads had to adhere to and regulated the charge for grain elevators. In 1873, the Texas Grange was organized with the prime intention of fighting for railroad legislation. Half of the delegates that were elected to the Texas Constitutional Convention of 1875 were members of the movement. After the convention, railroad companies were forbidden from buying or controling competing lines, and cities were prevented from issuing bonds to pay for the construction of railroads. Rates and fares were fixed by the legislature.

After the nationwide financial panic of 1873, growth in the membership of the Grange increased dramatically, and by 1874, there were some 268,368 paying members. By 1875, this had increased to 850,000. The organization was most strongly represented in Illinois, Minnesota, Iowa and Winsconsin, states where many railroad regulations were imposed. During its battles with the railroad companies, the Grange was sued by its adversaries, with many cases being heard in the United States Supreme Court.

Numerous rulings were given in favor of the Grange. As the organization grew, it began to take on more of an economic role. It established cooperative grain elevators and mills, and set up buying cooperatives, cutting out the middlemen and so reducing prices. Critics, however, claimed that the Grange itself had beccome a middleman.

Although much of the Grange's activities were aimed against the railroads, this was by no means its sole purpose, a concept reinforced in a report to the executive committee in 1874, which stated, "Unfortunately for our order, the impression prevails to some extent that its chief mission is to fight railroads and denounce capitalists. It is a work of time to remove these erroneous impressions, and to prove that we do not wage a meaningless aggressive warfare upon any interst whatever..." The group had interests in mail delivery, and in the 1870s, campaigned for rural free delivery (RFD); by the turn of the century, the scheme was widespread. It was staunchly pro-temperance; it railed against tobacco products, and argued for a system of progressive federal income tax.

As time progressed, however, it seemed that the movement attracted many of the individuals it sought to control: it was thought that new enrolments secretly had allegiance to the middlemen and the railroads, and that many were hoping to secure discount prices. Membership of the Grange dropped during the late 1870s, and its political influence became minimal. By 1879, there were fewer than 250,000 members, and during the 1880s, there were little over 100,000.

Grain elevators were important to the storage and shipment of grain. Invented in 1842 in Buffalo, New York, by Joseph Dart, who had earlier developed a steam-powered mechanism (a "marine leg") for scooping grain out of the hulls of ships directly into storage silos. Early grain elevators and bins were constructed of wood and prone to fire; later types were constructed of steel or reinforced concrete. The elevator's silos, bins, and tanks were emptied by gravity flow, sweep augers and conveyors— blended and weighted—into railroad cars, or barges, or, later, trucks, and shipped to the end users of grain, such as mills.

CLOSING THE FRONTIER, 1880-1920

CONSTRUCTION OF TRANSCONTINENTAL RAILROADS, DURING THE FINAL DECADES OF THE 19TH CENTURY, HAD STRONGLY CONTRIBUTED TO THE CLOSURE OF THE FRONTIER IN THE WEST. IN SO DOING, IT HAD INVESTED AMERICAN SOCIETY WITH ITS UNIQUE CHARACTER.

America's Progress, painted by George Crogutt in 1873, depicted an allegorical female hovering goddess-like above the westward moving pioneers, and came to symbolize the virtue of taming the western frontier, what was considered America's "manifest destiny." In 1890, however, the frontier was declared closed on the occasion of the U.S. census.

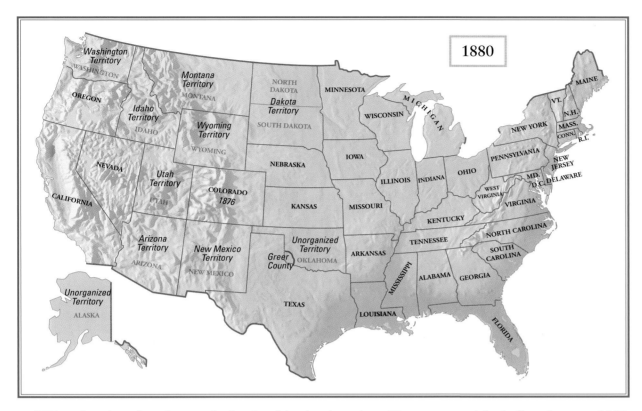

1880

By 1880, the frontier of settlement had effectively ceased to exist. The spread of population was largely down to the railroads.

A frontier of settlement had existed in the American West up to and including the year 1880, although in fact the unsettled area was fragmented by sporadic bodies of settlement that meant, in the words of the superintendent of the U.S. Census in 1890, "there can hardly be said to be a frontier line." The frontier was closed. In just 25 years, the far western frontier had been settled, three million families had established farms on the Great Plains, and the vast continent no longer seemed to be limitless. Key to the spread of the population had been the railroads.

In 1893, at the Columbian Exposition in Chicago, which celebrated the 400th anniversary of Columbus' discovery of the New World, Frederick Jackson Turner, a historian from the University of Wisconsin, published a controversial thesis—*The Frontier in American History*—in which he maintained that the conquest of the western frontier had been the single most important event that had invested American society with a special and identifiable character.

The Turner Thesis, as this analysis of history was subsequently called, argued that the settlement of the western frontier had been the nation's "formative experience," which had shaped its character and values. Turner believed that the western expansion had brought about certain traits in the new American people: as the settlers moved ever westward, they had become increasingly divorced from the European way of life; they demonstrated optimism, rugged independence, were adaptable, self-reliant, and displayed great ingenuity.

While Turner's thesis was believable in part, it did tend to ignore the fact that the federal government had been largely responsible for encouraging the pioneers to spread westward. After all, the government had organized the initial explorations of the country by Lewis and Clark (1804–06), the detailed surveys that resulted, and the later Pacific Railroad Surveys (1853–55), while it was the Army that had begun to confine the tribes of Native Americans to reservations, leaving the frontier relatively free for settlement by the flood of pioneers. Furthermore, the availability of free land had been a strong lure for the settlers,

Frederick Jackson Turner (1861–1932), a historian teaching at the University of Wisconsin expounded a theory, in 1893, that American history was based on the influence of the frontier in shaping the character of the American people.

Closing the Frontier 1890

European settlement, by 1890
1812 Date of statehood, to 1890
Western railroad constructed, 1869–97
Railroad land grant
Indian Reservation, by 1930
Area of Ghost Dance religion
Indian battle

1. Central Pacific RR–Union Pacific RR, 1869
2. Northern Pacific RR, 1883
3. Atchison, Topeka, and Santa Fe RR, 1883
4. Southern Pacific RR, 1883
5. Great Northern RR, 1893

The closure of the frontier had put immense pressure on Native Americans, now confined mainly to reservations. The rise of the Ghost Dance cult among the indigenous population was one last attempt to assert themselves, but it was doomed to failure.

while land grants had been made available by the government for the funding of railroad construction. Nevertheless, the search for new frontiers had become a potent symbol for Americans—and much later, that spirit would be encouraged by President John F. Kennedy, prompting man's exploration of outer space and the ocean depths.

The closure of the frontier had severe consequences for the country's Native Americans. Pushed off their tribal lands and forced into reservations, paradoxically, they were encouraged to assimilate with the settlers. Native American children were sent away to boarding schools, with the intention of socializing them and instructing them in the ways of the "white man." Eventually, many aspects of their daily life

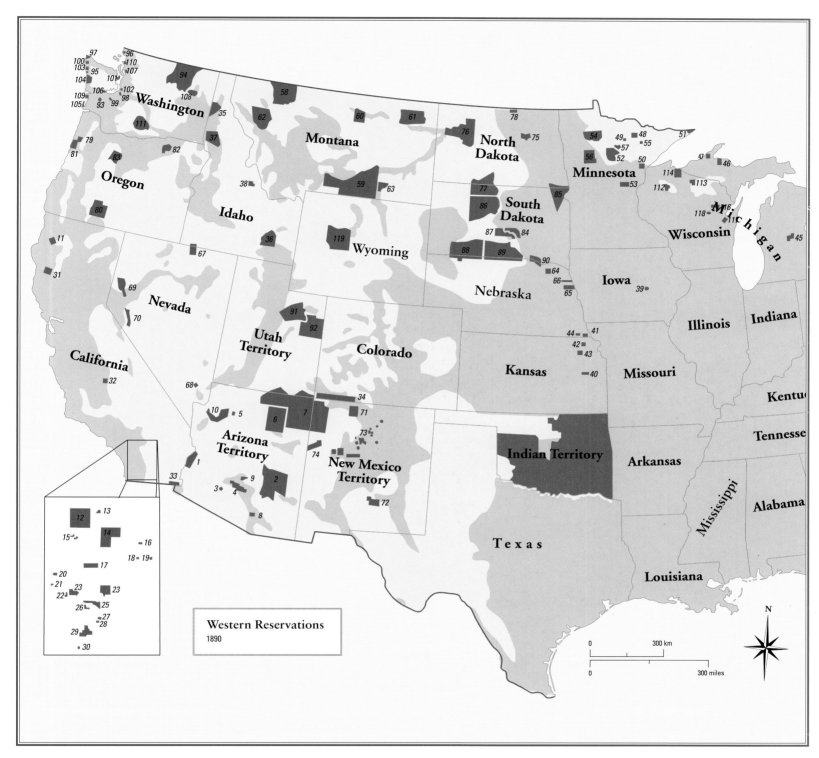

Washington
97 96 110 107
100 95 101
103 104
109 106 102 98
105 93 99
111
79
81 83
Oregon
80
11
31
Nevada
69
70
California
32

94
58
35 62 60 61
37
Montana
38
59 63
Idaho
36
119
Wyoming
67

78
76
North
Dakota
75
77
South
Dakota
85
86
87 84
88 89
90
Nebraska
64
66
65

54 49 48 55
57
56 52 50
53
114
112 113
Minnesota
118 116 117
Michigan
Wisconsin
45

Iowa
39
Illinois
Indiana
Missouri
Kansas
40
42 43
44 41

Kentu
Tennesse
Alabama

91
92
Utah
Territory
Colorado
68
10 5
6 7
34
71
73
74
New Mexico
Territory
72
1
33
3 4
9
8
2
Arizona
Territory

Indian Territory
Arkansas
Mississippi
Texas
Louisiana

12 13
15 14 16
18 19
17
20
21 23 23
22 25
26 27
28
29
30

Western Reservations
1890

N

0   300 km

0   300 miles

changed, including their traditional dress, their housing, their sources of food, their religion, and their entire livelihoods.

The Indian tribes were not the only ones to be treated as a different class of citizen in the United States. The immigrant Chinese also suffered at the closure of the frontier. While originally they had been encouraged and even welcomed to the United States, where they were used as cheap labor on the railroads and in other industries, prejudice against them had remained rife, and in 1882, the government introduced the Chinese Exclusion Act, which effectively closed the borders of the United States to further Chinese immigration.

Indian reservations were dotted throughout the western states by 1890, the largest being in what would become Oklahoma following the discovery of oil.

THE LAND GRANT ISSUE

THE RAILROADS CONTINUED TO EXPAND DURING THE 1880s, ENCOURAGED BY THE FEDERAL GOVERNMENT. BUILDING A RAILROAD WAS A COSTLY VENTURE, AND BANKS WERE RELUCTANT TO LEND MONEY, SO LUCRATIVE LAND GRANTS WERE MADE AVAILABLE TO ENABLE THE RAILROADERS TO PROGRESS.

As a result of its land grants, the Burlington & Missouri River RR, in 1872, posted this enticing advertisement, offering "Millions of Acres" for sale in Iowa and Nebraska, on 10 years credit, at 6 percent interest and "low prices." It goes on to offer "extraordinary inducements on freight and passage afforded to purchasers and their families."

Opposite In 1884, as part of their advertising campaign, the Democrats published a map (top) showing the amount of land purported to have been granted to the railroads by the government. The reality was, however, somewhat different.

PRODUCTS WILL PAY FOR LAND AND IMPROVEMENTS!

MILLIONS OF ACRES

View on the Big Blue, between Camden and Crete, representing Valley and Rolling Prairie Land in Nebraska.

IOWA AND NEBRASKA LANDS

FOR SALE ON **10** YEARS CREDIT BY THE

Burlington & Missouri River R.R. Co.

AT 6 PER CT. INTEREST AND LOW PRICES.

Only One-Seventh of Principal Due Annually, beginning Four Years after purchase.

20 PER CENT. DEDUCTED FROM 10 YEARS PRICE, FOR CASH.

LAND EXPLORING TICKETS SOLD

and Cost allowed in First Interest paid, on Land bought in 30 days from date of ticket.

Thus our Land Buyers GET A FREE PASS in the State where the Land bought is located. These TERMS are BETTER at $5, than to pre-empt United States Land at $2.50 per Acre.

EXTRAORDINARY INDUCEMENTS on FREIGHT and PASSAGE are AFFORDED to PURCHASERS and THEIR FAMILIES.

Address GEO. S. HARRIS, LAND COMMISSIONER,
or T. H. LEAVITT, Ass't Land Comm'r, Burlington, Iowa.

Or apply to

FREE ROOMS for buyers to board themselves are provided at Burlington and Lincoln.

Without assistance from the U.S. government, railroad construction between 1860 and 1900 would certainly have been greatly curtailed. Land grants were made available by Congress to the railroad companies, since private banks were afraid that the railroad companies would need a long time to pay off their debts and were reluctant to lend them money. To remedy the situation, railroads received millions of acres of public land, which they sold to make money, enabling them to lay their tracks. Four out of the five U.S. transcontinental railroads were built with this type of assistance from the government.

The land-grant bills made government gifts of public land to the railroad companies in exchange for laying track in specified areas. As

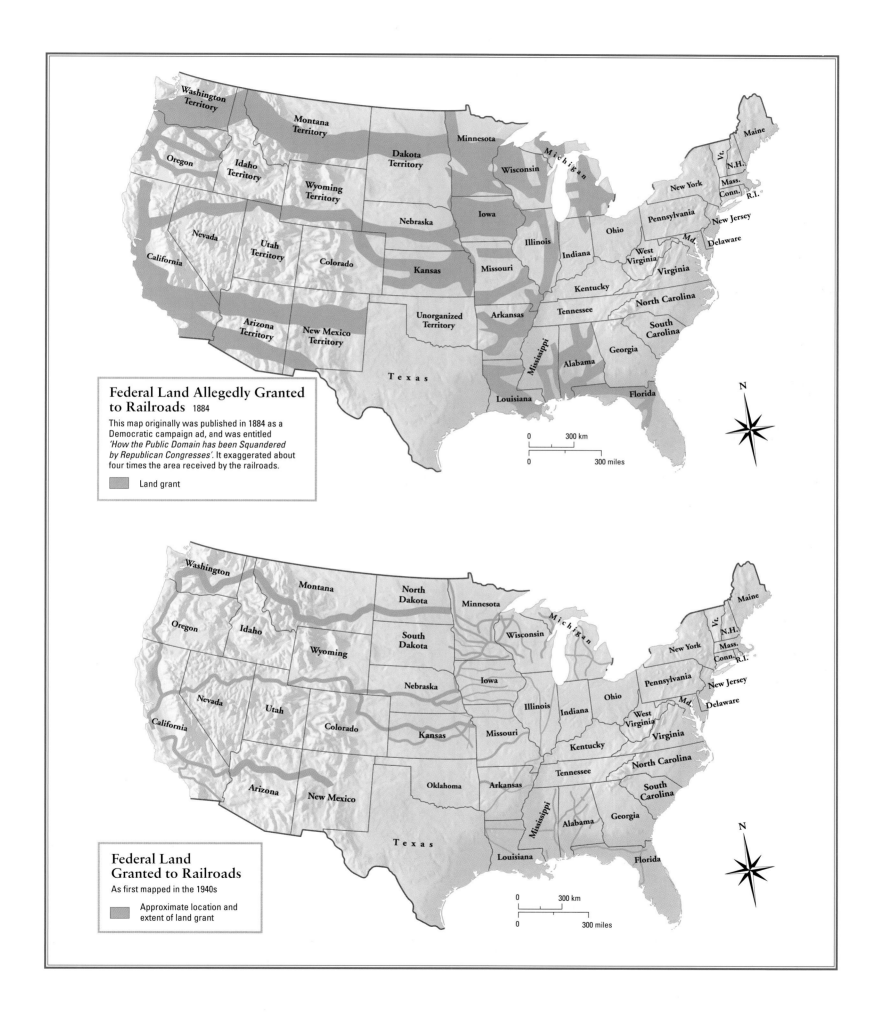

Federal Land Allegedly Granted to Railroads 1884

This map originally was published in 1884 as a Democratic campaign ad, and was entitled *'How the Public Domain has been Squandered by Republican Congresses'*. It exaggerated about four times the area received by the railroads.

▇ Land grant

Federal Land Granted to Railroads

As first mapped in the 1940s

▇ Approximate location and extent of land grant

the value of land increased, both the railroads and the government gained financially. The railroad companies would then sell their profitable lots of land and use the proceeds to pay for materials and labor with which to continue their expansion. By this method, the construction of the railroads became entwined with the sale of land, and provided a substantial amount of the capital required to finance future railroad projects. Land sales were encouraged in the United States and Western Europe through advertising by the railroads. In this way both immigration and westward migration were accelerated by the development of the railroads.

The first major railroad land grants had resulted from the 1862 legislation that allowed the transcontinental railroad to come into being. The Union Pacific and Central Pacific railroads had been granted 400ft (122m) rights-of-way plus 10 square miles (25.9sq km) of land for every mile (1.6km) of track built. While this amount of land seemed substantial, the parcels did not share a common border, being laid out in a checkerboard design. Seen on a map, the railroad track would snake across this checkerboard, with parallel lines drawn 10 miles (1.6km) to the left and 10 miles to the right. The railroads were given the odd-numbered sections on each side of the railroad right-of-way, meaning they would have 5 square miles (13sq km) of land on each side of the track.

Shortly after the meeting of the two railroad companies at Promontory Point and the completion of the first transcontinental railroad in 1869, land grants ceased to be public policy. Many people had voiced dissent at the long-term sense of giving away so much land to private companies. Between 1850 and 1870, more than 129 million acres (52 million ha)—seven percent of the continental United States—had been ceded to just 80 railroad companies. Most of that land lay west of the Mississippi, and the value of the grants totaled more than a staggering half billion dollars.

The responsibility for surveying and mapping the areas of the land grants fell to the U.S. General Land Office. Hundreds of maps of the United States, and individual states and counties were produced, indicating the precise parcels of granted land and

This large-scale grant map, of Franklin County, Arkansas, dated 1893, shows the shows the typical checkerboard pattern of railroad land grants. The dark shaded areas were granted to the Little Rock & Fort Smith RR. Maps such as this were used by land speculators to advertise railroad lands that were made available for sale to the public.

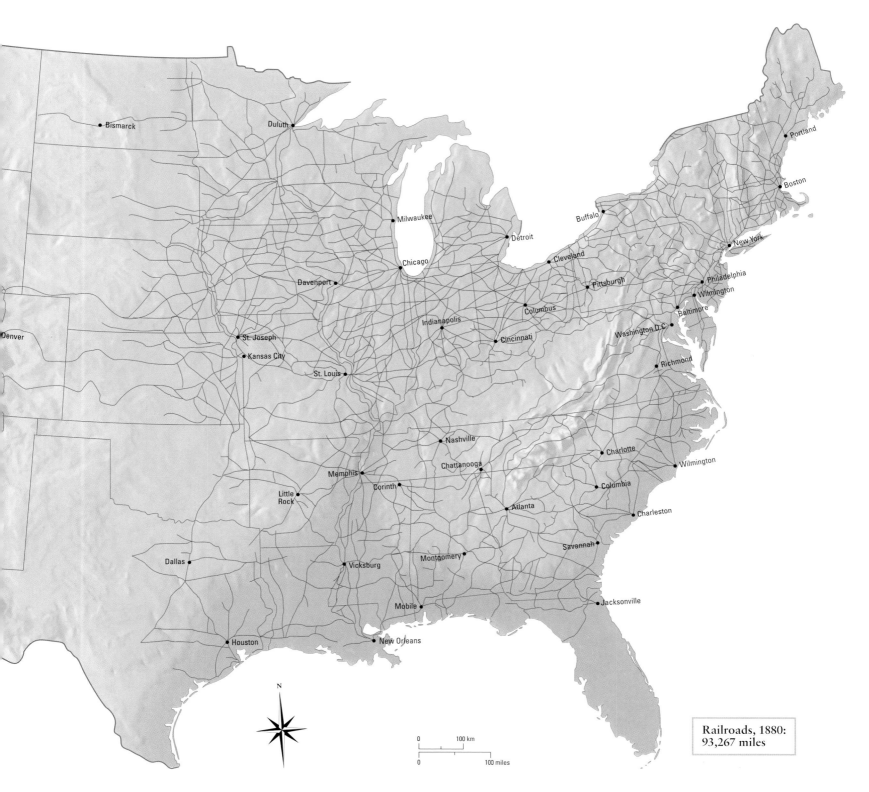

Railroads, 1880:
93,267 miles

showing the railroad rights-of-way. These land-grant maps were also used by speculators to advertise railroad lands that were to be made available for sale to the public. In the late 1860s, most western railroads had established land departments and bureaus of immigration—many of which had offices in Europe—to sell land and promote foreign settlement in the western United States.

The government land-grant maps themselves had misrepresented the true size of the granted areas, however, and it is likely that intense competition between speculators led to them distorting their

By 1880, the railroads were spreading farther west, and a second transcontinental link was provided by the Santa Fe and Southern Pacific railroads.

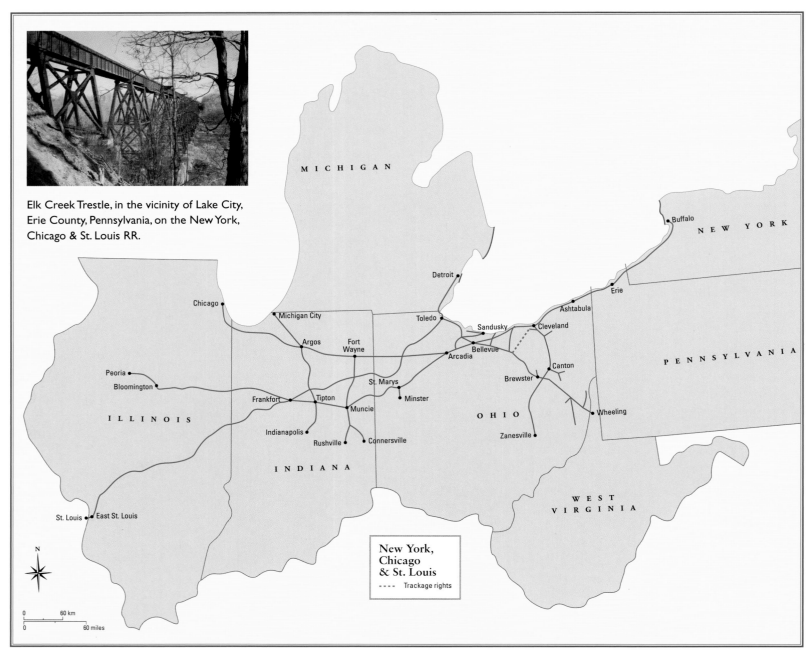

Elk Creek Trestle, in the vicinity of Lake City, Erie County, Pennsylvania, on the New York, Chicago & St. Louis RR.

New York, Chicago & St. Louis
- - - - Trackage rights

The New York, Chicago & St. Louis RR began operations in 1882 with a line from Buffalo, New York State, to Chicago. It became famous for its Nickel Plate freight service, which earned it the nickname "Nickel Plate Road." It was owned by the New York Central for a short while in 1916, and eventually merged with the Norfolk & Western RR in 1964.

railroad maps. For example, the Illinois Central RR had been granted land along its path in 1850. John W. Amerman's book, *The Illinois Central Rail-Road Company Offers for Sale Over 2,000,000 Acres Selected Farming and Wood Land* (New York, 1856) shows an outline map of Illinois with the Illinois Central RR highlighted by a heavy black line; stations are shown spaced along the line, suggesting the proximity of towns along the tracks, which was misleading. During the early 1880s, scale, area and the routes of the railroads were manipulated to create a false impression in favor of the railroad companies.

The land-grant topic was highly political and controversial. In 1884, a Democratic Party campaign advertisement, entitled *How the public domain has been squandered by Republican Congresses,* exaggerated by about four times the amount of land that had been made available to the railroads.

Despite the criticism of the land grants, they helped to bring West and East together; goods could be sent to market more cheaply; shipping costs were reduced; and thousands of jobs were created as a result of both railroad construction and the new settlements that were created.

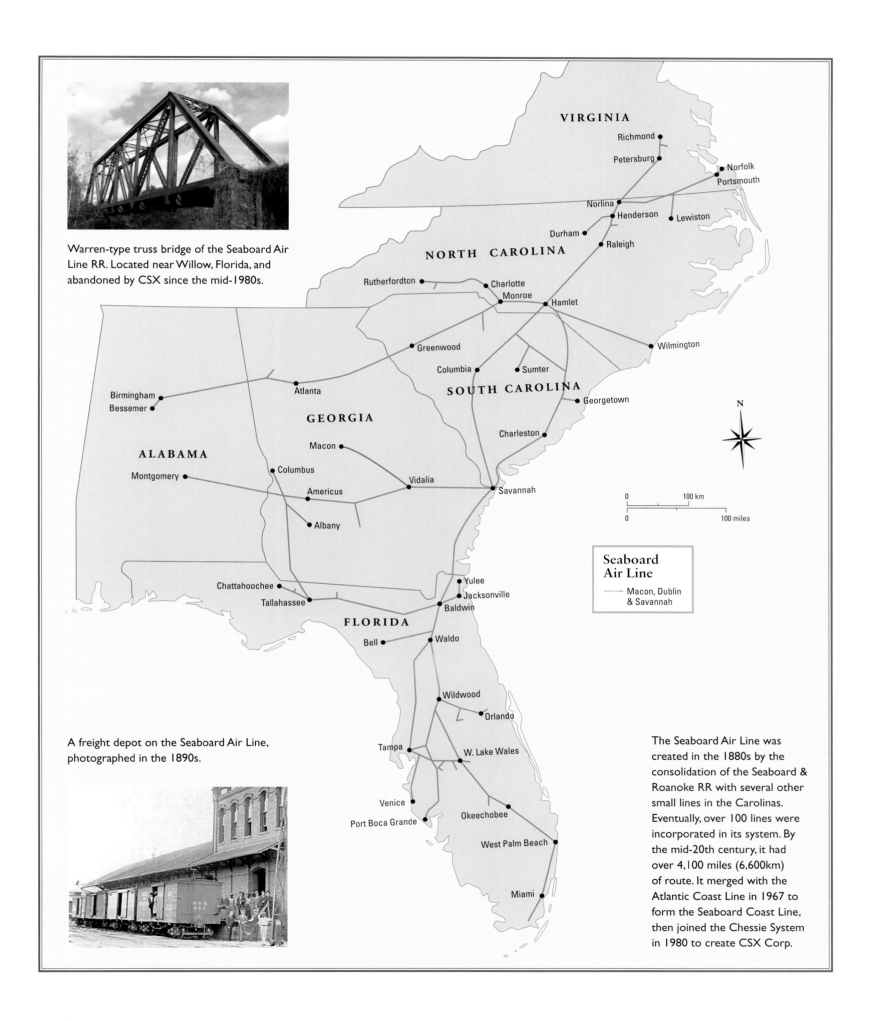

Warren-type truss bridge of the Seaboard Air Line RR. Located near Willow, Florida, and abandoned by CSX since the mid-1980s.

A freight depot on the Seaboard Air Line, photographed in the 1890s.

Seaboard Air Line
— Macon, Dublin & Savannah

The Seaboard Air Line was created in the 1880s by the consolidation of the Seaboard & Roanoke RR with several other small lines in the Carolinas. Eventually, over 100 lines were incorporated in its system. By the mid-20th century, it had over 4,100 miles (6,600km) of route. It merged with the Atlantic Coast Line in 1967 to form the Seaboard Coast Line, then joined the Chessie System in 1980 to create CSX Corp.

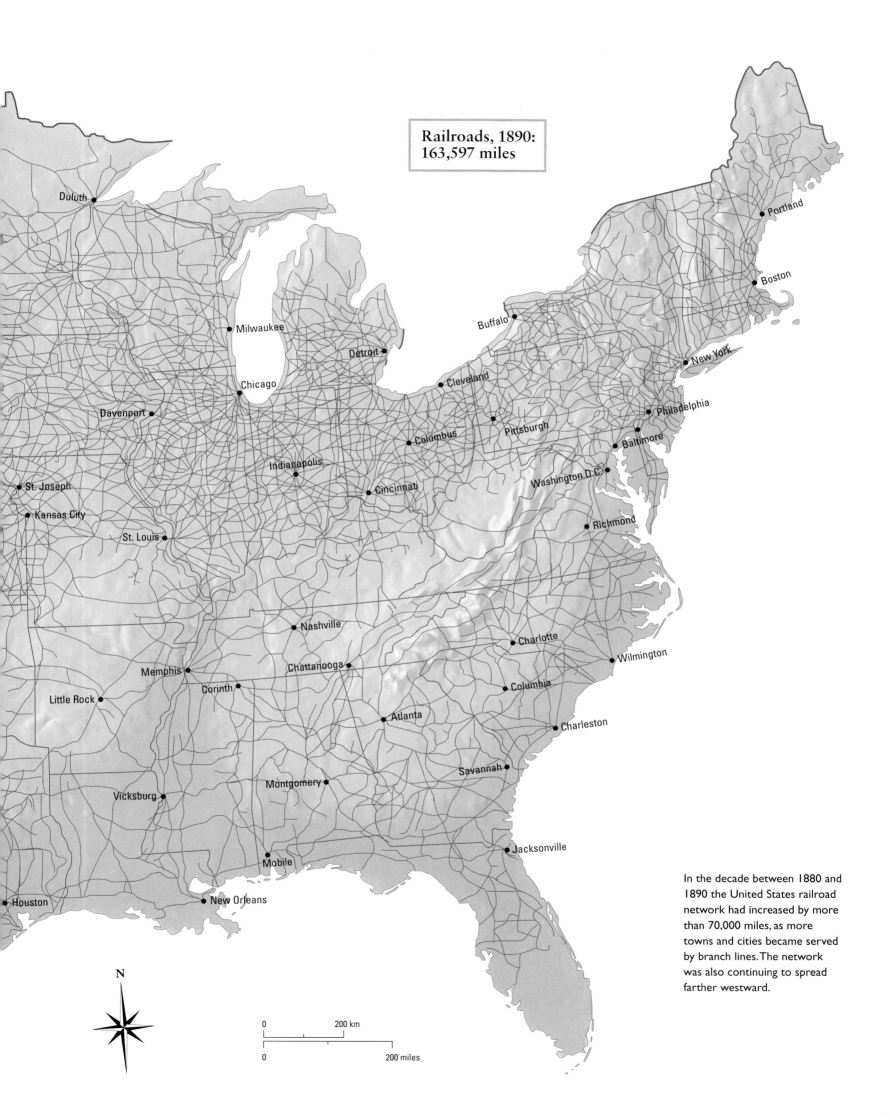

Railroads, 1890:
163,597 miles

In the decade between 1880 and 1890 the United States railroad network had increased by more than 70,000 miles, as more towns and cities became served by branch lines. The network was also continuing to spread farther westward.

N
0   200 km
0   200 miles

LOCOMOTIVE DEVELOPMENTS, 1880-1900

TOWARD THE END OF THE 19TH CENTURY CAME ADVANCES IN SCIENCE AND TECHNOLOGY, ENABLING THE DEVELOPMENT OF MORE POWERFUL, MORE EFFICIENT ENGINES. IN TANDEM WITH THIS CAME THE SEARCH FOR ALTERNATIVE SOURCES OF FUEL FOR STEAM LOCOMOTIVES.

As steam locomotives grew larger, so their consumption of fuel and water increased. There had always been a plentiful supply of fuel, since the United States had huge reserves of wood and coal. Even so, thought was given to possible alternative fuels. The first regular use of oil as a fuel for locomotives seems to have been in Russia in 1882, when Thomas Urquhart, superintendent of the Grazi Czaritzin Railroad, developed a suitable system; by 1885, 143 engines had been converted to burn oil. American engineers kept an eye on developments in Europe, and those features that were considered to be suitable for American conditions were tried or adapted and developed for their particular needs. For example, valves for the distribution of steam in the cylinders had always presented problems with lubrication and wear. Piston valves were introduced successfully on the North Eastern Railway in England in 1887, and were in use in the United States by 1898.

The growing size of locomotives meant that more coal and water had to be carried if more frequent or longer water-replenishment and refueling stops were not to cancel out any gains in speed made possible by increases in power. In Europe, fuel economy for other reasons had led to experiment with compound expansion, in which steam was fed to one or more cylinders at boiler pressure, and then exhausted to another cylinder or cylinders for further expansion. Theoretically, steam exhausted from one cylinder at about half boiler pressure could exert the same force on another piston of twice the surface area.

In 1889, 33-year-old Samuel M. Vauclain was general manager of the Baldwin Locomotive Works—his

THE RAILWAY AGE

father was one of those who had built the locomotive *Old Ironsides*. He invented the "tandem compound" system which used high- and low-pressure cylinders mounted one behind the other. By 1893, he had refined the system sufficiently for the Atchison, Topeka & Santa Fe RR to take delivery of the first of an order for 86 successful 2-10-2s.

Other types of compounding were developed, probably the most successful being that conceived by Alfred de Glehn in France, first used in 1886. His system employed four cylinders, two outside the frames at high pressure, and two low-pressure cylinders between the frames. Two similar systems were developed in the United States, one by Vauclain and another by Francis J. Pitkin of the American Locomotive Company (ALCO). Both claimed savings of up to 20 percent in fuel.

Meanwhile, other engineers were showing interest in the possible use of electric traction, particularly on mountain lines with long tunnels and on other lines with tunnels, within city limits, where smoke from steam locomotives could prove a health and safety hazard.

At the end of the 19th century, railroads were firmly established, and travel by train could be accomplished in reasonable comfort from the Atlantic to the Pacific in under six days.

With the dawn of a new century came a change in locomotive design to reflect technological discoveries and to give a more modern appeance to rolling stock. This technical drawing shows the Atchison Topeka & Santa Fe's Decapod Tandem Compound engine, built by ALCO around 1902.

Camelbacks and High Wheelers

A POPULAR LOCOMOTIVE WAS THE "CAMELBACK." IN 1877, JOHN E. WOOTTEN, OF THE PHILADELPHIA & READING RR, IMPROVED THE STABILITY OF A WASTE-ANTHRACITE BURNING LOCOMOTIVE WITH ITS CHARACTERISTICALLY WIDE FIREBOX, BY PLACING THE GRATE ABOVE THE REAR DRIVERS ON A NEW DESIGN OF 4-6-0.

On Wootten's design, the cab was placed above the firebox, and the fireman stoked the grate from an unprotected platform on the tender. A machine of this type was sent to Europe, but owing to restricted tunnel clearances in France and Italy, the cab had

An example of a 4-6-0 camelback built by the Baldwin Locomotive Works for the Central Railroad of New Jersey.

to be moved forward and lowered. Thus was born the "camelback," also known as the "Mother Hubbard." The wide firebox became known universally as the Wootten firebox, and was used worldwide. Various designs of camelback were built, but a second, rudimentary cab had to be provided, usually mounted off the end of the firebox, to protect the fireman. The design lasted well into the 20th century, used on some very large locomotives.

With reliable brake systems, it was possible to run at higher speeds, and by the late 1880s, the thoughts of engineers turned to maximum speeds as high as 100mph (160km/h). To keep piston speeds at reasonable levels, designers increased the diameters of the driving wheels. Locomotives, with these taller drivers were known as "high wheelers"; most were 4-4-0s, and a few were 4-4-2s, but all were more sophisticated than the standard American type. Typical high wheelers were those turned out to the designs of William Buchanan of the New York Central & Hudson River Railroad.

The most famous of the New York Central's high wheelers was No. 999, which hauled the crack *Empire State Express*. On May 10, 1893, No. 999, with a light train, covered a measured mile of slightly downhill track west of Batavia, New York, in 31.2 seconds—a speed of 112.5mph (181km/h). This was claimed as a record, but was later the subject of much controversy. Nonetheless, No. 999's 80in (61cm) drivers and 24in (61cm) piston travel undoubtedly gave it the potential for very high speeds.

The ultimate example of a camelback. This massive 0-8-8-0 articulated locomotive was one of three built by ALCO for the Erie RR in 1908. Two firemen were needed to stoke the huge grate. It weighed 205.5 tons.

A pair of Baldwin 4-4-2 camelbacks built for the Atlantic City Railroad in 1896 regularly ran the 55.3 miles (89km) between Atlantic City and Camden, New Jersey, at an average start-to-stop speed of 70mph (113km/h) and could develop 1,450hp at that speed.

The advance of technology was nowhere more widely evident than in motive power. Toward the end of the 19th century, the steam locomotive was climbing rapidly out of the form from which it had first developed. It was growing in size following the introduction of continuous train brakes and stronger couplings, which enabled much longer and heavier trains to be operated. This, in turn, led to the need for more powerful "pusher" locomotives on the long, steep grades of the Alleghenies in the

While the engineer of a camelback locomotive enjoyed the protection of the cab, the fireman had to make do with a rudimentary shelter at the rear.

East, and the Sierra Nevada, the Rockies, and their outliers in the West. In freight and pusher service, the greater the number of driving wheels, the better the traction; and, as speeds were low of necessity, small wheels gave high pulling power. On the other hand, passenger-train speeds were becoming ever higher and loads much less, so that large driving wheels were the order of the day. Some high wheelers had drivers as tall as 86in (218cm). But it was the details that were improved—to reduce maintenance, increase power output, reduce fuel consumption, and so on. The external appearance of locomotives was changing, as well, with the advent of larger-diameter boilers.

American locomotives could be built large because the physical dimensions of the early railroads were not inhibited by tunnels and bridges to anything like the extent they were in Europe, and in Britain in particular. There is little doubt that Russian railroads were strongly influenced by American engineers and built locomotives of much the same dimensions; their choice of the 5ft (1,524mm) gauge was probably no coincidence.

Be that as it may, by the end of the 19th century, locomotives in the United States were rapidly increasing in size and power. Ten driving axles became popular for freight locomotives, particularly pushers, while, for passenger trains, the ten-wheeler locomotive replaced the eight-wheeler. The 4-4-2, or "Atlantic," was popular, as the addition of the trailing axle permitted a wide firebox of the Wootten type and a correspondingly larger boiler. By the turn of the century, the salient characteristics of the American steam locomotive were established and being used to the full.

A 4-4-2 high wheeler of the Pennsylvania RR. The large-diameter driving wheels allowed locomotives to run at high speeds while keeping piston speeds at an acceptable level.

Rise and Fall of the Electric Interurbans

In the 1890s, the use of electric streetcars spread from the cities to rural areas with the introduction of "interurban" networks or, as they were known in Canada, "radials," because they spread out from the city hubs in a web-like, radial pattern.

The Yakima Valley Transportation Company Interurban RR opened in 1907, connecting Yakima, Selah and Wiley City, Washington. Its passenger service ceased in 1947, but the line ran freight until 1984. The City of Yakima acquired a portion of the track to run as a tourist operation by Yakima Valley Trolleys.

The interurban trolley seemed such a powerful idea, particularly in the American Midwest. The steam railroads had no interest in connecting small towns with any kind of frequent service, for the large locomotives took a long time to stop and then get up to speed again. Trolleys, on the other hand, were suited to quick stops and starts, smooth acceleration, and long runs at high speed. The later American interurban cars appeared unstoppable—majestic machines that could out-accelerate a steam locomotive and, given a favorable headwind, out-race an airplane. They were an intimidating 3ft (91cm) higher than a streetcar and twice as heavy.

The technology was easily adaptable to long distances. Using low-loss, high-voltage lines to transmit the power, and step-down transformers and rectifiers spaced along the track to feed the accustomed 600 volts dc to the car, power losses were kept to the minimum. The first of the interurbans, in Sandusky, Ohio, and Portland, Oregon, in 1893, folded quickly, largely because hardware and reliability still presented problems. Nevertheless, pressure mounted for the construction of new interurban lines.

Not only did large stretches of the country need tying together, but people were convinced that their town was "nowhere," a backwater, unless it had an interurban connection. So the networks grew and grew from the Midwest, where Ohio alone had nearly 3,000 miles (4,800km) of track, and it was possible to take a 217-mile (349km) trip between Cincinnati and Toledo. The Northeast and the South also fell under their spell, with property values rising everywhere, and the giant railroad companies started to acquire control of the upstart interurbans. In the West, where such men as Henry E. Huntington and his Pacific Electric streetcar company were building furiously, it was possible in Los Angeles, in 1905, to make a profit of 60 percent on property held for just a month. By 1913, plans were complete to construct a grand interurban connection from New York to Chicago, which would be called the "Air Line."

The technology used to run electric streetcars was applied, in the early 20th century, to interurbans connecting cities and towns—transporting freight and passengers. In urban areas they ran on the tracks of existing streetcars; between towns, new tracks were laid on their own rights-of-way. Interurban lines were prolific in the Midwest. People could ride from upstate New York to Wisconsin on a connecting interurban line. In the 1920s, when automobiles became more popular, the interurbans began to lose popularity and, within the next 20 years, all but disappeared.

Two beautifully appointed cars were built for the Air Line, and stock was sold, but the bubble was ready to burst. It cost more and more to bring each new passenger into the system, and as city centers grew more congested, the 60–70mph (95–110km/h) speedsters had to crawl through town. Most ominous of all, roads were improving and interurban passengers were growing ever more vulnerable to the siren call of the automobile. The interurbans had been magnificent machines, though, in their short golden age, though, with names like the Orange Limited, the Muncie Meteor, and the Red Devil. They are all gone now. The only remaining interurban run in the United States is the South Shore Line, which uses modern rolling stock and connects South Bend, Indiana, to downtown Chicago.

One of the best known of the early interurban lines was the Chicago, North Shore & Milwaukee RR. Beginning in 1891 as the Waukegan & North Shore Rapid Transit Co., a trolley line for the city of Waukegan, 36 miles (58km) north of Chicago, Illinois, it was extended south to Lake Bluff and became the CNS & M Electric RR when it was extended farther to Chicago.

Eighteen-ninety-five saw the first haulage by electric locomotives of main-line trains on standard gauge. The Baltimore & Ohio RR tunneled under the city of Baltimore, and the sections between the Waverley and Camden stations—about 3 miles (5km)—were electrified by the Westinghouse Electric Company in 1895 to eliminate the smoke nuisance created by steam locomotives. At first, a conventional train, including a coke burning locomotive with steam shut off and the valve gear in mid-gear, was hauled by pairs of Bo + Bo electric motors through the tunnel sections. This was the forerunner of the Baltimore Belt System. The electrification was at 600volts dc on the overhead system. Because of the high current demand, instead of a contact wire, an overhead rail supported from insulators was provided, and current collected by a pantograph arm with a shoe that ran along the rail. The locomotives were of the "steeple-cab" type with four gearless traction motors. This pickup system was later replaced by a third rail.

THE ADAPTABLE STREETCAR

FROM THE 1890s TO THE MID-1920s, STREETCAR NETWORKS GREW IN NUMBERS AND IN SIZE, AND THE STREETCARS BECAME BIGGER, FASTER, SAFER, AND MORE COMFORTABLE. HOWEVER, THESE IMPROVED VEHICLES SOMETIMES PROVED UNPOPULAR WITH THE TRAVELING PUBLIC.

Open streetcars known as "breezers" were a welcome relief in the hot summer months. This car ran on 8th and Central Avenues, Minneapolis, Minnesota, in 1894. Its curtains could be drawn to shield against the sun, or if the weather was less clement. The driver, however, stood on an open platform at the front.

In the early years of the 20th century, the small, four-wheeled vehicles that had replaced the horsecars were themselves succeeded by longer, heavier cars carried on pairs of four-wheel trucks, and wooden bodies were replaced by steel. Another innovation, not always welcomed by the passengers, was the trend for those networks that operated cars with open-sided bodies to phase them out in favor of designs with fully enclosed bodies and glazed windows. In the early days of the trolley, there was little difference in comfort between closed and open cars, because on both types, the open platforms at front and rear had little more than a waist-high dashboard for weather protection. Nevertheless, when summer came, the public wanted open cars, and even in Canada, the closed cars would be put into storage and out would come the "breezers."

Many companies possessed two fleets of streetcars, one open and one closed. The transit lines hated the expense and inefficiency of this, but they were partly to blame. To increase passenger revenue, they had encouraged people to take weekend and vacation excursion tours and special trips. How many people at the beginning of the 20th century had any other way to feel the cooling rush of air as they spun through meadows and woods at a galloping 15mph (24km/h) on a hot July day? Streetcar companies financed and built parks at the ends of their lines to encourage leisure traffic. These "trolley parks" were often fanciful places with picnic grounds, bandstands, dance halls. games fields, scenic railways, or roller coasters, lit and powered by electricity from the same sources that supplied the trolleys. There was Luna Park, Washington, D.C.; Overlook Park, Ohio, with its automated piano; Willow Grove Park, Pennsylvania, with its Electric Fountain, lit at night by multicolored electric lights; and countless others. Ravinia Park, Illinois, even had the Chicago Symphony Orchestra.

Despite this, the companies hated the open cars, although they loved the revenue they brought in. The open benches and full-length step rails encouraged people to leap on and off cars while they were in motion, so increasing accident rates. Worst of all, from the companies' point of view, passengers could avoid the conductor and "beat the fare." As fare collection plans evolved in the closed cars, the open cars disappeared from all but the hardiest tourist lines.

Some streetcars, such as the San Francisco cable-cars still in use today, were half-and-half varieties, offering fully enclosed seating at one end, or open benches at the other. However, during inclement weather, passengers tended to desert the open seating and huddle in the enclosed section.

As much as the public loved open cars, the trolley companies resisted demands to provide two sets of cars for good and bad weather, or even to have two sets of bodies, as was tried in Baltimore and a few other places. In Baltimore, the Union Railway & Electric Co. thought it the height of efficiency to buy one set of trucks and wheels, and two sets of bodies for its new fleet in 1902. Thus 110 enclosed bodies sat idle in spring and summer, until each fall they replaced the airy, awning-bedecked open car bodies. To overcome the problem of having so much expensive equipment lying idle for half the year, several designs—called "convertibles"—attempted to combine the best features of both open and closed bodies.

Some of the earliest attempts to obviate the need for two fleets of cars, or two sets of bodies, were the half-and-half designs known as "California" cars, such as those still in use on San Francisco's cable-car system. The flaw in the design was that on sunny days everyone wanted to be outside, but when it rained, people huddled inside, so half the car's capacity was always unused.

As with many of the innovations in streetcar design, the true convertible seems to have had its beginnings in Canada. In Toronto in 1904, cars were designed with removable side panels that could be changed in the sheds. Some single-ended cars were built as "nearside convertibles," with only one side (the one away from traffic) removable. Others were more flexible and could be changed quickly, "in case of a change in the weather." Brill had one with straight-sided panels that slid up into the roof. There was also the Duplex design, which used curved sliding panels; these last were known as semiconvertibles.

Open cars and convertibles both died out during World War I. The dangers of boarding open cars, especially as traffic, and the transportation companies' preoccupation with fare dodging increased, meant that only a few tourist-type open or convertible cars survived into the 1920s and 1930s. One exception was in New York City, where the convertible cars remained in day-to-day service throughout Brooklyn until after World War II. Perhaps the secret of their longevity was the open metal grillework that replaced the windows in summer and kept passengers from losing an arm or leg in the brutal New York traffic.

RAILROADS TO THE PACIFIC 1893–1900

AFTER THE ORIGINAL RAILROAD TO THE
PACIFIC HAD BEEN COMPLETED IN 1869,
OTHERS FOLLOWED, HELPING TO OPEN UP
VAST SWATHES OF LAND ACROSS THE WEST,
AND PARTICULARLY IN THE NORTHWEST,
WHERE SEVERAL VIED FOR TRAFFIC.

Opposite: By 1893, when the Great Northern Railroad was completed, linking Minneapolis and St. Paul with the West Coast, there were several routes to the Pacific, all of which played major roles in opening up the western states to migrants from the East.

By 1890, the Union Pacific/Central Pacific line across the United States, which had become known as the Overland Route, had been joined by three more railroads to the Pacific coast. These were the Northern Pacific and the Southern Pacific, both completed in 1883; and the Atchison, Topeka & Santa Fe, completed in 1888.

The Northern Pacific route began at the twin cities of Minneapolis and St. Paul, in Minnesota, and headed westward through southern North Dakota and Montana. It ran parallel to the border with Idaho before crossing to Spokane, Washington State. Then it passed through the Cascade Mountains, dropped down into Portland and on to Seattle. The line had been built with government subsidies and massive land grants, which included all of

Railroads to the Pacific

- - - - - Major railroads with date of completion

1889 Date of state admitted to Union after 1870

CANADA

Rocky Mountains

Great Northern (1893)

Missouri

• Helena

MONTANA
1889

Northern Pacific (1883)

NORTH DAKOTA
1889

Bismarck •

MINNESOTA

Duluth •

AHO
890

Short Line (1882)

omontory Point •

Ogden •

Salt Lake City •

WYOMING
1890

Platte

Cheyenne •

Union Pacific (1869)

Minneapolis • St. Paul

WISCONSIN

Mississippi

Madison •

IOWA

Omaha •

• Des Moines

Chicago •

NEBRASKA

Lincoln •

Atchison •

Santa Fe Extension to Chicago (1888)

• Springfield

ILLINOIS

UTAH
1896

Denver & Rio Grande (1883)

COLORADO
1876

• Denver

Pueblo •

Colorado

Santa Fe (1883)

Kansas Pacific (1870)

Arkansas

KANSAS

Abilene •

Topeka •

Kansas City

St. Louis •

Jefferson City •

MISSOURI

Dodge City •

Pacific (1888)

ARIZONA
1912

• Phoenix

Santa Fe •

• Albuquerque

Canadian

OKLAHOMA
1907

Oklahoma City •

ARKANSAS

Little Rock •

Mississippi

rn Pacific (1883)

NEW MEXICO
1912

• El Paso

Rio Grande

Texas & Pacific (1882)

• Dallas

TEXAS

Colorado

Austin •

Southern Pacific (1883)

Houston •

San Antonio

Streveport •

LOUISIANA

MISSISSIPPI

• Jackson

Red

Baton Rouge •

New Orleans •

MEXICO

Gulf of Mexico

The work of the great railroad builder J.J. Hill, the Great Northern ran from the Mississippi at Minneapolis and St. Paul all the way to Seattle in the West, with extensions into Montana, Oregon, California, and over the border into Canada.

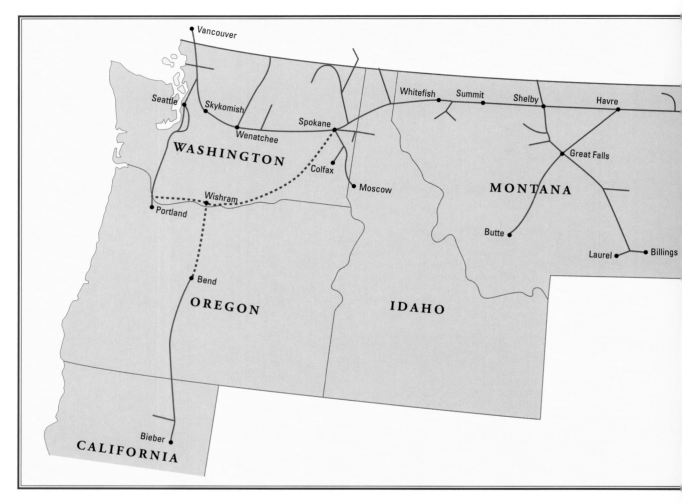

present-day Yellowstone Park. It was not the most direct of routes to the Pacific Northwest, however, and it had many steeply graded sections that tested the mettle of the early locomotives.

Way to the south, the Southern Pacific ran all the way down through California, from San Francisco to Los Angeles, then across into Arizona near the border with Mexico. Its route stayed close to the border as it passed through New Mexico and across Texas into Louisiana, finally reaching New Orleans. The Southern Pacific played a major role in developing California, since it enjoyed a near monopoly on north–south traffic, and it became very influential in state affairs, having politicians from both parties in its pocket. In 1885, the Southern Pacific took over the Central Pacific's portion of the Overland Route. On two occasions, the Southern Pacific came to the aid of the population of California: in 1905, after the Imperial Valley floods, and in 1906, following the San Francisco earthquake.

Westward from Chicago, the Atchison, Topeka & Santa Fe Railroad (known simply as the Santa Fe) provided a truly great route to the Pacific coast. It ran through Dodge City, Kansas, Albuquerque, New Mexico, and on to Los Angeles, crossing seven states, three time zones, and three great mountain ranges. The total route length was 2,223 miles (3,577km). The Santa Fe went on to become probably the most well-known railroad in the United States, running such famous express trains as the steam hauled *Chief* and diesel powered *Super Chief*. At the peak of the steam era, during World War II, when an efficient service of very heavy trains to the West Coast was a national necessity, only two locomotives were needed for the entire journey, which took two days.

One of the original syndicate involved in building the Canadian Pacific railroad was James Jerome

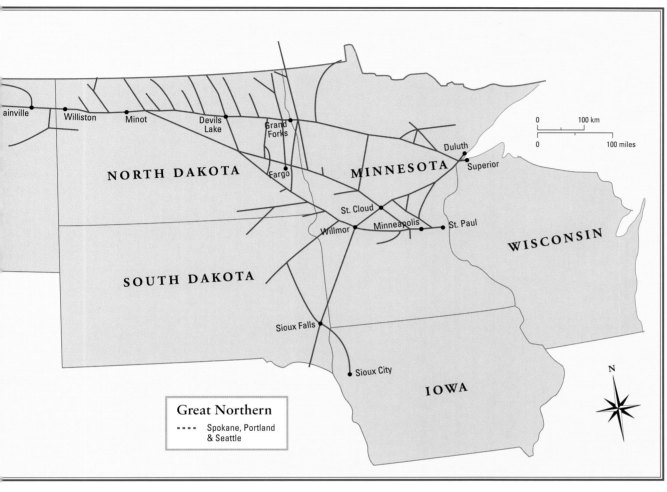

Great Northern
- - - - Spokane, Portland
& Seattle

Hill, who had substantial business interests in the United States. He had urged that the CP be routed south of Lake Superior, into U.S. territory, to link up with those interests, but he was outvoted. As a result, he resigned from the project and set about promoting a rival transcontinental line in the United States, which became known as the Great Northern. This railroad had its headquarters at Minneapolis/ St. Paul, Minnesota. Work began in 1887, a route being forged across northern North Dakota, Montana, and Idaho. Meanwhile, the western portion of the line was being built from Seattle across Washington State and up into the Cascade Mountains. The onset of winter in 1892 made the work in the mountains arduous, but on January 6, 1893, the two tracks met in the snow high in Stevens Pass.

In addition to competing with the Canadian Pacific, the Great Northern also had a rival in the shape of the Northern Pacific. The NP was saddled with debt and heading for bankruptcy following the stock market plunge of 1893, which set off five years of financial panic. By 1900, J.J. Hill's banker, J.P. Morgan had hatched a plan to take over the NP and hand it to Hill to run along with the Great Northern. Morgan and Hill also took over the Chicago, Burlington & Quincy RR, combining all three under the Northern Securities banner. Eventually, Hill's railroad activities would earn him the name "the Empire Builder," which later would be applied to a Great Northern express train in his memory.

By the turn of the century, the Union Pacific had completed its Oregon Short Line across Idaho to Portland, Oregon, in 1884, while in August 1893, the Minneapolis, St. Paul & Sault Ste. Marie Railway (Soo Line) had linked Minneapolis/St. Paul with Portal, on the border between North Dakota and Canada. This provided a connection with the Canadian Pacific and a through route to Vancouver.

James Jerome Hill (1838–1916), pictured around 1890. From Wellington County, Upper Canada (now Ontario), he relocated to the USA to build the Great Northern transcontinental railroad. "What we want," Hill said, "is the best possible line, shortest distance, lowest grades, and least curvature we can build. We do not care enough for Rocky Mountains scenery to spend a large sum of money developing it." Hill planned the route himself, traveling on horseback.

Consolidation and Legal Issues, 1900-10

The first three decades of the 20th century saw consolidation rather than expansion, although some new railroads were built. However, many were being extended, merged, taken over, leased and otherwise changed by control or sale.

The industrialized Northeast's dense network of large and small railroads had grown faster than anywhere else in the country, although those in some other regions were catching up rapidly. The railroads were the most important single factor in the development of modern America. As large railroad corporations grew and became more powerful, it suited them either to acquire smaller roads or to squeeze them out of business. Many had serious financial problems and were glad to be rescued by more prosperous concerns.

In 1901, the Baltimore & Ohio, the oldest U.S. railroad, had a large slice of its stock acquired by Pennsylvania RR, and Leonor F. Loree was installed as president. He immediately commenced a major program of route improvement, which included reducing grades and curves, and doubling many miles of track. He also secured a large interest in the Reading RR, which in turn brought in the Central Railroad of New Jersey, already under Reading control. The Central passed fully into control by the Pennsylvania after a few years.

In 1910, Daniel Willard became president of the B & O. In the same year, B & O acquired the Chicago Terminal Transfer Railroad, which was renamed the Baltimore & Ohio Chicago Transfer Railroad. Further acquisitions extended the B & O's area of operations from New York City in the East to Chicago in the North, and St. Louis, MO, in the West. By 1929, B & O operated 5,658 miles (9,105km) of railroad and owned 2,364 locomotives.

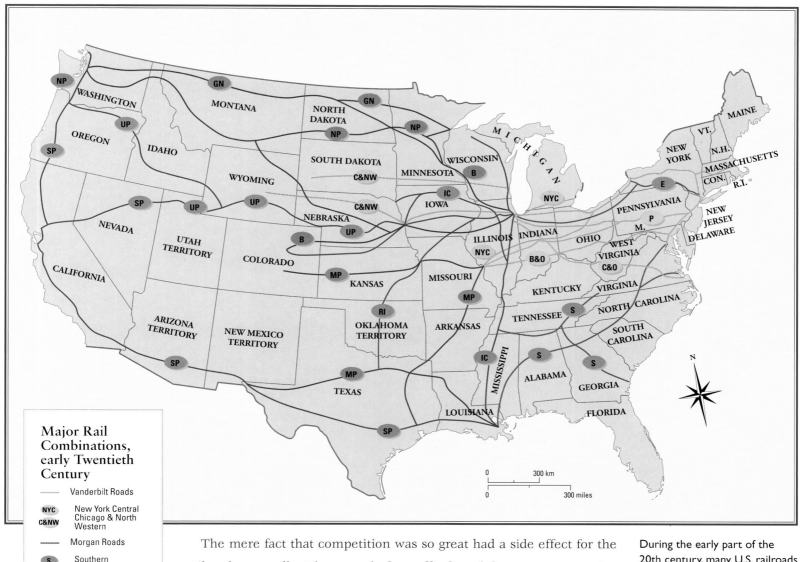

Major Rail Combinations, early Twentieth Century

———	Vanderbilt Roads
NYC	New York Central
C&NW	Chicago & North Western
———	Morgan Roads
S	Southern
E	Erie
———	Pennsylvania Group
P	Pennsylvania
B&O	Baltimore & Ohio
C&O	Chesapeake & Ohio
———	Harriman Roads
UP	Union Pacific
SP	Southern Pacific
IC	Illinois Central
———	Hill Roads
GN	Great Northern
NP	Northern Pacific
B	Burlington
———	Gould System
MP	Missouri Pacific
———	Rock Island System
RI	Rock Island

The mere fact that competition was so great had a side effect for the railroads generally. The struggle for traffic forced down rates to a point where none but the strongest roads could earn a profit. Although there were agreements to maintain rates, these were just pieces of paper and there was practically no limit to the rebates extorted by the shippers and their agents under threat of diverting traffic to other carriers. There was discrimination and undue preference in the most insidious and corrupting form. While many industries prospered by these practices, the railways suffered proportionately.

In the 10 years to 1900, the number of freight cars had increased by 64.5 percent and locomotives by only 29.5 percent, indicating better utilization as well as increased locomotive haulage capacity. Passenger cars too had increased, but by a smaller figure than freight cars, 41.2 percent. The figures indicate the intensive development that had been characteristic of American railroads over the decade. The demand for increased transport along established lines encouraged the laying of double tracks. There was considerable investment in improving facilities,

During the early part of the 20th century, many U.S. railroads merged or were taken over by more prosperous companies. The major consolidations are shown on this map.

Alexander Cassatt, President of the Pennsylvania Railroad, and other major railroad executives worked to strengthen the Commerce Act, preventing unscrupulous carriers from giving preferential rates to particular customers or for certain types of traffic.

easing gradients, and realigning routes, which was made possible by reducing or withholding dividends to stockholders.

Earnings from both passenger traffic and freight were low, and attempts by the carriers to increase these rates to compensate for mounting expenses n 1900 brought forth more protests to the ICC and to Congress. The so-called Elkins Amendment to the Commerce Act strengthened its provisions, forbidding special rates, rebates, or other devices granting undue preference to any individual or species of traffic. In addition, the publication of tariffs was made obligatory, and any practice on the part of carriers to transport any article at a lower rate than that named in the tariffs was prohibited under penalty.

While Senator Elkins gave his name to the legislation, it was in fact a joint effort on the part of railway executives under the leadership of President Cassatt of the Pennsylvania Railroad to root out the demoralizing and destructive practices of unscrupulous corporations, which threatened to disgrace the transportation system and lead it to financial disaster.

In 1906, the ICC got what it wanted. On June 20, Congress approved the Hepburn Bill, which gave it authority to prescribe rates in place of those that, after complaint and hearing, it pronounced unjust, unreasonable, or discriminating. Even so, in 1907, although railroad

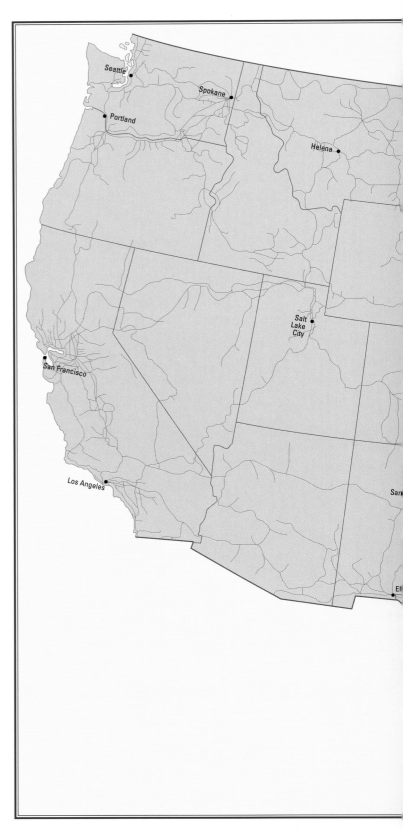

managers had accepted the act in good faith, little progress had been made in implementing it, and suits were filed questioning the right of Congress to delegate to any tribunal the authority to establish an interstate rate.

It was not until 1910 that the position was finally clarified, and the Commission received almost absolute authority over the rate making phase of railroad management. Not only was it authorized to

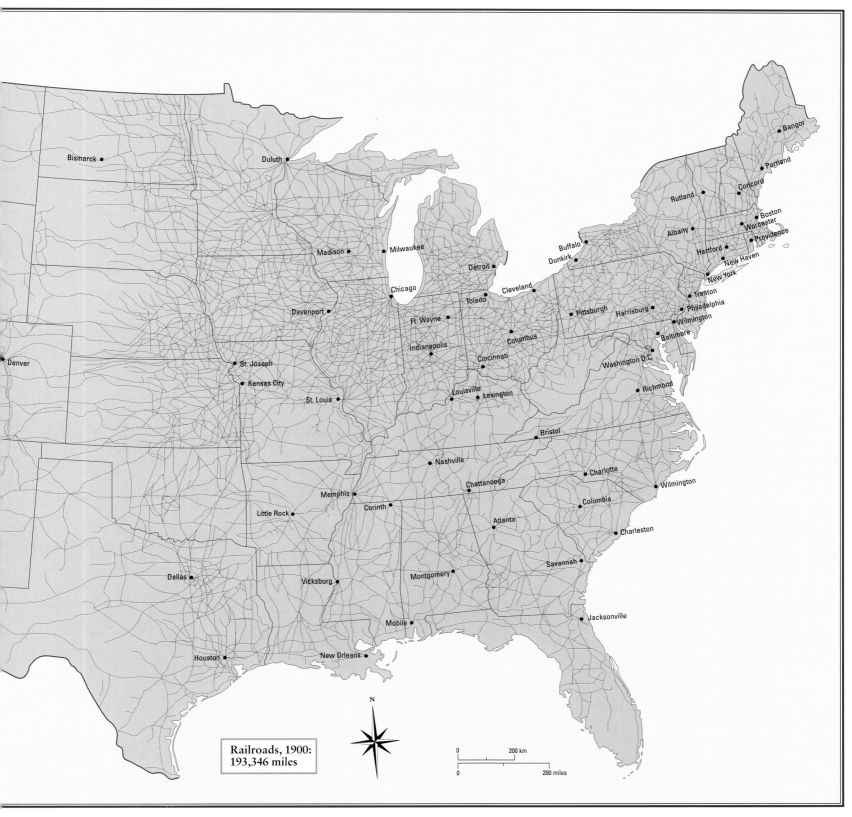

Railroads, 1900:
193,346 miles

N

0   200 km

0   200 miles

suspend rate increases until the circumstances had been investigated, but the act imposed the burden of proof on carriers to justify any proposed rate advances. The immediate effect of this was to put the brakes on expansion and construction. The mileage in the six years following the passing of the act showed a drop of 34 percent compared to the six years before. Receipts from freight dropped by $30 million a year.

By 1900, the total length of U.S. railroads had grown to 192,556 miles (309,880km). The densest part of the network remained in the industrialized Northeast.

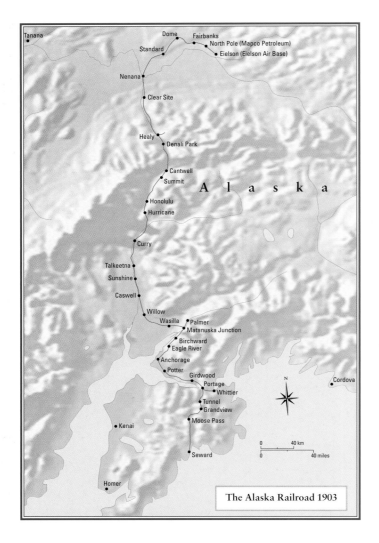

The Alaska Railroad 1903

The effects of stringent regulation were not the only things to affect the railroads. For the fifth time in eight decades, they were again caught in the middle of financial panic in the fall of 1907. In the very heyday of their usefulness, the railroads found themselves in a situation that lost them $300 million, or over 11 percent of earnings in one calendar year. Prompt and drastic retrenchment was essential, which reduced the payroll by nearly 18 percent in 1908. The recovery of the national economy and the railroads from this financial panic was not complete until 1910.

The effects of this stringent regulation on railroads would have a lasting effect on their fortunes. Altogether, the first three decades of the century saw many changes in the railroads of the United States as a result of the regulations, together with natural disasters, a world war, and government policies that resulted in financial failures, mergers, and company buyouts.

By 1900, U.S. railroads were working 192,556 miles (309,880km) of single track and 14,074 miles (22,649km) of auxiliary track (lengths of double line, passing loops, etc, which indicates the increased volume of traffic over some routes), and had 52,154 miles (83,931km) of sidings, giving a total track length of 258,784 miles (416,461km). In addition, they operated 37,663 locomotives, 34,713 passenger cars, and 1,365,531 freight cars.

Work began on the first railroad in Alaska in 1903, with 50 miles (80km) of track being laid north from Seward on the coast. In 1910, another 71 miles (114km) were added. Four years later, Congress voted to fund construction and operation of the railroad through to Fairbanks, at an estimated cost of $35 million. The Alaska Railroad was finally completed in 1923, when President Warren G. Harding drove in the golden spike at Nenana, one of the state's largest cities at the time.

The harsh winter climate of Alaska can make keeping the tracks clear a difficult task. One solution was the steam powered blower, such as the White Pass snowplow, built in 1899 in Skagway, Alaska.

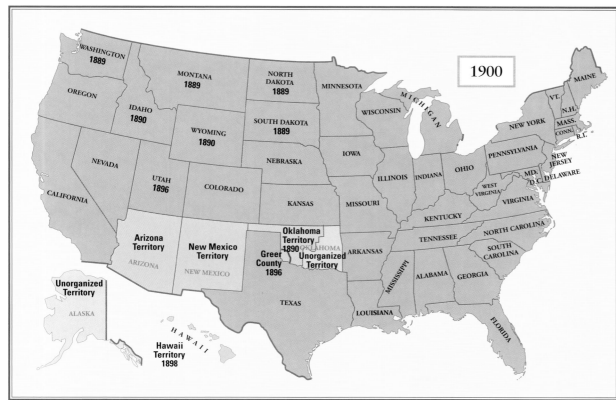

Abandoned 0-4-4 locomotives at the mouth of the Solomon River, Seward Peninsula, Alaska. Originally, they ran on the Council City & Solomon River RR, which was built during the Alaskan gold rush. The railroad closed in 1916.

In 1900, Arizona, New Mexico, Oklahoma, Alaska, and Hawaii were still classed as territories. The part played by the railroads in encouraging growth in the first three at least must have contributed to their eventual elevation to full statehood.

REROUTING, 1900–04

THE EAST AND WEST HAD BEEN CONNECTED BY THE ORIGINAL
TRANSCONTINENTAL LINE, BUT FINANCIAL PROBLEMS BESET THE
SOUTHERN PACIFIC AND UNION PACIFIC RAILROADS. AS PART OF
THE REVITALIZATION PLAN, THE TRACKS WERE IMPROVED TO
ACCEPT HEAVIER ROLLING STOCK.

Railroads had grown in importance, while the mileage covered by their operations and the potential traffic were also giving rise to physical growth. The early tracks and trains had been small and relatively light, but by the turn of the century, the sheer volume of traffic meant that the permanent way and bridges (particularly trestles) needed strengthening, many curves needed straightening, and gradients required easing. In some areas, new alignments, cutoffs, and even abandonment of some parts of routes were necessary.

A prime example was the original transcontinental route, which had been completed in 1869. It was soon found that little revenue was generated by through traffic from the East, and although local traffic produced much of the income, this was still modest, since development of the country was slow at first. As a result, the railroad was starved of revenue and passed into administration. Then Edward H. Harriman took the railroad in hand and used his extraordinary energy to make it pay.

Only 30 years after it was completed, the Union Pacific and Southern Pacific had to pay a huge price for the speed and cheapness of the original work. As early as 1869, a Federal commission had criticized the location and route of the Central Pacific through the Sierra Nevada in these words:

"The curvature was excessive and needlessly sharp. Throughout a large portion the ascents and descents had been multiplied needlessly. Grades of 70 to 80 feet per mile (1.3 percent to 1.5 percent) had been introduced where one of 53 feet per mile (1.0 percent) would have sufficed, and grades of 53 feet per mile where one half that rate of ascent was required. In the Humboldt Valley between Lake Humboldt and Humboldt Wells, the difference in elevation of a little over 1,100 feet had been overcome by ascents and descents amounting to 6,232 feet in a distance of 290 miles."

The Lucin Cutoff ran in almost a straight line from Ogden to Lucin, across the Great Salt Lake, cutting out the heavily graded section that ran around the north of the lake, and which was expensive to operate. In doing so, however, it isolated the historic meeting place of the Union Pacific and Central Pacific railroads at Promontory Point.

In fairness, it should be remembered that the track in question had been completed seven years ahead of the original estimate and, at the time of construction, facilities were very crude compared with what was possible 30 years later. It was also claimed that "A good deal of improvement was purposely left to the future, when traffic developments should justify the expense."

By 1900, "developments" in traffic had made the task of reconstruction and improvement essential, and they had to be put in hand. This involved tearing up and replacing much of the old track, abandoning some sections altogether to construct new ones, additional tunneling to ease gradients and curvature, and replacement of wooden trestles by steel bridges.

The original route between Summit, in west Omaha, and Lane ran for 21 miles (34km). Even though the two towns were only 12 miles (19km) apart, the land between them was rolling and partly unstable. The Omaha Cutoff, which replaced the original track, runs in a straight line, and to keep it as level as possible, construction involved excavating 2.8 million cubic yards (2.14 million cubic meters) and filling about 4.0 million cubic yards (3.0 million cubic meters) of embankment. At one point, the embankment is 65ft (20m) high; at just over a mile long, it required some 1.5 million cubic yards (1.1

Originally, engineers envisaged that the track for the Lucin Cutoff would be carried across the Great Salt Lake on a long wooden trestle bridge. In the end, however, only 12 miles (19km) of trestle were built; the remainder of the causeway was an earth embankment. Even so, over 38,000 wooden piles were used, equating to a section of forest 2 miles (3km) square.

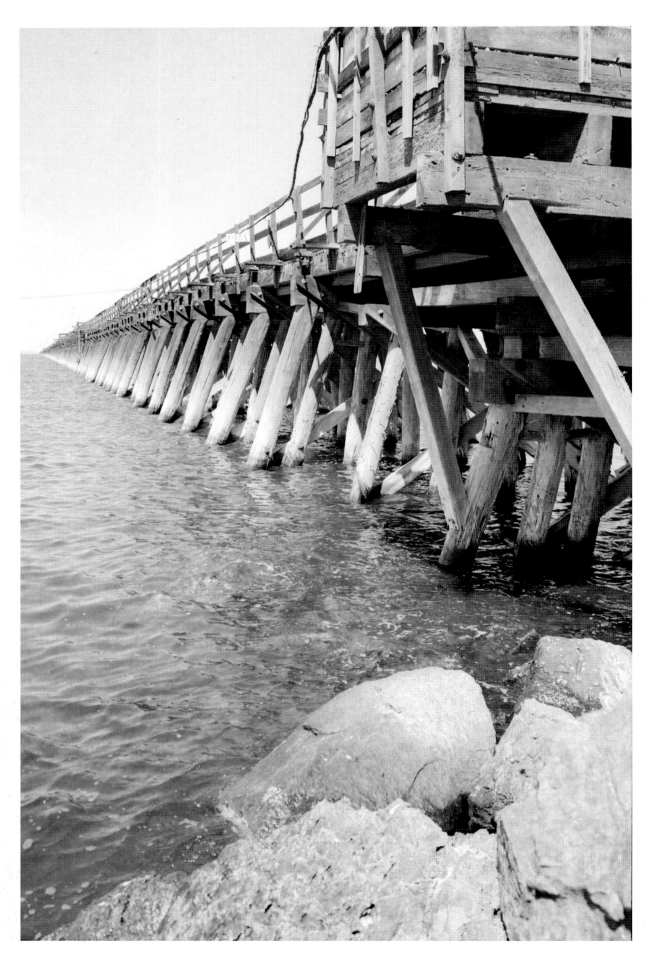

million cubic meters) of dirt. Another fill, across Little Papillon, took the track 89ft (27m) above the floor of the valley and was 3,100ft (945m) long.

Perhaps the best-known rerouting project is the Salt Lake, or Lucin, cutoff across the Great Salt Lake, in Utah, completed in 1904. This saved 43½ miles (70km) over the original line around the northern end of the lake, which was heavily graded with many curves. Unfortunately for history, it removed the track from the original point connecting east and west at Promontory summit, about 30 miles (48km) west of Brigham City, where there is now a commemorative museum. The meeting place is designated the Golden Spike National Historical Site; the original line was finally abandoned and the rails lifted in 1942.

From Sacramento, California, eastward, the line had to climb the western flank of the Sierra Nevada, and from Roseville, the climb was 7,000ft (2,134m) in 140 miles (225km) to Donner Pass, about 30 miles (48km) west of the Nevada state line. Bridges were strengthened, and track realigned to ease gradients and curvature. The ruling gradient was reduced to 1 in 42 (2.4 percent), although some sections were still as steep as 1 in 38 (2.63 percent). Protection of the track from avalanches needed a total of 40 miles (64km) of snow sheds and 39 tunnels. Track was relaid to take the heavier rolling stock necessitated by Edward Harriman's revitalization program.

The transcontinental railroad changed the nature of the country through which it passed and helped open up the West. In less than 30 years, Omaha became the third largest packing station for meat products in the country; Fremont, 30 miles (48km) northwest of Omaha, grew from nothing into a thriving city; the prairie became a great agricultural region as well as an exporter of livestock and minerals; Lexington, on the Platte River, grew on the site where South Cheyenne Indians had burned a freight train in 1867; Laramie, Wyoming, became a mining center with railroad workshops; and, some 200 miles (322km) to the west, Green River became the junction for the northward route, via Idaho, to Portland, Oregon, and Seattle and Spokane in Washington.

At the point where the causeway crosses, the Great Salt Lake is 30 miles (48km) wide. The causeway itself rises 17ft (5m) above the water, while the width at the top is 16ft (4.8m). Construction was carried out by 3,000 men, working night and day, the bridge being built in two sections from opposite shores of the lake and meeting in the middle. A steamboat, the *Promontory*, was floated on the lake to tow barges with supplies and provisions for the construction camps.

EASTERN CITY ROUTES

IN THE EAST, COMPETITION FOR PASSENGERS BETWEEN THE
MAJOR CITIES WAS INTENSE, NOWHERE MORE SO THAN ON THE
NEW YORK–CHICAGO ROUTE. PUBLICITY-CONSCIOUS RAILROADS
INTRODUCED NAMED LUXURY TRAINS, AND THE IDEAL OF
"CHICAGO IN 24 HOURS" FROM NEW YORK WAS SOON BETTERED.

The New York Central RR had its *Empire State Express*, while the Pennsylvania RR had the *Pennsylvania Limited*. The Vanderbilts controlled the NYC, and the president of the Pennsylvania was Alexander J. Cassatt. To say that there was considerable rivalry between them is an understatement; fortunately they confined their hostility to undercutting each other's rates and rival services.

The New York Central & Hudson River RR, and its ally, the Lake Shore & Michigan Southern RR, operated the

Many early railroads followed rivers and watercourses because they meant easy grades. The New York Central enjoyed this benefit on its route to Chicago.

Water Level Route, so called because it ran for the most part in sight of water (notably the Hudson River) and therefore was relatively easily graded. Its route distance between New York and Chicago was 961 miles (1,547km). The rival "mountain" route of the Pennsylvania Railroad negotiated 1-in-50 (2 percent) grades and climbed to 2,193ft (668m) across the Alleghenies, but it had a shorter route of 912 miles (1,468km) and, moreover, called at Philadelphia on the way. An overall average speed of 40mph (64km/h) does not seem much by today's standards, but it was very creditable in the last few years of the 19th century. Stops along the way were necessary, since locomotives had to be changed, water replenished, and attention given to train service requirements.

In New York City, the two railroads had separate stations: the New York Central had its Grand Central Terminal (remodeled and enlarged in 1900) in Manhattan, but the Pennsylvania's terminal was across the Hudson at Exchange Place, Jersey City. They shared the same terminal in Chicago, however, in La Salle Street. The

Built by ALCO, this 4-4-0 high wheeler, No. 999 of the New York Central, was said to be the first steam locomotive to have exceeded 100mph (160km/h) when in service hauling the *Empire State Express*.

rivalry became intense when, in 1902, the New York Central introduced a new luxury train, called *The Twentieth Century Limited*, which cut the time between the two cities to 20 hours—an average of 48mph (77km/h).

The inaugural train on June 15, 1902, consisted of only five wooden-bodied cars—two sleepers, a diner, a buffet car, and an end-platform observation car. It was hauled by a high-wheeler of the same type as the speed-record holder, No. 999 (which resides today in the Chicago Museum of Science and Industry). On the day the *The Twentieth Century Limited* was inaugurated, it was challenged by the

Pennsylvania RR, which introduced the *Pennsylvania Special*, running its 912 miles (1,468km) also in 20 hours—an average of 45.6mph (73km/h).

While both trains left New York City from different stations in different directions, sharing the same station in Chicago caused the most rivalry. Since they both departed from La Salle Street at the same time (12.40pm) for the journey to New York on parallel tracks, there was usually a race over the first few miles to Gary, Indiana.

The Twentieth Century Limited was one of the most famous of U.S. express trains. Although the inaugural service was hauled by a 4-4-0 Atlantic locomotive, more powerful engines were required as the train grew in popularity and became heavier. Here, it is pulled by a 4-6-0.

So successful were these trains that patronage grew quickly; by 1903, two trains for each road were often necessary. Special rolling stock was built, steel cars being introduced in 1903, and upgraded at regular intervals as one railroad attempted to outdo the other. Trains became longer and heavier, so larger steam locomotives were soon required.

The New York Central terminal in Manhattan was approached by tunnel. Some 700 trains in and out of Grand Central every day produced considerable smoke nuisance, and by the early 1900s, the pollution had given rise to serious concern. This was compounded in 1902 by a serious accident in

Chicago's La Salle Street station, destination for the rival express services from New York, operated by the New York Central and the Pennsylvania.

the approach tunnel, when a train overran a stop signal obscured by smoke, and 15 people were killed. In 1903, the New York legislature passed a law prohibiting the use of "smoking locomotives" south of the Harlem River (effectively south of 125th Street) after July 1, 1908. The railroad had to act, or it would be barred from its prestigious and conveniently located Manhattan terminal. The railroad chose electrification.

The B & O had earlier used electric locomotives in its tunnels running under the city of Baltimore, while the New Haven RR had electrified some of its Connecticut branch lines on the third-rail system at 600 volts dc. This was the system chosen for the lines into Grand Central.

A total of 35 electric locomotives were built by the American Locomotive Company (ALCO) and General Electric, being delivered in 1906, and electric haulage was introduced in 1907, the changeover point being Wakefield. In 1913, electrification was extended to Harmon, some 33 miles (53km) from New York City on the east side of the Hudson River, where steam locomotives were exchanged for electric, and vice versa,

Locomotive No. 999 of the New York Central hauled the *Empire State Express* to a record speed of 112mph (179km/h.

and where a large locomotive depot was built. The New Haven RR, which shared Grand Central Terminal, had a changeover point, also on the east side of the river, a couple of miles (3km) away at Croton. Electric multiple-unit cars were introduced on local services.

Pennsylvania's terminal being in Jersey City meant that travelers to New York had to complete their journey by ferry. In 1900, the "Pennsy" acquired the Long Island RR, and, after a study of possibilities for bridges and tunnels, in 1904, it began construction of Pennsylvania Station on Manhattan Island. Sited between Seventh and Eighth Avenues, and 31st and 33rd Streets, it was in a good position. A twin tunnel was constructed under the Hudson, and four single tunnels under the East River, which, together with a double-track main line across the Hackensack Meadows, connected the new terminal to its road east of Newark, New Jersey. All these lines were electrified, again on the 600 volt dc, third-rail system. The new Pennsylvania Station was opened in 1910 and electric haulage in and out of the terminal began, with steam locomotives being changed for electric, and vice versa, at a station called Manhattan Transfer, where it was also possible for passengers to make cross-platform interchange with the Hudson subways.

On November 24,1912, the *Pennsylvania Special* was renamed *Broadway Limited*. The name was coined, not to honor the entertainment industry, but in recognition of the fact that much of the route between New York and Chicago was quadruple track—a subtlety that was probably lost on most travelers. Both roads were obliged to introduce steel rolling stock, since wooden cars were banned from using the tunnels.

A crowd poses in front of the Pennsylvania RR's car, No. 3998. This was the largest electric locomotive in the world, when it was first introduced during the early 1900s to run through the subway line into New York City.

Natural Disasters

NATURAL DISASTERS WERE NOTHING NEW. FROM THEIR VERY
BEGINNINGS, NORTH AMERICAN RAILROADS HAD TO FACE
STORMS IN ALL SEASONS, AND SPRING FLOODS CAUSED BY THE
MELTING OF ACCUMULATIONS OF WINTER SNOW. THEY ALSO HAD
TO CONTEND WITH EARTHQUAKES, AND LANDSLIDES.

An earthquake caused severe damage to San Francisco in 1906, but help was at hand from the railroads, which shipped in supplies and evacuated refugees to safety—despite the fact that many of the tracks had been badly warped and rendered impassible by trains.

Many lines followed watercourses, with the tracks often only a few feet above normal high-water level, making them vulnerable to flooding; others endured washouts and destruction by torrential rain in the hills and mountains. Lines west of the Mississippi followed or crossed many rivers that could turn into rushing torrents, irrespective of season. The Mississippi itself has been responsible for much railroad destruction.

When the San Francisco earthquake of 1906 devastated the city, the railroads also suffered—but not so seriously, and they played a significant role in the rescue work. On the first day of the disaster, railroads delivered food from Los Angeles by special fast freight, and moved 1,073 carloads of refugees away from the city. Between April 18 and May 23, the Union Pacific and Southern Pacific together took in 1,603 carloads of supplies and carried out 224,069 refugees, absorbing costs that amounted to over $1 million.

In his *Short History of American Railways* (1925), Slason Thompson wrote: "The bears of the stock exchange in New York did not fail to take note of the calamity. The psychological tremor that struck San Francisco was felt across the continent and shook more than $1 billion of market value out of railroad securities. Between April 17 and May 20 the shares of the leading companies sold off all the way from 6 to 48 points. Industrial stocks showed their sympathetic sensitiveness to anything affecting

Above After the earthquake in San Francisco came the conflagration, as fires swept through the city. Helpless citizens could only stand by and watch. This photograph clearly shows the cable car track in the center of the devastated road. *Left* Many of the wooden frame houses of San Francisco simply toppled over as their foundations were disrupted by the earthquake.

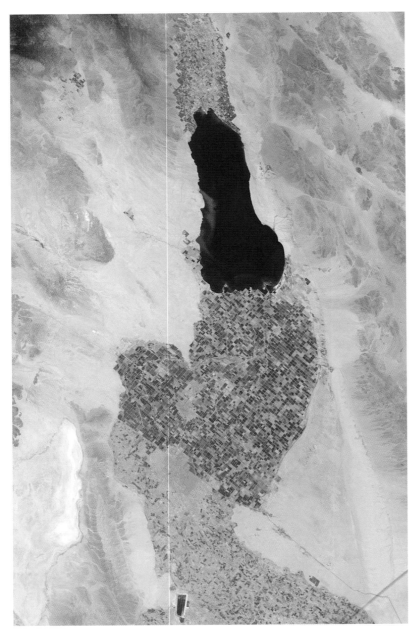

The Salton Sea today, as seen from a satellite orbiting the earth. The floods that led to its formation threatened the fertile Imperial Valley. Thanks to the help of the Southern Pacific Railroad, the valley was saved.

the railways by even greater losses."

As willing rescuers, railroads have played their part in dispensing first aid to the injured in almost every state, and mostly have been taken for granted. Another illustration is the way the Southern Pacific saved the Imperial Valley after the floods of 1905.

Today, Imperial Valley is known as a rich section of southern California, famed for its glorious climate and golden harvests—both agricultural and mineral. Geographically, it is a depression in the earth's surface about 100 miles (161km) long and 35 miles (56km) wide, and was once covered by water to a depth of 300ft (91m) at its deepest part. Originally, it formed part of the Gulf of California, but in time the Colorado River formed a barrier of silt, leaving the upper stretch a great salt lake. Slowly, the water evaporated and an arid basin, called the Salton Sink, was left. There is geological evidence that from time to time in the past, the Colorado broke through the barrier, and the process that formed the Sink was repeated several times.

In 1902, a canal was dug from the Colorado River at Pilot Knob, opposite Yuma, Arizona. The Sink was renamed Imperial Valley, and 400 miles (644km) of ditches were dug to irrigate 100,000 acres (40,470ha) of land. The railway, a branch of the Southern Pacific, arrived in 1904, bringing with it more than 10,000 settlers, and numerous townships were established. The capacity of the canals and ditches was quadrupled, and by the beginning of 1905, 120,000 acres (48,564ha) of reclaimed land were under cultivation. The soil was so rich that it would produce almost anything. The air of the valley was so dry that men could work in a shade temperature of 120°F (49°C) without exhaustion.

Nobody seems to have realized that the bottom of the valley was far below the level of the Pacific Ocean. In 1904, silt from the Colorado clogged up the canal, and the California Development Company cut a new intake from the river, but failed to provide head-gate control. In February 1905, it flooded, but not seriously. A second flood followed shortly afterward, and in March, the volume of water, increased by the rapid melting of snow, enlarged the size of the intake. The breach increased in size so rapidly that no amount of plugging with piles, brushwood, and sandbags was of any use. Water flowed into the valley through a breach 100ft (30m) wide at the rate of 90,000cu.ft (2,547cu.m) a second; a new Salton Sea was forming.

As the valley filled, the town of Salton, parts of the nearby Indian Reservation, and a long section of the Southern Pacific railroad siding were flooded. The Southern Pacific RR mounted a lengthy rescue operation, during which the railroad poured in a great deal of money and resources to achieve

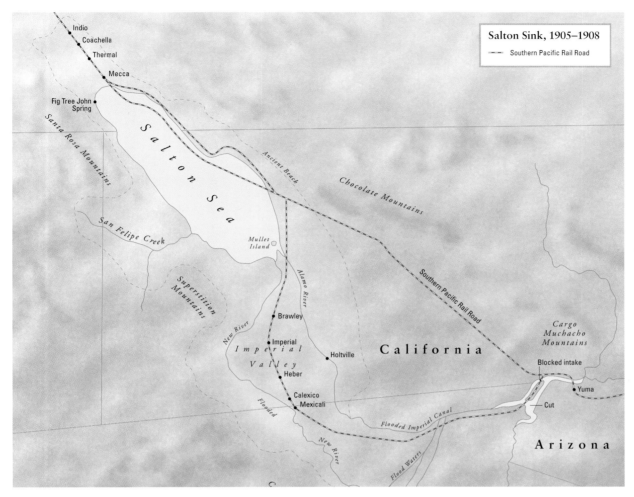

Salton Sink, 1905–1908
--·-- Southern Pacific Rail Road

The lack of head-gate control on the new canal intake from the Colorado River led to the flooding of Imperial Valley in 1905. In the process, a long section of the Southern Pacific Railroad was inundated and a new Salton Sea was formed.

Presidents William Howard Taft (*top*) and Theodore Roosevelt (*above*) urged Congress to reimburse the Southern Pacific Railroad for its great efforts in saving Imperial Valley, but with little success.

a successful final conclusion, as remarkable in its way as its operations during the San Francisco earthquake. The flooding was finally checked in 1907 by a dike, built with the aid of railcars that dumped boulders into the floodwaters. The Southern Pacific spent $3.1 million on rescuing Imperial Valley, and although Congress was urged by both President Theodore Roosevelt and his successor, William Howard Taft, to reimburse the claim in some measure "for coming to the rescue of the Government at the instance of President Roosevelt in a great emergency," as Taft put it, the claim was never honored. In January 1911, the Senate House Committee on Claims reported a bill appropriating $773,000, but it was not taken any farther. In 1916, it was claimed that the farmers in the Imperial Valley expected to earn a sum equivalent to the interest on $500 million.

To quote Slason Thompson again: "In this splendid piece of rescue work the Southern Pacific simply added to the long list of sacrifices American railroads have made for the communities they serve only to experience the traditional ingratitude of republics."

Another disaster befell the cities, towns, and settlements in Ohio in March 1913. Floods inundated an area of about 315 square miles (816sq.km), with Columbus at its center, when between 7 and 8in (18 and 20cm) of rain fell in four days, following wind damage that had already disrupted telegraph and telephone communication. The Pennsylvania Railroad probably suffered most, but other railroads also affected were the New York Central, "Big Four," Erie, Baltimore & Ohio, Hocking Valley, Wabash, and other small railroads serving the flooded area. This time, the direct money loss was estimated at $300 million.

New Constructions, 1906–10

IN THE EARLY PART OF THE 20TH CENTURY, PLENTY OF NEW
CONSTRUCTION WAS CARRIED OUT BY NORTH AMERICAN
RAILROADS. MANY MAJOR CITIES SAW THE ERECTION OF
MAGNIFICENT TERMINAL BUILDINGS, SOME OF WHICH WERE
AMONG THE FINEST STRUCTURES IN THE WORLD.

A contemporary illustration from *Century* magazine showing the excavation of the new Grand Central Terminal, New York, in 1907.

In 1906, the New York Central began constructing a tunnel to replace the ferry that had long been its only way to run trains from Detroit across the Detroit River into Windsor, Ontario. The river is over half a mile (0.8km) wide and in places is 50ft (15m) deep, with an uneven bottom and a 2mph (3km/h) current. To avoid steep approach gradients, it was decided to construct a tubular tunnel on the riverbed rather than a bored tunnel beneath it.

To provide a graded bed for the tubes, the river was dredged at that point to a depth of 74ft (22.5m) below the lowest surface level. Sections of tube 260ft (79m) long were constructed 5 miles (8km) upstream, loaded on pontoons that were launched sideways, and floated down river to be sunk into position. Supreme accuracy was essential so that sections could be placed and joined to form a continuous tunnel. The internal diameter of

The grandiose interior of New York's Grand Central Terminal, with its ornate moldings, imposing windows, and the magnificent four-faced clock on top of the information booth, its most recognizable icon. Each of the four clock faces are made from opal, and both Sotheby's and Christie's have estimated its value to be $10m-$20m.

each concrete-lined tube was 23ft 4in (7.1m), and they were encased in concrete so as to form in cross-section a solid rectangle, the function of which was to exclude water completely.

The tunnel opened on October 16, 1910, and, together with the approaches, measured 2.4 miles (3.9km) in length. To avoid smoke and ventilation problems, trains were hauled through the tunnel between Detroit and Windsor by electric locomotives operating from 600 volt dc third rails. Six were delivered initially in 1909 by General Electric, which was responsible for the whole scheme. As far as is known, the tunnel has never developed any structural defects.

The new (1910) Pennsylvania Station in New York City has been described as one of the great monumental edifices of the world. The part visible from the streets was of classical proportions, but the work of reaching Manhattan began across the Hudson at Harrison, in the New Jersey hinterland. The double-track Hudson River tunnels were built at a depth of 97ft (30m) below mean water level, but the line emerged at Manhattan's 10th Avenue to enter the main terminal building. The tunnels were about 9ft (3m) below mean water level at the highest point. For the Long Island Line trains, there

The interior of the Pennsylvania Station, showing the complex, vaulted, glazed roof. The station contained 11 island platforms and 21 standing tracks.

The magnificent Pennsylvania Station, with its classical facade, was built on Manhattan Island in 1910. It was a massive building, covering an area of 28 acres (11ha). Trains approached through tunnels under the river and were electrically hauled for that portion of the journey.

were four tunnels under the East River, which emerged on the Long Island shore in Queens.

The station and yard covered an area of 28 acres (11ha) with 16 miles (26km) of tracks and siding space for 386 cars. There were 21 standing tracks in the station and 11 island platforms; the capacity of the tunnels feeding the station has been estimated at 144 trains per hour. The station was opened to traffic in September 1910, nine years after the franchise was granted by the City of New York. It was demolished in 1966.

Pennsylvania Station was one of a number of great stations built in that era. On June 4, 1911, the Chicago & North Western opened its new station in Chicago on Madison Street, and Canal

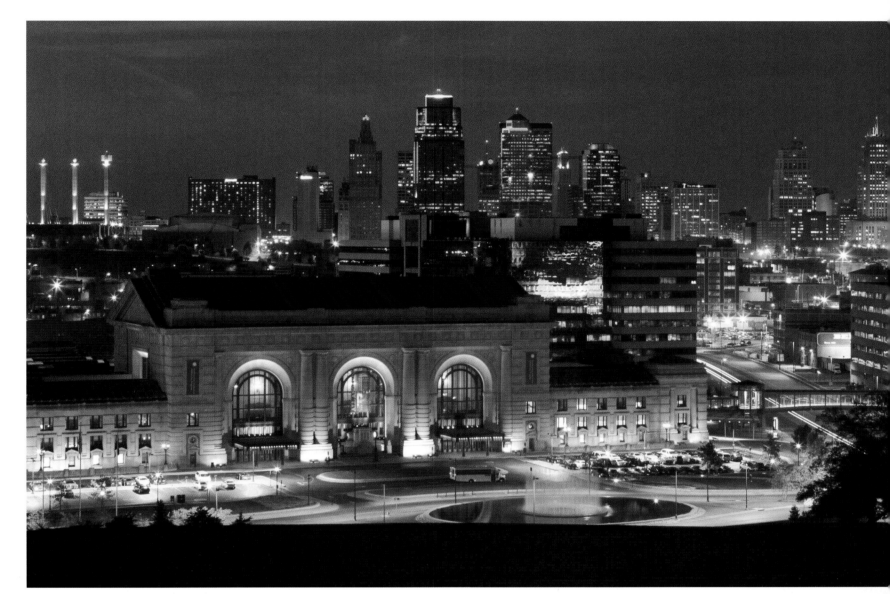

and Clinton Streets, moving its passenger services from the old Wells and Kinzie Street site on the north side to the west side of the city. The total cost was $23.75 million.

Twelve railway systems united to provide Kansas City Union Station, and the list includes all those railroads entering Kansas City in 1906. When the scheme was first promoted, it included a new belt line around the northern end of the city, with the station on an entirely new site. The main buildings and train shed covered 18 acres (7ha), an area exceeded only by the Pennsylvania and Grand Central stations in New York. The station was not a terminal as such, since the tracks ran right through.

Another grand station to be built was the Union Passenger Station on Massachusetts Avenue in Washington, D.C., which was completed and opened on November 17, 1907. Built by the Washington Terminal company in agreement with the Baltimore & Ohio RR and a subsidiary of the Pennsylvania, the terminal was for the joint use of the Southern, the Washington Southern, the Chesapeake & Ohio, and "such other companies as might be admitted to the use of its facilities and connections." Expenses and revenue were to be charged separately against the tenant companies in proportion to their use. Under Act of Congress, all other railroad stations in the city were abandoned, together with their approaching tracks.

At the turn of the 20th century, the Kansas City Terminal Railway, controled by the 12 railroads serving Kansas City, chose a new location for the train depot, since the original was prone to flooding by the Kansas and Missouri Rivers. The new building was erected south of the central business district, above and away from the floodplain. Jarvis Hunt's design had a main hall for ticketing, and a perpendicular hall extending over the tracks for passenger waiting. The Beaux-Arts station opened on October 30, 1914, the third-largest railroad station in the country.

LEGISLATION AND LOSSES, 1900–16

DESPITE THEIR APPARENT OPULENCE, AMERICAN RAILROADS WERE BEING SLOWLY STIFLED IN THE FIRST DECADE OF THE 20TH CENTURY. TOUGH REGULATIONS AND INCREASING COSTS COMBINED TO CUT THEIR INCOMES. AT THE SAME TIME, SOME OF THE INDUSTRY'S LEADING LIGHTS PASSED AWAY.

By 1910, restrictive legislation, both state and federal, together with increasing materials and labor costs, slowly but surely were eroding the railroads' ability to pay their way. Between 1900 and 1910, everything affecting their operation had increased in price, except the one thing they all had to sell: transportation. This had been fixed by legislation. By contrast, all their essential commodities increased by an average of a little over 2 percent per annum. Any other industry would have added these increases to their selling prices; being unable to do so, the railroads incurred additional expenses of $250 million over the decade. An application to the Commission for increased rates was denied in 1911, owing to a misinterpretation of railroad profits, dividends having been counted twice. There was also an optimistic anticipation on the part of the Commission of heavier traffic, which did not materialize. An increase in expenses did come about, however, and the next few years showed a marked shrinkage of net income.

About this time, a number of the leading personalities involved in developing the railways died. Alexander J. Cassatt, president of the Pennsylvania RR since 1899, died in 1906 at the age of 66, before he could see the completion of his crowning glory. He had great foresight, and remarkable gifts as a railway engineer and executive. His monument was the great double-track tunnel under the Hudson River, the magnificent Pennsylvania Station, the four tunnels under the East River, and the Great steel-arch bridge over "Hell Gate" that connected with the New Haven road. The monument erected to him

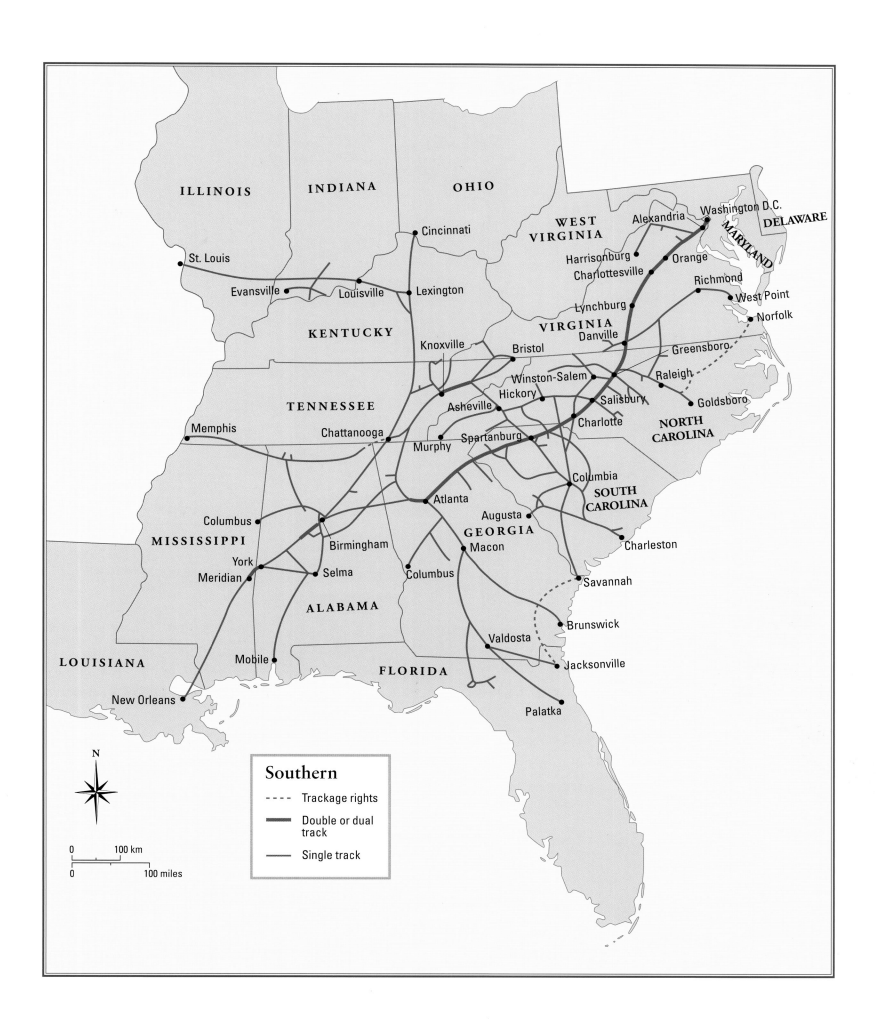

ILLINOIS
INDIANA
OHIO
WEST VIRGINIA
Cincinnati
St. Louis
Alexandria
Washington D.C.
DELAWARE
MARYLAND
Harrisonburg
Orange
Charlottesville
Richmond
Evansville
Louisville
Lexington
West Point
Lynchburg
Norfolk
KENTUCKY
VIRGINIA
Danville
Knoxville
Greensboro
Bristol
Winston-Salem
Raleigh
Hickory
Salisbury
Goldsboro
TENNESSEE
Asheville
Charlotte
NORTH CAROLINA
Memphis
Chattanooga
Spartanburg
Murphy
Columbia
SOUTH CAROLINA
Atlanta
Augusta
Columbus
GEORGIA
Charleston
Birmingham
Macon
York
MISSISSIPPI
Selma
Savannah
Meridian
Columbus
ALABAMA
Brunswick
Valdosta
LOUISIANA
Mobile
Jacksonville
FLORIDA
New Orleans
Palatka

N

Southern

- - - - Trackage rights

▬▬▬ Double or dual track

──── Single track

0   100 km

0   100 miles

Completed in 1916, New York's Hell Gate Bridge is a steel arch railroad bridge spanning the East River, and connecting Astoria in the borough of Queens with Randalls and Wards Islands. Originally, it carried four tracks (two passenger and two freight), but today has only three.

in Pennsylvania Station bore the inscription: "Alexander Johnston Cassatt, President, Pennsylvania Railroad Company, 1899–1906, whose foresight, courage, and ability achieved the extension of the Pennsylvania Railroad System in New York City."

Edward H. Harriman died in 1909 at the age of 61. It has been said of Harriman that wherever he touched a piece of railroad property, the result was an improved and more profitable service to the public at reduced rates. There was one exception to this: the Chicago & Alton RR, which he left rehabilitated and improved—but impoverished. Harriman is perhaps best remembered for his reconstruction of the Union Pacific line. The most difficult task facing his engineers was the easing of the gradients on the section of line over the Black Hills. His board had laid down a maximum gradient of 43ft (13m) to the mile (1.6km), 1 in 123 (0.81 percent). This involved constructing a new line over all manner of natural hazards. In addition, curves were eased on each side of Sherman summit, which itself was lowered 247ft (75m) by boring a 1,800ft (549m) tunnel, and the 6,000ft (1,829m) long Aspen tunnel was also constructed.

Harriman was responsible for the reorganization and consolidation of minor railroads south of the Mason Dixon line. This involved bringing together practically all the southern lines that had suffered in the financial panic of 1893, following the collapse of the stock market, to make four trunk lines: the Southern, the Atlantic Coast Line, the Louisville & Nashville, and the Seaboard Air Line. Together, they operated 20,000 miles (32,200km) of track. Harriman also helped to place the Illinois Central in the forefront of railroad progress.

James Jerome Hill died in 1916 at the age of 78. He was a farsighted man, and many unconnected with the railroads will long remember him for his thought and foresight. Among railroad men, he was known as the Empire Builder, a title earned by his work through the whole of the Northwest, from Lake Michigan to Puget Sound in Washington State. He was deeply involved in two great transcontinental projects, the Great Northern and Northern Pacific railroad systems, and laid the foundations for their eventual consolidation with the Chicago, Burlington & Quincy RR.

Another personality to pass away in this decade, at the age of 75, was Edward Payson Ripley, president of the Atchison, Topeka & Santa Fe railroad from 1895. He too was one of the great railroad builders. The passing of these influential men perhaps signified the end of an era.

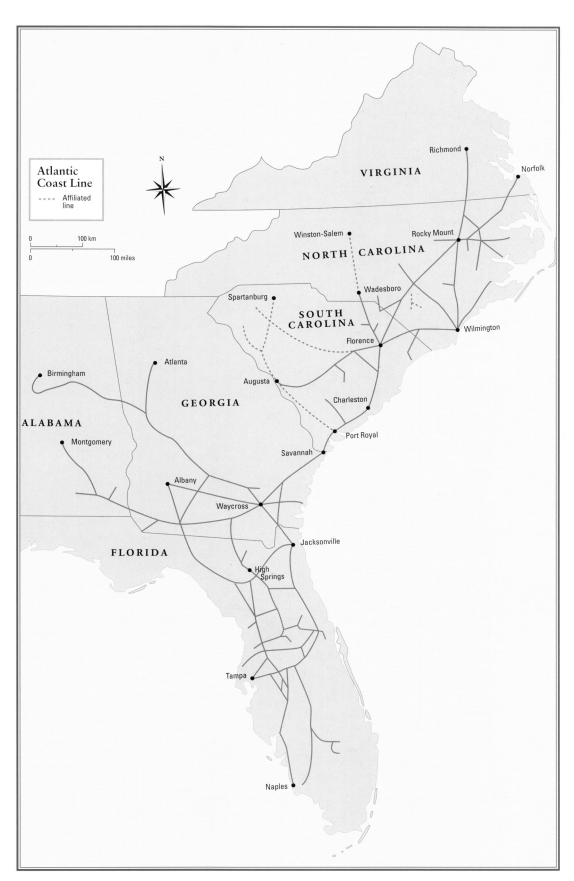

Another railroad that owed its existence to Edward H. Harriman was the Atlantic Coast Line.

Growth of the Steam Locomotive, 1900-1928

THE LIGHT CONSTRUCTION OF THE EARLY RAILROADS HAD AN INFLUENCE ON ROLLING-STOCK DESIGN. USUALLY, LOCOMOTIVES WERE EQUIPPED WITH FOUR OR SIX DRIVING WHEELS; BY THE TURN OF THE CENTURY, HOWEVER, THEY HAD SIX, EIGHT, AND EVEN TEN COUPLED WHEELS.

In the 1860s and 1870s, the classic American eight-wheeler (4-4-0) was giving way in passenger haulage to the ten-wheeler, and in freight haulage to the "Mogul" (2-6-0) and "Consolidation" (2-8-0) types for freight. Around the beginning of the 20th century, these were replaced by the "Atlantic" (4-4-2), "Pacific" (4-6-2), and "Mountain" (4-8-2) types for passenger trains; the "Mikado" and, later, "MacArthur" (2-8-2) and "Santa Fe" (2-10-2) types took over freight haulage.

Other wheel arrangements were also used on freight and banking (pusher) locomotives. A two-wheel trailing truck was provided underneath the firebox, which had grown in size, to give a larger grate for more power output. By the 1920s, the demand for yet more power resulted in even larger fireboxes, which required four-wheel trailing trucks for support. Among the best-known designs representing

An IIS 2-10-0 Decapod heavy freight locomotive built for the Pennsylvania RR by Baldwin.

INCREASE IN LOCOMOTIVE SCALE 1837—1918

1837

Sandusky built for Mad River & Lake Erie RR in 1837.
Total weight of loaded engine and tender 16,000lb (7,257kg).

1851

Governor Merey built for Michigan Southern RR in 1851.
Total weight of loaded engine and tender 67,000lb (30,390kg).

1860

Locomotive built for Hudson River RR in 1860.
Total weight of loaded engine and tender 108,000lb (49,000kg).

1880

Locomotive built for New York, Pennsylvania & Ohio RR in 1880.
Total weight of loaded engine and tender 160,000lb (72,574kg).

1895

Locomotive built for St. Louis, Vandalia & Terre Haute RR in 1895.
Total weight of loaded engine and tender 219,000lb (99,336kg).

1902

Locomotive built for Missouri Pacific RR in 1902.
Total weight of loaded engine and tender 283,000lb (128,336kg).

1904

Locomotive built for Baltimore & Ohio RR in 1904.
Total weight of loaded engine and tender 474,000lb (215,000kg).

1911

Locomotive built for Chesapeake & Ohio RR in 1911.
Total weight of loaded engine and tender 493,000lb (223,621kg).

1918

Locomotive built for Baltimore & Ohio RR in 1904.
Total weight of loaded engine and tender 668,000lb (303,000kg).

A 2-8-0 Consolidation freight locomotive. These locomotives were true workhorses of the railroads during the late 19th and early 20th centuries.

these types were the "Hudson" (4-6-4), "Berkshire" (2-8-4), "Northern" (4-8-4), and "Texas" (2-10-4); their names gave an indication of the railroads for which they were first developed.

With the introduction of steel for freight car frames and the adoption of automatic couplers and automatic air brakes, longer and heavier trains became possible, which suited the American market. By the early 1900s, 5,000- and 6,000-ton trains became the norm on many lines, trains being up to a mile (1.6km) long. With long, single-track stretches of road, it was beneficial to run the longest possible trains between any two points. This called for extremely powerful locomotives,

As train weights increased, so the problem of steep gradients became more acute. Making headway uphill was not the only problem: it was often difficult to stop a long, heavy train on the steepest downhill gradients. Pusher locomotives had been employed since early times on the mountainous lines, and some had been specially developed for that purpose. In 1900, it was quite common to find two at the end of a long, heavy coal train as well as a "helper" at the head. Invariably, these were of the small-wheeled type, and their number of axles grew as their duties became more onerous. Even with the newer upgraded tracks, the weight had to be spread as much as possible. While the pioneering

An 0-6-6-0 articulated freight locomotive built for the New York Central RR. Big, rugged locomotives of this type had great hauling capacity. They often took the place of two locomotives on heavy freight trains, providing a saving in crews and fuel.

Stourbridge Lion of 1829 weighed 8 tons, Baldwin's *Santa Fe* (2-10-2) of 1903 weighed 143.5 tons.

For most North American railroad men, the ideal locomotive should be big, powerful, rugged, and mechanically simple. As the locomotive increased in size, its appetite for fuel and water grew—as did its tender. No steam locomotive is complete without its tender (unless it is a tank locomotive, which carries its fuel and water on the same frame). Originally, tenders were kept as small as possible, because they were a non-revenue-earning load. The simple tender carried on two four-wheel trucks soon became too small to allow a long-distance train to complete its journey without stopping for replenishment.

The "Pacific"-type locomotive built by ALCO in 1924 still had a double-truck, eight-wheel tender,

A restored Consolidation 2-8-0 locomotive, originally built by Baldwin in 1916 for the Lake Superior & Ishpeming RR in Michigan. This locomotive remained in service for switching and hauling freight until 1956.

and it could carry 15 tons of soft coal and 10,000 gallons (36,850 liters) of water. This was a more-or-less standard size of tender for the era. By way of contrast, the Northern Pacific 2-8-8-4 Mallet of 1928, also built by ALCO, had a tender with a capacity of 27 tons of coal and 21,200 gallons (80,242 liters) of water, carried on two six-wheel trucks. (Of course, a Mallet of that size was almost the equivalent of two "Consolidations.")

By 1917, the number of locomotive builders in the United States had been reduced to three: the American Locomotive Company (ALCO), Baldwin Locomotive Works, and Lima Locomotive Company. The last had its roots in a locomotive builder established in 1880, Carnes, Agather & Company, with a works in Ohio. It also produced sawmill equipment and, since logging railroads had particularly light and rough tracks, it added a special articulated type of locomotive invented by a Michigan lumberman, Ephraim Shay. These were double-truck locomotives, usually with double-truck tenders,

This 2-10-2 freight locomotive, known as the Santa Fe type, is shown as part of a triple header. Note the massive tender necessary to keep such a monster fed and watered.

all the wheels—including those of the tender—being driven through bevel gears from a longitudinal shaft, which was connected flexibly to each end of the crankshaft of a two- or three-cylinder vertical engine. The Shay locomotive was particularly flexible, coping with the dips and rises of the hastily laid, uneven track of logging outfits far better than any conventional locomotive.

Lima began building conventional locomotives in 1912, from which time they became the company's chief product. When the federal government took over the railroads in December 1917, representatives of the three builders formed a committee of the United States Railroad Administration (USRA) to develop 12 standard types of locomotive for wartime service. These included a six-wheel switcher, a "Santa Fe," a "Pacific," a "Mountain," and two Mallets—a "light" 2-6-6-2 and a "heavy" 2-8-8-2. The only previous example of a "Mountain" (4-8-2) had been built in 1911 by ALCO's Richmond, Virginia, plant for the Chesapeake & Ohio Railroad.

The USRA locomotives were good, pleasing, well-proportioned designs. They had a large number of interchangeable parts and, being mass-produced, they came off the production lines fast with low unit costs. In less than two years, 1,830 were turned out by the three manufacturers. This example of efficient design and standardization made good economic sense—but it was swiftly abandoned when the railroads were returned to private control in 1920.

The 2-8-2 configuration was most often referred to as a Mikado (sometimes nicknamed "Mike"), but also referred to as a MacArthur type. The arrangement allows the firebox to be placed behind, instead of above, the driving wheels, permitting a large, wide and deep firebox. This example is the Pennsylvania RR's locomotive No. 520, shown here on display at the Pennsylvania Railroad Museum, Strasburg, Pennsylvania.

Shay locomotives were designed to climb steep grades, swing around hairpin curves and negotiate the temporary tracks of logging operations. Unlike standard steam locomotives, Shays are driven by direct gearing to each wheel, which allows smooth, even flow of power. Shays also had to be powerful enough to haul heavy loads from the woods to the mill. In 1911, West Virginia led the nation with more than 3,000 miles (4,828km) of logging track. All that remains are 11 miles (17.70km) at the Cass Scenic Railroad State Park, restored as they were in the early 1900s. Shay No. 2, shown here filling up at a water tower, is a "Pacific Coast" type—the only one used east of the Mississippi—a souped-up, 70-ton, three-truck Shay. It features superheat, a bigger firebox, lower gear ratio, steel cab, and steel truck frames.

THE MALLETS, 1904–20

ABOUT THIS TIME, A SIGNIFICANT EUROPEAN DEVELOPMENT IN LOCOMOTIVE DESIGN BEGAN TO INTEREST AMERICAN ENGINEERS. THIS WAS THE ARTICULATED, OR DUPLEX, TYPE OF LOCOMOTIVE, INVENTED BY THE FRENCH ENGINEER ANATOLE MALLET AND PATENTED BY HIM IN 1885.

The articulated, or duplex, locomotive comprised two engine units fed by a common boiler. The rear engine was mounted rigidly to the locomotive's frame, while the forward unit was pivoted to the first. The result was a very powerful machine.

Briefly, the Mallet locomotive may be described as two engine units supplied with steam from a single boiler, one engine unit being attached rigidly to the locomotive bed, while the other, the forward unit, is connected to the first by a vertical hinge joint. Mallet's original thinking had been to make this a compound locomotive, with the cylinders of the rear, fixed unit receiving steam at boiler pressure and exhausting into the cylinders of the front unit.

The natural conservatism of early 20th-century American locomotive engineers restricted innovation to the addition of more and more wheels, fed from ever larger boilers. Some 10- and even 12-coupled-wheel designs resulted. It was J.E. Muhlfeld, the Baltimore & Ohio's superintendent of motive power, spurred on by the B & O's president, who introduced the Mallet locomotive to the United States. This was to have far-reaching consequences.

The B & O was working trains of 2,000 tons over the Alleghenies, and three "Consolidation" locomotives were needed—one hauling, two pushing—to work such a train over the Sand Patch gradient.

This restored 2-6-6-2 Mallet type locomotive was built in 1928 by Baldwin for the Weyhauser Lumber Company in Washington State. Today, it sees service on a tourist line in the Black Hills.

Muhlfeld calculated that he could use a Mallet to replace two of the locomotives and crews, and reap the benefits of higher thermal efficiency with compounding. He designed an 0-6-6-0 Mallet and ordered it from the American Locomotive Company (ALCO). It was delivered in 1904—just in time to be exhibited at the St. Louis Exposition. At the time, it was the largest locomotive in the world (if only briefly), and weighed 167.25 short tons.

Muhlfeld's Mallet incorporated a number of firsts. It introduced U.S. railroads to the Walschaerts valve gear (until then, Stephenson's link-motion had been the normal type); it employed steam assisted reversing gear; and (later) it was fitted with an early form of mechanical stoker. On test on the Sand Patch grade, No. 2400 easily accomplished the task normally undertaken by two "Consolidations" and burned a third less coal. Indeed, one authority on articulated locomotives claims a 38 percent saving between 1905 and 1910.

Having no separate guiding axles, No. 2400—affectionately known as *Old Maud* by its crews, after a fabulously strong strip-cartoon mule of the period—was unstable at speed, so it was confined to pusher work until something even bigger came along. Then it was relegated to switcher work, where it remained in service until 1938.

Baldwin Locomotive Works was not slow in recognizing the benefits of Mallet locomotives, and even profited from a lesson learned from the operation of *Old Maud* on the Sand Patch grade. While it clearly demonstrated the potential of the articulated, compound-type locomotive for sustained running with heavy trains, it was clear that guiding wheels were needed. In 1906/7, Baldwin built 30 2-6-6-2 Mallets for the Great Northern Railway's Cascade Division, which operated through the Rockies. They were designed primarily for head-end service between Spokane and Leavenworth, Washington, but five were reserved for helper service.

Next in the field was the builder of *Old Maud*, ALCO, who delivered to the Erie Railroad three of the biggest Mallets ever made. These too had no leading axle, and were 0-8-8-0s weighing 205.5 tons. So big was the firebox of these locomotives that they were built as camelbacks, the cab being close behind the stack, which was not appreciated by the engineers. Two firemen had to be provided to feed the 100sq. ft (9.3sq.m) of grate—a grate area of about 50sq.ft (4.6sq.m) was considered to be the limit of firing for one fireman—and they rode in a very rudimentary shelter behind the firebox. These locomotives were used on the road up to Gulf Summit grade, east of the Susquehanna, Pennsylvania.

The use of two firemen was not economic and gave rise to the invention of the mechanical stoker. A design was developed for the Pennsylvania Railroad in 1905, but it was about 1920 before satisfactory models were in general use. The Archimedes' screw provided the answer. Placed in a trough or pipe, the spiral screw was driven by a small steam motor and carried coal from the locomotive's tender to the grate. One slight disadvantage of mechanical stokers was that only small-size coal could be used, but means were soon found to obtain the necessary size of coal by grading.

As one road adopted the Mallet, so others with severe gradients soon followed suit, and it was not long before even bigger locomotives were being built. Another attraction, of course, was that train weights and lengths could be increased if Mallets were used for head-end power, with another Mallet as pusher on steep grades. The limit to the size of locomotive was the restriction placed on the diameter (and length) of the boiler that could be accommodated. Some rather strange beasts appeared, but in the end, these gave way to reason. In all, it is estimated, that approximately 3,100 Mallet locomotives were built for service on American railroads.

To some extent, the spectacular success of the various Mallet designs overshadowed the steady progress made in improving the "conventional" steam locomotive during the same period. Boiler efficiency was increased by a number of devices, but the invention of the superheater in 1897, by the German engineer Wilhelm Schmidt, was probably the greatest advance in this field.

At best, the steam locomotive is not very efficient at converting energy into power, but the superheater enables much better use of the steam generated in the boiler. The superheater allows the temperature of the steam to be raised without increasing its pressure and, hence, to expand more in the cylinders, so producing more work for the same volume of water evaporated. Increases of 25–30 percent in power output over a similar unsuperheated locomotive can be obtained.

The superheater consists of a reservoir divided into two compartments. The first compartment receives steam from the boiler, feeding it through tubes that run back and forth in the boiler flues. Here the heat of the gases increases the temperature of the steam, which then is fed into the second chamber for supply to the cylinders. Schmidt return-bend superheaters were generally adopted from about 1910.

In Europe, locomotives were developed with inside cylinders as well as outside cylinders, but

The French engineer Anotole Mallet was responsible for the concept of the articulated, or duplex, locomotive. It effectively combined two locomotives in one, thus producing a powerful machine that was ideal for hauling heavy trains.

the extra complication was never popular on North American railroads, since it required more maintenance, which often was more difficult. In the 1920s, there was some interest in three-cylinder locomotives, but again, the extra complexity forced their discontinuance. Mallet locomotives were the exception, but all their cylinders were external. The Mallet compound was an additional complication, and it had a disadvantage: the fact that the high- and low-pressure cylinders were not coupled led to "choking" when the two sets of wheels did not synchronize, so Mallets were never suitable for high-speed haulage.

One of three Mallets supplied to the Erie RR by ALCO. The fire grate of these locomotives was so large that they had to be built as camelbacks.

This 0-8-8-0 Mallet type of the New York Central RR is of conventional design. Note the massive cylinders.

CAR DESIGN, 1900–25

EARLY PASSENGER CARS HAD BEEN OF WOODEN CONSTRUCTION,

BUT THE PROJECTED OPENING OF THE MANHATTAN TERMINALS,

APPROACHED BY RELATIVELY DEEP TUNNELS, AND THE

INCREASING COST OF LUMBER, PROMPTED THE DESIGN OF MORE

FIRE-RESISTANT PASSENGER CARS IN 1904.

The Pennsylvania RR decided to abandon wooden cars on grounds of safety; in any case, by this time, suitable lumber was becoming scarce and had increased in price dramatically, so the change to steel cars also made a lot of sense economically. By 1907, a practical design had been developed and tested, and large-scale production began. By 1913, no more wooden cars were being produced for domestic service. Despite this, the wooden car was slow to disappear; even in 1920, some 60 percent of the nation's car fleet was still made of lumber, and a few wooden cars remained in commuter service as late as the 1950s.

One result of the introduction of steel cars was a dramatic increase in train weight. Cars were longer (up to 80ft/24m), and although they looked very similar to the wooden cars they replaced, the designs involved the fitting of massive underframe support sills. Added to this was the use of concrete floors for fire resistance,

Many specialized freight cars were developed. This is an early refrigerated boxcar.

cast-steel endframes, and cast-steel, six-wheel trucks with massive wrought-steel wheels. The result was a very heavy car of 80–90 tons, which would last 50 or more years in service. This all taxed motive power and increased fuel costs. During the 1920s, an effort was made to reduce car weights by replacing steel with aluminum, but this was largely confined to commuter cars. Heavyweight steel cars remained for a long time on long-distance trains.

Freight cars too were growing in size and weight. In 1900, the standard open-top hopper car was constructed from riveted steel plates and had a capacity of 50 tons, a weight when empty of 21 tons, and a volume of 2,035cu.ft (57.6cu.m). Between 1912 and 1925, the coal car grew from 50 through 70 to 100 tons capacity. The 100-ton car had an empty weight of 30 tons, giving a weight on each axle of 32.5 tons—a punishing load on rail joints, even though freight train speeds at the time were relatively low, at around 35mph (56km/h). A wide variety of freight cars were in use: flatcars, boxcars, tankcars, refrigerated boxcars, gondola cars, and covered hopper cars. Boxcars came in various sizes, but typically were of 40–50 tons capacity and up to 60ft (18m) long.

Refrigerator cars were already in existence in 1878, and at first they used water-ice as the refrigerant. Automated ice-bunker systems had been developed by the early 1900s and could carry a 30-ton load plus 5 tons of ice. A car of this type weighed up to 65 tons.

Steel railroad cars were much safer than their wooden predecessors, but they increased train weights considerably.

This steel built railroad car has a rear, open air, observation deck, where passengers could stand and admire the view with only a railing preventing them from plumeting to the tracks as the train sped onward.

INDUSTRIAL TURMOIL

THROUGHOUT THEIR HISTORY, U.S. RAILROADS HAVE BEEN
INVOLVED IN LABOR DISPUTES, BUT THE WORST OCCURRED
TOWARD THE END OF THE 19TH CENTURY AND IN THE YEARS
FOLLOWING WORLD WAR I.

I n the early 1990s, workers in U.S. industry were forming unions to protect their rights. Many employers of the time had little respect or sympathy for their employees, and tried their utmost to keep wages low. Not surprisingly, this led to discontent among workers, and on occasion they expressed that discontent by walking off the job, sometimes with violent consequencies. In 1892, for example, a failure to agree terms between management and workers at the Carnegie Steel plant in Homestead, just

The Carnegie Steel plant at Homestead, near Pittsburgh, Pennsylvania, dominated the town. In 1892, there was a strike by workers over pay and conditions, which led to a bloody confrontation with Pinkerton men hired to break their blockade. In time, the workers returned, but to lower wages and longer hours. Andrew Carnegie, owner of the plant, was roundly condemned for his treatment of the steel workers and spent much of the rest of his life making philanthropic gestures to atone.

outside Pittsburgh, led to a 13-hour gun battle between strikers and strikebreaking Pinkerton detectives. Three detectives and seven steel workers lost their lives. Eventually, the National Guard was called in to quell the trouble. Workers were evicted from their company owned homes and many were arrested. Such tactics broke the strike and prevented union organization within the steel industry for 40 years.

In June 1893, the Stock Market crashed, setting off what became known as the Panic of 1893, which led to five years of severe depression. Many businesses went under and vast numbers were put out of work; over half of U.S. railroads became bankrupt. At George Pullman's sleeping-car

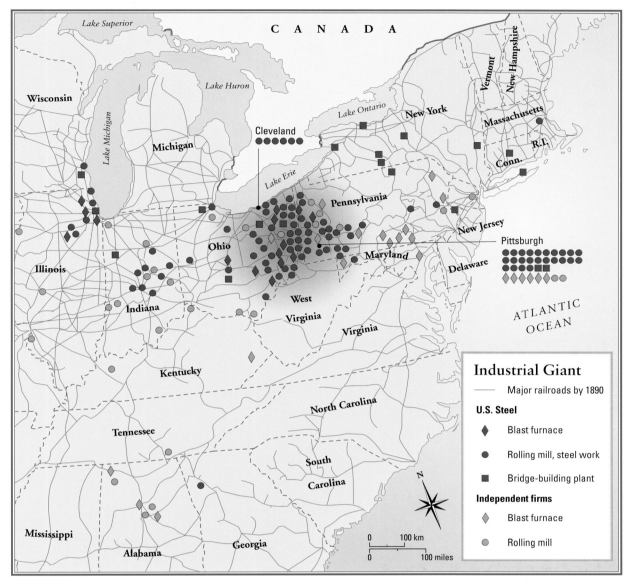

Lake Superior

Lake Huron

Lake Ontario

Lake Michigan

Lake Erie

Wisconsin

Michigan

Cleveland

New York

Massachusetts

Vermont

New Hampshire

R.I.

Conn.

Pennsylvania

Illinois

Ohio

Indiana

New Jersey

Pittsburgh

Maryland

Delaware

West Virginia

Virginia

ATLANTIC OCEAN

Kentucky

North Carolina

Tennessee

South Carolina

N

Mississippi

Alabama

Georgia

0   100 km

0   100 miles

Industrial Giant

—— Major railroads by 1890

U.S. Steel

◆ Blast furnace

● Rolling mill, steel work

■ Bridge-building plant

Independent firms

◆ Blast furnace

● Rolling mill

By 1900, aided in no small part by the railroads, the United States had become an industrial giant. The major steel manufacturing plants were centered on the Northeast, where the proliferation of roads ensured easy transport of raw materials and finished products.

A contemporary illustration showing troops confronting rioters during the Pullman Boycott—with disastrous consequences.

plant in Chicago, 2,000 of the workforce were dismissed; the remainder faced a reduction in hours and an average cut in wages of 25 percent. The company was also its workers' landlord, having built a town for its employees alongside the plant. Despite the reduction in wages, Pullman refused to reduce their rents to make life a little easier.

Finally, on May 11, 1894, Pullman's workers walked out. Many were members of the American Railway Union (ARU), and they turned to its leader, Eugene Debs, for help. At first, Debs sought to arbitrate between the strikers and Pullman, but the company would not meet the union. The ARU called for a national boycott, which came into effect on June 26, instructing its members to keep the mail moving, but to leave Pullman cars idle.

Within three days, the strike had spread throughout the railroad industry, involving 50,000 workers. Matters took a turn for the worse when a union meeting at Blue Island, Illinois, erupted into violence, the strikers derailing a locomotive and destroying railroad yards. In response, the government obtained an injunction against the strike, allowing federal troops to be sent in to protect the mail. Far from defusing the situation, this prompted angry strikers, again at Blue Island, to obstruct the tracks with baggage cars.

Opposite These contemporary sketches record some of the individuals and events of the Pullman Boycott in and around Chicago. Top, left to right: George Pullman, Cushman Davis, and Eugene Debs. The scenes show a blockade of railcars, individuals applying to become deputies at the U.S. marshal's office, a roundhouse, and deputies trying to move a car at Blue Island.

Soldiers from Company C of the 15th U.S. Infantry, tasked with protecting the U.S. mail during the Pullman Boycott, pose with the train in which they patrolled the tracks.

The strikers' violent behavior turned public opinion against them, and following the arrest of Debs and other union leaders, the strike collapsed on July 11, with the only stipulation that workers be rehired in their previous jobs. In fact, many were not taken back. Moreover, Pullman workers were forced to sign agreements that they would not join a union on pain of dismissal.

Between 1898 and the beginning of World War I, many railroads recovered from the hard times of the Panic of 1893. During the war, the railroads had been under the control of the U.S. Railroad Administration, which had increased railroad workers' wages substantially. The railroads were returned to private ownership in 1920—with a huge deficit, rolling-stock shortages, and high labor costs. Another economic turndown postwar compounded the problems. With falling prices, the railroads sought to reduce wages, seeing the labor surplus caused by the depression as a means of breaking the power of the unions.

To pressurize its workers, the Pennsylvania RR contracted out some locomotive repair work to Baldwin, even though its own shops could have handled the work. Other railroads followed suit. Then, in June 1922, the Railway Labor Board (RLB) allowed a 7 percent reduction in shopworkers' wages. When it came into effect on July 1, railroad workers across the country walked out. It was the beginning of the Great Railroad Shopworkers Strike of 1922. Within three days, the RLB had given permission to the railroads to hire strikebreakers, promising government protection. The railroads housed the strikebreakers in barbed-wire compounds protected by armed guards. These became the focus of abusive confrontations between strikers and "scabs." The confrontations escalated from abuse to violence. Then, on July 8, came the news that strikers had been shot and killed in Buffalo and Cleveland. Groups of strikers began beating up strikebreakers and subjecting them to mock lynchings. There were shootings too.

The government obtained injunctions to make support of the strike a criminal offense. Federal marshals, sent to arrest strikers, were stoned. Trains were sabotaged, equipment damaged, and there were bombings. In one town in Texas, martial law was declared. When federal troops put down the trouble, more were sent to other railroad shop towns in Texas.

By August, with much rolling stock in a poor state of repair, crews were refusing to operate trains they considered unsafe, while their unions were threatening to bring everything to a halt. Finally, using interference with the U.S. mail as a reason, the government obtained an injunction that made it a criminal offense to interfere with trains and equipment, to prevent their repair, intimidate others, to congregate near railroad facilities, or ask anyone to stop work. So wide ranging was this injunction that it broke the strike, albeit gradually. It ended in 1928, when the last strikers returned to work on the Pennsylvania RR. The outcome of the strike was the Railway Labor Act of 1926, which stipulated that both sides in a dispute should go through a rigorous mediation procedure in an effort to prevent strikes. No more would labor disputes end in violent confrontations and even murder, but rather would be entrusted to the argument of lawyers.

Transcontinental Railroads, 1900–20

IN THE EARLY 20TH CENTURY, THE ESTABLISHED
NORTH AMERICAN TRANSCONTINENTAL RAILROADS
WERE EXTENDING THE REACH OF THEIR LINES. ON
BOTH SIDES OF THE CANADIAN BORDER, YET MORE
TRACKS WERE BEING LAID TO THE PACIFIC COAST.

The Northern Securities grouping of the Great Northern, Northern Pacific, and Chicago, Burlington & Quincy railroads, planned by banker J.P. Morgan and railroad pioneer J.J. Hill, finally came to fruition in 1901. The inclusion of the Burlington, as the CB&Q was known, gave the GN and NP access to Chicago and many other cities in the Midwest, as well as in the East. The other transcontinental railroads also had their own preferred partners among the Midwestern grange railroads. The Union Pacific, for example, had a connection with the Chicago & North Western; the Southern Pacific worked with the Rock Island; while the Santa Fe had its own grange lines. There was one major grange line that did not have any kind of transcontinental connection, however, and that was the Chicago, Milwaukee & St. Paul Railroad, which was known simply as the St. Paul in those days, but subsequently became more famous as the Milwaukee Road.

The way things were shaping up, it looked as though the St. Paul would be surrounded and cut off from routes to the Pacific coast. Moreover, finding a new, viable route to the Northwest appeared a difficult prospect; the Great Northern and Northern Pacific had taken the best. Even so, in 1905, work began on the St. Paul's Pacific Extension. The railroad already had a line that ran from Minneapolis/St.

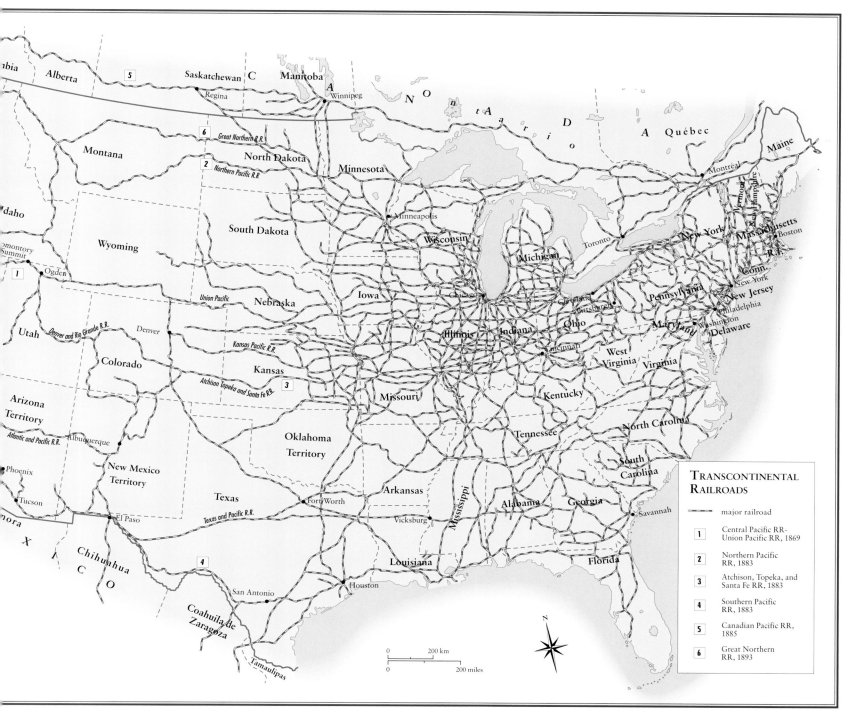

TRANSCONTINENTAL RAILROADS

——— major railroad

1 Central Pacific RR-
Union Pacific RR, 1869

2 Northern Pacific
RR, 1883

3 Atchison, Topeka, and
Santa Fe RR, 1883

4 Southern Pacific
RR, 1883

5 Canadian Pacific RR,
1885

6 Great Northern
RR, 1893

Paul to Aberdeen in northern South Dakota. This was the jumping off point for the new route. Track was laid across the southwestern corner of North Dakota and into Montana, passing through Miles City and across the Continental Divide to Butte. Because the Great Northern and Northern Pacific had already occupied the only suitable gap between the Selkirk and Bitterroot Mountains, the St. Paul was forced to push its way through the Bitterroots, boring numerous tunnels and building endless soaring trestle bridges. More engineering challenges presented themselves as the railroad crossed the Cascades through Snoqualmie Pass. The line continued across Washington State to Seattle, while at Tacoma, the St. Paul built a seaport so that ships could berth alongside waiting freight cars. The line was completed in 1909, a golden spike ceremony being held at Garrison, Montana. As with other transcontinental

By 1900, the eastern half of the United States was crowded with railroads, while there were many transcontinental lines providing a choice of east–west links. Finding another route to the Pacific, particularly in the Northwest, was a difficult prospect for the Chicago, Milwaukee, St. Paul & Pacific.

The Rocky Mountains were a major barrier to railroad companies pushing westward. Finding a route through was difficult and often required innovative feats of engineering. Here, the peaks of the Rocky Mountains of Alberta, Canada, dominate the turquoise waters of Moraine Lake, elev. 6,265ft (1,910m), located in what is now Banff National Park.

lines, the St. Paul opened up the country it ran through. It encouraged settlers to fill the new towns along its route, opening land offices in the eastern states and in Europe. Thousands flocked to the new lands, which seemed to hold out so much promise. That promise was fulfilled for a few years, but in 1917, Montana entered a prolonged dry spell and crops began to fail. Many farmers lost their livelihoods, and things would get worse: the Great Depression was just around the corner.

The St. Paul was not faring well either. Its port at Tacoma had not attracted the business expected, while the Great Northern and Northern Pacific had a stranglehold on connections west of the Twin Cities; they insisted that any traffic bound for their yards on the Pacific coast be passed to them at St. Paul to be hauled west. Only in Butte, Montana, and Washington State could the St. Paul interchange cars with another major railroad, the Union Pacific. Moreover, 600 miles of the line had been electrified, and the company was locked into a deal with the Montana Power Company that obliged it to buy a certain amount of power, whether it needed it or not. The Pacific Extension had been financed with loans, and the repayments were crippling. Eventually, in 1925, the Chicago, Milwaukee & St. Paul became bankrupt. It resurfaced in 1928, then fell victim to the Great Depression in 1935, not appearing again until after World War II.

In the meantime, other lines were being built to extend the transcontinental network. For example, in 1907, the Union Pacific completed a connection between Los Angeles and Salt Lake City in Utah. In 1909, the Western Pacific was completed between Salt Lake City and Oakland, California.

In 1904, following a suit by the government, the Supreme Court had ordered that Northern Securities be broken up, although the Great Northern and Northern Pacific retained a 48 percent share each of the Burlington and continued to cooperate closely. That cooperation included building the Spokane, Portland & Seattle Railway, extending their lines to Portland.

Another major transcontinental railroad grouping had come about in 1900, when E.H. Harriman had put the Union Pacific and Southern Pacific under common management. Like Northern Securities, however, the Supreme Court took a dim view and ordered that they be split, which occurred in 1913.

In Canada, meanwhile, two rivals to the Canadian Pacific had struck out west-northwest from Winnipeg, both heading for Edmonton, Alberta. The Canadian Northern (started in 1899) and the Grand Trunk Pacific (begun in 1903) strove to open up different parts of the intervening country, but they were never very far apart. The Canadian Northern ran abreast of the Canadian Pacific in the

Chicago,
Milwaukee,
St. Paul & Pacific

▬▬ Double or dual track

— Single track

canyons west of Kamloops and eventually reached Vancouver, while the Grand Trunk Pacific continued northwest through virgin territory to Prince Rupert. Both of these railroads, and the lines connecting with them from the East at Winnipeg, fell into financial difficulties and were kept going during World War I by substantial government loans. In 1922, all of these lines were amalgamated with the Grand Trunk and the Intercolonial to form the huge Canadian National Railways, a publicly owned company that worked alongside the privately owned Canadian Pacific.

The Chicago, Milwaukee, St. Paul & Pacific Railroad pushed its line westward from Aberdeen in South Dakota. After reaching Butte in Montana, it was forced to forge a route through several mountain ranges on its way to Seattle in Washington State.

During an icy blizzard, the first double header steam train prepares to go through the Chicago, Milwaukee, St. Paul & Pacific Railroad pass, cut through the Bitter Root Mountains, Idaho, in 1909, transporting a carload of workers with little more than shovels.

U.S. Railroads During World War I, 1914–18

THE UNITED STATES RAILROADS FACED A MASSIVE INCREASE IN FREIGHT BUSINESS DURING WORLD WAR I. WHILE ROLLING STOCK AND FUEL COSTS ROSE, THERE WAS A SHORTAGE OF LABOR AS MEN LEFT TO JOIN THE ARMY. THE GOVERNMENT TOOK CONTROL OF THE RAILROADS FOR THE DURATION OF THE HOSTILITIES.

The first effect of World War I on the American economy was to create a remarkable boom in exports, from which the railroads were able to benefit by means of considerable increases in the amount of freight they carried. At first there was a massive increase of 260 percent in the freight that was exported via the railroads, and then a further 37 percent by the time the United States entered the war in 1917.

The Commerce Law prevented the railroads from reaping the true benefits of this increase in traffic, however, unlike profiteers in industry, who lost no time in increasing their prices and thereby doubling or even trebling their profits.

During the course of the war, the prices of locomotives doubled, the cost of passenger cars rose by 18 percent and of freight cars by 50 percent, while the price of fuel rose by over 80 percent. On August 29, 1916, Congress passed an act authorizing the president, in time of war and "through the Secretary of War," to assume total control of the transportation system. America entered the war on April 6, 1917,

Troop trains made use of whatever vehicles were to hand. Freight cars were often pressed into service.

Opposite A novel form of military transport. This highway truck has had its conventional wheels and tires replaced by flanged steel wheels.

With many men having enlisted in the Army or Navy, the railroads had to employ women to help service locomotives and rolling stock.

A World War I propaganda poster urging railroad shop workers to contribute to the war effort by keeping locomotives running.

and five days later, a group of senior railroad executives pledged their cooperation in the war effort and created the Railroad War Board (RWB). Among the problems the board had to face were labor difficulties caused by employees rushing to join the army, and a huge amount of freight for the war effort that choked every eastern rail yard and port.

The RWB's efforts to deal with these problems failed, and on December 28, 1917, President Woodrow Wilson placed the nation's railroads under the control of the government through the United States Railroad Administration (USRA) agency, appointing his son-in-law, William G. McAdoo, then Secretary of the Treasury, as Director General of Railroads. Some years before, McAdoo had been in charge of construction of the Hudson & Manhattan Railroad, now the Port Authority Trans-Hudson (PATH), between New York City, Hoboken and Newark, New Jersey.

Among other acts, McAdoo discharged all railroad presidents, eliminated all competition between railroads, and awarded a flat increase of $20 per month to all employees who earned less than $46 a month. At the same time, it was decreed that the railroads should accept the average of their net operating income for the three-year period ending June 30, 1917, "as just and reasonable compensation." The fact that the lean year to June 30, 1915, had been included effectively robbed the railroads of at least $100 million a year while the guarantee lasted.

Additionally, the USRA ordered and assigned to the railroads more than 2,000 new locomotives and 50,000 freight cars of standardized design.

When America entered World War I, there were some 240,000 miles (386,232km) of track in the United States. Rolling stock and railroad rights-of-way were being taxed to their utmost, and while there was a shortage of around 117,000 freight cars, some 700 miles (1,127km) of double track were added, together with a large number of new and enlarged freight yards.

Federal control of the railroads came to an end

Keep 'em Going!

Every bad order Locomotive is a Prussian soldier. Every live Locomotive is an American soldier. Let us get on top of the Prussian Locomotives and make American soldiers out of them."

on September 1, 1920, when they reverted to fully regulated, private operation. The result of nearly three years of government management, however, was an enormous deficit. The country's railroads were then desperately short of rolling stock, while their labor costs had risen significantly.

The USRA's net operating income for the 26 months of control fell short of the guaranteed payments by an incredible $714 million; damage claims amounted to an additional $677 million.

One beneficial legacy of the war years and governmental control of the country's railroads were the 12 standardized locomotive designs to which wartime and postwar locomotives were built—some even as late as 1944.

Although mounting artillery pieces on railroad flatcars made them easy to move, it did restrict the direction in which they could be aimed.

Railroad passenger cars were converted into makeshift mobile hospital wards to care for the war wounded.

President Woodrow Wilson (top) ordered that the railroads be placed under the control of the government during World War I. This was done through the United States Railroad Administration; Wilson's son-in-law, William G. McAdoo (above) was appointed Director General of Railroads.

By 1916, U.S. railroads had a combined route length 254,037 miles (408,822km).

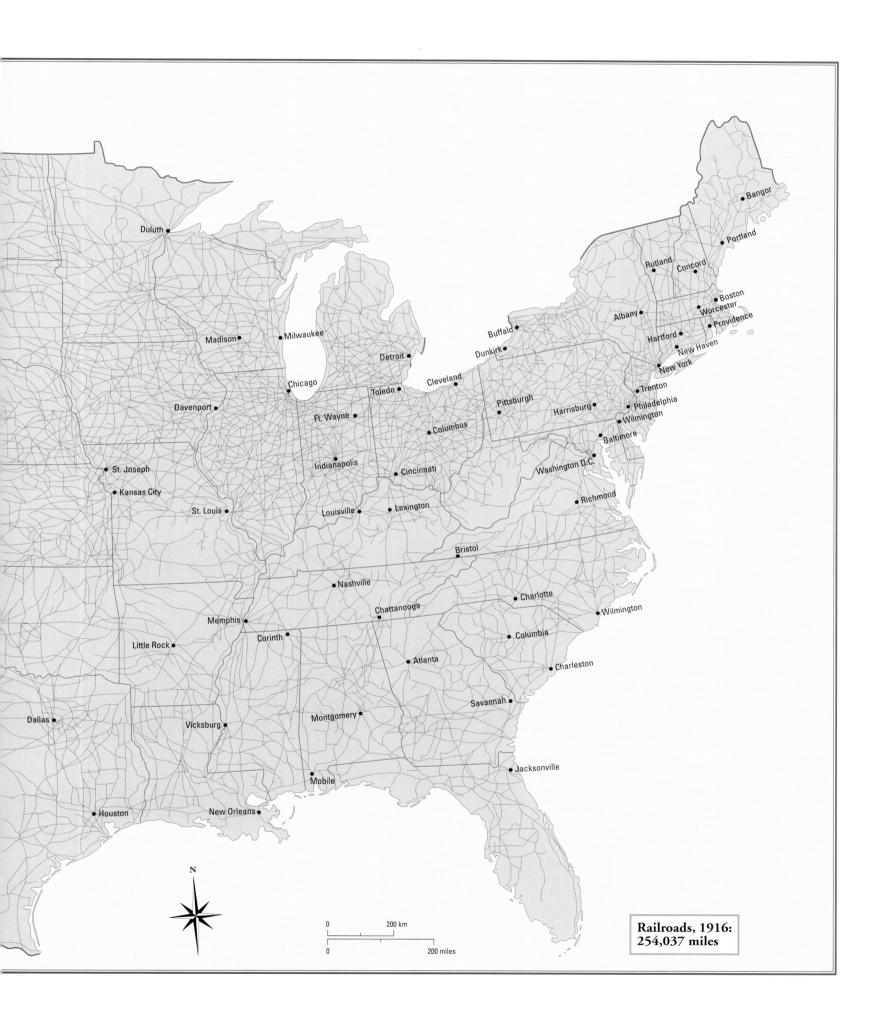

Railroads, 1916:
254,037 miles

ICC REGROUPING AND ELECTRIFICATION, 1903–30

ATTEMPTING TO EVEN OUT COMPETITION AFTER WORLD WAR I, THE INTERSTATE COMMERCE COMMISSION PREPARED A PLAN TO COMBINE THE RAILROADS INTO A NUMBER OF GROUPS. MEANWHILE, ELECTRIFICATION WAS SEEN AS THE ANSWER TO OVERCOMING SOME OF THE OBSTACLES TO STEAM OPERATION.

In 1920, Congress asked the Interstate Commerce Commission (ICC) to prepare a plan for grouping the railroads while at the same time preserving competition and existing routes of trade. The aim was to create some 19 groups from existing railroads in such a way that the cost of transportation on competing routes would be the same—or, to quote the ICC, to "equitably parcel out the weak sisters."

It was 1929 before the commission published its recommendations. Broadly, they were that subsidiaries would remain with their parent companies, short lines would be assigned to the connecting trunk line, and affiliates of the Canadian roads would remain with either Canadian National or Canadian Pacific; a few railroads were assigned to joint ownership of more than one system. The plan would have resulted in the following main railroad companies: Boston & Maine, New Haven, New York Central, Pennsylvania, Baltimore & Ohio, Chesapeake & Ohio-Nickel Plate, Wabash-Seaboard Air Line, Atlantic Coast Line, Southern, Illinois Central, Chicago & North Western, Great Northern-Northern Pacific, Milwaukee Road, Burlington, Union Pacific, Southern Pacific, Santa Fe, Missouri Pacific, Rock Island-Frisco

Nobody was happy; after much agonizing and many proposed changes, some of which were the result of altered circumstances, Congress withdrew its original request in 1940.

Electrification had never played a major part on American railroads (apart from the special tunnel

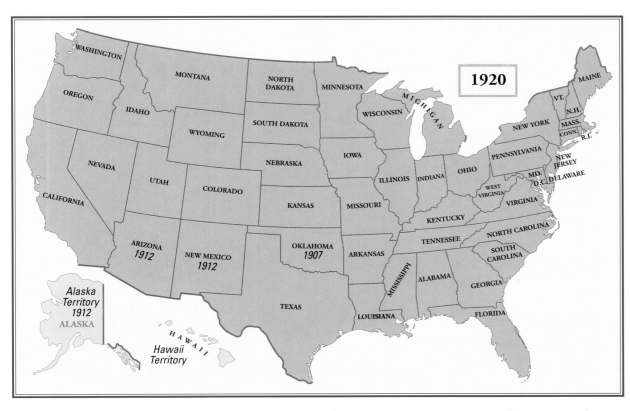

By 1920, growth in the western United States, encouraged by the existence of the railroads, ensured that Arizona, New Mexico, and Oklahoma were granted statehood.

schemes mentioned already) and was confined mainly to mountain sections or urban areas, where it could be justified by traffic density.

Following the New York Legislature Act of 1903, the New Haven RR chose to electrify from Woodlawn, New York, to New Haven, with alternating current at 11 kilovolts, 25Hz, single phase with overhead conductors. Before the turn of the century, the New Haven, which was a heavy-duty, high-traffic-density railroad, had electrified some branch lines using low-voltage direct current. To work into the NYV terminal, its electric locomotives were designed also to operate from 600 volts direct current with a third-rail pickup. Electric operation began in 1907. It was eminently successful and later extended.

A gearless, bipolar electric locomotive belonging to the Milwaukee Road. Built by General Electric during World War I, these locomotives made use of low-power electric motors, the armatures being attached directly to the axles. The result was a unique and silent machine.

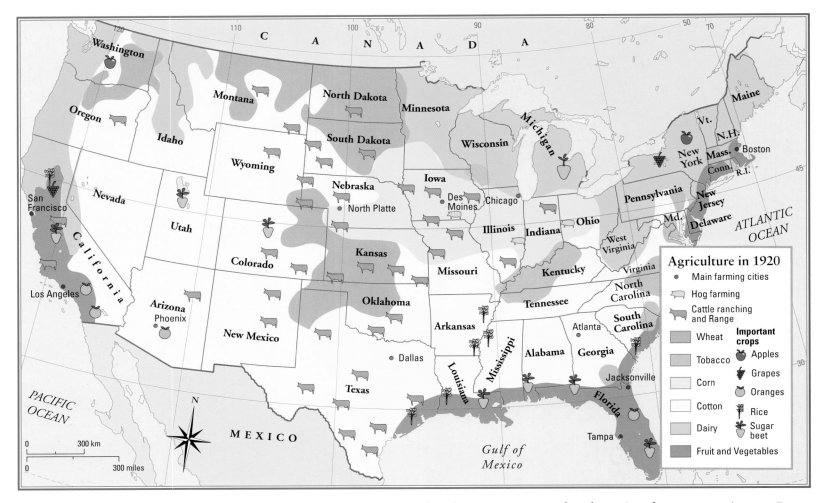

Agriculture in 1920

● Main farming cities

Hog farming

Cattle ranching and Range

Wheat

Tobacco

Corn

Cotton

Dairy

Fruit and Vegetables

Important crops

🍎 Apples

🍇 Grapes

🍊 Oranges

Rice

Sugar beet

By 1920, wide swathes of the United States were being put to a variety of agricultural uses. The railroads were an essential method of shipping produce from one part of the country to markets in other parts.

The Butte, Anaconda & Pacific Railroad was a mining railroad serving the copper mines at Butte, Montana. By 1911, it employed a considerable amount of electrical plant in the mines and decided to electrify its rail operations to take advantage of the economy of electric traction. The system of electrification was 2,400 volts direct current with overhead conductors. It opened in 1913 and continued for many years.

In 1915, the Norfolk & Western electrified 56 miles (90km) of line in the region of Iaeger and Blufield,

in the southwest corner of West Virginia, to remove the need to run steam locomotives over 2 percent grades and through the Elkhorn Tunnel, both of which were severe obstacles to steam operation. Electrification produced an increase in line capacity and lasted for 35 years, by which time, a realignment had obviated the need. The system was alternating current at 11 kilovolts, 25Hz, single phase.

In 1925, the Virginian RR began electric operation between Roanoke, Virginia, and Mullens, West Virginia, a section notoriously difficult for steam operation, which in 1916 was worked unsuccessfully by the 377-ton, 2-8-8-8-4 triple Mallet. Electrification enabled heavier trains to be run twice as fast as steam. Again, the system was

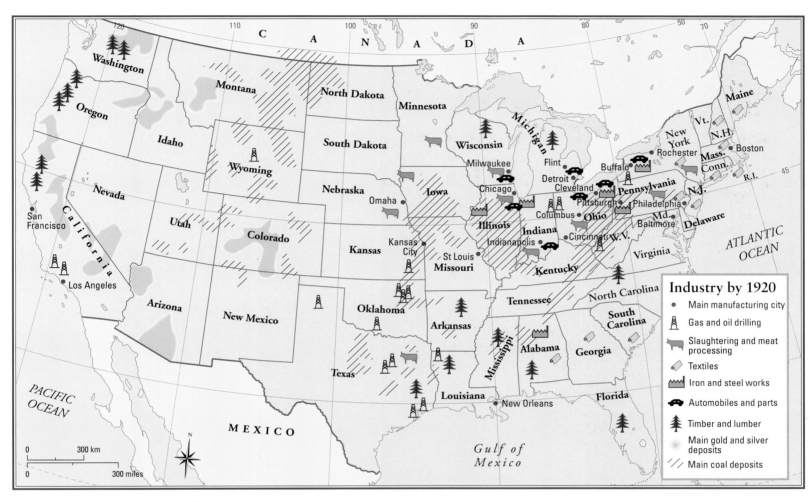

Industry by 1920

- Main manufacturing city
- Gas and oil drilling
- Slaughtering and meat processing
- Textiles
- Iron and steel works
- Automobiles and parts
- Timber and lumber
- Main gold and silver deposits
- Main coal deposits

alternating current at 11 kilovolts, 25 Hz, single phase.

Electrification in the mountainous region of the Continental Divide was an attractive proposition, and in 1916, the Milwaukee Road put 30 electric locomotives into service on freight, followed by another 12 on passenger trains. The first section, from Harlowtown, Montana, to Avery in northern Idaho was followed by the section from Othello, Washington, to Tacoma, with a northward branch to Seattle. In nine years, the Milwaukee Road produced savings of $12 million over steam operation. In this case, the system chosen was 3,000 volts direct current.

The Pennsylvania terminal line into New York City was electrified initially (1910) with third-rail direct current, at the time principally to conform with that of its subsidiary company, the Long Island RR. In 1915, the Pennsylvania electrified the line from Philadelphia to Paoli, Pennsylvania, on the alternating-current system at 11 kilovolts, 25 Hz, single phase. With electrification

Industry, too, needed the railroads for transporting raw materials and finished products. While much of industry was located in the eastern half of the country, where the railroad network was most widespread, important raw materials, such as coal, oil, and lumber were found all over the country.

Specialized freight cars belonging to the Minneapolis, St. Paul & Sault Ste. Marie RR (Soo Line): a slatted boxcar for moving livestock (facing page) and a typical hopper car for minerals, etc (left).

from New York to Washington, D.C., and Philadelphia to Harrisburg, Pennsylvania, in mind, the single-phase system was extended to Wilmington, Delaware, and Trenton, New Jersey. The line into New York City terminal was switched to alternating current to meet the line from Philadelphia. With the exception of surburban services in the New York City area, no further electrification took place until after World War II.

Mention has been made of the growth of the interurban railroads during the early part of the 20th century. Some were successful, and were enlarged and extended. However, the interurban did not enjoy a monopoly for long; the automobile and the extension of paved highways began to make inroads into the interurbans' business for short journeys. The majority of interurbans did not last much beyond 1930, after which the automobile began to eat into the railroad business. In an attempt to fight back, many railroads formed bus and truck subsidiaries; some even entered the airline business. But times were about to become worse—the Great Depression was on its way.

The advent of the motor truck and development of the highway system caused severe problems for the US railroads. Much freight traffic was lost to the trucking companies.

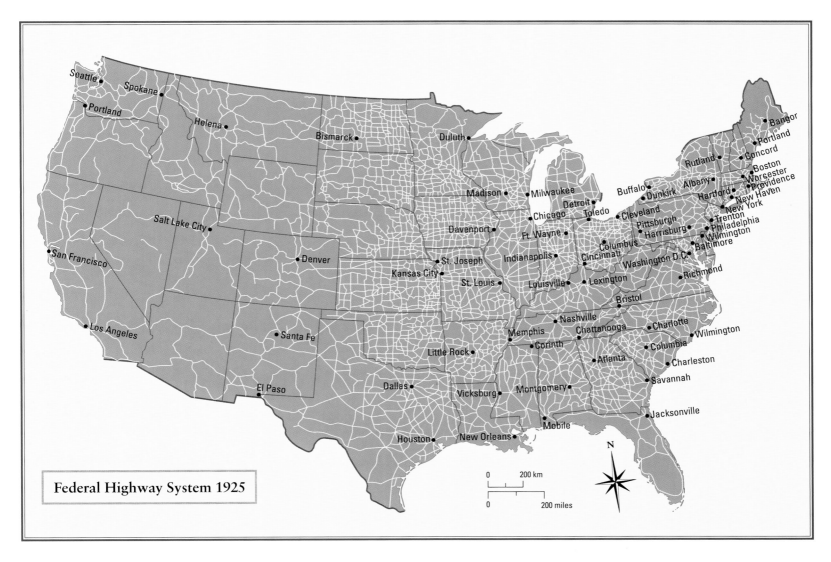

Federal Highway System 1925

0   200 km

0   200 miles

N

As the 1920s progressed, the railroads had to face competition from automobiles and trucks. A spreading highway system meant that they no longer had a monopoly on passenger and freight traffic.

The production-line manufacture of automobiles, pioneered by Henry Ford's Model-T, put the nation on wheels and hit the railroads' passenger traffic hard. In fact, they never recovered.

Fare Dodgers and Safety Cars, 1920s

TOWARD THE END OF THE SECOND DECADE OF THE 20TH CENTURY, STREETCAR OPERATORS WERE LOSING INCOME THROUGH FARE DODGING, WHILE PASSENGER NUMBERS WERE BEGINNING TO DROP. NEW INNOVATIONS IN CAR DESIGN WERE SEEN AS THE ANSWERS TO THEIR PREDICAMENT.

Open streetcars made it easy for passengers to hop on and off—and easy for them to dodge paying the fare. They could be dangerous too.

The costly problem of fare dodging, which had plagued the streetcar operators for years, was addressed by two important innovations—pay-as-you-enter (PAYE) cars and Peter Witt cars. Today, it is hard to imagine any other fare paying method than giving the money for the fare (or showing your transit card) to the driver. Almost all local buses are one-man operated; it is almost as if there was never any other way. When PAYE was first introduced, in Montreal, Canada, in 1904, the idea that a passenger should pay when getting on to a streetcar was revolutionary, but by 1915, the idea had spread to Toronto and soon followed in most parts of North America. Of course, open cars did not lend themselves to the pay-as-you-enter method, which requires passengers to board only through the front entrance, and this was another factor that led to their being phased out.

The second fare payment innovation was the idea of Peter Witt, the commissioner of street railways in Cleveland, Ohio. Immediately after World War I, Witt designed a fare paying scheme and car layout that became standard among many streetcar companies as they sought the most efficient way of getting passengers on and off the cars. This type of car and its cousin, the nearside car, were designed so that people entered a large holding area at the front of the car and left from the center, where the conductor stood. The best seats were in the rear, and to get to them, passengers had to pass the conductor and pay their fares. This logical pattern greatly reduced boarding delays; as a result, Peter Witt cars spread throughout the world. In North America, cities such as Toronto, Buffalo, Baltimore, and Philadelphia had them, but Milan, Italy, was the last city to use them in large numbers, which it still does.

Peter Witt cars, particularly the smaller, later versions, used the most modern techniques to reduce weight, and increase comfort and safety. The cars had such features as steel-arch-roof bodies with improved ventilation, air operated doors, and better motors and performance.

Introduced in 1916, the Birney Safety Car was seen by many operators as the salvation of the streetcar industry, which was under increasing threat from its new competitors, the automobile and the motor bus.

By the late 1910s, despite the phasing out of open-bodied cars and the reduction in fare dodging brought about by pay-as-you-enter and Peter Witt cars, many streetcar systems were struggling for survival. While Henry Ford's Model "T" and its ilk put millions of ordinary people on the road, costs and wages were rising as passenger numbers leveled off. In addition, the motor bus was rapidly gaining in popularity and becoming a serious rival to the streetcar. The industry, with some equipment now 15 or 20 years old, was also suffering from what today would be called an infrastructure problem. So when Charles Birney designed a new type of car for trolley operator Stone & Webster, which promised to solve these problems, manufacturers and transit companies alike rushed to place orders.

The new Birney Safety Car was a clever mixture of modern and antique. Recalling the days of the horse-drawn car, when some companies introduced small one-horse cars called "bobtails" as an

Peter Witt, Commissioner of Street Railways for Cleveland, Ohio, designed this form of car, in which passengers entered at the front and left from the center. That way, they could not avoid passing the conductor.

economy move, the Birney reverted to a short-wheelbase, single-truck layout for minimum weight and low unit cost. New technology included the smooth-arch roof and a stressed-steel-skin construction that routed structural loads through external body panels, thereby reducing the weight and bulk of the frame. A key strategy was one-man operation, which was achieved by the use of the new deadman switch on the controller, and by an interlock on the doors so that the car could not move if they were open. Smaller wheels and high-efficiency, compact motors allowed for a lower overall height. On paper, at least, it seemed a surefire winner, and thousands of Birney Safety Cars were made between 1916 and 1921.

Although the wide, low, well-rounded design gave the cars the appearance of competence, in practice they fell short. The passengers were the first to notice: a rocking, porpoising ride, because of the short wheelbase and light weight, led the public to christen the cars "Galloping Gerties" and "Rocking Horses." Because only one of the two doors would usually be in use at a time, boarding congestion was a constant irritation. The companies found that their problems had been staved off only temporarily by the new cars. Although possibly understandable, it was both shortsighted and naive to believe that a transformation in public attitudes as fundamental as that brought about by the automobile and the bus could be countered by some tinkering with the hardware.

Following their arrival in the 1880s, electric streetcars quickly became the dominant form of urban and interurban transportation. By the 1920s, however, their supremacy was under serious threat from the rise of the automobile and the motor bus. In 1920, almost every city in the United States with a population of more than 10,000 had streetcars. The number of street railway companies had grown to more than 1,000, and annual passenger numbers had risen from around 410 million in 1890 to more than 13.7 billion. During this period, the only serious threat to the dominance of the streetcar had come from "jitneys"—shared-ride taxi services operated with automobiles or small motor buses that ran along fixed routes for a fixed fare of one nickel, or "jitney." The first large-scale use of jitneys began in Los Angeles in 1914, and by the end of that year, the city had more than 800 in service. The jitney craze then spread quickly throughout the United States, and by the end of 1915, the number in use nationwide had topped 62,000.

The streetcar companies, some of which had lost up to half of their passengers to jitneys, reacted swiftly, successfully lobbying their local and state authorities to regulate the operation of these unwelcome rivals. The restrictions placed on the jitney operators included minimum route lengths and hours of operation, limits on routes allowed, and compulsory public-liability insurance, which typically cost them 25–50 percent of their net earnings. The effect on the jitneys was rapid and dramatic: by the end of 1916, there were only 6,000 of the vehicles still operating.

For the streetcar companies, however, the problems created by the jitneys were merely a foretaste of worse troubles ahead, in the form of competition from the automobile and the motor bus. During the 1920s, automobile ownership in the United States—encouraged by rapidly improving vehicle design, falling prices, and paved roads—rose from 8.1 million to 23.1 million. Meanwhile, bus passenger numbers had grown steadily from near-negligible in 1920 to more than 2 billion in 1929. Thanks to this growth in automobile and bus usage, and in some cities the expansion of subway and elevated railway systems, annual streetcar passenger numbers began to fall in 1923. By 1929, they had dropped to about 11.8 billion and clearly were in long-term decline.

Jitneys—unregulated, shared-ride taxi services—caused serious problems for the streetcar companies. Running on fixed routes with a single fixed fare, they took up to half the passengers from some companies. When regulations were put in place to control their operation, however, many soon disappeared.

The Great Depression and Receivership, 1930s

THE RAILROADS WERE NOT IMMUNE FROM THE EFFECTS OF THE DEPRESSION, AND TO MAKE MATTERS WORSE, THEY WERE FACING STIFFER COMPETITION FROM THE AUTOMOBILE AND AIRLINES. MANY BECAME BANKRUPT; IT WAS NOT UNTIL THE POSTWAR BOOM OF THE 1940s THAT THEY BEGAN TO RECOVER.

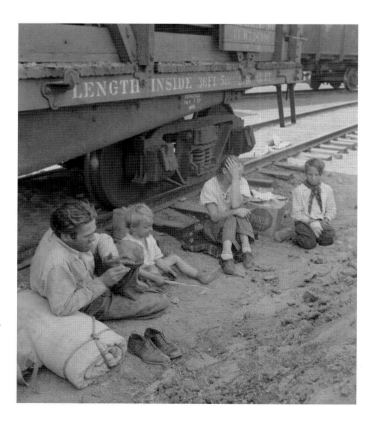

During the Depression years, unemployment soared as companies went out of business. The unemployed headed westward, to California, in the hope of finding work, many "riding the rails" for free by jumping on to freight cars. In the late 1930s, this man traveled with his family and all their possessions in bundles, headed for Toppenish, in the Yakima Valley, Washington, in search of a new life.

The Great Depression, which began with the Stock Exchange crash in October 1929, did not result in an immediate, complete economic collapse, but went in a series of dips and temporary recoveries until the economy reached its low point in 1933. An enduring image of the human cost of the Great Depression is of transients "riding the rails" in search of a new future. At its peak, the army of jobless totaled four million, and hundreds of thousands of these chose to cross the United States in search of work on the great rail networks, such as the Great Northern, Union Pacific, Southern Pacific, and Pennsylvania railroads, many of them following the seasonal harvests.

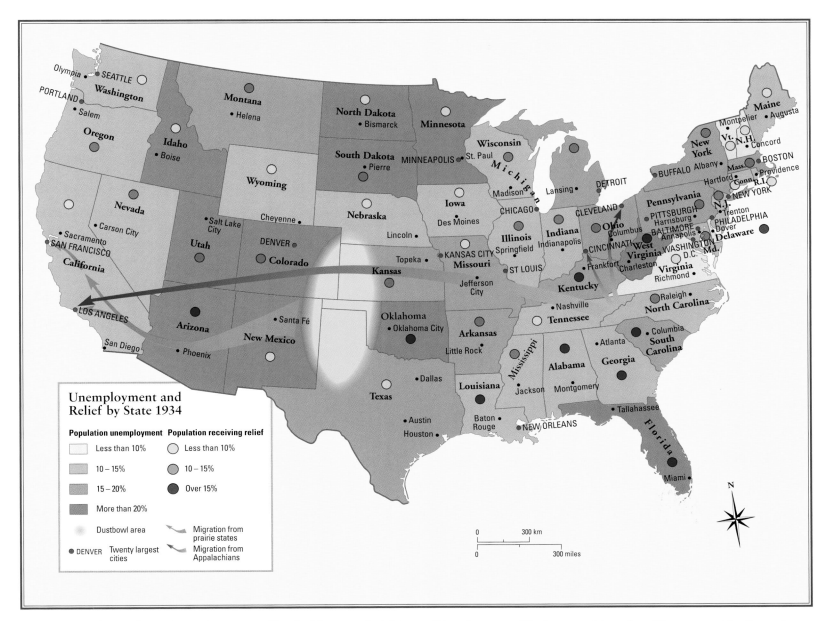

Unemployment and
Relief by State 1934

Population unemployment | Population receiving relief

Less than 10% | Less than 10%

10 – 15% | 10 – 15%

15 – 20% | Over 15%

More than 20%

Dustbowl area

DENVER Twenty largest cities

Migration from prairie states

Migration from Appalachians

0   300 km

0   300 miles

N

For vast numbers, the only option was a "free" ride on a freight car. The chances of being caught and ejected were high—in 1932, the Southern Pacific alone recorded 683,457 trespasses—but for many desperate itinerants, the cost was even higher. According to the Interstate Commerce Commission's annual reports, during the decade 1929–39, 24,647 trespassers were killed and 27,171 were injured on the nation's railroads.

The Depression's financial costs to the railroads were also high, since there was a huge decrease in revenues from both passengers and freight. The results were clear at the Baldwin Locomotive works, which, together with ALCO, accounted for most of the U.S. locomotive building business. As the Depression began to bite, Baldwin's chairman robustly stated, "I have seen the grass, at times, grow six inches high in the Baldwin Locomotive works. It is not six inches high now. Therefore, why worry?" In 1932, however, Baldwin sold only six locomotives. In 1929, it had been considered among the most solid of companies, with assets of over $20 million. In 1934, its assets had dwindled to under $3.5 million, while it made a loss of more than that for the year and was having trouble meeting its interest payments.

The catastrophic effects of the Great Depression in the 1930s are starkly revealed in this map, which traces the dire state of unemployment and governmental relief, and the reaction of desperate people on the move in search of work.

President Hoover had refused to listen to the advice of his Treasury Secretary, Andrew Mellon—"Liquidate labor, liquidate stocks, liquidate the farmers, liquidate real estate..."—since he did not believe that the government should provide direct state aid. Instead, he promoted the idea of "voluntary cooperation" between business and government. However, when it became clear that recovery from the crisis would take much longer than first thought, Hoover put in place a series of programs that were intended to combat the economic and social problems, such as the Emergency Relief Organization, the National Credit Corporation, and the Reconstruction Finance Corporation, which gave billions in aid to

In the throes of the Depression, dust storms wreaked ecological and agricultural havoc on the American and Canadian prairies. A result of decades of intensive farming without crop rotation among cotton, corn and grain farmers, the storms promoted erosion, which was exacerbated by severe drought. As hundreds of tons of topsoil were blown off barren fields, dust clouds blackened the sky all the way to Chicago. An exodus set out from Texas, Arkansas, Oklahoma, and the surrounding Great Plains—many riding the rails— with over 500,000 Americans left homeless. Canadians fled to urban areas such as Toronto. The photograph shows the most devastating storm approaching Stratford, Texas, in 1935, after which the region became known as the Dust Bowl.

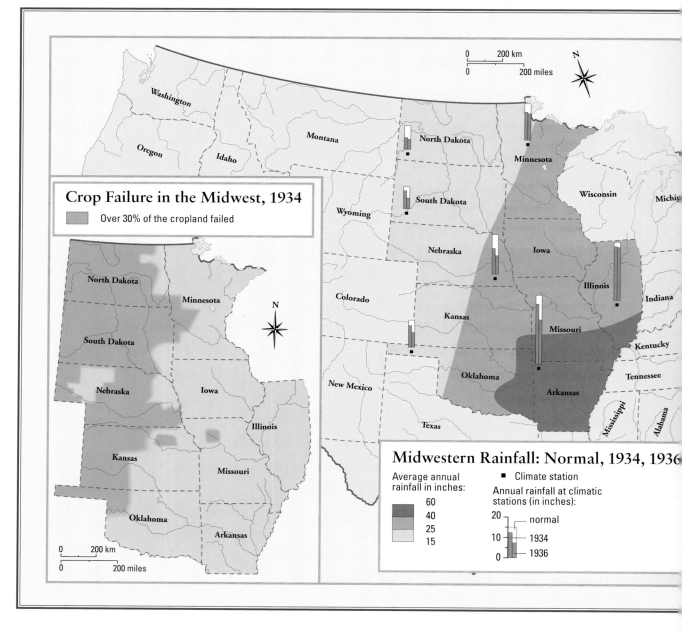

Crop Failure in the Midwest, 1934

Over 30% of the cropland failed

Midwestern Rainfall: Normal, 1934, 1936

Average annual rainfall in inches:

60	
40	
25	
15	

▪ Climate station

Annual rainfall at climatic stations (in inches):

20 — normal
10 — 1934
0 — 1936

state and local government, and made loans to banks, mortgage associations, and other businesses, including the railroads. He also encouraged public works with the aim of creating jobs. As part of this policy, there was an acceleration of the construction schedule of the Boulder Canyon dam, ultimately to be known as the Hoover Dam.

When Hoover's measures failed to improve matters, it was seen as proof that the government needed to take a more active role in the economy to aid recovery. President Roosevelt, newly elected in 1932, blamed the power of big business for causing an unstable economy. His New Deal proposed the remedy of empowering farmers (with aid programs) and labor unions, and increasing taxes on corporate profits. Despite this, the effects of the Great Depression continued throughout the 1930s and until well after the outbreak of World War II. From 1935, however, Roosevelt's Works Progress Administration (WPA), which was formed with the aim of putting people back into work, employed millions of Americans on federal funded projects. Almost three-quarters of this was construction work. The WPA built 650,000 miles (1,046,000km) of highways and streets, 78,000 bridges, and 700 miles

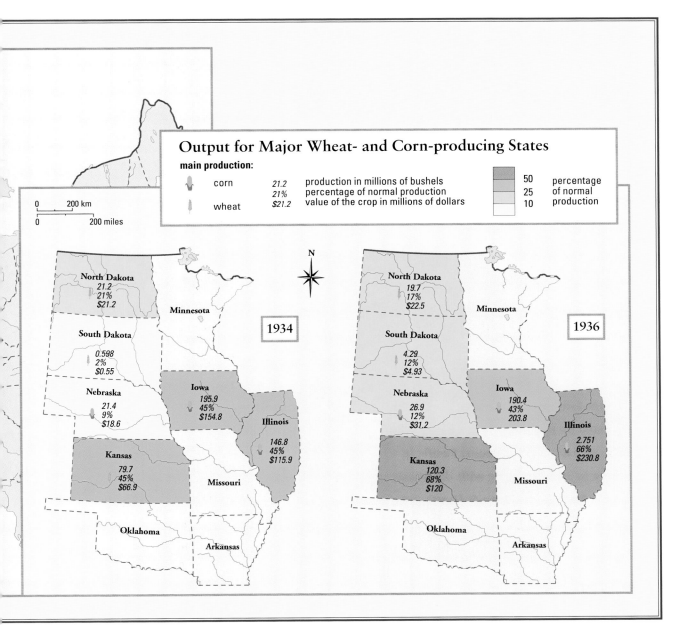

Output for Major Wheat- and Corn-producing States

main production:

corn   21.2   production in millions of bushels
       21%   percentage of normal production
       $21.2 value of the crop in millions of dollars

wheat

50   percentage
25   of normal
10   production

1934

North Dakota
21.2
21%
$21.2

Minnesota

South Dakota
0.598
2%
$0.55

Nebraska
21.4
9%
$18.6

Iowa
195.9
45%
$154.8

Illinois
146.8
45%
$115.9

Kansas
79.7
45%
$66.9

Missouri

Oklahoma

Arkansas

1936

North Dakota
19.7
17%
$22.5

Minnesota

South Dakota
4.29
12%
$4.93

Nebraska
26.9
12%
$31.2

Iowa
190.4
43%
203.8

Illinois
2.751
66%
$230.8

Kansas
120.3
68%
$120

Missouri

Oklahoma

Arkansas

In the mid-1930s, a reduction in rainfall in the Midwest caused serious problems for farmers. Crops failed and livelihoods were destroyed, all adding to the westward move of population.

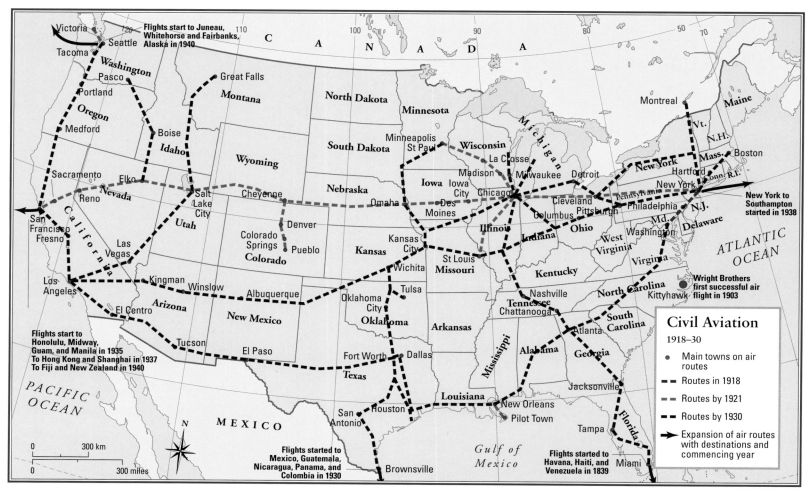

Civil Aviation
1918–30

• Main towns on air routes
--- Routes in 1918
--- Routes by 1921
--- Routes by 1930
➤ Expansion of air routes with destinations and commencing year

As if dealing with the competition from highway transport wasn't enough, after 1918 there was a significant growth in domestic air transport within the United States. This made inroads into the railroads' passenger traffic.

(1,127km) of airport runways. It also constructed 125,000 public buildings and sports facilities, as well as many sewers, dams, and other utilities.

The Great Depression hit the railroads every bit as hard as industry generally. They were under a double burden, however, because of the increased attraction of road and air transport. The effect was inevitable. Business declined; there was less freight and even fewer passengers. Services were cut, and locomotives and cars were put into storage (some were even scrapped). Many railroad corporations became bankrupt, including such major railroads as the Frisco (St. Louis-San Francisco), Missouri-Illinois, Milwaukee Road, and New Haven. The strongest survived, but in a weakened state. By 1939, close to one-third of the United States' total mileage of track belonged to companies in receivership. Their future fortunes were mixed. The Frisco came out of receivership in 1947, a result of its receipts being boosted by revenues from increased traffic during World War II. The Missouri-Illinois was taken under the control of the Missouri Pacific in 1929, when the latter was reorganized, and emerged from bankruptcy in 1944, merging with the Mississippi River & Bonne Terre Railroad in 1945.

The New York, New Haven & Hartford Railroad eventually swallowed up nearly all the railroads in Connecticut, Rhode Island, and southeast Massachusetts, and was a primary connection between many places and New York City. It was a heavy-duty, intense-traffic railroad, more on the European style than American. It operated an intense suburban service out of New York, and had electrified its main line in the 1920s. Despite four-fifths of New Haven's stock being owned by the Pennsylvania RR, and the fact that it had an interest in the Boston & Maine, the Depression played its part here, too, the company

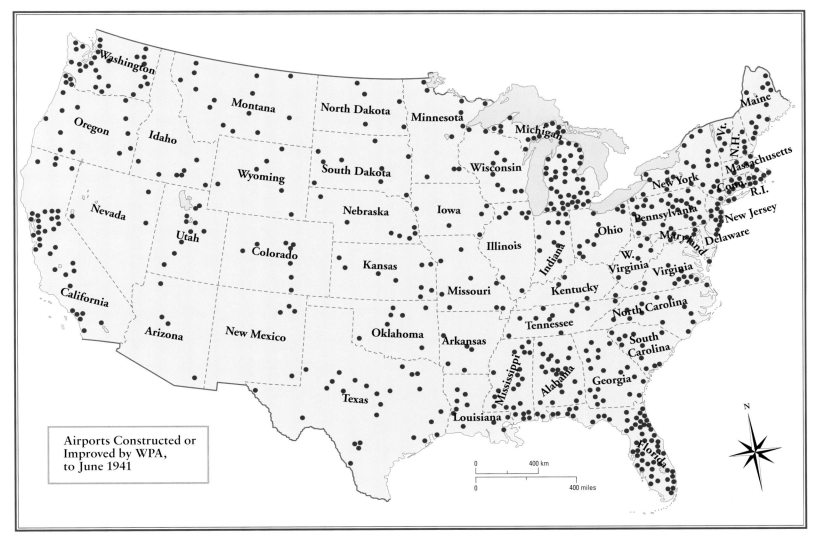

Airports Constructed or
Improved by WPA,
to June 1941

becoming bankrupt in 1935. Reorganization involved pruning much of its branch-line network, and upgrading plant and rolling stock on the main line. In 1938, it introduced "piggyback" services—double stacking containers on flatcars—and it switched to diesel power for many of its mainline trains. Traffic increased considerably during World War II, but it was not until 1947 that the New Haven completed its reorganization. Hardly had this happy state been reached when, in 1948, control passed into the hands of Frederic C. Dumaine, Patrick B. McGinnis, and others. The New Haven's fortunes quickly plummeted to new and greater depths. Experienced executives were dismissed, and new management was hired, leading to turmoil. McGinnis assumed the Presidency in 1954; in 1956, he became president (and, in 1962, chairman) of the Boston & Maine; he resigned in 1963.

Many battles raged between stockholders and management, and some dubious accountancy (which had valued the road at over double its worth) was exposed when McGinnis departed for the Boston & Maine in 1956. It took another six years to get the New Haven back into reorganization, and seven years more before it was healthy enough to be involved in a merger with the Penn Central. McGinnis' financial dealings culminated in a prison sentence for receiving kickbacks on the sale of B & M's streamlined passenger cars, ending his career in railroading. Many other railroads were involved in similar financial wrangles, but these examples illustrate the kind of problems besetting railroads in the late 1930s and the postwar era.

Among the tasks undertaken by the Works Progress Administration during the 1930s was the construction or improvement of airports across the country. These all helped boost air services, at the expense of the railroads.

Streamlined Steam

WHILE THE DEPRESSION TOOK A HEAVY TOLL ON MANY U.S. RAILROADS, SOME WEATHERED THE STORM WITH SUCCESS. THEY TOOK ON NEW ROLLING STOCK, IMPROVED THEIR OPERATING PRACTICES, AND INTRODUCED PRESTIGE, INTER-CITY EXPRESS TRAINS WITH GLAMOROUS NAMES AND SLEEK NEW LOOKS.

Although the Depression hit many railroads hard, there were still success stories. The Union Pacific, for example, enjoyed impeccable credit in the capital markets throughout the Depression, being able to afford new locomotives and even new, streamlined diesel trains, despite the fact that it connected only 36 communities of 10,000 people or more. Even among the harder-hit railroads, the picture was not all gloomy: along with bankruptcies, reorganizations, and mergers, there were improvements in operating methods, new construction techniques, upgrading of tracks, new signaling, and ever larger and more powerful locomotives.

One major railroad that made it through the Depression without going bankrupt was the Pennsylvania. Having made an early start on electrifying its main artery from New York City to Washington, D.C., it completed the conversion of its New York terminal to high-voltage alternating current in 1933. In 1935, electrification was extended through Baltimore, Maryland, and Washington

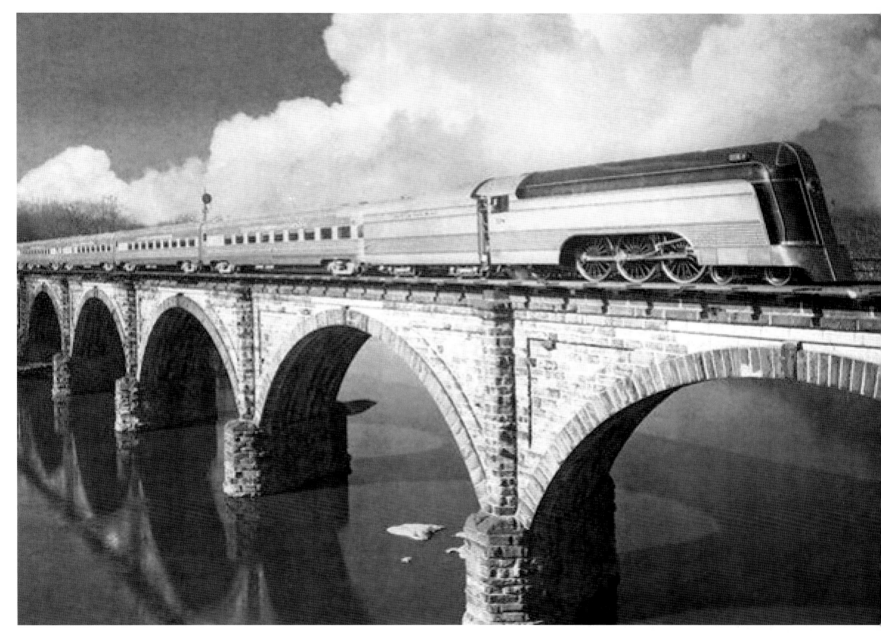

to Potomac Yard in Alexandria, Virginia. It was further extended in 1938 from Paoli to Harrisburg, with the intention of going on to Pittsburgh, Pennsylvania.

The New York Central leased the "Big Four"—Cleveland, Cincinnati, Chicago & St. Louis—in 1930, and it weathered the Depression as well. The NYC continued to develop its prestige passenger services, and its crack train, *The Twentieth Century Limited*, was so popular that it frequently ran in many sections. The record number had been achieved just before the Depression, when on January 7, 1929, it ran in seven sections, carrying a total of 822 passengers. Now it included sleeping cars, with single rooms, barbers, fresh- and salt-water bathrooms, valet and ladies' maid services, and manicurists. Stock-market reports were available, as were the services of a stenographer.

New Pullman cars were introduced with single and double rooms, some with drawing-room accommodation, restaurant cars, club lounge, and a rear observation lounge. An express parcels and post-office car was included as required.

From 1927, motive power for the NYC's main passenger trains had been provided by a new design of

The distinctive, sheet stainless steel clad *Crusader* was the most famous and stylish of the Reading RR's streamlined, 4-6-4 Pacifics. The streamlined trains operated between Jersey City, New Jersey, and Reading,

Opposite Built by ALCO and based on the lightweight, 4-4-2, Atlantic type, the streamlined locomotives operated by the Milwaukee Road made the fastest regular running during the steam era. They were used to pull the *Hiawatha* expresses inaugurated in 1935.

4-6-4 steam locomotive by ALCO. The type was developed with successive batches, until by 1948, there were 275 in total, all except 10 having been delivered by ALCO. The latter were built by Lima and allocated to the Boston & Albany RR, which had been leased by the NYC in 1900. In 1932, the New York City to Chicago schedule was cut to 18 hours, in 1935 to 16½, hours, and in 1936 to 15½ hours.

Meanwhile, the Pennsylvania's rival *Broadway Limited* continued to prosper. Through the 1920s, the train was hauled mainly by 4-6-2 Pacifics of the famous K.4 class, until they were replaced by electric locomotives as far as Harrisburg, Pennsylvania, in 1938. In 1926/7, more powerful steam 4-8-4 M.1 locomotives, built in the Pennsy's own Altoona shops, took the express over the Alleghenies between Altoona and Pittsburgh, negotiating the Horseshoe Curve. From Pittsburgh, a K.4 would take the train on to Chicago; similarly, on the run to New York City, a K.4 would take over at Altoona.

The Chesapeake & Ohio RR introduced a new, all-air-conditioned train, the *George Washington*, which ran between Washington, D.C., Newport News, Virginia, Louisville, Kentucky, and Cincinnati, Ohio. Clearly, the race was on to win as much traffic as possible. In this period, and following World War II, it was fashionable to name principal trains. There were many examples, such as: *Panama Limited* (Illinois Central RR), Chicago–New Orleans; *Overland Limited* (Chicago & North Western/Union Pacific/Southern Pacific), Chicago–San Francisco; *Super Chief* (Santa Fe), Chicago–Los Angeles; *Daylight* (Southern Pacific), San Francisco–Los Angeles; *City of Salina* (Chicago, Burlington & Quincy RR), Kansas City–Salina, Kansas; *The Flying Yankee* (Boston & Maine/Maine Central), Boston–Bangor, Maine; and *Twin Cities 400* (Chicago & North Western), Chicago–St. Paul and Minneapolis, Minnesota, with the proud boast, "400 miles in 400 minutes!"

In the 1930s, streamlining was very much the fashion in industrial design, and many railroads attempted to update the look of their trains with streamlined locomotives, along the lines of the diesels. The public associated diesels with state-of-the-art passenger services, and steam was considered old-fashioned. While not all railroads could afford the luxury of these fine, but expensive, trainsets, publicity-conscious managements began to employ the new breed of industrial designers to give their trains a modern appearance. Among the most famous associated with railroads of the early 1930s were Henry Dreyfuss, Raymond Loewy, and Otto Kuhler, who respectively styled the NYC's *The Twentieth Century Limited*, the Pennsy's *Broadway Limited*, and the Milwaukee Road's *Hiawatha* in an attempt to give steam power an up-to-date, sophisticated image in the face of the diesel threat. Loewy was particularly associated with the striking appearance of the R-1 and GG-1 electric locomotives, but his talents were also applied to steam locomotives, notably the duplex, high-speed T.1 4-4-4-4.

The Milwaukee Road had been reorganized as the Milwaukee, St. Paul & Pacific Railroad in 1925, but in 1935, it declared bankruptcy again. Despite this, the 1930s and 1940s saw the railroad involved in several notable developments. One was the introduction of *Hiawatha*, the 100mph (160km/h), steam

This strikingly streamlined Hudson class locomotive was designed by Henry Drefuss and built by ALCO for the New York Central RR. It was used to haul The Twentieth Century Limited express during the 1930s.

Built in 1936 by Lima Locomotive Works, this 4-8-4 streamlined locomotive was one of five similar engines delivered to the Canadian Northern Railway. They were used for hauling passenger trains between Toronto and Montreal.

powered streamliner that operated between the cities of Chicago, Milwaukee and St. Paul. The train was a great success, and Hiawathas were introduced on other routes. The Milwaukee's own shops produced the cars for the Hiawathas; indeed, they built most of the company's freight and passenger cars, and many of its locomotives. Again, the postwar boom helped to bring the Milwaukee Road out of bankruptcy.

Otto Kuhler styled the 4-6-4 *Hudson*, which had driving wheels of 7ft (2.13m) diameter, for the Milwaukee Road's *Hiawatha*. For a time, this seemed to be an effective answer to the high-speed, lightweight diesel streamliners. These and similar designs of steam locomotive for other roads were used until the last days of steam, when diesels replaced them, particularly where grades were encountered with heavy passenger trains.

Much of the so-called streamlining on both diesel and steam locomotives was bogus, being little more than styling to create a new image, with little attention paid to aerodynamics. As a result, much of it "aged" very quickly—rather as last year's styling gimmick does in the automobile industry—and was soon discarded, particularly if it hampered access for maintenance.

Streamlining was often superficial cladding on the exterior of a locomotive. This glimpse inside the cab of the Norfolk & Southern RR's locomotive No. 611 reveals a confusing mass of valves and controls for brake and throttle, and rather stark conditions for the engineer.

ALTERNATIVE MOTIVE POWER

FACED WITH THE REDUCTION IN PASSENGER TRAFFIC, THE
RAILROADS WERE FORCED TO SEEK COST CUTTING MEASURES.
ONE WAS TO REPLACE STEAM, WITH ITS ATTENDANT EXPENSIVE
AND COMPLEX MAINTENANCE REQUIREMENTS, WITH MORE
ECONOMIC FORMS OF MOTIVE POWER.

With the industrialization of the eastern states and the ever expanding programs of road building and improvement, many former railroad passengers opted for personal transportation in the form of the automobile. The first to feel the effect of this were the railroads' lighter loaded branch and secondary lines. The same was not true of the less-industrialized states of the Midwest, whose railroads were confident that they could continue to attract a commercially viable flow of passenger traffic. They reckoned they could do this if "limited-stop" trains were introduced. To achieve this, however, it would be necessary either to increase the water carrying capacity of existing locomotive tenders, or to abandon steam locomotives in favor of internal-combustion-engined trains. There was a limit to the former option, while the latter form of motive power needed to be developed.

In the 1920s, a few railroads had experimented with vehicles powered by internal-combustion engines—some with diesel switcher locomotives, but many more with self-propelled passenger vehicles (railcars). The latter were mainly gas-electric passenger cars, one of which would usually replace a two- or three-car local train and be operated by a smaller crew. There was a saving in maintenance because such a car needed less servicing and was instantly available. By 1930, there were many such cars, the most successful being built by the Electro-Motive Company of Cleveland, Ohio, who had produced around 500 between 1922 and 1929. Electro-Motive built the cars and their transmission systems, while power was provided by Winton gasoline engines.

Another company involved in the development of self-propelled railcars was formed by Harry P. Edwards in 1917. The Edwards Railway Motor Car Company ceased motor car construction in 1942, but had manufactured over 130 rail cars, sold to 50 different railroads in 19 different countries in the

Western Hemisphere. Edwards cars were simple, well built, and rugged, with a low purchase cost. There were two basic styles; the 1920s Model-20, and a 1936 streamlined Model-21, reminiscent of the *Zephyrs*.

By 1936, there was a relatively small number of various types of diesel-engined locomotive. ranging from switchers to road diesel units. The first three diesel-electric locomotives in the U.S. were switchers, built in 1918 by General Electric. One went to the Jay Street Connecting Railroad, one to the U.S. Army, and one to an industrial concern in Baltimore, Maryland. Commercial success came in 1924, following a tour with a demonstrator by GE/Ingersoll-Rand. This resulted in production by ALCO/GE of five locomotives, the first of which, No. 1000, was sold to the Central Railroad of New Jersey in October 1925. Several factors made diesel locomotives desirable. In an ailing industry, where cost savings were needed, a unit that could run nearly continuously, be operated economically, and comply fully with local smoke-abatement laws was seen to be just what the railroad managers needed for switching and transfer work. By 1936, there were 200 such locomotives operating in the United States and Canada.

Built by Electro-Motive Corporation, during the 1920s, the Doodle Bug was a self-propelled passenger car suitable for interurban use. It had a gasoline engine and electric transmission.

If switchers were so desirable, what about road locomotives? The first experimental road locomotives in North America were built by the Canadian Locomotive Company, engineered by Sir Henry Thornton in 1925, for the Canadian National. They were powered by four- or eight-cylinder motors built by Beardmore, of Glasgow, Scotland. In 1929, one of these twin-unit locomotives made a passenger trip from Montreal to Vancouver to demonstrate its long-range capability. It completed the 2,937-mile (4,727km) run in 67 hours.

The first two diesel-electric locomotives in the United States were delivered to the New York Central in 1928 and 1929, one for freight and one for passenger haulage in the Putnam division. The first suffered a succession of failures, but the second performed better, although neither of these experimental locomotives was wholly satisfactory. Moreover, the railroad men, fiercely loyal to steam power, did not care for them; also, there was a lack of adequate service and maintenance facilities.

The self-propelled, diesel powered railcar West Virginia Central M-3, affectionately known as *Salamander*, was built in 2000 by the Edwards Railcar Company (reformed in 1997), from original Edwards drawings of 1922. The 48-seater travels two scenic routes on the lofty Cheat Mountain at Cheat Bridge, West Virginia.

Perhaps the most important event in American diesel locomotive history came about by the lucky collaboration of Hal Hamilton and Carl Salisbury. The former founded the Electro-Motive Engineering Company of Cleveland, Ohio, while the second was chief engineer of the Winton Engine Company, also of Cleveland, which had built the successful gas-electric, self-propelled railcars mentioned earlier. A third person was also a significant contributor in the field of electric transmission. This was Richard (Dick) Dilworth, who later had a major influence on the design of diesel-electric locomotives. He became chief engineer of the Electro-Motive Company on January 1, 1926, and was an active contributor until he retired in 1952.

DIESEL-ELECTRIC LOCOMOTIVES, 1930-44

THE EARLY DIESEL-ELECTRIC LOCOMOTIVES SOON PROVED THAT THEY COULD ACCELERATE FASTER AND RUN LONGER DISTANCES BETWEEN SERVICING THAN TRADITIONAL STEAM LOCOMOTIVES. THEY WERE IDEAL FOR THE STREAMLINED PRESTIGE TRAINS OF THE 1930s, AND PERFORMED WELL IN FREIGHT SERVICE.

General Motors Corporation purchased the Winton Engine Company in June 1930, and, in December 1930, the Electro-Motive Company, which would become GM's Electro-Motive Division (EMD). This was the beginning of the story of diesel-electric traction in the United States. Despite a number of efforts to introduce alternative forms of power, diesel-electric was the chosen system in the 1930s, and it has remained the most practical form of motive power for locomotives.

In 1933, Ralph Budd, president of the Chicago, Burlington & Quincy RR, visited the Chicago World's Fair and was impressed by the Winton diesel engines he saw powering the Chevrolet model assembly plant. At the time, he was engaged in the design of a high-speed, lightweight, self-propelled train, and this engine was just what he needed. It was the right size, had a low specific weight, and developed the right output. The CB & Q design was for three-car, articulated unit, the cars being constructed from stainless steel, and it was intended to run long distances at higher than usual speeds. Called the *Pioneer Zephyr*, the train employed a modified design of Winton's 8-201A eight-cylinder, two-stroke engine with electric transmission from General Electric, and was capable of over 110mph (177km/h). It was built by the Edward G. Budd Company and delivered to the CB & Q on April 18, 1934.

The *Pioneer Zephyr* weighed only 97½ tons and was immediately successful in drawing public attention to a new era. Generally, this train is considered to be the single most important factor in introducing the diesel-electric locomotive to road passenger service. After a short period of trial,

The streamlined diesel-electric *Pioneer Zephyr* was a striking sight. The train played a major role in introducing diesels into passenger service.

Operated by the Chicago, Burlington & Quincy RR, the diesel hauled Pioneer Zephyr made a stunning debut in 1934, when it ran from Denver, Colorado, to Chicago, Illinois—1,015 miles (1,634km)—in 13 hours 5 minutes, an average of 76.61mph (123.29km/h)

Zephyr Trip
Denver to Chicago
1,015 miles
13 hours, 5 minutes

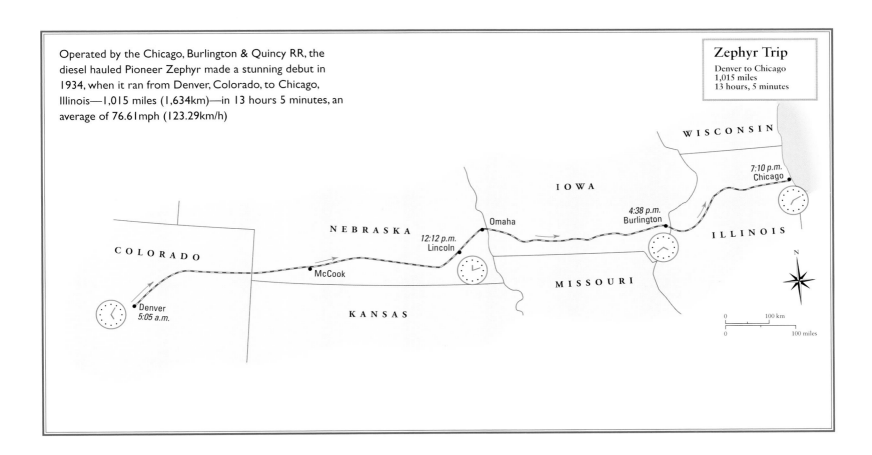

WISCONSIN

IOWA

7:10 p.m.
Chicago

NEBRASKA

Omaha

4:38 p.m.
Burlington

ILLINOIS

12:12 p.m.
Lincoln

COLORADO

McCook

MISSOURI

N

Denver
5:05 a.m.

KANSAS

0 100 km
0 100 miles

Coming or going, the *Pioneer Zephyr* was a striking looking train. Its bodywork, as shown in the rear observation car, was formed from highly polished stainless steel.

on May 26, 1934, it ran from Denver, Colorado, to Chicago, a distance of 1,015.4 miles (1,634km), in 13 hours, 4 minutes, and 58 seconds—an average speed of 76.61mph (123.29km/h)—exceeding 100mph (160km/h) at several points in the journey. It entered regular service between Lincoln, Nebraska, and Kansas City, Missouri, in November 1934. Later, in 1938, a fourth car, a Dinette, was added.

The innovative Union Pacific Railroad had already ordered a three-car, articulated, streamlined train, which was even lighter than the *Zephyr*, since its construction made extensive use of aluminum. It was built by the Pullman Standard Car Company in Chicago, and weighed 85 tons. Named *The City of Salina*, it made an extensive tour in February, 1934. Apparently, it was not quite what was wanted, as shortly after, a longer articulated train was built, consisting of a power car and six trailers, two of which were sleepers and one a day car. This was also powered by a Winton engine, a V-12 201A of 900hp; later, this was changed to a V-16 201A of 1,200hp. Then the train was named The City of Portland. In all, seven generally similar units were built between 1934 and 1936. Only the first had a single engine: the second had a 900hp booster engine, and the remaining five had 1,200hp booster engines. Another six units followed in 1937, all with a single 1,200hp engines.

Meanwhile, in 1935, the Burlington Road had added two more three-car trainsets and two four-car sets. Eventually, all carried names; the *Flying Yankee*, which ran between Boston, Massachusetts, and Bangor, Maine, was probably the best known in the East. All the *Zephyrs* have been preserved in railroad museums. Gradually, power cars began to lose ground to locomotives, but, in whatever form, diesel-electric power began to take a firm hold, especially in prestige expresses. Other famous named trains introduced in this period included the New Haven's *Comet*, B & O's *Royal Blue*, Santa Fe's *Super Chief*, and Chicago & North Western/Union Pacific's *City of Los Angeles*.

In May 1935, Electro-Motive completed a prototype passenger locomotive with a total rating of 3,600hp. It was a twin-unit, in reality two separate, identical, 1,800hp halves coupled together. Each unit weighed 120 tons and had two 12-cylinder, 900hp 201A engines with electric transmission. Although a successful demonstrator, it had a short life and was retired in 1938. A similar single locomotive for the Baltimore & Ohio, built in August 1935, had a much longer life and was used to haul the Royal Blue, which ran between New York City and Washington, D.C. In 1937, it passed to the Alton, when one driving-cab end was restyled; later, it became the property of the Gulf, Mobile & Ohio RR on merger in 1949. Subsequently, it was restored to its original design and livery.

Later in 1935, a 3,600hp, twin-unit locomotive was introduced, and this set the scene for the concept of the multiple-unit passenger locomotive, which became the standard for many years. It was the forerunner of the E-series, which developed from 1,800hp to 2,400hp per unit over the next 19 years. In the same year, General Motors began construction of its diesel locomotive manufacturing plant at La

Grange, Illinois. There it developed its own version of the Winton engine, a simplified design, tailored to locomotive work, which became the EMD 567 series of 8-, 12- and 16-cylinder engines.

Diesel locomotives soon showed that they could accelerate faster than steam locomotives, take curves at higher speeds, and run greater distances without service stops. Moreover, if they were good for passenger trains, they would be equally good, if not better, for freight, so attention turned to the development of freight units for long-distance haulage. In 1939–40, the first EMD freight locomotive made a national tour of a number of railroads, including the Santa Fe.

The freight demonstrator was a four-unit, 5,400hp (4 x 1,350hp) locomotive. On its maiden trip, it took 66 cars from Kansas City, Missouri, to Los Angeles efficiently and economically. Known as the model FT, the first were ordered by the Santa Fe, being delivered in 1941. Although wartime restrictions limited production, no fewer than 555 A-units and 541 B-units had been delivered by 1945, most semi-permanently coupled as A + B pairs.

The diesel-electric locomotive seemed the answer to the railroad man's prayers. The first railroad to turn to diesel-electric freight locomotives was the Santa Fe. With long runs through desert country, it had always had water-supply problems for its steam locomotives. Apart from a relative shortage of water, much of what there was gave problems with scale and other deposits in steam locomotive boilers, leading to increased maintenance costs and downtime. Diesel fuel was also relatively cheap, while diesel

Built by Pullman for the Union Pacific RR in 1934, the *City of Salina* was a three-car articulated train that made extensive use of aluminum in its construction.

The first U.S. railroad to turn to diesels was the Santa Fe. Its EMD F7 locomotives were ideal for the terrain in which the railroad operated, and hauled famous passenger trains such as the *Super Chief* and *El Capitan*. This locomotive sports the company's distinctive *Warbonnet* paint scheme, and its famous "Indian Head" logo.

locomotive efficiency was high—about three times the typical 6–7 percent efficiency of comparable steam locomotives. So it was not surprising that the Santa Fe heralded the purchase of the first 68 FT models from EMD.

One drawback was initial cost—a little over twice that of a comparable steam locomotive. Another was the railroads' considerable investment in steam-locomotive servicing plant, repair facilities, coal depots, and water supplies, not to mention the men and materials needed to keep steam locomotives running. There was no escaping the fact that with steam locomotives went dirt and pollution: they threw out large quantities of smoke and cinders, and although that is one of the attractions to the steam enthusiast today, it didn't help to run the railroads.

The diesel-electric manufacturers began their marketing campaigns well before World War II. Fuel and operating economies were highlighted, as was the reduction in servicing facilities. The high purchase price was countered by the claim that savings in operational costs would recoup more than the price difference over a very short period. This could easily be demonstrated with switchers: with their higher availability, fewer diesel-electric locomotives—probably only half the number of steam—would be needed to do the same amount of work. Passengers would be won back by the vision of new, fast, clean motive power that didn't shower them with cinders. The United States, rapidly becoming a nation of automobile drivers, would be attracted back to the railroads.

Even so, some steam railroads were skeptical; a few even remained opposed to the very idea of diesels. Soon after World War II, however, many of the smaller railroads and most of the larger ones had succumbed. Among the few that held out against diesels was the Norfolk & Western, a coal hauler from the Appalachian coalfields to the port of Norfolk, Virginia. The company designed and built its own locomotives at Roanoke, and many of those, it claimed, were more than a match for the diesels.

Before World War II, other manufacturers besides GM had begun manufacturing diesel-electric locomotives. ALCO and its Schenectady, New York, neighbor, General Electric, produced a large range of switchers and line locomotives using ALCO diesel engines and GE electrics. Baldwin combined with Westinghouse to build a similar range. Finally, toward the end of the war, Fairbanks-Morse entered the field with its novel, two-stroke, opposed-piston engines.

Economy and low price went together, and this was understood by General Motors. From the start, GM saw the advantage to the railroads of highly standardized products, and the flexibility to meet haulage demands by running relatively small locomotives coupled in two, three, or four units as the occasion demanded. This was also understood by the ALCO-GE combination, but Baldwin still adhered to the time-honored railroad tradition of custom design; consequently, its products were more costly and often cumbersome.

Opposite An early EMD diesel freight locomotive, built for the Atchison, Topeka & Santa Fe RR, being washed down before being put back into service during World War II.

Fairbanks-Morse also introduced a line of standardized locomotives for all applications, but they were late arrivals, appearing in August 1944. Their lightweight, opposed-piston engine had been supplied almost exclusively to the U.S. Navy during World War II. It had been very well regarded by Navy engineers, but it was never taken up by the railroads in large quantities.

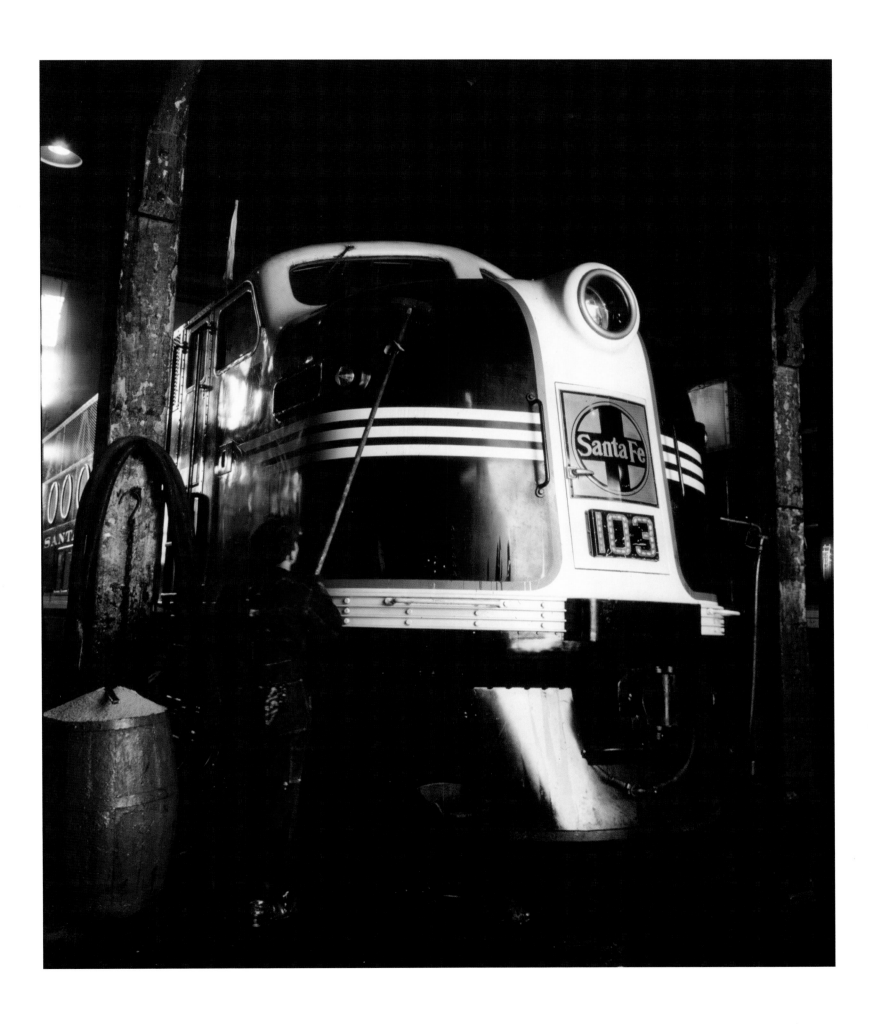

HEAVY STEAM, 1930-50

DESPITE THE CHALLENGE FROM DIESEL ENGINES, STEAM FREIGHT
LOCOMOTIVES WERE BECOMING BIGGER AND INCREASINGLY
POWERFUL. STEAM CONTINUED TO WOO PASSENGERS WITH
FASTER TRAINS AND IMPROVED FACILITIES—UNTIL WORLD WAR II
BROUGHT MORE PASSENGERS THAN COULD BE HANDLED.

In 1930, Baldwin Locomotive Works delivered this 2-10-4 Texas type locomotive to the Santa Fe for freight work. Known as *Madam Queen*, it remained in service until 1953.

As freight trains grew in weight, so locomotive power was increased to meet the need for heavier haulage, and to avoid double-heading, except where it was necessary to use helpers on severely graded lines. By 1950, the Mallet-type articulated locomotive was well established as a freight hauler over the more mountainous lines, but perhaps the first popular freight locomotives for heavy hauling at relatively low speeds were first the 2-8-0 then the 2-10-2.

The first 2-10-2s were built for the Santa Fe RR, and from then on, the wheel arrangement was known as the "Santa Fe" type. It was developed in two ways: with a four-wheel trailing truck as a 2-10-4, or "Texas," to support a larger firebox; and with a four-wheel leading truck for greater stability as a 4-10-2, or "Overland." Some three-cylinder "Overlands" were built for the Union Pacific and Southern Pacific. The last "Texas," produced by Baldwin for the Santa Fe RR in 1938, had the highest piston thrust of any steam locomotive, and with 6ft 2in (1.88m) driving wheels, it was capable of reaching high speeds.

A notable and rare type for North America was the S.515 "Union Pacific." This was a three-cylinder 4-12-2, of which 88 were built by ALCO for the Union Pacific during 1926–30. It was an interesting design for two reasons: it was a rare example of a non-articulated, multi-cylinder locomotive; and it represented the limits of a rigid driving wheelbase—30ft 8in (9.35m). Also, it had a rare American example of Nigel Gresley's combination valve gear. The long wheelbase restricted its use to roads with only moderate curvature. "Union Pacific" locomotives were operated for 10 years on main-line work, subsequently being relegated to lesser duties.

For general-purpose freight, the 2-8-2 ("Mikado" until 1941; "MacArthur" thereafter) and its development, the 2-8-4 ("Berkshire"), were built in large numbers. The Louisville & Nashville RR took its final delivery of "Berkshires" as late as 1949.

Articulated locomotives were built mainly to provide greater power for roads with special characteristics, particularly heavy grades with severe curvature. They were the largest and most powerful steam locomotives to be built, but there were only about 2,800 of them spread over 22 main-line railroads. The first examples were compounds and were restricted largely to helper or yard work, since they were unable to work at acceptable speed on main lines. In articulated locomotives, the rear, fixed engine worked at boiler pressure, exhausting steam into the front, pivoted engine. Not being physically coupled, the front and rear engines tended to get out of "phase," and the exhaust from the high-pressure engine was choked by the low-pressure engine.

The later articulated locomotives—2-6-6-0, 2-8-8-0, and derivatives—were capable of road work at speeds of up to about 25mph (40km/h) with heavy trains. The design was expanded to some immense machines, even triple locomotives with six cylinders, and 2-8-8-8-2 or 2-8-8-8-4 wheel arrangements,

The ultimate articulated steam locomotive, the Union Pacific's 4-8-8-4 "Big Boy." Twenty-five of these huge machines were built between 1941 and 1944 by ALCO. Each was designed to pull a 3,600-ton train unaided over a 1.14 percent grade. The last was retired in 1961.

A 4-6-6-4 "Challenger" and 4-8-8-4 "Big Boy" of the Union Pacific double heading a freight train on Sherman Hill, Wyoming in the mid-1940s.

but they had so many practical limitations that they were never produced in significant numbers.

Compound expansion was dropped by American locomotive builders around 1924, because simple expansion was so much more flexible and produced a greater tractive effort at starting. Even so, fewer than 500 four-cylinder, simple locomotives were built. The more modern types had larger driving wheels of 67–70in (170–178cm) diameter and were capable of operating at over 60mph (97km/h), with power outputs of up to 7,000hp indicated. The best known were the Union Pacific's "Challenger" 4-6-6-4s of 1936, made by ALCO; the type was named for a passenger train for which its 80mph (129km/h) speed capability was needed.

Union Pacific operated 105 "Challengers," and a further 149 had been built for six other roads by the early 1940s. While, sometimes, they were used on passenger trains, their main duty was to haul heavy freight trains at speeds approaching those of passenger trains. One UP "Challenger"' has been preserved in running order and is used occasionally on long--distance excursions.

The ultimate in articulated steam locomotive design was reached with the aptly named 4-8-8-4 "Big Boy." This was a 1941 design, also for Union Pacific, and again from ALCO. Over the next three years, 25 of these immense locomotives were built; they were the largest conventional steamers of all—more than 130ft (39m) long, 16ft 2in (4.9m) high, and (with tender) weighing 552 tons (the tender alone weighed over 150 tons). They developed no less than 7,000hp and could generate a starting tractive effort of 135,375lb (61,406kg). The "Big Boy" was an express freight locomotive, designed to run at up to 80mph (129km/h), and to take 100-car trains over the formidable Sherman Summit. At times, the trains were so heavy that two of these giant locomotives were needed to maintain speeds in the region of 40mph (64km/h) up "The Hill."

To satisfy their large appetites, these and the later "Challengers" were provided with 14-wheel tenders of a novel design, carrying 28 tons of coal and 24,000 gallons (90,840 liters) of water. They were intended principally for the long, heavy drag from Cheyenne, Wyoming, up through the Wasatch Range in Utah, and on to Salt Lake City. Each "Big Boy" cost $265,174. Today, a few have been preserved and reside in railroad museums, awe inspiring examples of the ultimate in steam locomotive size and power.

To quote from Henry B. Comstock's delightful book, *The Iron Horse*: "The engines were deliberately 'overbuilt' to withstand the punishment of eighty miles per hour speeds, and during World War Two they occasionally topped seventy with heavy troop trains. However, they were at their vocal best when they drummed up Weber Canyon out of Ogden [Utah], punctuating each beat of their exhaust with a towering black exclamation mark."

The Pennsylvania Railroad and USRA apart, standardization of design was almost nonexistent in the steam era. Most railroads considered that their own designs were necessary to meet their own particular requirements. To quote E. Thomas Harley, from an article published by the American Society of Mechanical Engineers (ASME) in 1979: "It has been said, with some overstatement, that the steam locomotive standard was 'N.T.A.' (no two alike). Be that as it may, American Railroads and Builders provided what the U.S. required, locomotives that were relatively crude and simple, yet powerful and reliable. Nevertheless the U.S.A. built the largest and most powerful steam locomotives ever produced."

The steam locomotive fleet reached its peak at 70,000 in 1924, then steadily dwindled. There were 40,000 in 1944, and only 29,000 by 1949, when commercial steam locomotive production ceased in the United States. The last steam locomotive in regular service on a road carrier dropped its fire for the last time in 1960. Of those remaining in 1949, only 8,000 had been built after 1925, suggesting that the diesel-electric mainly replaced worn-out steam locomotives at or near the end of their economic lives, and not a large number of modern, high-capacity steam locomotives, as has been suggested.

Locomotive No. 4449 is the only surviving example of the Southern Pacific Railroad's powerful GS-4 class of steam locomotives. The GS-4 is a streamlined 4-8-4 (Northern) type; the GS is said to stand for "Golden State", a nickname for California, where the locomotive was operated in regular service, or "General Service." Built by the Lima Locomotive Works in Lima, Ohio, for the SP in May, 1941, it received its bold red-and-orange paint scheme for the *Daylight* passenger trains, which it hauled for most of its career. The locomotive was retired from active service in 1957 and placed on static display in Oaks Park, Portland, Oregon. In 1974, it was restored to operative use in the second American Freedom Train, which toured the United States for the American Bicentennial celebrations. Since then, No. 4449 has been operated an excursion service throughout the continental U.S., and is seen here on a visit to Toronto's Union Station, Canada.

Railroads During World War II, 1939-45

IN THE COURSE OF WORLD WAR II, THE RAILROADS BECAME THE TRANSPORTATION BACKBONE OF THE NATION, MOVING VAST QUANTITIES OF SUPPLIES AND MUNITIONS, AND LARGE NUMBERS OF MEN ACROSS THE UNITED STATES, AT THE SAME TIME MAINTAINING REGULAR PASSENGER AND FREIGHT SERVICES.

The railroads were vital in World War II for transporting huge numbers of military personnel across the country to embarkation ports on the Pacific and Atlantic coasts.

Following the outbreak of World War II in Europe, the American government's Neutrality Act of 1937 was altered to permit war materials to be sent to the Allied nations fighting Germany. At home, steps were taken to build up the Army and Navy. All this increased both freight and passenger traffic, but, unlike in World War I, no steps were taken to exercise federal control over the railroads. Even when the Japanese bombing of Pearl Harbor, on December 7, 1941, prompted the United States' entry into the conflict, the railroads remained in control of their affairs and were able to direct their best efforts where they were needed.

Overall, freight traffic doubled and passenger business quadrupled, much of the extra freight

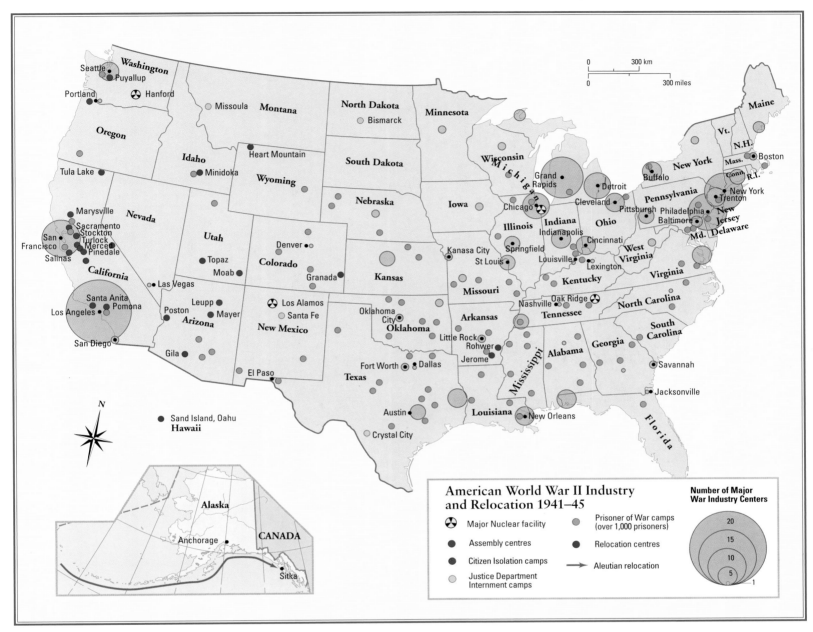

American World War II Industry and Relocation 1941–45

☢ Major Nuclear facility

● Assembly centres

● Citizen Isolation camps

○ Justice Department Internment camps

○ Prisoner of War camps (over 1,000 prisoners)

● Relocation centres

→ Aleutian relocation

Number of Major War Industry Centers

20

15

10

5

1

traffic being the movement of war materials from factories to ports on both sides of the continent. In addition, the railroads took on the shipment of oil to east-coast refineries following attacks on coastal shipping by German submarines. It was said that every six minutes, a troop train set off for an embarkation port, while a freight train carrying war materials left every four seconds.

The greatest burden fell on the lines leading to the Pacific coast. To aid the passage of a far greater number of trains than that for which they were equipped, the technology of modern signaling, in the form of Centralized Traffic Control (CTC), was applied to great advantage.

One problem faced by all the railroads during the war was a shortage of manpower. Thousands of skilled men and women left their jobs with the railroads for military service; the Southern Pacific alone lost 11,000 in this way; over 1,300 men and women of the Pennsylvania Railroad never returned, having lost their lives during the conflict.

Traffic peaked around the beginning of 1943, then dropped gradually until 1946. Motive power, particularly for freight, was stretched to the limit, and although there was a shortage of steel, the War

During World War II, the railroads experienced a significant rise in both freight and passenger traffic as they shuttled personnel, materials, and munitions around the country to meet the needs of the U.S. war effort. Passenger traffic increased fourfold, and included the movement of prisoners-of-war and internees.

Production Board permitted some new building. To save time, however, construction was restricted to locomotives of tried and proven designs or, at most, limited developments of existing types.

One design chosen by the Pennsylvania Railroad was the Chesapeake & Ohio's Texas (2-10-4) freight locomotive; 125 more were built, the work being shared between the Pennsylvania's own Juniata shops and Baldwin's between December 1942 and December 1943. Many regarded them as the finest freight locomotives ever to have run on the Pennsylvania.

The switcher diesel was well established by the outbreak of war, and the first generation of passenger and freight diesels was already being built. The construction of passenger diesels was halted between 1940 and 1944, although diesel freight locomotives and switchers continued in production for a time.

At the end of World War II, in the summer of 1945, the railroads could breathe a sigh of relief. They had weathered 15 difficult years, first with the Depression and then with the war. They had done a magnificent job moving men, supplies, and munitions, all the while handling regular passenger and freight traffic. In the public eye, the railroads' role had been amply reinforced by war as the backbone of transportation. Most people assumed—as did the railroads—that this situation would remain, at least

In addition to personnel, the railroads moved vast amounts of war materials and equipment. Here, Sherman tanks are given a rousing sendoff as they leave the factory on flatcars.

As they had done in World War I, the railroads turned to women to keep the trains running when many of their male employees had left to enlist. These "wipers" of the Chicago & North Western Railroad clamber aboard a giant H-class locomotive in Clinton, Iowa.

A freight train hauled by a Santa Fe locomotive gets ready to leave the Corwith Yard, Chicago, for the West Coast in the winter of 1943.

for the foreseeable future.

Returning servicemen, having made sacrifices overseas, saw things differently. Their dream was a job, a family, and an automobile. The automobile manufacturers, released from wartime restrictions, responded, and sales soared. Demands for highway improvements were voiced and seen by politicians as a vote catcher, so they underwrote a boom in highway construction. Tax funds for new highways became plentiful, and truckers took to the new highways, capturing short- and medium-haul business from the railroads, whose deliveries were less favorable.

Internal air traffic also began to increase, while the aircraft manufacturers, who had benefited from advances in technology brought about by the war, produced airliners like the Douglas DC-7 and the Lockheed Constellation, both developments of highly successful wartime transport planes. The cost per passenger seat fell below that of prewar prices, and flying gained a "popular" image. Meanwhile, the truckers' success encouraged them to enter the long-haul business, particularly for the carriage of light manufactured goods using articulated (tractor and semi-trailer) vehicles. Gasoline was cheap, made possible by the vast production of the Texas, Oklahoma, Louisiana, and California oilfields, plus the newly tapped reserves of the Middle East, which helped trucking companies and airlines to lower their rates and become very competitive with rail.

The Chicago & North Western RR's classification yard, Chicago, Illinois, in 1942. Yards such as these were vital to the shipment of war materials.

Opposite With the railroads being such a vital part of the war effort, the locomotive shops were kept busy night and day.

Diesel engines needed far less by way of servicing compared to steam locomotives. Here, a Santa Fe EMD is being prepared for another run of the *Super Chief* express.

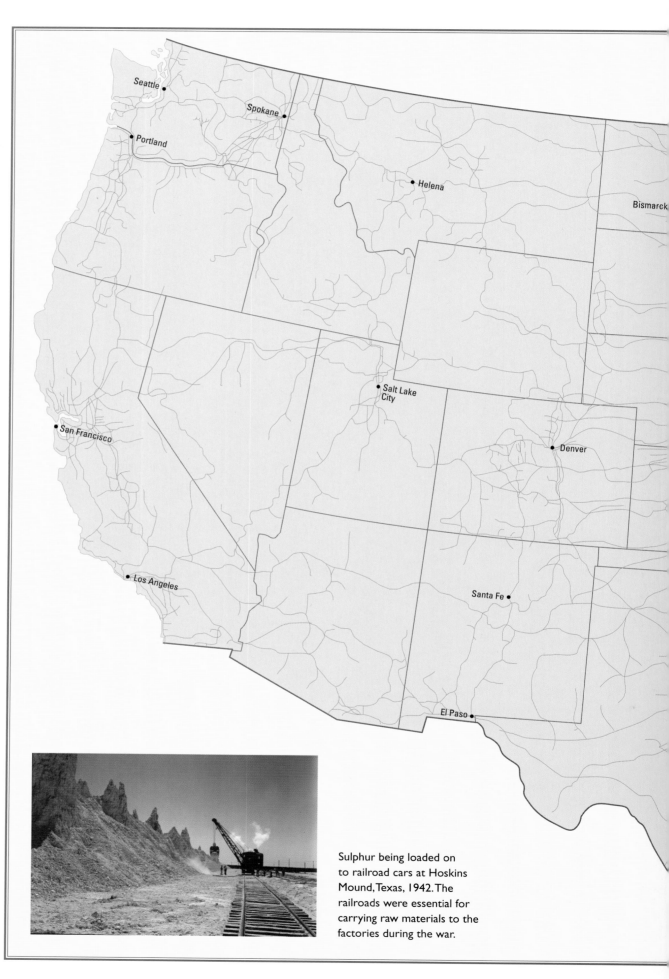

Sulphur being loaded on to railroad cars at Hoskins Mound, Texas, 1942. The railroads were essential for carrying raw materials to the factories during the war.

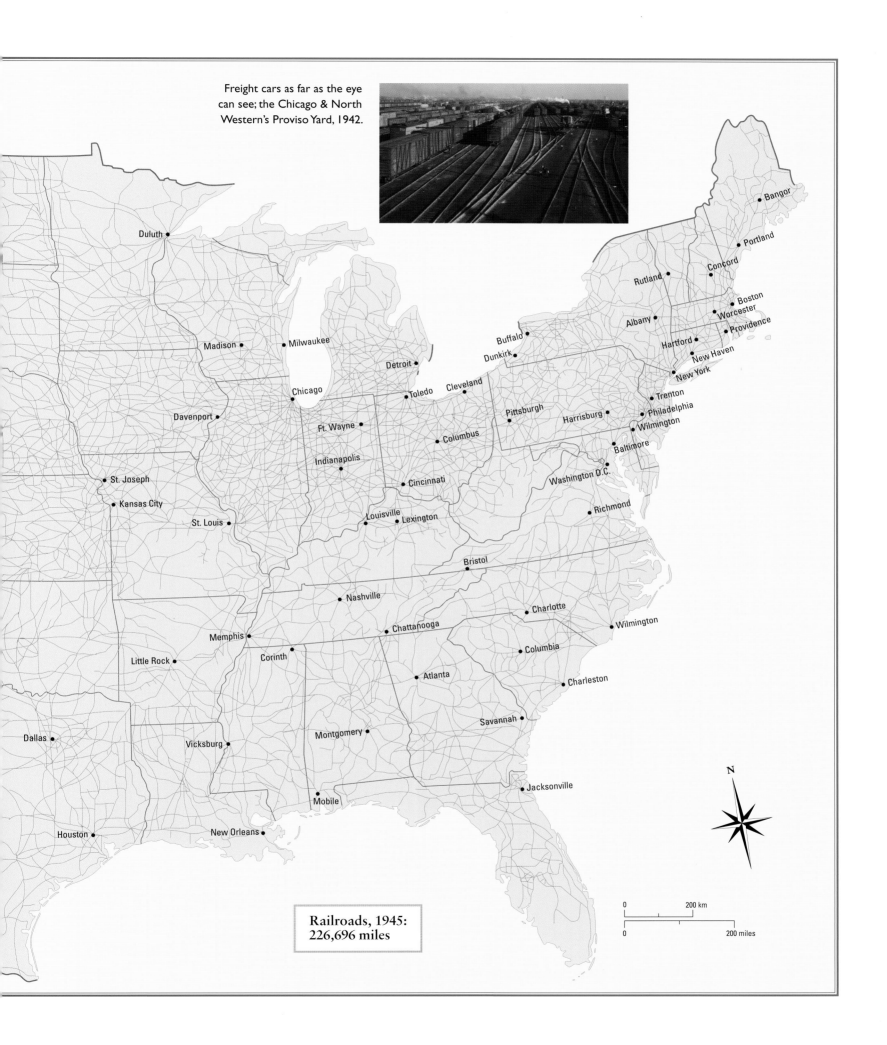

Freight cars as far as the eye can see; the Chicago & North Western's Proviso Yard, 1942.

Railroads, 1945:
226,696 miles

N

0   200 km

0   200 miles

Oil-Burning, Cab-Forward Locomotives, 1900-60

NORMALLY, STEAM LOCOMOTIVES WERE COAL FIRED, BUT IN THE OIL PRODUCING REGIONS OF THE UNITED STATES, RAILROADS BENEFITED FROM SWITCHING TO OIL. THIS ALTERNATIVE FUEL ALSO LED TO SOME INTERESTING LOCOMOTIVE DESIGNS, NOTABLY THE "CAB-FORWARD" OF THE SOUTHERN PACIFIC.

The Southern Pacific's "cab-forward" locomotives were developed for hauling heavy freight on the steeply graded line between Sacramento and Donner Summit.

Although coal was the normal fuel for steam locomotives, there had also been interest in using oil, but it was not until the American oilfields began to produce large surpluses in the late 19th and early 20th centuries that the price became attractive. Railroads with access to the oilfields of the South and west now began to take an interest. Even so, many railroads were slow to adopt oil as a fuel for steam locomotives, because it required much more careful handling. The regular steam-locomotive firebox could be adapted to burn oil without difficulty, but special burners and firing techniques had to be developed. On the other hand, some railroads were forced to burn soft coal from local coalfields. One such was the Chesapeake & Ohio, and photographs of many of their trains are notable for the large volumes of black smoke emitted by the locomotives when working hard.

In addition to the ready availability of fuel oil to some railroads, there were other advantages to burning oil in steam locomotives. Oil has greater calorific value than coal, that is it burns hotter. Moreover, in a coal fired locomotives, the fire itself gradually became clogged with ash, reducing its heat output; with an oil burner, this did not occur, no dirt or dust being produced. The locomotive cab also remained cleaner, and the fireman had time to help the engineer by keeping a lookout on the track. On a coal burner, when the firedoor was opened at night, the glare could distract the engineer; this did not happen on an oil burner.

The tender of an oil burning locomotive was normally of the same overall design as that of a coal burner, except that the oil was contained in a large tank. As a rule, this would be mounted at the rear, with the water tank toward the front.

The principle oil producing regions were Texas, California, the Gulf, Oklahoma, and Kansas, and the railroads of these areas began to switch to oil burning locomotives. The Southern Pacific was one of the first railroads to turn to oil in the early 1900s; the Santa Fe soon followed.

Were it not for oil, the famous Southern Pacific "cab-forward" locomotives would not have been possible. In all, 250 of them were built. The first AC-4 was a conversion from a Baldwin 2-8-8-2. Later, a four-wheel truck was substituted to improve curving. There were also some AM 2-6-6-2s. In the class names, "AC" stands for "articulated Consolidation," and "AM" for "articulated Mogul." Both types were Mallet locomotives. They provided an effective answer to the problem of heavy haulage over the "Hill"—the tortuous stretch that climbs the western slopes of the Sierra Nevada in California, between Sacramento and Donner Summit, close to the Nevada state line. This section abounds in a succession of snow sheds—20 miles (32km) or more of them—and has a ruling grade of 1 in 37.7 (2.65 percent). A situation existed on the line through the Cascades between Eugene and Klamath Falls, Oregon, and Redding, California, where many single-line tunnels exist. Even diesels can get a little short of breath on this line!

The last cab-forward locomotive, No. 4294, was withdrawn from traffic by the Southern Pacific in 1958, having entered service in 1944. Today, it is preserved in the California State Railroad Museum at Sacramento.

A double-headed freight train is hauled through Altamont Pass by Southern Pacific AM-2 Mogul 4-6-6-2 "cab-forward" locomotives in 1936. The cab was placed at the front of the locomotive to prevent the crew from being asphyxiated by the exhaust gases as the train ran through the many snow sheds on the line.

POSTWAR PROBLEMS, 1945-60

FALLING TRAFFIC, WORN-OUT ROLLING STOCK, RISING COAL

PRICES, OVERMANNING, AND HIGH WAGE DEMANDS COMBINED

TO MAKE LIFE DIFFICULT FOR THE RAILROADS AFTER WORLD

WAR II. MAJOR CHANGES WERE NEEDED, AND THE DIESEL

LOCOMOTIVE WAS THE CATALYST FOR THOSE CHANGES.

In 1944, railroads handled nearly 80 percent of passenger-miles between cities. By 1950, this had dropped to 47 percent, and by 1960, to 29 percent. Freight did not fare quite so badly; nonetheless, it was down from 69 percent in 1944 to 44 percent by 1960. What had gone wrong? There were several reasons for this drop in traffic. With the end of the war in sight, railroad managers had made smug assumptions that business would continue more or less as usual. Investment in track, locomotives, and rolling stock had not kept pace with demand; a substantial amount of the locomotive fleet was old and worn out, and represented a major cost sink, which the war had exacerbated. Very few locomotives had been built between 1942 and 1945.

Coal prices were jacked up by strikes in the Appalachian coalfields. This increased fuel costs for railroads from the East through the Midwest, the latter having higher haulage costs to add to the higher fuel bill. Railroad workers demanded higher wages, and every railroad union bargained for higher pay, with walkouts in most grades. By 1951, there were still almost as many railroad employees as in 1944, yet although railroad revenue had fallen steadily during this period, employees' wages had risen by as much as 53 percent. Something had to change.

In fact, attitudes and employment levels had not altered much since the early years of the century. Despite the universal use of reliable continuous brakes, the numbers of trainmen differed very little in 1950 from 1905; the same applied in other fields.

The diesel locomotive loomed as a serious challenge to steam. Many railroads were quick to see the diesel-electric's advantages; others would fight almost to the death to keep steam. In the main, the big locomotive builders fell into the latter category, even though ALCO had a lucrative arrangement with

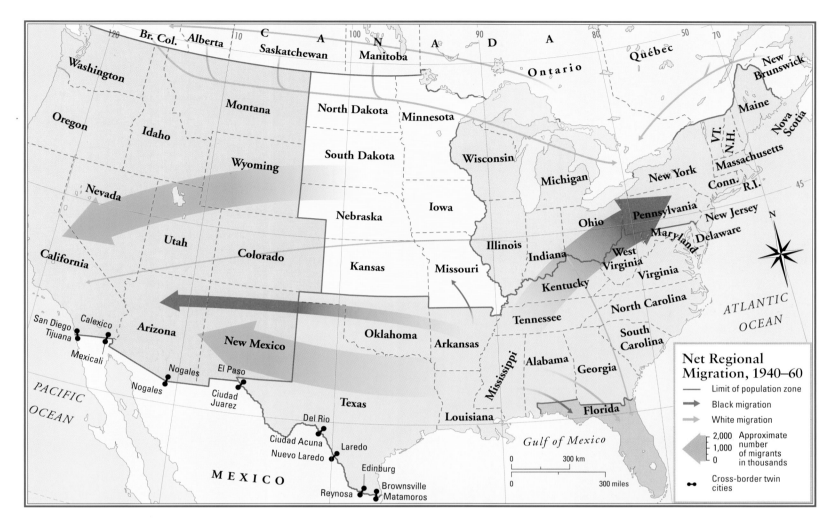

Net Regional
Migration, 1940–60

— Limit of population zone
→ Black migration
→ White migration

2,000 Approximate
1,000 number
0 of migrants
in thousands

●●● Cross-border twin
cities

0 — 300 km

0 — 300 miles

GE for diesel-electric work, and Baldwin acquired Lima Locomotive Works in 1950.

There could be no doubt that a wholesale switch to diesel power would bring sweeping changes. It would offer greater flexibility in operation, and much less labor-intensive servicing and maintenance work. It also promised much greater standardization in locomotive design and manufacture. As we have seen already, many railroads stuck to the conviction that they were best served by locomotives designed specifically for their needs. Undoubtedly, this was true with steam locomotives, but for diesels, it was quite another story.

In the road diesel field, the Electro-Motive Division (EMD) of General Motors enjoyed a virtual monopoly for a number of years. It researched railroads' needs very thoroughly and came up with a very flexible concept: the relatively low-powered unit that could be coupled to one or more similar units to form one high-powered locomotive, which could be operated by a single crew. A great deal of experience had been obtained during the war, demonstrating what diesels could do.

The Santa Fe's president, Fred Gurley, probably was the diesel's greatest salesman. In a speech in 1916, he said of the diesel, "Time does not permit a discussion of all its virtues; sufficient to say it is the best which man's ingenuity has produced for our service." *Life* magazine took this up in 1947 and, with a big photospread, made the observation, "Last year 90 percent of the locomotives ordered by railroads were diesels." Except for the Norfolk & Western, which continued building its own steam locomotives until 1953, the last steamer on United States railroads was ordered in 1947.

Population movements have always had an effect on the railroads. Trains have carried migrants from one part of the country to another in search of perceived better opportunities. Moreover, the resulting increases and decreases in local populations have led to changes in demand for railroad services. Over the period of 20 years between 1940 and 1960, there have been major movements from the poorer areas of the South to the more prosperous Northeast and West Coast.

Built by ALCO between 1941 and 1960, the RS-1 four-axle, diesel-electric locomotive had the longest production run of any diesel in the United States. By its side is a restored Fairmount railcar.

However, the diesel-electric protagonists had a big battle on their hands. The change to diesel power would affect not only machines, but also people and their jobs. In the eyes of the American locomotive industry, General Motors was an outsider. How could it possibly know what the railroads really needed to run their businesses? But with an outsider's eye, GM could see very well what was needed to pull the railroads out of their doldrums. It rejected design collaboration, refusing to be a party to the traditional railroad-company/locomotive-supplier relationship. Indeed, on one famous occasion, when a railroad wanted to help in the development of a diesel locomotive, GM refused its offer to underwrite the cost of testing. When asked why, GM replied, "So you fellows won't tell us how to build it."

Standardization in high-volume production—GM's basic manufacturing credo—would be impossible if each individual customer wanted a different locomotive design. High volume meant efficient production methods, low production costs, low material costs—and low prices to customers. EMD had already shown that, with the flexibility conferred by electric transmission, a good general-purpose, diesel-electric locomotive could successfully handle a much wider variety of traffic over many different routes, grades, etc, than any steam locomotive. That being the case, customized design was no longer necessary.

An EMD BL2 four-axle road switcher built by General Motors. The letters "BL" stood for "Branch Line," indicating that the locomotive was intended for light traffic and switcher work.

One famous episode in American railroad history calls to mind Henry Ford and the Model "T," of which he is alleged to have said, "You can have it any color you like, so long as it's black." A certain railroad persisted in asking for a series of design alterations to the diesel it wished to order, so GM finally delivered an ultimatum: "We'll build you a locomotive. You tell us what color you want it painted and we'll be responsible for everything else. We'll send you the locomotive without charge, with one of our men in it to supervise. You run the locomotive for six months. At the end of that time, you send us either the locomotive or the money." Six months later, the railroad paid—and ordered five more locomotives of a standard EMD specification.

The big three locomotive builders all went into the diesel business. Baldwin—now known as BLH, following its merger with Lima and Lima owned Hamilton in 1950—built standardized diesel-electric switchers, mainly with Westinghouse electrical equipment. BLH ceased building locomotives in 1956, by which time it had produced around 3,000 for the American market. It fell into the trap of trying to satisfy the demands for custom design, and did not survive.

On the other hand, ALCO understood the need for a high degree of standardization and, while its arrangement with General Electric for transmission equipment endured, it became an effective competitor to EMD. ALCO saw the need for high-horsepower units and pioneered the 2,000hp locomotive, which could be used singly or in multiples for both main freight and passenger work.

The first was put into service on the New York, New Haven & Hartford RR in 1941, working the Shore Line between Boston, Massachusetts, and New Haven, Connecticut. The New Haven had been one of the pioneers among eastern railroads in the use of diesel locomotives, its first switcher entering service in 1931. This was the first 600hp switcher to be manufactured by ALCO-GE.

General Electric broke off its partnership with ALCO in 1952. Although the latter continued using GE electrical equipment for a time, as did its offshoot, Montreal Locomotive Works (MLW), it built its last diesel in 1969.

The final diesel builder to enter the field was Fairbanks-Morse in 1944. It had made gasoline-engined railcars early in the century, but now produced an opposed-piston diesel engine with a good power/weight ratio of particular interest to railroads. It built complete diesel-electric locomotives with GE or Westinghouse electrical equipment in its shops near the Illinois state line at Beloit, Wisconsin. Its first 1,000hp switcher went to the Milwaukee Road on August 8, 1911. F-M assembled both switchers and road diesels for a number of years, but dropped out of the United States market in 1958.

GE had been early in the market, but concentrated chiefly on the smaller industrial switcher market, being well occupied otherwise with electric locomotives and multiple units. It produced a four-unit set that operated on the Erie RR as a test laboratory during 1954–9, after which it was sold to the Union Pacific. Two of the units originally had 1,200hp engines, while the other two had 1,800hp power plants. For UP service, all were equipped with 2,000hp engines.

Nicknamed "U-Boat," the U25B was the first diesel-electric locomotive produced by GE after its split with ALCO. At the time of its introduction, it was the most powerful diesel road locomotive available in the United States.

GE did not begin building large locomotives seriously until 1959, when it introduced the U25B road switcher of 2,500hp, having sold 10 road switchers of 1,800hp to Mexico in 1956. Today, it is the only serious competitor to EMD.

By 1960, it is estimated that approximately 34,000 diesel-electric locomotives had been built for U.S. railroads, with a further 3,500 for Canada and Mexico.

The diesel locomotive was probably the catalyst for a host of changes that railroad managements knew had to be made. The cost of labor to operate trains remained high. Steamers required a crew of two for each locomotive used on a train; fuel and watering facilities were needed at frequent intervals on every line, and each had to be manned; and servicing and repairs were much more labor-intensive for steamers than for diesel-electrics. The switch from steam to diesel would be revolutionary, not least in its effect on the size of the workforce. There was much hardship, and there would have been even more if train crews had been reduced still further. The unions fought tooth and nail to keep communities together where sometimes the livelihoods of whole townships were bound to the railroads.

PASSENGER AND FREIGHT CAR EVOLUTION, 1920-50s

AS RAILROADS DEVELOPED FAST, LONG-DISTANCE SERVICES, THEY PUT PRESSURE ON PASSENGER CAR BUILDERS TO PRODUCE LIGHTER AND MORE COMFORTABLE VEHICLES. BY THE LATE 1950s, HOWEVER, THE PASSENGER MARKET WAS COLLAPSING. FREIGHT CARS, MEANWHILE, BECAME LARGER AND MORE SPECIALIZED.

Railway Post Office cars were fitted with a hook to collect the mail bag as the train sped through a station.

B y the 1920s, some 100,000 travelers slept in Pullman beds every night. The heavyweight passenger cars were built like tanks and offered a service life of 50 or more years. During the worst part of the 1930s Depression, however, the Pullman company was losing money heavily. People were traveling less and, at the same time, the interstate highway construction program, funded by the taxpayer, was eating into the rail passenger business.

Change was forced on Pullman and other railroad car builders by the need to cater for higher speeds with more comfort over longer distances. Only under heavy pressure from the railroads did Pullman modify its rigid attitude and concede that it had to move away from building very heavy cars. It did introduce private-room accommodation, but it was slower to build lighter vehicles. The advent of the experimental diesel trains in the early 1930s showed that passenger cars could be made from something other than 1/4in (6mm) steel plate. Lightweight aluminum and stainless steel, together with carefully designed trucks, brought weight down. Even so, providing such amenities as air conditioning and its power supply left the new streamliner cars still in excess of 60 tons apiece. The large-scale introduction of air conditioning began in 1930, and by 1936, there were some 5,800 cars so equipped.

Another notable device that began to appear in the 1930s was the disc brake, which the Budd Company began marketing in 1938–9, although it was not in general use until the mid-1950s. Disc brakes were quieter than shoe brakes, and saved on wheel wear.

In 1940, the U.S. Department of Justice filed a complaint against Pullman's monopoly of the sleeping-car business. This had been tolerated by the railroads because Pullman's pool of cars could be moved around the country to wherever they were most needed. In 1947, Pullman was forced to separate its car building from its operating division, creating Pullman Inc., Car Builder. The sleeping-car operation, the Pullman Company, was sold to the 57 railroads over which it ran its cars.

No other major innovations appeared until the 1950s. While 3,000 new cars had been ordered in 1945–6, they were essentially copies of earlier models; even by 1950, only 15 percent were lightweights. At the time, economic conditions did not favor a full-scale replacement of cars, and as passengers deserted the railroads for the automobile and air travel, few new cars were ordered. Long-distance travel was still in demand, however, and continued for the next decade. In 1957, the Pennsylvania began operating its own parlor cars, and one by one, the other railroads pulled out of the Pullman operation. In 1958, when the New York Central started to run its own sleeping cars, the first commercial jet airliners, which would take most business away from Pullman, went into service.

Among many attempts by the railroads to lure passengers back was the dome car, which gave passengers a panoramic view of the most scenic parts of a route. They were few in number, however, as were the Santa Fe's "Hi-level" cars. By 1955, the passenger market had collapsed generally; new car construction was stopped, and obsolescent vehicles retained. It was a dismal picture, symbolized at the end of 1960 by American Car & Foundry quitting the market altogether.

Although it could have been better, freight traffic held up fairly well, with bulk traffic, the kind of haulage suited to rail, retaining a fair market share. Again, steel had replaced lumber in the construction of freight cars in the early 1930s, and welded-steel structures were being designed and adopted for hopper cars to reduce dead weight. It was possible to increase the payload from 70 to 82 tons within the gross rail load limit of 210,000lb (95,256kg) in force at the time. Since then, there has been an increase in payload as rail load limits have been raised in the wake of stronger tracks.

High-capacity flatcars were introduced in 1933, enabling road vehicles to be transported great distances. From the 1950s, the flatcar grew to a length of 89ft (27m); at the same time, autorack and "piggyback" carriers were introduced. Boxcars grew to a length of 86ft (26m). Various devices were introduced to cushion loads from shunting and other knocks. Many other special-purpose cars have been introduced, with tankcars particularly reaching a capacity of 12,000 gallons (45,420 liters) by 1960. The range of special freight cars is interesting in its diversity. For example, there are cars for hauling hot metal, steel billets, poultry, pickles, vinegar, milk, livestock (horses, cattle, pigs), military equipment of all kinds, atomic waste, and bridge components.

Tankcars for carrying milk were just one innovation among many when it came to the design of freight cars.

The dome car provided a high-level observation point, giving passengers a panoramic view of the passing countryside.

Bulkhead flatcars had sturdy end-walls, to prevent loads shifting beyond the ends of the car. Loads typically carried were lumber, pipe, and steel slabs.

THE NEW INTERURBANS, 1930-41

DESPITE THE INROADS OF THE AUTOMOBILE AND MOTOR BUS—
AND THE IMPACT OF THE WALL STREET CRASH OF 1929, AND
THE GREAT DEPRESSION THAT FOLLOWED IT—THE STREETCAR
BUILDERS AND THOSE OPERATORS WHO HAD NOT SWITCHED TO
BUSES WERE NOT GOING TO GIVE UP WITHOUT A FIGHT.

The bankrupt North Shore Line turned to the streamlined Electroliner to revive its fortunes in the early 1940s.

Streetcar design had changed little during the 1920s, and by the end of the decade, the industry realized that higher standards of vehicle performance and passenger comfort would be essential if it wanted to avoid extinction. In 1931, the J.G. Brill company produced a series of 10 high-speed railcars, known as Bullet cars because of their radically streamlined noses. The Bullet car, probably the first trolley ever to be tested in a wind tunnel, was Brill's bid to revolutionize the high-speed interurban market. It was the first American trolley to sell streamlining to the traveling public, and was introduced after tests by the aerodynamicist Professor Felix Pawlowski, of the University of Michigan, showed a 42 percent increase in efficiency resulting from its streamlined shape and aluminum body. One of the largest customers for Bullet cars was the Philadelphia & Western (P&W), which put them in service at the end of 1931. Even as the Depression decimated the interurban lines, P&W traffic increased, for the public loved the new cars and their speeds of up to 85mph (137km/h). The P&W's successor, the Southeastern Pennsylvania Transportation Authority (SEPTA), continued to run them on its Red Arrow Lines, and they spent a phenomenal 60 years on the main line. The P&W's Bullet cars never ran as trolleys, because they drew their power from a third rail, not from overhead wires, but they probably traveled farther, faster, and more profitably than most other streetcars.

Another notable attempt to revitalize interurban streetcar travel began in 1938, when the St. Louis Car Company (SLCC) started work on its Electroliner vehicles. At the time, the major railroads were beginning the transition from steam to diesel and introducing new locomotive designs called streamliners. Stealing a bit of thunder from these eye-catching models, the sleekly streamlined, articulated, four-car Electroliner was designed specifically to revitalize the bankrupt North Shore Line (the Chicago, North Shore and Milwaukee Railroad), which ran between Chicago, Illinois, and Milwaukee, Wisconsin. When the shovel-nosed speedster went into service in 1941, it far exceeded expectations, and passenger numbers on the line doubled in one year.

The Electroliner was a huge leap forward for interurban lines, and among the improvements it offered were true air conditioning, soundproofing, and hydraulic shock absorbers. There was even a luxurious bar, where passengers could munch Electroburgers while cruising at 90mph (145km/h) as the 1,000hp of the Electroliner's eight motors whisked them toward Chicago's Loop. Only two Electroliners were built, however, and when the North Shore Line gave them up in 1963, Red Arrow Lines of Philadelphia took them over. There, renamed Liberty Liners and in the same livery as the Bullet trains of 1931, they ran until 1979. After they were retired, they were acquired by museums—one is now at the Rockhill Trolley Museum in Rockhill Furnace, Pennsylvania, while the other is at the Illinois Railway Museum, in Union, Illinois.

Built by the St. Louis Car Company, the Electroliner was an articulated four-car trainset that did much to generate renewed interest in interurbans.

THE LAST GREAT STREETCAR

IN 1929, OVER 50 LEADING MEMBERS OF THE STREETCAR INDUSTRY GOT TOGETHER TO PLAN A MODERN, STANDARDIZED REPLACEMENT FOR NORTH AMERICA'S AGING AND DIVERSE FLEET OF TROLLEYS. THE RESULT WAS THE PCC, A STREETCAR THAT BECAME A WORLDWIDE FAVORITE AND IS STILL IN USE TODAY.

Alongside their development of new interurbans, Brill and SLCC were active in the production of new urban streetcars. Brill introduced its Master Unit streetcars in 1929, and the two companies shared the production of 20 streamlined cars for the Capital Transit Company of Washington, D.C., which were delivered in 1935. More importantly, both companies were members of an industry consortium called the Electric Railway Presidents Conference Committee (ERPCC), which was set up in 1929 to develop a modern, standardized streetcar design. Headed by Dr. Thomas Conway, who had ordered the Brill Bullet cars for the Philadelphia & Western, its membership consisted of 28 streetcar operating companies and 25 manufacturers.

After five years of intensive effort, the committee completed a total redesign of every component of the streetcar. Mechanical improvements concentrated on smooth, rapid acceleration and a whisper-quiet ride. As for the exterior skin, it was to be expected that the "dream streetcar"—known as the PCC (a shortened form of ERPCC)—would take the aerodynamically inspired streamliner shape. Steam locomotives of the day had received the same treatment from such industrial designers as Norman Bel Geddes and Raymond Loewy, as had many other vehicles and home appliances. Although they were far from the perfectly aerodynamic teardrop shape, the PCC prototypes resembled nothing else then running on U.S. trolley tracks. As a fitting inaugural gesture for this new breed of streetcar, Frank Sprague, the man who had started the whole business in 1877, rode in a prototype PCC car shortly before his death in 1934.

SLCC and Pullman-Standard rushed them into production; the first to be delivered was Brooklyn 1001, which went into trial service with the Brooklyn and Queens Transit Company, New York, in May

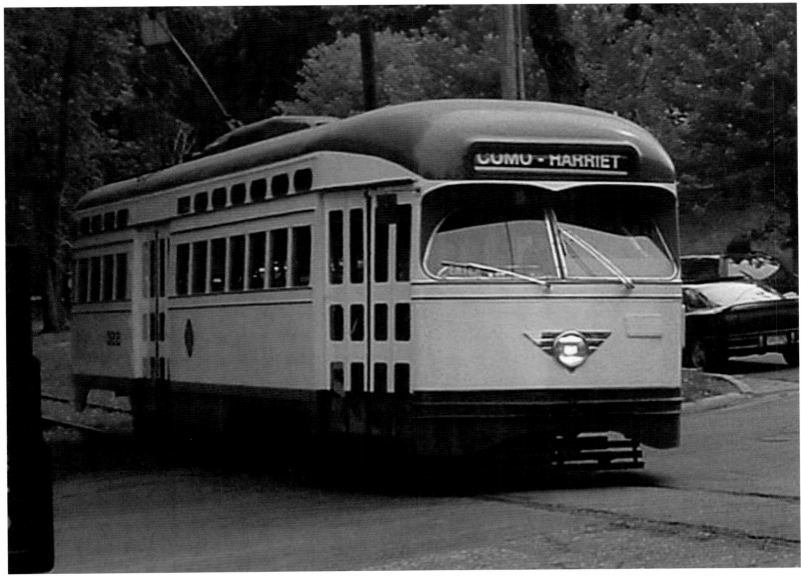

1936. The first to enter actual revenue service was Pittsburgh 100, the second PCC to be built, which was delivered to the Pittsburgh Railways Company two months later. For a streetcar designed by a committee, the PCC streamliner was overwhelmingly successful, and production totaled more than 5,000 in North America, where SLCC made 3,966 and Pullman-Standard 1,057. Another 15–20,000 more were manufactured under license by factories in Europe, and hundreds still run on routes throughout the world more than 70 years after their debut. Philadelphia, San Francisco, and Boston operate some, as do several cities in Europe and in Latin America. PCC technology also formed the basis of rapid-transit trainsets for urban railroads in Boston, Brooklyn (New York), Chicago, and Cleveland.

National production priorities during World War II halted most assembly lines for automobiles, buses, and home appliances, but trolleys, which consumed no scarce gasoline or rubber tires, remained in production and regained a measure of importance in city transportation systems. Pullman-Standard kept its PCC production lines open, but shortages of raw materials meant that the chrome trim in the interiors had to be abandoned, paint being used instead, and some of the rubber inserts that gave PCC cars their quiet ride were omitted. Pullman-Standard simplified the interior trim and eliminated a few compound-curved metal panels for ease of manufacture, but these cars still gave sterling service for

The PCC was an enduring design that found favor around the world. Remarkably, although the prototype was tested in 1934, many examples of this streetcar remain in service.

In the 1930s, the Brooklyn and Queens Transit Company, in New York, operated a substantial trolley network throughout Brooklyn, illustrating the value of this form of public transport system. The B&Q was the first streetcar company to trial the PCC car in 1936.

the duration of the war and long after.

When you enter a PCC car today, it is disconcerting to see a driver's seat like that of a bus, with accelerator and brake pedal, and a petite speedometer, but no steering wheel, only a row of switches across the dashboard. The foot pedal replaced the old hand controler, resulting in much smoother acceleration. There were three discrete brake systems on the PCC: a regenerative brake, which fed stopping energy back into the power grid; a compressed-air system; and an emergency magnetic system, which clamped down on the tracks. A 19-ton vehicle needed all the stopping power it could muster, especially in the fall, when wet leaves littered the tracks. The wetness wasn't a problem—it actually improved steel-to-steel friction—but the leaves were worse than sheet ice, as any veteran driver would attest.

The later, postwar PCCs, called all-electric because they had electric "fail-safe" brakes instead of air brakes, had an additional row of "standee" windows running along the top of the car. Because of the rakish "chopped and dropped" windows on earlier PCCs, standing passengers could not see their stops. The new windows, which helped to overcome this problem, were allegedly copied from those of the buses of the time. This was only fair, because buses had borrowed heavily from the PCC in their styling. Also of note on these newer PCC cars was a long dorsal pod containing ventilating fans, which, curiously, were never used by the PCCs operated by the Toronto Transportation Commission. The fans were removed, but the pods were left in place.

Toronto operated more PCCs by far than any other Canadian city. In all, 745 streamliners saw service there between 1938 and 1995, and in the 1950s, the city was operating the largest fleet of PCCs in the world. Some PCCs were produced for Toronto by SLCC and Canadian Car & Foundry, acting in partnership. Others, built by SLCC and by Pullman-Standard, were bought secondhand from U.S. cities, such as Louisville, Cincinnati, Cleveland, Birmingham, and Kansas City. All were similar in size—slightly less than 47ft (14.4m) long—and, of course, used the nonstandard Toronto wide gauge of 4ft 10 7/8in (1.5m). Most of the earlier, prewar cars and those that had been acquired secondhand were disposed of in 1983.

Later examples of the PCC had a long pod on the roof containing ventilating fans.

Although it had been a member of the ERPCC, Brill opted out of PCC production, preferring to develop its own new streetcar, the Brilliner. Intended as a competitor for the PCC, the Brilliner was launched in 1938 and had bodywork styled by Raymond Loewy. Brill sold only 40 of them, however, including 25 to Atlantic City and 10 to Philadelphia's Red Arrow Lines. The Atlantic City Brilliners remained in service until 1955, while those in Philadelphia—which were the last streetcars Brill ever built, in 1941—ran for more than 40 years until their retirement in 1982.

The PCC was the most successful of all streetcar designs, and in many cities it helped to slow the conversion from streetcars to buses, but the long-term decline in streetcar patronage continued unabated. In the United States, annual passenger numbers were down to just under 6 billion by 1940, less than half of what they had been in 1920. They rose again to around 9 billion during World War II (when fuel and tire rationing hit private automobile use), but dropped rapidly after the war, slumping to under 4 billion in 1950, and just 133 million in 1980, by which time only a handful of North American cities were operating regular streetcar services.

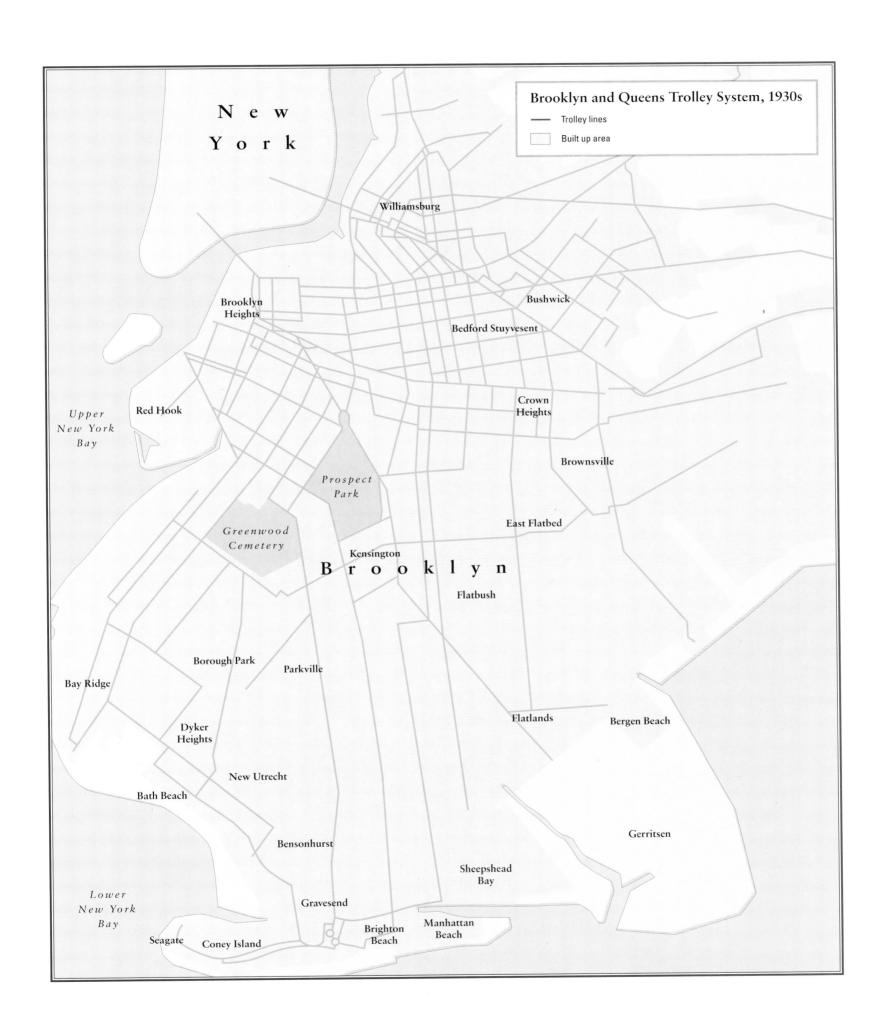

Brooklyn and Queens Trolley System, 1930s

—— Trolley lines

☐ Built up area

New York

Williamsburg

Brooklyn
Heights

Bushwick

Bedford Stuyvesent

Red Hook

*Upper
New York
Bay*

Crown
Heights

Brownsville

*Prospect
Park*

East Flatbed

*Greenwood
Cemetery*

Kensington

B r o o k l y n

Flatbush

Borough Park

Parkville

Bay Ridge

Flatlands

Bergen Beach

Dyker
Heights

New Utrecht

Bath Beach

Gerritsen

Bensonhurst

Sheepshead
Bay

*Lower
New York
Bay*

Gravesend

Manhattan
Beach

Seagate

Coney Island

Brighton
Beach

Railroad Mergers and Deregulation, 1960–95

THE LAST THREE DECADES OF THE 20TH CENTURY SAW
MAJOR CHANGES TO U.S. RAILROADS AS THEY FOUGHT TO
STAY IN BUSINESS. MERGERS HELPED MANY SURVIVE, WHILE
DEREGULATION, REVISED LABOR PRACTICES, AND IMPROVED
EQUIPMENT LED TO INCREASED PROFITABILITY.

By 1960, the situation on America's railroads was reaching a crucial point, which can be seen from what happened to rail traffic over the preceding 30 years. In 1930, passenger traffic movements on the railroads reached 32 billion, but fell to 19 billion in 1933. They rose to a peak of 71 billion in 1943, then fell to 64 billion in 1946, to 32 billion in 1950, and finally to 21 billion in 1960. Freight, on the other hand, began at 42 billion in 1930, fell to 28 billion in 1933, rose to a peak of 65 billion in 1943, and seesawed mainly between that figure and 58 billion in 1960, with a low of 52 billion in 1949.

The last steam locomotive was retired in 1960, by which time diesel reigned almost supreme (there was still a significant amount of traffic operated by electric traction). Passenger traffic receipts were falling, although the pace of fall had slowed. On the other hand, freight receipts were holding up fairly well. The implications were obvious. As a passenger-carrier, rail seemed to be in terminal decline, but the freight side of the business was in fair shape, with the possibility even of increasing its share of the market. Inevitably, changes would be required if the railroads were to remain viable businesses.

By 1960, diesel-electric locomotives had changed the face of railroad operation—but so, too, had highway vehicles and airplanes. With falling freight and passenger traffic, and decreasing revenue, railroads had to merge to survive. Big was beautiful, or so it seemed to many railroads struggling to compete with other modes of transport, as well as with each other.

The diesel revolution put new life into American railroads. By 1960, 27,000 diesels had replaced some 40,000 steam locomotives in the United States. Canada, too, soon retired its last steam locomotives, in 1962. Steam maintenance facilities disappeared fast, steam workshops quickly being converted to diesel repair shops or being shut down entirely. Whole communities were affected. There had been other cost cutting strategies, too. Centralized Traffic Control (CTC) had been introduced before 1950, making train movement safer and more efficient. By 1965, it was accepted as the safest form of traffic control then available. By clearing signals and operating switches directly from his desk, the dispatcher had complete control of a train's progress. Soon the radio and computer added another dimension to railroad operation. Two-way radio communication between train crews and control towers became normal. Then, new computerized systems for tracking the movement of locomotives and cars appeared, of which TOPS (Total Operations Processing System) was perhaps the most successful.

Probably the most crucial innovation was the hot-box detector. Freight train operation had long been plagued by axleboxes that ran hot. These could cause train fires, or soften and melt the axles, causing a derailment. One of the prime duties of crewmen was to keep axleboxes under observation, but with increasingly long trains, they could not always spot the wisps of smoke or flame in time. The new hot-box detectors were trackside heat-sensing devices that could detect trouble on a passing train and not only send a radio a warning to the train crew, but also indicate the precise location of the faulty axlebox.

Deregulation in 1980, with the passing of the Staggers Act, enabled the U.S. railroads to expand into the specialized carriage of commodities such as coal, carried in hopper cars, and liquids in tank cars.

Despite these innovations, the railroads were clearly struggling in the 1970s. Many solutions, even nationalization, were suggested. Such proposals got nowhere, owing to strong conservative opposition; almost every other proposal put to Congress had a feature that some senators or representatives threw out. Clearly, however, planning and action at national level were needed. Railroads had been hamstrung by regulating legislation since the 1880s. In the late 1970s, President Jimmy Carter had partly deregulated trucking and the airlines. This put additional pressure on the freight railroads, and they demanded parity of treatment. In 1980, at last this was granted by the passing of what came to be known as the Staggers Act, Rep. Harley Staggers (Democrat, West Virginia) being chairman of the House Commerce Committee at that time.

By 1963, the total route length for U.S. railroads was down to 214,387 miles (345,013km). The network matched the population and industry spread of the country, the Northeast remaining the best served area.

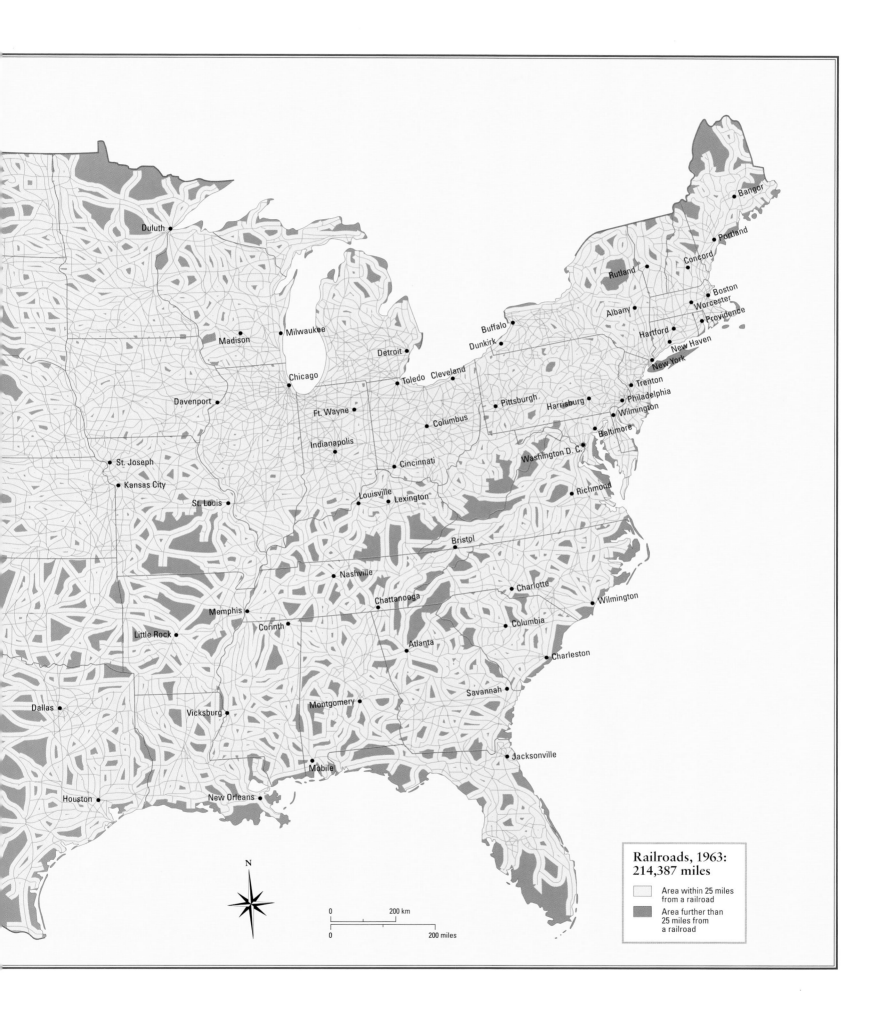

**Railroads, 1963:
214,387 miles**

☐ Area within 25 miles
from a railroad

■ Area further than
25 miles from
a railroad

A new sight on U.S. railroads from April 1, 1976 was the new livery and logo of Conrail. The Consolidated Rail Corporation was a federally-funded takeover of the major railroad companies in the northeast, which were in financial dire straits.

The Staggers Act significantly altered the terms under which railroads and shippers could agree freight charges. Henceforth, railroads could offer volume discounts and other tariff incentives, which formerly had been prohibited. The ICC would supervise only those tariffs where there was a real transportation monopoly, which was considerably less than 20 percent of the total. Railroads and shippers could negotiate their own contracts privately. Withdrawal of services and closure of loss making lines became easier.

The 1980 deregulation enabled the railroads to expand their carriage of coal and grain, automobiles, and intermodal containers, among other forms of traffic. Railroad investment, meager for too long, increased. The Act also encouraged the development of that specialized class of railroad, the regional line. Such companies could take on lines with low flow densities and operate them profitably. Some of them were quite long. The Wisconsin Central, for example, operated over 2,000 miles (3,200km) of route, and had 115 locomotives and 5,135 cars. It was formed in 1987 by purchase of the former Lakes States division of the Soo Line. Its main line linked Chicago with Minneapolis and extended into Ontario. Another regional was the Iowa Interstate, which took over the Soo Line's main line between Council Bluffs in Iowa and Bureau in Illinois. Like the WC, the Iowa Interstate also acquired failing railroads in other parts of the world, with the aim of revitalizing them.

The postwar merger era had really started earlier than 1980, some say in the late 1940s, when six roads merged to form three. These were the Gulf, Mobile & Ohio with the Alton (the new GM&O subsequently was merged into its near-parallel competitor, the Illinois Central); the Denver & Rio Grande Western with the Denver & Salt Lake; and the Chesapeake & Ohio with the Pere Marquette, a small road that operated mainly in Michigan. Then there was the merger in 1957 of the Louisville & Nashville RR with the Nashville, Chattanooga & St Louis.

At first, only the smaller roads began to disappear. Then, in 1963, the Chesapeake & Ohio acquired the celebrated old Baltimore & Ohio; in 1973, the latter, together with the Western Maryland, became a subsidiary of the Chessie System, as did the C&O itself. In 1964, the Norfolk & Western acquired two smaller roads and leased two others. The big news of that year, however, was the announcement that the arch-rival Pennsylvania and New York Central were to merge to form the Penn Central; the merger was completed in 1968, the ICC stipulating that the New Haven Railroad (NYNH&H RR) should also be included.

At the time of merger, both the NYC and PRR were in the black, but the new company immediately

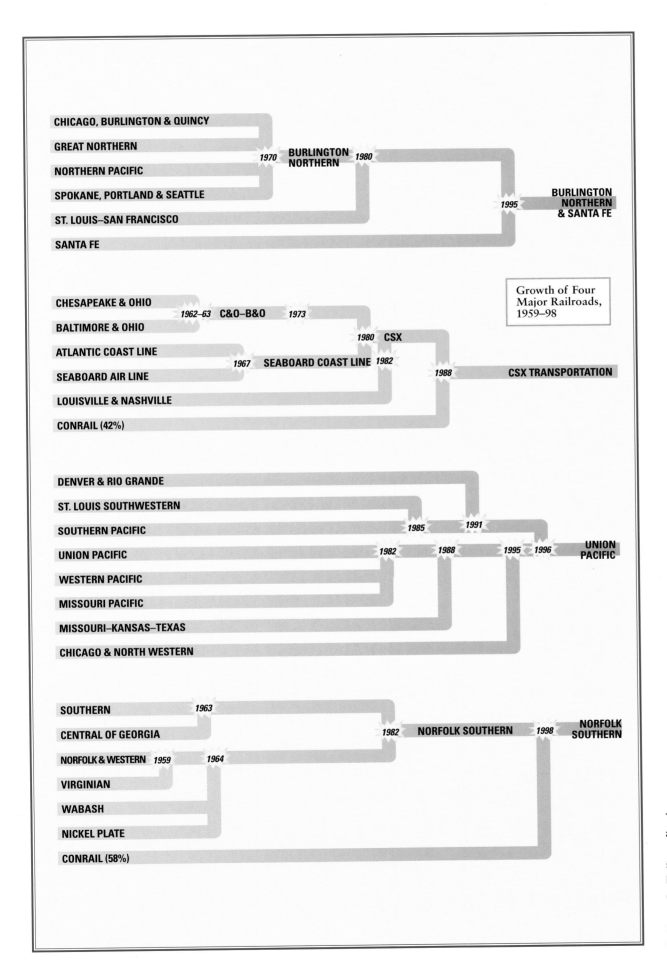

Growth of Four
Major Railroads,
1959–98

CHICAGO, BURLINGTON & QUINCY

GREAT NORTHERN

1970 BURLINGTON NORTHERN 1980

NORTHERN PACIFIC

SPOKANE, PORTLAND & SEATTLE

1995 BURLINGTON NORTHERN & SANTA FE

ST. LOUIS–SAN FRANCISCO

SANTA FE

CHESAPEAKE & OHIO

1962–63 C&O–B&O 1973

BALTIMORE & OHIO

1980 CSX

ATLANTIC COAST LINE

1967 SEABOARD COAST LINE 1982

SEABOARD AIR LINE

1988 CSX TRANSPORTATION

LOUISVILLE & NASHVILLE

CONRAIL (42%)

DENVER & RIO GRANDE

ST. LOUIS SOUTHWESTERN

SOUTHERN PACIFIC 1985 1991

UNION PACIFIC 1982 1988 1995 1996 UNION PACIFIC

WESTERN PACIFIC

MISSOURI PACIFIC

MISSOURI–KANSAS–TEXAS

CHICAGO & NORTH WESTERN

SOUTHERN 1963

CENTRAL OF GEORGIA 1982 NORFOLK SOUTHERN 1998 NORFOLK SOUTHERN

NORFOLK & WESTERN 1959 1964

VIRGINIAN

WABASH

NICKEL PLATE

CONRAIL (58%)

This graph indicates the growth and decline of track mileage in 10 selected states. Notice the steep rise during the second half of the 19th century. In most cases, there was a peak around 1920, after which a steady reduction occurred for the remainder of the 20th century.

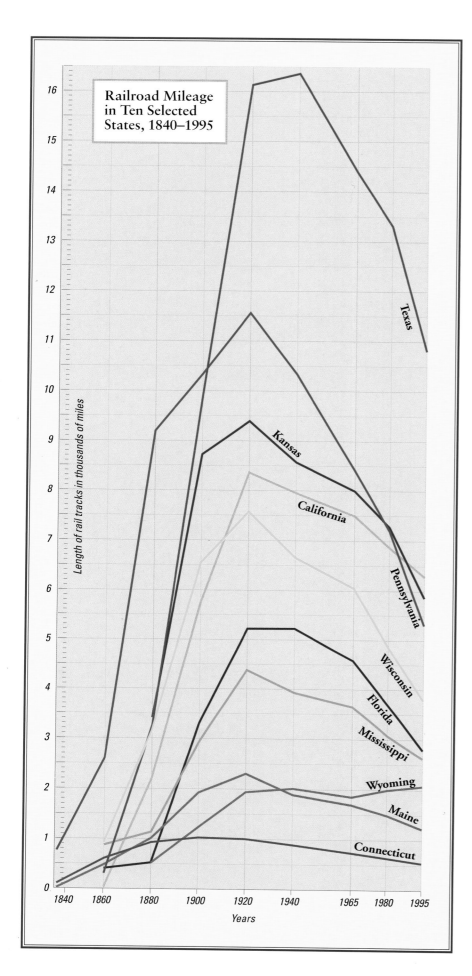

Railroad Mileage in Ten Selected States, 1840–1995

Length of rail tracks in thousands of miles

Texas
Kansas
California
Pennsylvania
Wisconsin
Florida
Mississippi
Wyoming
Maine
Connecticut

Years

ran into heavy deficits. None of the merging railroads had really prepared in practical terms for the change; the managements of the NYC and PRR, having long regarded each other as opponents, failed to mesh. Working systems and practices were not integrated, and each "team" sought to impose its own methods on the whole system. This failure to integrate management was accompanied by a failure to promptly combine the physical assets, which was what the merger had promised. Former competing NYC and PRR lines continued, in effect, to compete. Meanwhile, the deindustrialization of the region that the Penn Central served removed traditional sources of traffic; the four-track main lines, about which both companies had boasted in the past, became burdens, still attracting taxes and maintenance costs, but without the traffic to justify them. The Penn Central traded for only two years before becoming the biggest single bankruptcy in United States history. The cataclysm of this failure, and the parlous state of the "anthracite roads" in the same region, created a situation with which the free market economy was unable to cope effectively, so the federal government felt obliged to step in. After long proceedings, Consolidated Rail Corporation (Conrail) was inaugurated on April 1, 1976, to take over the failed and failing lines.

Conrail, a government owned Class I railroad, was feared by some influential Americans as a fateful step toward dreaded railroad nationalization, a concern already aroused by the establishment in 1971 of Amtrak, the government financed passenger-train operator. Conrail would do well, however, and eventually return to the private sector. Apart from the Penn Central, it incorporated the Erie Lackawanna, Lehigh Valley, Lehigh & Hudson River, Reading, and Central of New Jersey railroads, together with the jointly owned Pennsylvania-Reading Seashore Lines. One of its early moves was to sell the Northeast Corridor lines (Washington–New York–Boston, as well as Philadelphia–Harrisburg)) to Amtrak, while retaining trackage rights. It shed the burden of about 6,000 miles (9,656km) of low-traffic route by selling to short lines or agreeing to operate with subsidy. Its commuter services were steadily hived off to other operators.

Conrail was the largest freight carrier in the East, operating in 12 states plus the District of Columbia, as well as in the Canadian province of Quebec. After many trials and tribulations, the new railroad, managed by L. Stanley Crane, recently retired president of the Southern Railway, was able to adopt a new approach to railroading. Crane tackled the train-crew problem by avoiding the traditional management posture of confrontation. The unions cooperated, and by adroit negotiation and bargaining, a new labor structure was worked out. Another of Crane's initiatives was to encourage new marketing techniques that focused on the most important commodities: grain, coal, automobiles, intermodal, etc. Trains ran to time more frequently, and operation became more reliable. In a relatively short time, Conrail began running at a profit, and Congress was persuaded to authorize the sale of its stock to the public. Conrail had shown that railroads could be a profitable, successful, and even exciting business.

Elsewhere in the United States, hard pressed railroads were seeking refuge in mergers; the closure of loss making lines entailed a protracted and bureaucratic negotiation with the ICC, and, despite the Staggers deregulation, was not always successful. The ICC also approved or disapproved mergers,

The railroads branched out into the transportation of newly completed automobiles from manufacturers on specialized, double- and sometimes triple-deck rail cars called autoracks. Automobiles could be quickly and easily loaded and unloaded.

Opposite ver the years, the survival of many railroads depended on mergers or takeovers. This illustration shows the genesis of four major roads over four decades in the second half of the 20th century.

Amtrak was set up by Act of Congress to take over loss making passenger services from the other railroads. In the main, its services ran over tracks that belonged to those railroads, but its trains didn't always receive the priority they required to run to schedule, which caused problems for passengers. This map shows its major routes in the year of its inauguration.

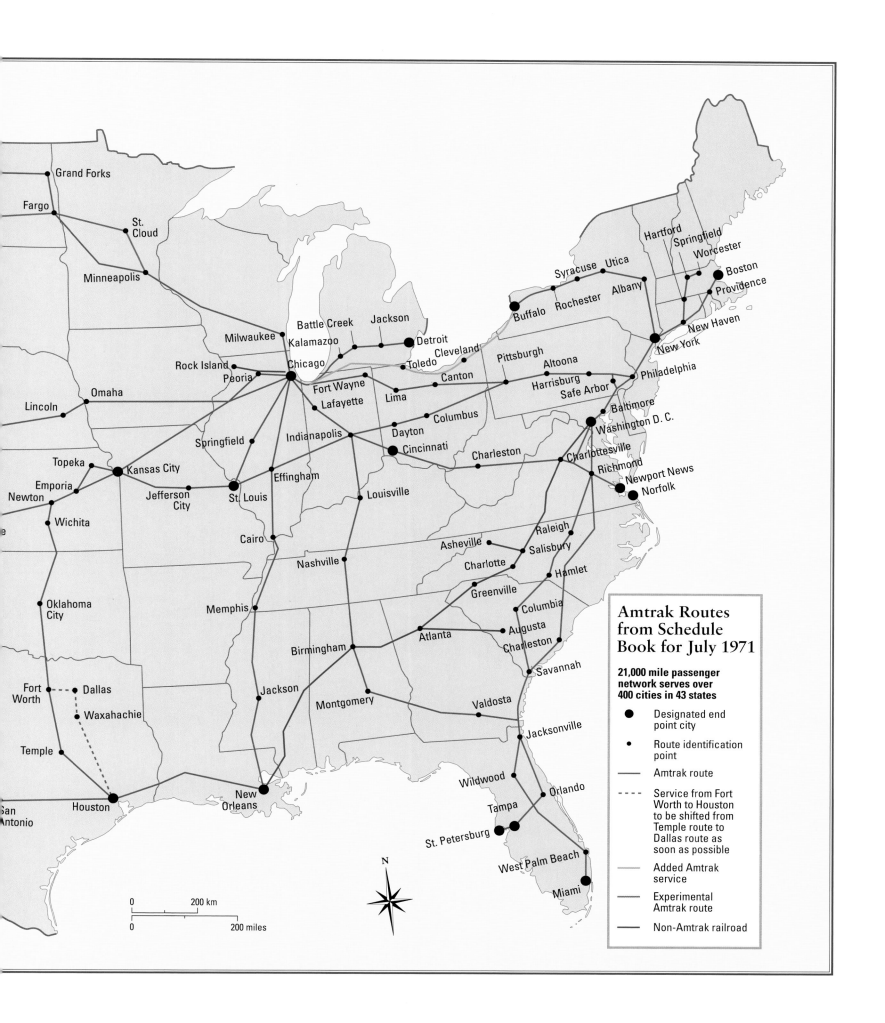

Amtrak Routes from Schedule Book for July 1971

21,000 mile passenger network serves over 400 cities in 43 states

- ● Designated end point city
- • Route identification point
- —— Amtrak route
- - - - Service from Fort Worth to Houston to be shifted from Temple route to Dallas route as soon as possible
- —— Added Amtrak service
- —— Experimental Amtrak route
- —— Non-Amtrak railroad

Grand Forks
Fargo
St. Cloud
Minneapolis
Milwaukee
Battle Creek
Jackson
Kalamazoo
Detroit
Cleveland
Rock Island
Chicago
Toledo
Pittsburgh
Altoona
Peoria
Fort Wayne
Lima
Canton
Harrisburg
Safe Arbor
Philadelphia
Lafayette
Columbus
Baltimore
Omaha
Springfield
Indianapolis
Dayton
Washington D.C.
Lincoln
Cincinnati
Charleston
Charlottesville
Topeka
Kansas City
Effingham
Louisville
Richmond
Newport News
Emporia
Jefferson City
St. Louis
Norfolk
Newton
Wichita
Cairo
Raleigh
Oklahoma City
Nashville
Asheville
Salisbury
Charlotte
Hamlet
Memphis
Greenville
Columbia
Atlanta
Augusta
Birmingham
Charleston
Fort Worth
Dallas
Jackson
Savannah
Waxahachie
Montgomery
Valdosta
Temple
Jacksonville
San Antonio
Houston
New Orleans
Wildwood
Orlando
Tampa
St. Petersburg
West Palm Beach
Miami
Syracuse
Utica
Hartford
Springfield
Worcester
Buffalo
Rochester
Albany
Boston
Providence
New Haven
New York

N

| 0 | 200 km |
| 0 | 200 miles |

another slow (but careful) process. The fate of the Chicago, Rock Island & Pacific illustrates the complexities. In 1964, the chairman of the Chicago & North Western, Ben Heineman, proposed a merger with the Rock Island (1964 was Rock Island's last year of profitability) and the Milwaukee Road into an Upper Midwest system, selling the lines south of Kansas City to the Santa Fe. The Union Pacific made a counterproposal that would have given it access to Chicago.

The proposal began the longest, most complicated merger so far handled by the ICC. Roads west of Chicago protested, some petitioned for inclusion, while others asked for a piece of the Rock Island. In 1973, the ICC proposed a restructuring of the railroad systems of the West around the Union Pacific, Southern Pacific, Burlington Northern, and Santa Fe. The railroads involved in the merger, other than the two principals, the Union Pacific and Rock Island, petitioned to dismiss the case and begin again.

The merger was approved by the ICC in November 1974, but several conditions were attached. The Union Pacific said that the merger now needed reevaluation, since the Rock Island of 1974 wasn't the Rock Island of 10 years before. The Rock Island filed for bankruptcy on March 17, 1975, and on August 4, 1975, the Union Pacific withdrew its offer. The ICC dismissed the case on July 10, 1976, and that was the beginning of the end of the Rock Island, which ceased operation on March 31, 1980. This was the first time the railroad industry had seen an abandonment of such magnitude. (The abandonment of the Milwaukee RR's transcontinental line in 1977 was not considered as being so drastic, because a rump of the Milwaukee survived; nor was the liquidation of the New York, Ontario & Western in 1957 seen as serious, since that railroad had been redundant from the year it was built.) In 1978, the Rock Island had operated more than 7,000 miles (11,000km) of lines.

The coal hauling Norfolk & Western Railway was remarkable for its long adherence to steam traction, and it was not until the late 1950s that diesels were accepted wholeheartedly. Thus it skipped the first generation of diesel locomotives. This economy of capital expenditure may have been a factor in the NW's solid financial position. It was able to merge with its competitor, the Virginian Railroad, and then, in 1982, the ICC approved its merger with the Southern Railway, to form the Norfolk Southern, which remains one of the major U.S. railroads.

In 1967, the ICC approved the merger of two rivals, the Atlantic Coast RR and the Seaboard Air Line. The latter, despite its title, was a railroad, competing with ACL for the Florida traffic as well as for freight over much of the South. The merged companies adopted the tautological name of Seaboard Coast Line. This merger also involved the Louisville & Nashville RR, which was controlled by the ACL. Then, in 1980, the SCL merged with the Chessie System to form the second of the big eastern railroads, the CSX.

In the West, the old competitors Great Northern and Northern Pacific amalgamated in 1970, together with the Chicago, Burlington & Quincy, to form the Burlington Northern. The deal also included the Spokane, Portland & Seattle and two lesser lines, the Colorado & Southern RR and the Fort Worth & Denver. Ten years later, the BN bought the substantial Frisco (St. Louis-San Francisco Railway), gaining penetration into Texas and Alabama. This made the BN the dominant western railroad, although it was run a close second by the Union Pacific, which acquired the Missouri Pacific, Western Pacific, and Missouri-Kansas-Texas railroads in the 1980s.

By the end of the 1980s, there were just 15 Class I railroads (then defined as those with gross

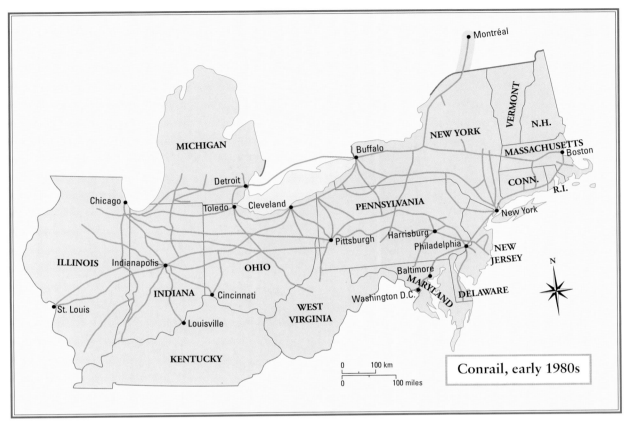

Conrail, early 1980s

Conrail worked tracks in the busy Northeast and was a successful reinvigoration of failing railroads in the region.

revenues of $50 million or more). These were the Burlington Northern, Union Pacific, Conrail, CSX, Norfolk Southern, Santa Fe, Illinois Central, Southern Pacific, Kansas City Southern, Chicago & North Western, Soo Line, Florida East Coast, Denver and Rio Grande Western, Grand Trunk (the Canadian National's U.S. lines), and Guilford Industries. The last of these was a type of corporation that was growing in importance, a company that acquired and held small- or medium-sized railroads that might well be physically separated. Another was RailTex, which was founded in 1984 and, within a decade, held and operated a score of lines totaling several thousand miles. Guilford Industries' main acquisitions were the substantial Boston & Maine and Maine Central railroads.

In addition to the Class Is, there were almost 500 Class II and III railroads. These included some big regional corporations as well as a multitude of short lines, mainly occupied in interchanging local traffic with the main-line companies.

Short lines could make low-traffic railroads profitable, largely because they were normally excluded from the pay-and-conditions settlements reached by the unions with the major companies. In this period, those bigger companies were under strong pressure from the brotherhoods, partly because there were too many of the latter, each striving to outdo the other. General railroad strike situations could occur, but could be brought to some kind of conclusion by actual or threatened federal intervention. The issue of retaining firemen on diesel locomotives was a long-fought battle, which took several decades to settle in a rational fashion. The longest strike was that undergone by the Florida East Coast RR, which lasted for years. In 1963, the FEC had refused to abide by a nationwide agreement on pay increases; the resultant strike included interpersonal violence and stoning of trains, as well as bombs on the track. Nonunionized staff, largely from management, became operating workers. Passenger-train conductors not only checked tickets, but also listed the names of passengers, to help in notifying next-of-kin if anything happened. The strike was not settled finally until 1973; by that time, the FEC had been able to impose all kinds of innovations that the railroad industry obviously needed and eventually was able to imitate. These included the abolition of the caboose, and the running of freight trains over the length of the railroad with just a two-man crew, instead of the three successive five-man crews that national railroad labor agreements had made obligatory (at this time, railroad labor was regarded by the public, quite rightly, as featherbedded).

In 1992, the ICC revised its classification of United States railroads. Henceforth, Class I railroads were those having income in excess of $250 million per year; Class II had operating revenues of between $20 million and $250 million; and Class III were those with less than $20 million. The only big demotion resulting from this change was that the Florida East Coast RR became a Class II, which reflected its regional significance. At that time, there were 15 companies that could be regarded as significant regional railroads.

By the late 1960s, with the general demise of long-distance passenger travel, and the loss of the mail contracts, which had provided a steady addition to passenger-train revenue, it was obvious that a radical change in the way railroads dealt with passenger traffic was needed. In its short life, the Penn Central had made some effort to reform services along its Washington–New York–Boston axis. Encouraged by the Department of Transportation, it tried a U.S.-built turbotrain between Boston and New York, and inaugurated a rapid inter-city service between Washington and New York, using the fast electric trains (Metroliners) that had been ordered by the PRR. Running fast trains over poor-quality track, plus managerial torpor (would-be passengers found it near-impossible to obtain timetables),

With cars designed by the Budd Company, the Metroliner was an electric express train service run by the Pennsylvania RR, Penn Central, and Amtrak, between Washington, D.C. and New York City from 1968 to 2006. The first-generation, self-powered cars were replaced by similar looking locomotive-powered sets in the early 1980s. The trip between Pennsylvania Station, New York, and Union Station, Washington, D.C. took 3 hours, and the train offered reserved business class and first class seating.

meant that both experiments failed. The Metroliners were put into store, to be resurrected later and operated at slower speeds.

It was clear that to compel railroads to continue passenger services could only result in bankruptcies. In 1970, therefore, the federal government stepped in to form an organization to cater for inter-city passengers. Amtrak was set up by Act of Congress that year as a government funded, private corporation to operate inter-city passenger trains. Twenty individual railroads elected to join Amtrak, four of them holding common stock. All preferred stock was held by the U.S. Department of Transportation.

The railroads were glad to shed their responsibility for passenger services; no longer would they be compelled to cross-subsidize passengers from freight revenue. Only the Southern Railway continued to run its own passenger service, out of pride, but within a few years, it had fallen into line. By 2000, Amtrak operated trains over 21,870 miles (35,200km) of route, and owned 780 miles (1,266km) of those routes, the Northeast Corridor and Philadelphia–Harrisburg. By virtue of these self-owned routes, it was the only substantial electrified railroad in North America. Amtrak also managed commuter trains under contract in Boston, the Baltimore-Washington area, Connecticut, Virginia, California, and elsewhere for various authorities and state agencies.

By 1983, Amtrak was carrying on its own services (that is, excluding its contract operations) almost 19 million revenue passengers annually, each traveling an average distance of 223 miles (359km). By the end of the century, passenger numbers exceeded 21 million, with an average trip of 280 miles (450km), although in the early 1990s, 22 million had been recorded,. This fluctuation in passenger traffic reflected the varying fortunes of Amtrak, being subject not only to the trends of economic life, but also to the varying outlooks of successive governments. On the whole, Amtrak fared better under Democratic regimes than under Republican, as might be expected from the political philosophies of those two parties. Both Democratic and Republican politicians were eager to cut Amtrak's expenses, however, provided those cuts occurred outside their own constituencies.

In the 1970s, a rolling Northeast Corridor Improvement Project was funded to rebuild the former Pennsylvania RR line to its proper standard. Amtrak received financial support for the purchase of new electric locomotives. Then came the new administration of President Ronald Reagan, however, which began a concerted effort to end Amtrak's funding. Amtrak fought back.

Originally, Congress had specified that Amtrak must cover at least 50 percent of its total operating expenses from fares, and Amtrak did reach this goal. In 1983, operating costs were $1,303 million against revenues of $605 million, but in 1987, revenues attained 58 percent of expenses. After that, there were falls and rises, and by the end of the century, it was recognized that Amtrak could be relied on to maintain at least a 50 percent level. Nothing had seemed good enough for the Reagan administration, however, which liked to portray Amtrak as an example of "government waste." Amtrak's president made a vigorous defense of the federal investment in the rail passenger business before Congress, overhauled the management, improved services, and increased the revenue/cost ratio. In the following decades, Amtrak went through other periods when its funding came under fire. In the struggle to maintain its cost/revenue ratio, train services were modified on many occasions, and from time to time, sizable cities found themselves deprived of a rail passenger service.

In the 1990s, only Amtrak's New York–Washington service was profitable. The really long-distance

President Ronald Reagan's budget of 1987 targeted Amtrak, the railroad that carried 21 million passengers a year, including 11.3 million in the Northeast Corridor, proposing to eliminate its Federal subsidy. The budget stated that "as a result, Amtrak would likely enter bankruptcy." Congress had rejected a similar proposal the previous year, but did reduce Federal support of Amtrak by $68 million, to $616 million the next year.

services, radiating from Chicago to the West Coast and Gulf, and from New York to Florida, were very popular with the public, but were serious loss-makers. Severe cuts were necessary to meet government pressure in 1995, but this also encouraged the so-called Section 403(b) arrangements, whereby individual states could subsidize their own Amtrak services. This allowed several services to be maintained or even introduced, although sometimes it was difficult to negotiate services covering more than one state. For example, a Portland–Boston service was subsidized by Massachusetts and Maine, but the intermediate state of New Hampshire, which the train also served, made no contribution; this would lead to serious difficulties in 2005.

Amtrak's state partnerships were especially rewarding in the West. The Pacific North West Rail Corridor scheme resulted in the introduction of the popular Cascade service between Vancouver British Columbia, Seattle, Portland, and Eugene, operated by Talgo tilting trains. With popular support, the State of California provided much investment to make possible the services of Amtrak California. The latter ran the San Joaquin Service (Sacramento–Oakland), Capital Corridor (San Jose–Sacramento), and Pacific Surfliner (San Luis Obispo–San Diego).

In the 1990s, Amtrak trains began to include cars for freight service. At a time when line capacity was increasingly scarce, it seemed sensible, and profitable, to use the Amtrak trains to carry high-value shipments as well as mail. Despite the extra station time needed to pick up and drop vehicles, this idea appeared to work quite well, although it was abandoned when Amtrak came under pressure in the new century. Mail service, which was beginning to make use of "Roadrailer" intermodal vehicles, was also abandoned.

The postwar decline in passenger traffic had put a severe brake on further improvements to passenger cars after the new, all-steel products of Budd and American Car & Foundry manufacture entered service. Moreover, when Amtrak took over passenger services, there were still many of the older, heavyweight cars around. Car builders either stopped making passenger cars or went out of business. American Car & Foundry left the business for good in 1961. Pullman and Budd held on for a little longer, mainly building for a limited rapid-transit car market. The Pullman Company's sleeping-car operation, controlled by a group of railroads, finally ended in 1968.

Amtrak began by purchasing the cars originally used by the railroads. It got rid of these as soon as possible, however, and achieved a changeover from steam heating to electric heating powered from the locomotive, that current also providing for lighting and air conditioning in place of under-car batteries. In 1973, federal funds were provided so that Amtrak could buy new cars. These were of stainless steel, arranged as coaches and coach-cafes, and ran on excellent, lightweight trucks of a 1956 design. More new cars were built by Pullman in 1975–6. They were hi-level cars with rather more luxurious fittings, and they filled Amtrak's desperate need for new sleepers and diners.

At the beginning, Amtrak placed a large-scale order for new diesel locomotives from GM. These proved to have some defects, which was not a good start, but it soldiered on with these units. In the 1980s, it bought new electric locomotives of GM manufacture, but Swedish origin. These were used

"Genesis" locomotives by GE were introduced in the 1990s, to provide motive power for passenger trains, such as the *California Zephyr*. The largest customer was Amtrak, which operated more than 200 on its routes. VIA Rail in Canada was also a major customer.

mainly with the new cars to reintroduce a Metroliner service between Washington and New York. In the 1990s, it received new-generation passenger locomotives from GM (F59PH type) and General Electric ("Genesis" type).

In the meantime, gas-turbine trains of both French and U.S. manufacture were introduced, being used mainly for regional services in New York; they were well liked, but the rise in oil prices in the 1970s made them too costly to operate. Amtrak had imported foreign trains for trials, and one of these, the Spanish Talgo tilting train, gave rise to orders for Amtrak North West services around Seattle. On the basis of other trials, the French Alstom company was chosen for new, high-speed, tilting trains for the Northeast Corridor. These were assembled in the United States. The service began in December 2000 with a single Boston–Washington round-trip, after which it was steadily extended. Various teething troubles were encountered, and for other reasons, the high speeds for which these trains had been built were not fully exploited. Nevertheless, they were a great step forward and resulted in significant gains of traffic.

A type of railroad that grew in importance was the commuter railroad. Following deregulation,

The Metra Line (ME) was originally built and operated by the Illinois Central RR, but purchased in 1987 by Metra (the Northeast Illinois Regional Commuter Railroad Corporation), to provide a commuter service for the Chicago, Illinois, and surrounding suburbs. Here a Metra train of high-capacity, double deck cars passes the locomotive depot on one of the busy commuter lines.

the main-line railroads ceased direct involvement in loss making commuter and suburban passenger operations. Local government and state agencies had to become increasingly involved in the provision of these services. In most cases, operation remained in the hands of the railroads on a contract basis, the authority providing the funds for improvements, new rolling stock, and promotion. In other instances, agencies owned the rights-of-way and operated the trains themselves, or the commuter lines were controlled by authorities responsible for the provision of all types of urban public transport: buses, subway, and rapid transit.

Often, these authorities had their roots in systems that had been established in the early part of the 20th century. An example was the Metropolitan Transportation Authority (MTA) of New York City, which was a public-benefit corporation of the State of New York. Created in 1965, it became responsible for almost all public transport in the New York City area. It had five subsidiaries, which operated the city's buses, subway, commuter rail (Long Island and Metro North), suburban buses, two tunnels, and seven bridges.

There were a score or so commuter railroads, some of them entirely or partly electrified; mostly, they operated over tracks of former main-line railroads, varying in size from a single route to a network like Chicago's Metra, which had nine routes and was planning more. New Jersey Transit (NJT) operated over 440 miles (708km) of line, 310 miles (499km) of which it owned, having taken over lines and passenger operations from Conrail, which Conrail itself had inherited from the Erie Lackawanna and Central of New Jersey railroads. NJT began to operate modern, electric, multiple-unit cars on many routes, with push-pull trains worked by electric and diesel locomotives on others. Commuter railroads were increasingly described as "heavy rail," to distinguish them from the growing number of Light Rail systems (essentially a modern form of trolley operation) and from rapid-transit lines. Probably the best known of the latter was New York Transit, which operated the New York Subway of more than 200 miles (322km).

In the 1980s, there were signs of improved prospects for the freight railroads, which would encourage a fresh wave of mergers in the 1990s. Partly thanks to new investment, partly to a more efficient deployment of workers, and partly to the sale of underused routes to regional and short railroads, the Class I railroads reduced their labor force from 458,000 in 1980 to just 182,000 in 1996. (In 1917, some 1.4 million people had been employed by railroads, a figure that had been cut by half in 1962.)

In the same 15-year period, the number of freight cars in use was halved, locomotive units were reduced by almost two-thirds, and track ownership by one third. At the same time, traffic revenue ton/miles increased by no less than 270 percent. Such a simultaneous reduction of costs and growth of revenue transformed the commercial situation of the big lines.

The merger of the Atchison, Topeka & Santa Fe (to give its full title) with the Burlington Northern was agreed in 1994, and received final approval from the ICC on July 20, 1995. The Santa Fe was one of the original railroads of the Southwest, serving many of the principal cities from Chicago, south to the Gulf of Mexico, and west to the Pacific at Los Angeles, Oakland, and San Francisco. It was one of several rail routes to the Pacific that had been completed in the 1880s. The Burlington Northern had more northerly routes from Chicago to the West Coast; the combined routes virtually blanketed the western half of the United States. The new railroad was known as the Burlington Northern Santa Fe

Corporation (BNSF). It owned 4,400 locomotives and 92,000 freight cars, and had a combined workforce of almost 41,000 operating 31,000 miles (49,888km) of track. However, the agreement was not reached without a struggle. Many shippers lost the chance of playing one railroad off against another, while other railroads argued that the new combination could give rise to unfair competition. In the final settlement, the Union Pacific was placated by being given trackage rights over a few key sectors of the new combination.

The Union Pacific itself was about to expand. Its chief executive officer together with its proactive board member (and head of its audit committee), Richard Cheney (future U.S. Vice-President), were introducing severe cost reductions while simultaneously looking for ways to expand. In April 1995, the UP acquired its one-time partner Chicago & North Western, which gave it access to Chicago over its own tracks. This merger was followed by some severe traffic disruptions because the two lines took a long time to merge on a practical basis, while, thanks to its cuts, the UP was not ready for extra business. Yet before properly digesting C&NW, in August 1995, the UP announced its intention to buy the Southern Pacific (which earlier had merged with the Denver & Rio Grande Western) in a $3.9-billion cash-stock deal. This merger took place in 1996, and by some measures, it made the UP the biggest of the U.S. railroads; not the most popular, however, for it resulted in crisis. Its already deteriorating safety and reliability performances meant that it was unable to cope with this enlargement. Cheney and his CEO

BNSF, a subsidiary of the Burlington Northern Santa Fe Corporation, was formed by the 1995 merger of the Burlington Northern and the Atchison, Topeka & Santa Fe RRs. It became one of four remaining transcontinental railroads and one of the largest networks in North America (second to Union Pacific). The railroad was among the top transporters of intermodal traffic, moving more grain than any other U.S. railroad. Seen passing West Palm Beach, Florida, in 2006, one of the affectionately dubbed "pumpkin" locomotives, No.7787, is displays BNSF's "New Image" paint scheme.

The Florida East Coast Railway (FEC), was formed in 1867 by tychoon Henry Morrison Flagler. Today the company only provides freight service, since passenger service was discontinued in 1968 after labor unrest that resulted in violence. Although in the past it has been a Class I railroad, it is now Class II, operating in the state of Florida on lines originally developed by Flagler. The FEC built the first railroad bridges to Key West, which have since been rebuilt into road bridges for vehicle traffic, and known as the Overseas Highway.

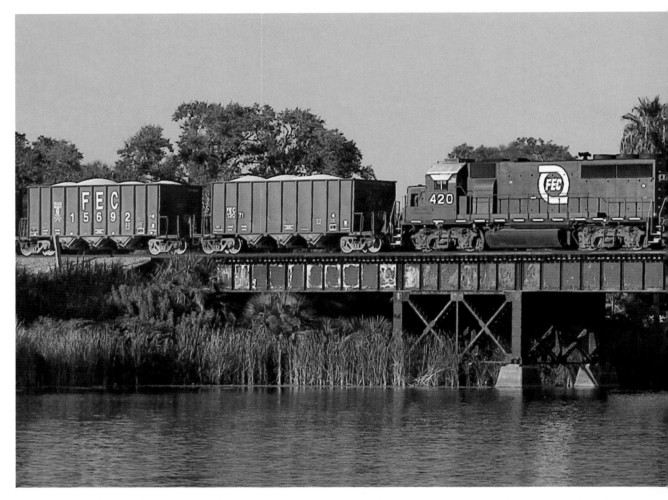

had succeeded in their campaign to capture and control the Southern Pacific, but it appeared that they had given little thought to what would happen afterwards.

Severe congestion began to occur, especially in Louisiana and Texas. Trains were blocked, sometimes for days, and traffic embargoes imposed. A state of near revolt grew among shippers, who were left without transportation. The Union Pacific proved unable to shift the grain harvest, and grain piled up not only in silos, but also in parking lots and even local stadiums. The cost of all this to the U.S. economy was reckoned to approach $4 billion; for the UP, it was reflected in operating losses that approached $1 billion. The only solution was to reverse the disastrous cost cutting program, invest hurriedly in new locomotives and cars, transfer more power to local managements, construct additional tracks at bottlenecks, and relieve the previously stressed and overworked staff. Even so, the Union Pacific's recovery took several years.

In 1998, the Illinois Central was merged into the Canadian National. Subsequently, the latter acquired the Wisconsin Central (and by virtue of a previous WC investment, thereby unenthusiastically obtained ownership of English, Welsh & Scottish, Britain's principal freight company). The CN expansion went smoothly and converted the railroad into a major U.S. carrier. Then the CN and BNSF negotiated for a merger that would have created something of an American super-railroad, but disillusionment resulting from the UP/SP chaos, among other things, meant that further mergers came under suspicion, and the Surface Transportation Board would not allow it.

Meanwhile, the Conrail problem was in course of solution. Beginning as a poor orphan under federal

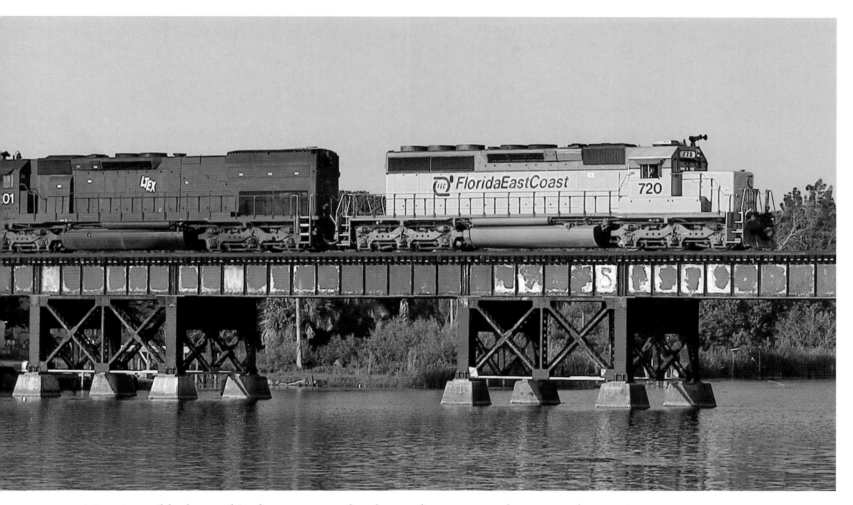

supervision, Conrail had turned its fortunes around and proved strong enough to succeed as a private company. Three railroads, the Norfolk Southern, CSX, and Conrail, competed for the eastern-states traffic, and Conrail was seeking a merger. There was a period of several years of secret negotiations, secret deals, and even secret denials, while in public there was a debate about what to do with Conrail. Both CSX and NS wanted to merge with it; whichever company won the deal would dominate the eastern market. Voices recommending that Conrail should join with a western railroad and thereby create what the United States had never had, a coast-to-coast railroad, were hardly noticed. In the end, the realization dawned that neither CSX nor NS could be allowed to swallow Conrail, and the two companies finally agreed to split it in 1997, the takeover being completed in 1999.

For several years, there was speculation about which company would swallow up the Kansas City Southern, the smallest of the Class I railroads. But the KCS was content to move in its own way, and its acquisition of Mexican lines, together with a traffic agreement with the Canadian National, seemed to assure its independence.

By 2000, therefore, there were five major railroads in the United States, together with the two major Canadian companies, the Canadian National and Canadian Pacific. In that same year, the Union Pacific was the biggest of the U.S. freight haulers (8.9 million carloads), closely followed by the Burlington Northern Santa Fe (8.2 million carloads). The two competing eastern roads, the CSX and Norfolk Southern, carried respectively 7.3 and 6.8 million carloads, while the Kansas City Southern trailed with just 0.93 million.

RENAISSANCE OF THE AMERICAN RAILROADS

CONTINUAL IMPROVEMENTS MADE TO THE ROLLING STOCK OF U.S. RAILROADS BROUGHT ABOUT NUMEROUS CHANGES IN LOCOMOTIVE AND CAR DESIGN, AND INNOVATIVE MEANS OF PROPULSION WERE EXPLORED. AFTER YEARS OF DIFFICULTY, THE REVIVAL OF THE RAILROADS WAS UNDERWAY.

An intermodal train carrying shipping containers and highway semi-trailers in "piggyback" service, on flatcars, passes through Cajon Pass, between the San Bernardino and San Gabriel Mountains, Southern California, in February, 1995.

Some stretches of main line had been electrified in the earlier part of the 20th century, but it was proving advantageous to replace electric traction with diesel. Diesel-electric locomotives gave railroad operators a great deal of flexibility, plus haulage capacity that at least equalled the ageing electric locomotives, many of which were overdue for replacement. Diesel-electric working over electrified routes meant that locomotives no longer had to be changed at the beginning and end of an electrified section. Before electrification was abandoned, however, sometimes special arrangements had to be made for tunnel ventilation.

In most cases, electrification had been adopted to meet a specific need: to improve haulage of heavy trains on long, steep grades, to work long tunnels with smoke problems, and so on. Exceptions were the electrification of the Pennsylvania Railroad in the 1920s and 1930s (from New York City to Washington, and Philadelphia to Harrisburg), and of the New York, New Haven & Hartford RR. On these, traffic densities were comparable to some of the busiest European routes, and electrification was seen as an investment of faith toward a better service.

Electrification from 1900

— Electrification 1900–1930
— Electrification After WWII
— Proposals of the 1970s

In Europe, the usual reason for electrification had been as a response to an increase in traffic intensity rather than an attempt to increase tractive capacity. In the United States, the capital for electrification could not be recouped easily, so there was little urge for further electrification. One by one, the electrified sections disappeared, the only significant exception being the Northeast Corridor with its high speeds and relatively high traffic density. The long freight hauls typical of other American roads, although technically suitable for electric haulage, did not usually result in the high traffic intensity that justified the cost of maintaining the electric supply and distribution system. Electrified sections of the Virginian RR were switched off in 1962, of the Milwaukee Road in 1972 and 1974, of the Norfolk & Western in 1950, of the Great Northern in 1956, and of the Northern Pacific in 1967.

An early electrification was the Butte, Anaconda & Pacific RR. Despite its grand title, it consisted of only 69 miles (110km) of line connecting copper mines at Butte in Montana with a smelter at Anaconda. It was electrified in 1913, and electric operation continued until 1967, by which time all but two of its 30 locomotives were 54 years old. In its last years, its locomotives worked also from Butte to Durant, using trackage rights over the Northern Pacific.

A few other lines remained electrified. Two of these were quite recent additions. The Black Mesa &

Unlike in Europe, electrification has never played a major role as a means of traction on U.S. main-line railroads. Some railroads did choose it to meet a particular need, such as combating pollution in long tunnels or improving haulage on long, steep grades. Subsequently, however, many systems were switched off in favour of diesel-electric traction.

A Pacer Stacktrain is a five-unit intermodal container car, using a specialized type of gondola to hold double-stacked containers. The train is shown here passing through Rochelle Railroad Park, Rochelle, Illinois, in 2005.

Lake Powell RR in northern Arizona had a single route, 78 miles (125km) long, opened in the early 1970s for hauling coal. It was electrified on the ac, single-phase system at 50 kilovolts, its high tension justified economically because it required only one substation. The Muskingham Electric RR of the Central Coal Company in Lancaster, Ohio, had a line only 20 miles (32km) long, which was electrified at 25 kilovolts, 60Hz. Coal was transported from mine to power station; again, there was only one substation. This operation was semi-automatic: the two electric locomotives were operated by remote control and not normally manned.

Freight cars were improved continuously through the last half of the 20th century, but many still had outdated features. One factor limiting the length or weight of freight trains had been the strength of the drawgear; another was the continued use of lumber in underframe construction. With the major purchases of freight cars in the late 1970s, however, these older cars tended to disappear. In the 1980s, one paradoxical result of the Staggers Act was a reduction in freight car orders from the railroads. Able now to reduce tariffs, they found that with reduced revenue per car-mile, capital investment in cars was less viable. Instead, they turned to leasing, and especially to the leasing company TTX (which was jointly owned by the railroads themselves). By 1987, two-fifths of freight traffic was handled by leased cars, and this percentage would rise still further later. Car orders would grow in the later 1990s, being largely for hoppers and gondolas for the unit coal trains, and flatcars for intermodal service. Orders for specialized covered cars for such commodities as grain, cement, and other bulk freight were also rising. Extra-large hoppers appeared for carrying low-weight materials like plastics. There was an increasing need for tankcars, especially for ethanol. However, a number of messy accidents had prompted a demand for chemical and other liquid cars that would be unlikely to leak in the event of an accident; chlorine producers were planning to replace their fleets with safer vehicles.

Because of the growing preference for specialized cars, fewer boxcars were ordered. For years, there had been talk of the imminent demise of the traditional boxcar, but it had survived because it could carry so many different kinds of load (and thereby was likely to obtain a return load, something that specialized cars rarely achieved). By the 1990s, however, the boxcar was virtually dependent on a handful of commodities, notably paper products such as newsprint. Shipments of these were in decline; moreover, it was increasingly difficult for a boxcar to make sufficient revenue runs in the year to pay back its capital cost. By 2006, the annual boxcar order was down to about 2,000 units, and it was expected to shrink further, probably to zero, within a few more years. To keep acquisitions to a minimum, partly for reasons of cost, and partly because existing car-builders were already having difficulty in raising their output, it was hoped to lengthen the working life of cars. The existing rule was that cars for interchange with other railroads (in effect, practically all cars) could not exceed 40 years of age, but there was discussion about extending this to 65 years.

What became known as intermodal traffic became widespread in the 1950s, initially with the carriage of road semi-trailers on flatcars, although the New York Central favored its own "Flexivan" container-on-flatcar system. The ICC's agreement that railroads carrying their own containers did not need to obtain truck-route certificates eased this process, as did the design of flatcars that could carry two trailers. Intermodal gave the railroads the opportunity of competing with the truckers' door-to-door capacity without the expense and delays of cargo transshipment en route. With the generous clearances of most U.S. railroads, it was possible to double-stack containers. Double-stacking was an innovation of the 1980s pioneered by the Southern Pacific. Now it is the standard method of shipping manufactured goods over long distances, steadily superseding the carriage of road trailers on flatcars (TOFC, or "piggyback"). The weakness of TOFC, apart from its unsuitability for double-stacking, was

A Roadrailer is a highway trailer, or semi-trailer, that is specially-equipped for use in railroad intermodal service. Due to their construction, the trailers can be pulled directly behind other freight, or even passenger, equipment without the use of trailer flatcars. Shown is the tailgate end of an Amtrak Mk V, can travel at speeds up to 100mph. (160.92km/h).

The caboose, which carried the train crew at the rear of the train, was phased out of service in the 1980s, and from then on the crew traveled in the locomotives. Also largely redundant because of the widespread use of intermodal and specialized cars, the traditional boxcar began to disappear from U.S. railroads.

that it entailed the haulage of the heavy sets of wheels that were needed by the semi-trailers for the highway sectors of their run. On the other hand, it did not need terminals equipped with hoists, as did containers. A close relative of "piggyback" was the freight car equipped with a set of tired wheels that could be raised or lowered, enabling it to run over both rail and highway. This was not widely used, although the "RoadRailer" version was successfully exploited by the Norfolk Southern and a handful of other operators.

A familiar vehicle to disappear in the 1980s was the caboose (or waycar), which originally carried the statutory three or four men of the train crew at the rear of the train. The Florida East Coast had shown it could be done, and the other railroads followed suit. The brotherhoods finally accepted that freight trains could run with two- or three-person crews, carried in reasonable comfort on the locomotives. To ensure that the last car of a train really was the last car, an End of Train Device (ETD) was attached to the rear car, usually on the rear coupler. The ETD incorporated a flashing red strobe light, a motion detector, and an air-brake-line monitor. Information on air-brake pressure and motion was transmitted automatically to a receiver in the locomotive cab, helping the engineer to handle trains a mile (1.6km) or more long with greater smoothness and safety than ever before.

An important facility to aid development was the Transportation Test Center near Pueblo, Colorado. This was set up by the Department of Transportation and was operated under contract by the

Association of American Railroads. The center had specialized test facilities, having been created originally to develop high-speed, surface-transport vehicles. There was a rail dynamics laboratory, a 15-mile (24km) ac-electrified test track for main-line use, and a 10-mile (16km) track equipped with third-rail dc and light-rail-type catenary for urban applications. In the early 1980s, a great deal of work was done at the center on magnetically levitated applications.

Released from wartime restrictions, diesel locomotive development was rapid in the last half of the 20th century. The first big freight diesel had developed 5,400hp in its units; soon, it became possible to have as much as 25,000hp at the head of a train. Where necessary, as on long. steep grades with heavy trains, another 10–15,000hp could be cut in anywhere from 50 to 100 cars back and operated from the manned unit by remote control. Dynamic braking was introduced, the traction motors being used as generators, which were driven via the wheels from the momentum of the train, producing current to be absorbed in resistances and dissipated as heat. On locomotives equipped with this system, there could be enormous savings of brake-block and tire wear.

From the start, diesel engine manufacturers sought to develop and improve their engines. From 1950, four-stroke engines with individual outputs for traction of 2,000hp from 16 cylinders were available; by 1960, this had reached 2,400hp. The 16-cylinder, EMD 567 two-stroke engine had reached 2,000hp by 1959 in its turbocharged form, and 2,500hp by 1963. Fairbanks-Morse also had a 2,400hp, two-stroke, opposed-piston engine as early as 1953. This was a development of their successful marine engine, but it was never as suitable as a railroad prime mover as the others.

Traditionally, switchers had been built as "hood" units, with a single cab at one end, while road passenger and freight locomotives were of the carbody type, whether driving (A-type) or booster (B-type), until about 1949. The majority, whether with four or six axles, had four traction motors. There were exceptions, among them Fairbanks-Morse, but it was never a major builder.

In the late 1940s, the first of what were termed general-purpose locomotives were introduced into road service. Based on the traditional switcher format, but with the cab located between a short nose and the main hood, these were dubbed road switchers. First in the field was ALCO, with its famous RS-2 of 1,500hp and later 1,600hp. Probably the best known, however, was the EMD 1,500hp GP7, introduced

The traditional "hood" style of locomotive, widely used on switchers, was eventually adopted for road service, too. Here a Chicago Central GP38 locomotive—one of 700 built for U.S. railroads—leads a freight train through northern Illinois in 1993.

as a general-purpose unit chiefly for secondary lines. Together with the later GP9, over 6,000 of these locomotives were delivered to U.S. railroads alone.

The hood style of casing suited the visibility requirements of yard and road operation. It also provided easy accessibility to the propulsion-system components. Given the relatively low speeds of freight trains in the United States, the absence of the streamlined nose and full-width carbody made little difference to aerodynamic drag. The road

The Union Pacific's first gas turbine-electric locomotive, or GTEL, used a gas turbine to drive an electric generator or alternator. The electric current produced then powered the traction motors. The units exceled when exerting full power to haul heavy loads over long over distances, but the system reached its peak between the 1950s and 1960s.

switcher form became the accepted second-generation standard for freight operation; with minor changes, it remains so to this day.

General Electric entered the road switcher market only in 1959, but when it did, it was with single-engine locomotives of 2,500hp against the 1,800hp then available from the EMD designs. ALCO had entered the field in 1946 with a design of similar power to EMD's, using electrical gear supplied by GE. The popularity of the road switcher grew rapidly, and the carbody locomotive dropped out of production with the last E9A/B in 1963.

Around the same time, certain railroads had become disenchanted with what they regarded as the manufacturers' fixation with electric transmission. In Europe, there were a few examples of locomotives in the 3,500–4,000hp range with high-speed engines and hydraulic transmissions. Between 1961 and 1963, Krauss-Maffei of Munich, Germany, exported 21 high-power diesel-hydraulic locomotives, each with two 2,000hp engines and hydraulic transmissions. Three of these went to the Rio Grande, and 17 to the Southern Pacific.

American conditions uncovered a number of problems, and the German locomotives were soon retired. There were other attempts by European manufacturers to break into the American market. One of these was by Sulzer Brothers of Winterthur, Switzerland, who sold a few 12- and 16-cylinder engines of 3,000 and 4,000hp (traction) to three United States railroads through Morrison-Knudsen of Boise, Idaho, in 1979–80. These went to the Southern Pacific, Burlington Northern, and Union Pacific. While operation was reasonably successful, the proposed licensee in the United States did not take up the option.

Another innovation, this time purely American, was the introduction of the gas-turbine locomotive. Gas turbines require less maintenance that diesel engines, and so long as they are exerting full power, they make good use of their fuel; at low power, however, their fuel requirement becomes inefficient. In those circumstances, only railroads hauling heavy loads over long distances could find the gas turbine of much use. One such railroad was the Union Pacific, which hauled heavy trains over the long line that climbs up to the Rockies between Cheyenne, Wyoming, and Ogden, Utah. After a production batch of 10 gas turbines, the UP ordered an improved batch of 15 4,500hp units from GE in the early 1950s. On the downhill trip, the turbine was cut out, there being a low-power supplementary diesel engine to provide what little power was needed. These locomotives worked well, but rising oil prices and the small difference between their performance and that of conventional diesel locomotives meant that the concept was not pursued.

One limitation on increased engine power, apart from suitable engines, was the direct-current generator, which had seemed to reach its limit at an input of about 2,800hp. In the early 1960s, silicon rectifiers had been introduced into railway traction, and development was fast, so that by the mid-

1960s, devices were small and reliable enough to enable three-phase alternators to be substituted. This removed the restriction on input power, paving the way for more powerful prime movers and, hence, single-unit locomotives.

In May 1966, GE handed over two U28Bs to the railroads for trials, and from that year on, all high-horsepower GE locomotives had alternators. EMD followed suit with 2,000hp GP38s and S38s in 1971, offering alternators as an option to dc generators. From January 1972, EMD began production of its Dash-2 range, all of which had alternators as well as other high-reliability innovations.

The pattern for the future had emerged with both four- and six-motor designs. Single-engine locomotives of up to 3,600hp were available by the late 1960s. Theoretically, fewer units per train were needed, but with the increased speeds over better tracks, three, four, and even five units could be found on very long and heavy trains.

Because of their steeply-graded lines over the Sierra Nevada and the Rockies, the Union Pacific and Southern Pacific persuaded both EMD and GE to break with tradition and produce some unique locomotives to their specific requirements. EMD DD35s were originally to be B-units to work between pairs of GP35s. They were 5,000hp locomotives riding on two four-axle trucks, each having two 16-cylinder 567D3A engines. Some 30 were produced in 1963–4. In 1965, a further 15 were delivered to the Union Pacific with cabs.

The crowning glory was the DDA40X of 6,600hp, built from 1969 to 1971. A total of 47 were produced for the Union Pacific, being known as "Centennials" in honor of the 100th anniversary of the Golden Spike ceremony of 1869. These, too, were carried on four-axle trucks, and had two 16-cylinder 645 E3A engines and "safety cabs."

The GE equivalents were of two designs. Between 1963 and 1965, 26 eight-axle locomotives, classified U50D, were built. They rode on four two-axle trucks, the drawgear being mounted on the truck. Each had two 16-cylinder FDL-16 engines, giving a total of 5,000hp. They had a GE version of the full-width safety cab. A second batch was to a six-axle design and weighed 208.5 tons each (the heaviest six-axle locomotives in the United States). Also of 5,000hp, they had two 12-cylinder FDL-12 engines.

The next change to locomotive outline came with the introduction of the so-called cowl design. Cowl units were produced originally for the Santa Fe RR to provide a more acceptable appearance than the typical road switcher for locomotives used on premier passenger trains. It was designed to create an airtight carbody that permitted troubleshooting and even maintenance en route, although in the main, that need had disappeared by then. With freight trains beginning to travel at speeds of up to 80mph (129km/h), there was renewed interest in reducing air resistance to improve fuel consumption. At the same time, the design permitted the use of a wider safety or "comfort" cab. Unlike the earlier carbody locomotives, cowl units were built on the road switcher principle, with a separate underframe; the cowl served merely to create an airtight carbody.

The road switcher provides an ideal locomotive for bi-directional working of a single unit. The cowl configuration does not, and it requires turning at each end of a run when used alone. They became common performers on Amtrak passenger trains, and it was not unusual to see two cowl units facing the same way at the head of a train, which was inconvenient when the terminal was reached and one, or both, had to be turned.

New developments to ensure high reliability and less maintenance were introduced over the years. As power ratings increased, so did the complexity of electrical controls to obtain optimum performance. To offset this, functions were grouped into discrete modules, and systems were devised to incorporate self-checking features to improve reliability. With the rapid development of electronic devices, constant monitoring of performance became possible, and defects could be spotted before they developed fully.

Until the early 1990s, the direct-current traction motor had dominated the field. It was familiar, highly developed, and reliable. But it had a snag: it needed substantial maintenance, especially of its commutator and brushes. It was also sensitive to overspeeding and required sophisticated anti-spin protection. Electronics changed all that. It became possible to employ alternating-current motors with ideal characteristics that were virtually maintenance-free.

Interest in ac power heightened in the 1980s. Early in the field in the United States was EMD with the F69PH-AC, a joint development with Siemens of Germany. Two locomotives were delivered to Amtrak in 1989, based on the well-known F40PH cowl type. The main changes were the engine, now a 12-710G3 of 3,000hp (traction); four asynchronous, three-phase traction motors; microprocessors for the control system; and a potential top speed of 110mph (177km/h)

Following the success of these prototypes, EMD introduced its S70MAC, which was based on the same control system. Hundreds were delivered, first to the Burlington Northern, and later to other railroads. The ac drive and three-phase, asynchronous motors provided much smoother operation, allowing far better control of wheel-slip under high power; these locomotives could use 45 percent of theoretical adhesion weight, as opposed to the 25 percent possible with conventional models. Although the latter were about a third cheaper, railroads purchased the newer three-phase models for the sake of their enhanced tractive performance. That enhanced tractive effort at low speeds was accompanied by a horsepower disadvantage at higher speeds, however, which was why the manufacturers began to look at the possibility of building such locomotives in a 6,000hp version.

By the end of the century, the standard freight locomotive, whether from EMD or GE, was a hood type with a full-width nose and a safety cab designed with special attention to crew safety and comfort. The wide nose became popular from 1990, and thereafter few new road units were delivered with standard cabs.

This, of course, is not the whole story. Apart from diesel locomotives, the 1970s and 1980s saw the return of fixed-formation, self-propelled vehicles in the shape of gas-turbine trains, known as the turbotrains. They enjoyed some initial success, but the French designed turbotrains did not meet U.S. standards of crashworthiness, and a later batch (produced by Rohr Industries) were heavier and not so economical. Later, Amtrak began to look again at European technology for high-speed trains, considering French, German, and Swedish designs; both German and Swedish trains were tried in the Northeast Corridor. In 1993, Amtrak borrowed a Swedish X2000 trainset, running it between Washington, New York City, and Boston. With diesel haulage, it was also taken for a nationwide tour. Later, a German ICE trainset was run over the same route and given the same nationwide treatment. The French TGV and Spanish Talgo were also studied, and one of the latter was operated between Seattle and Vancouver as the Mount Baker International.

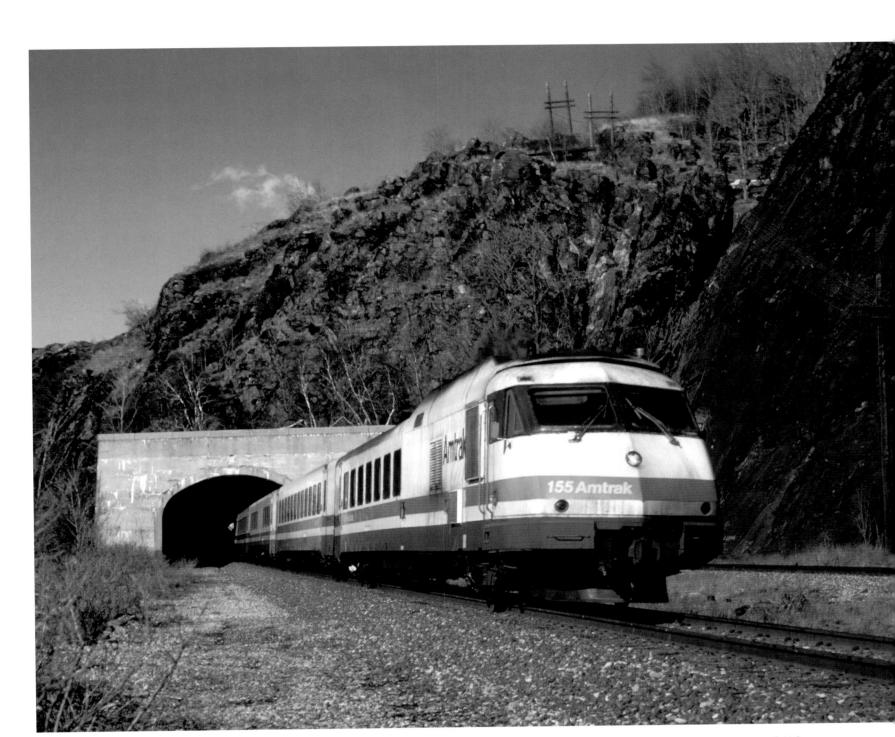

It became clear that a single, off-the-shelf train would not suit Amtrak. None of the trains they examined were found to meet all of the performance, aesthetic, and safety criteria. Amtrak was seeking a three-hour New York City–Boston running time, and this could be met only by a train with tilt technology, but the well-established Swedish X2000 tilt-train, with radial axles, did not have sufficient power for Amtrak's requirements.

Moreover, many people demanded an all-American approach, and Amtrak was seeking to establish its own identity with such a project. Already its designers were collaborating with the Henry Dreyfuss design company to produce models of what they would like the high-speed passenger train to be. It was hoped that a contract based on the approved model would be awarded, before the end of 1995, to one of three manufacturing consortiums to build 24 electric trainsets and two fossil fueled versions for use

Amtrak's turbotrain *Cold Spring* exits a tunnel near New York in February 1985. The French built, self-propeled, turbine-powered trainsets were first introduced to U.S. railroads in the 1970s.

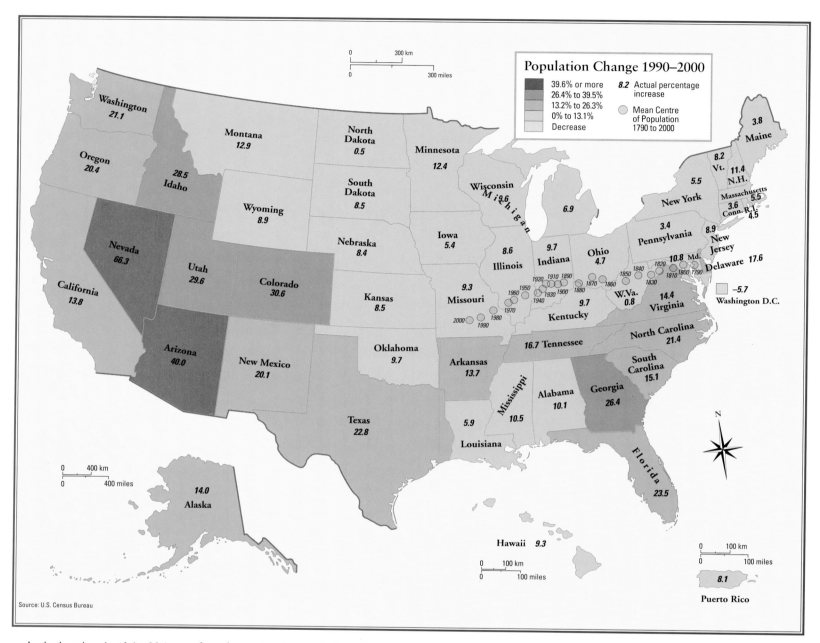

Population Change 1990–2000

- 39.6% or more
- 26.4% to 39.5%
- 13.2% to 26.3%
- 0% to 13.1%
- Decrease

8.2 Actual percentage increase

○ Mean Centre of Population 1790 to 2000

Source: U.S. Census Bureau

In the last decade of the 20th century, there were significant increases of population in the southeastern and western states. Such increases are bound to have a hand in shaping the railroads of the future.

elsewhere. In the end, the Talgo concept was accepted for Amtrak North West services. The low-slung Talgo cars were hauled by a full-height U.S. locomotive, the aesthetic mismatch obscured by some fancy screens masquerading as streamlining. These trains proved very successful, both technically and publicly. For the main requirement, high-speed tilting trains for the electrified Northeast Corridor, Alstom's French technology and the Canadian Bombardier company's manufacturing facilities were chosen for the production of 20 high-speed, tilting trainsets. At the same time (late 1990s), 15 locomotives that were not dissimilar to the power cars of the new sets were ordered for other services. The new trains were marketed as the Acela service and, despite some teething troubles, proved very successful. Each trainset consisted of a power car at each end, one first-class car, three standard cars, and a bistro car.

Meanwhile, in the 1990s, there was frequent talk of High Speed Rail (HSR) projects for passenger services. Studies were completed in 17 states, and the Clinton administration encouraged planning, provided the necessary funds were also committed by the relevant states. Texas had its own High

Speed Rail Authority, established in 1989 under the Texas High Speed Rail Act. In 1992, the authority awarded the Texas TGV Corporation a franchise to build a 590-mile (949km) network of high-speed lines linking Dallas, Fort Worth, Houston, Austin, and San Antonio, which would have exploited the technology of the celebrated 186mph (299km/h) French TGV. The franchise was cancelled in 1994, however, owing to difficulties in securing the necessary track rights-of-way and the failure to raise sufficient nongovernment funds.

There were other schemes, too, one of which looked at the possibility of using an unconventional form of land transport. A bi-state governmental commission of California and Nevada examined the feasibility of a high-speed link between Los Angeles and Las Vegas. The proposed system was Maglev (magnetic levitation), which by the 1980s had aroused a great deal of enthusiasm. Maglev was being promoted very actively in the 1970s and 1980s as a means of traveling over land at speeds as high as 300mph (483km/h).

The system employs a guideway (usually of concrete) rather than rails, the train floating with a clearance of up to 1in (2.54cm) on a magnetic field requiring no power expenditure, with no noise, and no need for maintenance. Frictionless forward motion is provided by a linear motor, using the track's permanent field for its excitation.

Major experiments in this technology had been carried out for more than a decade in Germany and Japan, using various forms of Maglev, and some very high speeds had been attained. However, there was not yet general acceptance of either the German or Japanese system as a practical or commercially viable, high-speed, high-density people-mover.

Concepts such as these, even though their achievement might have been slow in coming, helped to persuade Americans that the railroads were not merely a relic of the past. In any case, without the railroads, the flow of heavy goods and materials would have been exceedingly difficult to achieve. Pipelines could take bulk liquids; rivers, canals, and coastal shipping could carry other bulk loads, but were slow. The modernized American railroad system was moving vast quantities of a range of commodities speedily and efficiently. Moreover, it was considerably more fuel-efficient than most other modes of transport, and created relatively little pollution. With high traffic densities, far less labor was employed, and trains had become more responsive to modern needs.

American railroads, it seemed, were beginning to enter a new and extremely interesting era.

In April, 1976, the U.S. Department of Transportation tested new railroad technologies in western Colorado, with this experimental train. An electromagnetic current pulled the Linear Induction Motor Research Vehicle along an aluminium "reaction rail" set within a standard railroad track. Jet engines helped to reach a speed of 255mph (410km/h).

The *Cascades* train operated by Amtrak in partnership with the states of Washington and Oregon in the Pacific Northwest of the United States and Canada ran through a corridor 156 miles (251km) from Vancouver, British Columbia, south to Seattle, Washington, continuing 310 miles (499km) south via Portland, Oregon to Eugene, Oregon. The train was operated in a push-pull configuration with an EMD F59PHI locomotive at one end, and a de-motored EMD F40PH locomotive called a Non-Powered Control Unit (NPCU) at the other end. The passenger cars, produced by the Spanish company Talgo, were often called "cabbage cars" because they serve as both cab control car and baggage car. The cars are designed to passively tilt into curves, allowing the train to pass at higher speeds. Here, Amtrak No. 90253 heads a train at Everett, Washington State, in 2002.

U.S. Railroads in the New Century

WITH THE EXCEPTION OF LONG-DISTANCE PASSENGER SERVICES, THE EARLY PART OF THE 21ST CENTURY HAS BEEN GOOD FOR U.S. RAILROADS. FREIGHT TRAFFIC HAS INCREASED CONSIDERABLY, LEADING TO IMPROVEMENTS IN INFRASTRUCTURE AND EQUIPMENT; COMMUTER RAILROADS, TOO, ARE FARING WELL.

In the first years of the 21st century, the railroads continued to prosper. Wall Street, which until the 1990s, had regarded railroad stocks with suspicion, was recommending them as part of a balanced holding. *Fortune* magazine noted that in 2005, the railroads had the second highest growth rate of all industries, behind internet companies. Economic globalization, while it may have reduced traffic originating from some of the traditional U.S. industries, gave a chance for the railroads to grasp new traffic of the type they most desired, high flows over long distances. In the first five years of the new century, freight ton-miles rose by 18 percent. New technologies, like double-stack container trains and high-capacity autorack cars, were already in place to exploit the new opportunities, and new computerized management procedures speeded processes and reduced costs. Whereas the main concern of the railroads in recent decades had been gaining and keeping enough traffic to preserve them from decline and possible bankruptcy, by the turn of the century, their main anxiety was capacity bottlenecks. Hence there was growing investment in capital projects, including massive programs of double-tracking.

Meanwhile, increased demand for railroad transportation strengthened the industry's bargaining position. In the wake of the Staggers Act, to take advantage of the new freedom to fix rates, the railroads had concluded innumerable long- and medium-term contracts with shippers based on cut-price tariffs. In the new conditions, the railroads had little need to provide such inducements, so there was a steady

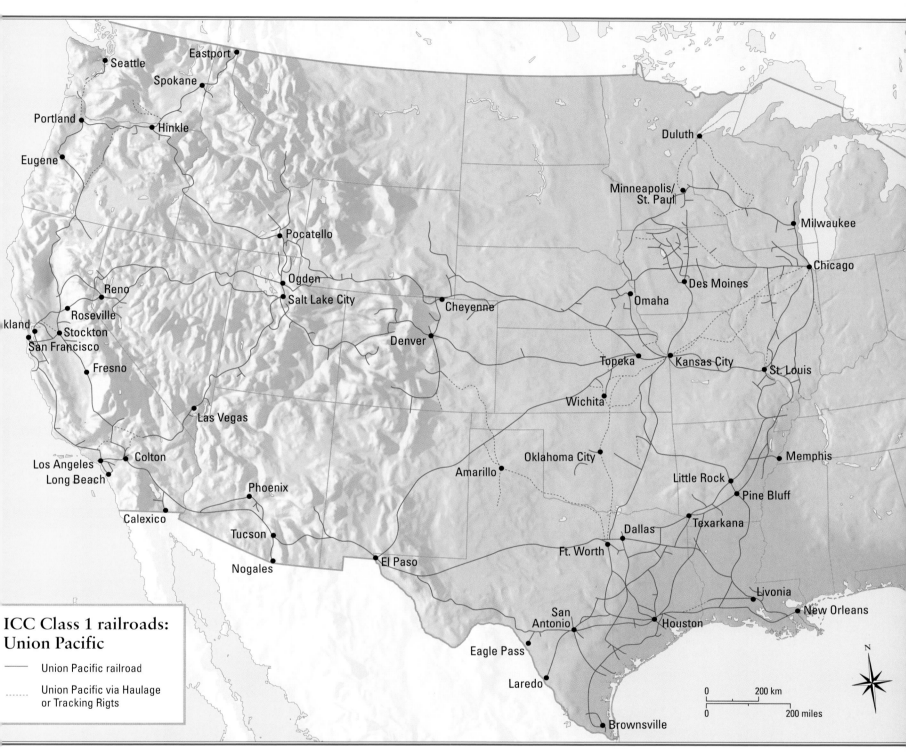

ICC Class 1 railroads: Union Pacific

— Union Pacific railroad

···· Union Pacific via Haulage or Tracking Rigts

rise of revenue as new higher tariffs replaced the old. Capacity limitations could mean that a railroad would not take on a new traffic flow unless it brought in as much revenue as the least profitable of the existing traffics. Shippers began to complain and even began to suggest a revision of the Staggers Act. They complained even more when the railroads felt strong enough to imitate the airlines by imposing fuel surcharges. However, their protests persuaded the Surface Transportation Board to prohibit this raise.

Although the federal government sought to obscure the threat of global warming, there was growing concern among the states and among the public. The railroads' comparatively small carbon footprint

The historic Union Pacific Railroad operates west and southwest from Chicago. Its network includes the original transcontinental route from Omaha to San Francisco.

The wreckage of two freight trains which collided head-on near Gunter, Texas, in May 2004. The trains collided just outside the small north Texas town, killing an engineer and injuring four other people. An increasing number of accidents on busy railroads prompted new legislation in 2007 to address the issue of rail safety in the 21st century.

became an additional incentive to favor rail transport. That same public, however, was alarmed by the increasing number of railroad accidents as increased traffic and the railroads' inability, or unwillingness, to find additional good-quality labor led to stressful situations. Derailments of freight trains carrying noxious substances, especially liquids, could cause severe local damage. Following a series of accidents on one eastern railroad, the Federal Railroad Administration in 2007 launched a mass offensive by safety inspectors, who reported over 3,000 safety violations on the railroad concerned over a period of three days. New legislation was discussed to enhance crew rest hours and to impose the latest train control system on all main lines.

The BNSF was the busiest railroad, shifting over 10 million carloads in 2006. About half of those loads were intermodal, a proportion greater than other railroads (although the Canadian Pacific was reporting over 40 percent intermodal). The next busiest (and probably the most overloaded) was the Union Pacific, with almost 10 million carloads. Next came the CSX and Norfolk Southern, each with more than 7 million, followed by the two Canadian companies, with the smallest of the Class I railroads, the Kansas City Southern, reporting almost 2 million.

While the rise of intermodal traffic (in which containers had long exceeded trailer-on-flatcar traffic) was the most noticeable trend, there were other changes that, on the whole, worked in the railroads' favor. One of these was the domestic demand for coal from the developing Powder River Basin in Wyoming. This coal was moved over long distances to a variety of destinations, and benefited particularly, but not exclusively, the BNSF. Capacity problems arose here, not greatly helped by the practice of overloading the coal hoppers, which, after a few years, resulted in an undesirable layer of coal dust over long stretches of main line. In 2006, the construction of a new line in Wyoming by the Dakota, Minnesota & Eastern RR to relieve the pressure was under discussion (the DM&E was one of the USA's several regional railroads, and this expansion would elevate it to a Class I railroad). Petroleum products also became a strong source of revenue. For small and even medium shipments, rail could often outperform pipeline. When ethanol became increasingly fashionable as a petroleum substitute, the railroads were ready to carry it.

The railroads' success in capturing much of the automobile industry's car distribution traffic in the late 20th century led to some disappointment in the early 21st, when car output fell. However, since this drop was due to overseas competition, there was compensation from the increased inflow of Japanese cars. A similar picture was seen in the steel industry, where declining U.S. output was partly replaced by an import traffic of steel slabs.

The ICC Class I Union Pacific railroad's network covers vast tracts of the United States. Here, locomotive No.3075 hauls a train of Swift Roadrailer units through a tunnel at West Marcel, California, in 2000.

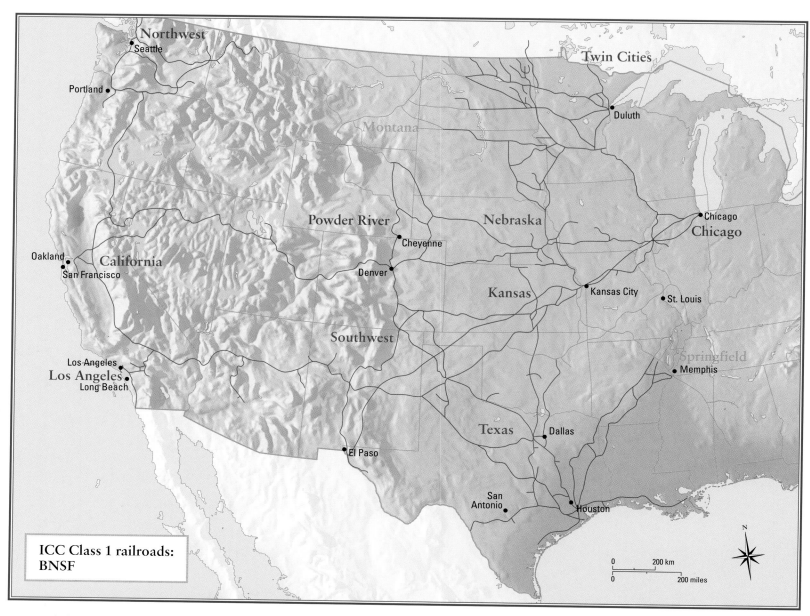

ICC Class 1 railroads:
BNSF

In 2006, the Burlington, Northern & Santa Fe was the busiest of the Class I railroads. Like the Union Pacific, its network covers a large area of the country to the west and southwest of Chicago, with three routes to the Pacific coast.

Carload traffic, once seen as unprofitable and with a doubtful future, has also rebounded. New IT programs make it easier to incorporate single or short trains into the long-distance block trains that reduce costs and speed services. Short lines and regional railroads, helped by federal tax credits, have responded with capital investment; in particular, a number have strengthened their tracks to take the new bigger freight cars. About a quarter of U.S. rail shipments are still handled by a short or regional line at some point in their movement. Another way of concentrating the smaller shipments is by the establishment of logistic centers outside main cities. Here small industries, warehouses, and short-distance highway services can locate, with the sponsoring railroad providing a rail link to the main line. Meanwhile, the Norfolk Southern's "RoadRailer" service was also showing the way to hold and gain smaller shipments of high-class merchandise; its services were extended to Canada and elsewhere. The BNSF also used this handy intermodal vehicle, as did Amtrak until it abandoned its mail service.

Four railroads serve the booming Pacific-coast ports, the Union Pacific and BNSF in the USA, while the Canadian National and Canadian Pacific handle the Vancouver traffic. However, the eastern railroads also benefit from traffic interchanged from those four. (In addition, the CSX holding company also owns Sea Land, a major container shipping line.) Despite an imbalance, with empty containers moving back to the ports, the traffic is highly remunerative, in contrast to previous decades when container traffic was only narrowly profitable. The export grain and mineral traffic to the ports is also unbalanced, with empty freight cars moving east, but here again it is still profitable business.

The twin ports of Los Angeles and Long Beach are the biggest source of international container traffic, followed by Oakland and Tacoma/Seattle. By 2000, there was serious congestion at these ports and considerable investment was needed. Trains to the harbor areas frequently traveled down main streets as well as crossing them at grade. In places, this still happens, but at Los Angeles, in particular, the picture has changed. There, trains are handled in the dock areas by Pacific Harbor Lines, which

A heavy hauling southbound BNSF stack train rumbles past the station at Emeryville, California, in 2005. Freight traffic on the ICC Class I railroad became increasingly busy at the beginning of the 21st century.

One of the lengthy freight trains of the CSX railroad, led by locomotive No.623, hauls a Southbound service through Folkston, Georgia, in 2006.

exchanges trains with the UP and BNSF outside the dock areas. The construction of the grade separated Alameda Corridor has enabled the completed trains to join the main lines without conflicts with highway traffic. The Corridor consists mainly of a concrete cutting; in 2007, it was being extended to Pomona, making a total length of 35 miles (56km).

To accommodate growing traffic, the UP began to double-track several hundred miles of its main line between Los Angeles and El Paso. Meanwhile, the BNSF was triple-tracking its line over the Cajon Pass, which it shared with the UP, as well as doubling most of its Chicago–Los Angeles main line.

In 2007, the ever resourceful Kansas City Southern was planning with Mexican partners to build a line across northern Mexico, from the port of Lazaro Cardenas to an interchange with the KCS at Nuevo Laredo. This would end the virtual monopoly of Asian container traffic by the UP and BNSF. A longer-

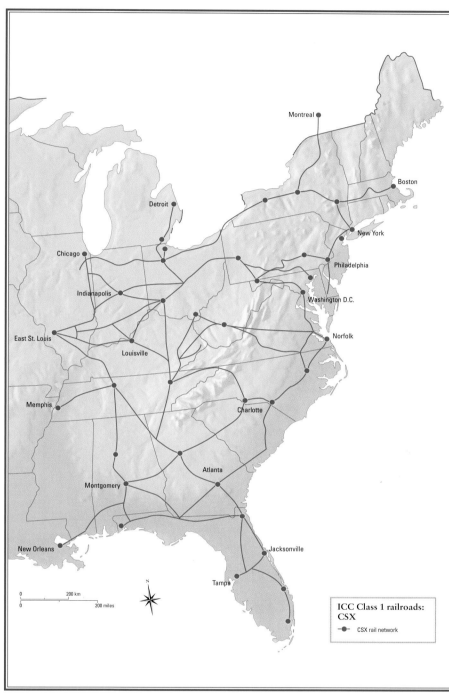

ICC Class 1 railroads:
CSX

— CSX rail network

term threat to that monopoly was the proposed widening of the Panama Canal, to enable container ships to sail directly to U.S. east-coast ports.

Continued traffic growth implied a need for more tractive power. In 1992, construction of new diesel locomotives had dropped to less than 400, but in the first five years of the new century, deliveries varied from 675 to nearly 1,200. General Motors had sold off its locomotive interest, the new company becoming Electro-Motive Diesel; its managers and designers stayed in place, but actual construction shifted to London, Ontario. In the ensuing years, it failed to overtake its competitor, General Electric, but nevertheless remained a substantial producer and innovator. The big railroads continued to favor high-power units. The Union Pacific received 1,000 EMD SD70M units in 1999, that being the largest order ever placed by a U.S. railroad. This model and its GE competitor were in the 4,400hp bracket;

The CSX is an eastern railroad, with routes spreading from Boston and Detroit in the North all the way down to New Orleans and Miami in the South. Its network reaches westward from New York, Philadelphia, and Washington, D.C., to Chicago, East St. Louis, and Memphis.

Union Pacific's switching locomotive, No. Y2315, is one of the ultra low emission diesel hybrid, or "genset" types operating out of Mira Loma, California.

EMD introduced a 6,000hp design, but this did not find great favor among the railroads. Most were seeking to replace older units on a "two for three" basis, and the existing 4,400hp locomotives were enough for that.

Contrary to what had once been thought, ac-motored diesels did not supersede conventional dc locomotives. The bigger railroads found it advantageous to buy both, using the ac types on their heavy bulk trains, and the dc variants for lighter, faster services.

Both builders designed new, or improved, diesel engines, partly to conform to increasingly tight federal emission standards. Really radical innovation in the field of fuel economy and pollution control was achieved by smaller niche companies, National Railway Equipment in Illinois, and Railpower Technologies. The latter, marketing its units as "Green Goats," was based in Vancouver British Columbia, but had a production facility at Schenectady, New York, the former home of the old ALCO locomotive company. Some of the designs ("gensets") had three small diesel engines, one or two of which cut out automatically when they were not needed. Others ("hybrids") had small generator sets that trickle charged batteries, from which power was drawn as necessary. All these designs achieved substantial fuel savings as well as pollution limitation. Initially, they were offered in the low-power range, mainly for switching or local freights. The Union Pacific ordered a substantial number of them for its lines in Texas and California, where state emission regulations were tightening. It also began experiments with a conventional unit fitted with a catalytic converter.

Another niche producer was Motive Power Industries, which had formerly specialized in the remanufacture of diesel locomotives. Its passenger diesel locomotive, the MP36, attracted orders in the new century. This was because new federal safety regulations required so many changes to the existing

The New Mexico *Rail Runner Express* was a commuter rail system serving metropolitan Albuquerque, New Mexico, on a BNSF right of way from Belen to Bernalillo; an extension was scheduled to open in 2008, to extend northward to Santa Fe. The Rail Runner's locomotives are diesel-electric MP36PH-3Cs built by Motive Power Inc. in Boise, Idaho, capable of running speeds in excess of 100mph (160.92k/h).

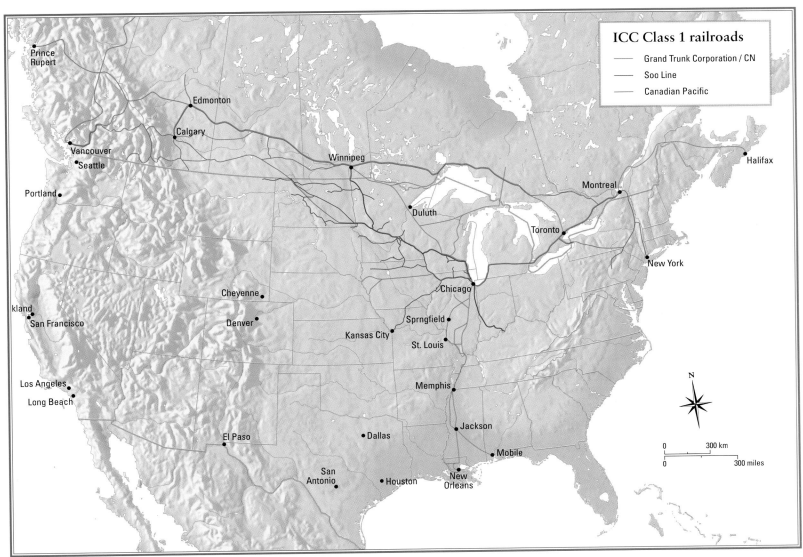

ICC Class 1 railroads

— Grand Trunk Corporation / CN
— Soo Line
— Canadian Pacific

GE "Genesis" and EMD F59PH that neither company thought further production worth the trouble, given that the passenger market was not large. This provided the opportunity for a small company like MPI to enter the field, and its first order was for Chicago's Metra lines.

New commuter railways continued to appear and old ones to expand. The traditional American distrust of government in business was outweighed by the inconvenience of congested highways; these lines were subsidized in various degrees from state or federal funds. New Mexico's State Runner Express, between Albuquerque and Bernalillo, for example, was expected to cover only 10 percent of its operating costs from ticket sales. The capital expenditure required by Nashville's Music City Star service, covering 32 miles (51km), was largely financed by the federal government. However, not all projects went forward; in 2006, the proposed Raleigh–Durham line in North Carolina, which had been in preparation for a decade, was abandoned when it did not meet new federal cost/benefit requirements. A line planned for Las Vegas also fell by the wayside when it failed to satisfy its regional transportation authority.

Several existing commuter authorities grew. The big and longstanding Chicago Metra system extended some of its lines, as did the Boston MBTA system. Florida's Tri-Rail double-tracked its 71-mile (116km) Miami–West Palm Beach line. In New York, contracts were placed for new tunnels, to give

Through takeovers, the two major Canadian railroads, Canadian National and Canadian Pacific have entered the U.S. railroad scene. Both operate routes to the Pacific coast in Canada. In the United States, the CN's activities are under the Grand Trunk name, while the CP has its own routes and those of the Soo Line.

The Tri-Rail commuter line extended 72 miles (115.87km) from Miami to Mangonia Park, north of West Palm Beach, Florida. The name referred to the three counties through which the line passed. The line was operated by South Florida Regional Transportation Authority from 1989, using CSX tracks. Pasenger cars were distinctive, double-deck units built by Bombardier.

the Long Island lines access to Grand Central Terminal, and to make possible a new Trans Hudson Express service.

The long-distance passenger operator, Amtrak, lacked a clear idea of its future as it faced increasingly onerous budget cuts year by year. It had started the century with the assurance, and possibly belief, that it was moving to a situation where its revenues would cover operating expenses. Despite cost cutting and useful traffic increases, this began to be seen as unlikely, and its president was replaced. The new incumbent seemed to know his business, which may have been his downfall. He was removed in 2005 by the Amtrak board, which consisted of government appointees. At that time, the federal government was proposing to eliminate federal funding, as part of its policy of breaking up Amtrak, with regional and state governments and maybe private investors taking over specific sectors. Amtrak's president had formulated a different long-term plan, looking to maintaining Amtrak's integrity while remedying some of its problems.

One of those problems was rehabilitation of worn-out infrastructure, although some progress had been made, with federal or state assistance. The electrification of the northern part of the New

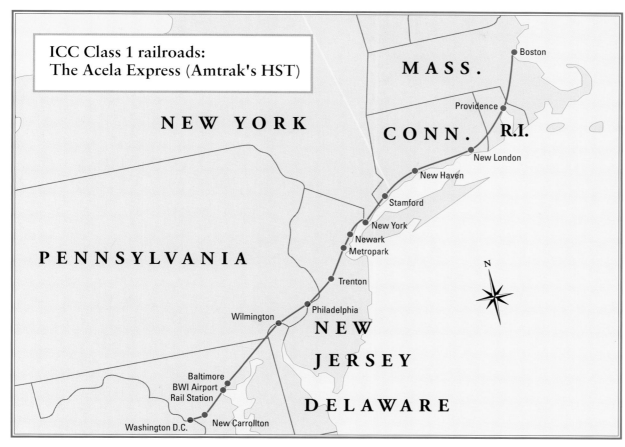

ICC Class 1 railroads:
The Acela Express (Amtrak's HST)

MASS.

Boston

Providence

NEW YORK

CONN.

R.I.

New London

New Haven

Stamford

New York

PENNSYLVANIA

Newark

Metropark

Trenton

Philadelphia

Wilmington

NEW

JERSEY

Baltimore

BWI Airport

Rail Station

DELAWARE

Washington D.C.

New Carrollton

N

Amtrak's *Acela Express* service relies on electric traction and tilting trains to provide a high-speed service through the Northeast Corridor.

York–Boston line in preparation for the Acela service had been a substantial work. The Pennsylvannia government participated in the rehabilitation of the Philadelphia–Harrisburg line with a view to enhanced train service. Another problem was timekeeping; by this time, nobody outside the Northeast Corridor expected Amtrak to run on time, for despite its incentive payments to the freight railroads over which it ran, the latter seemed unable to give Amtrak trains a clear run. Line congestion was the main cause, but some freight railroads seemed to give Amtrak trains a very low priority. At the hub of Amtrak's long-distance operations, Chicago, trains would be arriving many hours late on a regular

Amtrak's *Acela Express* was the United States' only true high-speed tilting train, when introduced in December, 2000. Operating at speeds between 75mph (120km/h) and 150mph (241km/h) on the sharply curved track of the Northeast Corridor, the tilting facitility meant that passengers were still assured of a comfortable ride.

basis, and hundreds of thousands of dollars were spent on hotel accommodation for passengers who had missed their connections. Amtrak's decision no longer to attach freight cars to its trains for high-value merchandise, an idea that at the time had seemed a good way to increase revenue, had no effect on punctuality.

On the bright side, the services provided in cooperation with the California and Washington State governments were popular, as was the new service of Acela tilting trains for the Northeast Corridor, despite a hiatus in 2005, when the Acela trains had to be withdrawn temporarily for precautionary replacements of brake discs. By 2005, Amtrak had won 50 percent of the Washington–New York passenger market.

Primary Canadian Railroads

FREIGHT IS THE ONLY SOURCE OF PROFIT FOR THE MAJOR
CANADIAN RAILROADS, BUT LOSS MAKING PASSENGER SERVICES
HAVE BEEN TAKEN ON BY A GOVERNMENT SUBSIDIZED OPERATOR.
INCREASED TRAFFIC WITH THE UNITED STATES AND ABSORPTION
OF U.S. LINES PAINT A ROSY FUTURE.

By the 1950s, the Canadian National and Canadian Pacific railroads were well into a program of switching to diesels, although they were a little behind the U.S. railroads; the CP's Montreal commuter service was long in the hands of immaculate maroon, gray, and gold steam locomotives, however, and it was not until the early 1960s that the two companies were totally equipped with diesels.

Over most of their trunk routes, the Canadian Pacific and Canadian National were in competition, although passenger services were pooled in the Montreal/Ottawa–Toronto service. They united in the 1950s to oppose the construction of the St. Lawrence Seaway, which seemed likely to rob them of their heavy traffic to the Atlantic ports. In this they were unsuccessful, but the Seaway was never the great success its proponents had forecast; moreover, it had the effect of causing the railways to improve their services, which stood them in good stead in the continuing struggle against highway operators.

The Canadian National was the bigger railroad of the two, although the Canadian Pacific, with its hotels, airline, ocean liners, and hyperactive public relations, was the better known. The CN management included men of ideas, but innovation tended to be stifled by its status as a crown corporation. It required government permission for any big changes, and it was subjected to more political pressure than the CP. Moreover, being an example of government participation in business, it was ideologically suspect in many quarters. Although its legislated goal was service rather than

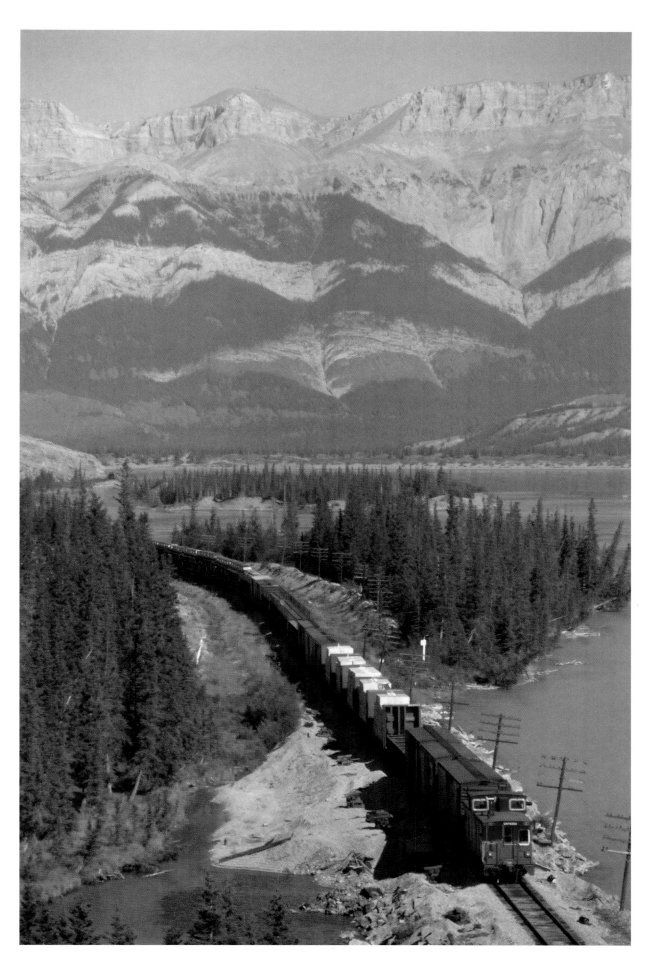

Amidst a backdrop of stunning natural beauty, a Canadian National Railroad freight train runs along the Athabasca River in Alberta's Jasper National Park.

profit, governments and taxpayers resented deficits. From the 1950s, there were heavy losses of high-value freight as the truckers benefited from highway improvements. Road transport had an undoubted advantage at the collection and delivery ends of a movement, whereas rail transportation was superior over the long haul. Both the CP and CN introduced trailer-on-flatcar services to meet this competition; later, containers made their appearance.

After secret negotiations, in the 1950s, the CP succeeded in purchasing Smith Transport, Canada's biggest highway operator. This gave it an enormous competitive advantage. The CN quietly began to woo another big trucking outfit, but despite a very persuasive letter to the minister in charge of transportation, the government refused to allow this purchase to proceed.

Nonetheless, from time to time, the CN did innovate. In the 1930s, it had been a pioneer in diesel traction and, for better or worse, it had introduced streamlined steam locomotives to Canada. In the 1960s, it pioneered differential pricing with its "Red, White, and Blue" scheme. In this, the days of the year were subdivided by color, the red days being those of high passenger traffic, and the other colors signifying lower levels; passenger tickets were priced high on the red days and lower on the others. The scheme worked insofar as it smoothed the peaks to the railroad's and passengers' benefit, but it did not end the losses incurred by passenger services. Both railroads, and the CN in particular, were obliged to provide loss making passenger services. The introduction of Budd diesel railcars on the shorter runs reduced losses, but only marginally. The highly publicized CP Canadian and CN Super Continental transcontinental services to Vancouver were trains of prestige rather than profit. Only the Montreal-Toronto service and its connections seemed to promise a profit. Cross-subsidizing passenger losses from freight revenues hampered the railways in their struggle to compete with highway operators.

BC Rail, known as the British Columbia Railway between 1972 and 1984, and as the Pacific Great Eastern Railway before 1972, operated in the Canadian province of British Columbia between 1912 and 2004. It was a Class II regional railway and the third-largest in Canada, operating 1,441 miles (2,320km) of mainline track. Owned by the provincial government from 1918 until 2004, the operations were sold to the Canadian National Railway. Photographed during the 1980s-90s, this freight train passes through Lillooet, British Columbia.

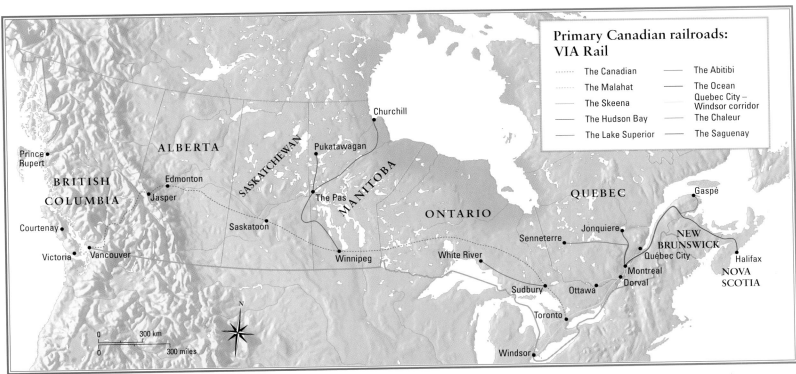

Primary Canadian railroads:
VIA Rail

- .... The Canadian
- .... The Malahat
- ——— The Skeena
- ——— The Hudson Bay
- ——— The Lake Superior
- ——— The Abitibi
- ——— The Ocean
- ——— Quebec City – Windsor corridor
- ——— The Chaleur
- ——— The Saguenay

In 1977, the railroads were relieved of their passenger problems when the government established VIA Rail, a crown corporation entrusted with all the passenger services (except commuter) formerly operated by the railroad companies. It had close parallels with Amtrak in the United States, but had fewer rights in relation to the passage of its trains over the railroad companies' routes and, moreover, was more subject to political pressures (its future was always subject to a government order-in-council, rather than an Act of Parliament). Hence, in most years, its management was preoccupied with resisting, or coping with, reductions in the government's financial support. As a result, it operates considerably fewer trains now than it did at the start.

VIA Rail took over the revolutionary Bombardier-built LRC (Light, Rapid, Comfortable) trains that had been on order. These were fast tilting trains intended primarily for the important Montreal–Toronto service. Unfortunately, they proved defective in many ways and spent much of their earlier years in the workshops. This was not a good start for VIA Rail, but on the whole, it did settle down and achieve what was intended—continuance of Canadian railway passenger service where it was socially crucial or otherwise desirable. By 2002, its revenues were almost two-thirds of costs, which in the circumstances was a good performance. Four-fifths of the passengers were accounted for by the Montreal–Toronto trunk route with its extensions to Quebec City and London, Ontario. The Toronto–Vancouver service was thrice weekly and tourist orientated. There were still classic long-distance trains from Montreal to the Maritime Provinces, and a large number of services in remote northern regions, often on a once-weekly basis.

In 2000, VIA Rail took the opportunity to purchase 139 European passenger cars built for overnight services through the Channel Tunnel that were never instituted. These were restyled as "Renaissance" cars, but their refurbishment for Canadian conditions, including the Canadian winter, proved expensive, and their integration was further held back when a court ruling obtained by a pressure group obliged VIA Rail to vastly increase its provision of handicapped-accessible accommodation on

Like Amtrak in the United States, VIA Rail was set up to relieve the Canadian railroads of the burden of operating loss making passenger services. It runs a number of named express trains between major cities.

the new trains. Elsewhere, the longstanding passenger service provided to James Bay by the Ontario Northland Railway continues, as does the Vancouver–Prince George service formerly provided by the Pacific Great Eastern, now BC Rail. In southern Ontario, the GO (Government of Ontario) commuter service, founded in 1967, using bi-level cars and operating in cooperation with the CN and CP, has been successful and has set an example for other North American cities. Montreal's Metropolitan Transport Agency took over and considerably renovated the electric and diesel commuter services provided by the CN and CP. In Vancouver, BC Transit has been established to provide commuter services.

In 1995, the government decided to privatize the Canadian National, with the proviso that no investor could purchase more than 15 percent. About two-thirds of the purchasers were U.S. institutions, and this accelerated the CN's trend toward becoming a North American, rather than simply a Canadian, corporation. Earlier, the CN had consolidated its U.S. assets, the Grand Trunk Western (Chicago to Detroit and Cincinnati) and the Duluth, Winnipeg & Pacific being fully integrated; later, the Central Vermont (Montreal–St. Albans) and Grand Trunk (Montreal–Portland) were sold to U.S. companies.

There was an increasing opportunity for United States–Canada traffic development. The CP had acquired the Delaware and Hudson RR and the Soo Line, integrating them into its own operations. Initially, the CN responded by rebuilding its St. Clair Tunnel between Sarnia and Huron so that it could accept double-stack container trains and the high autorack cars. Its next move was the purchase of the Illinois Central, a Class I railway extending from Chicago down to the Gulf of Mexico, with connections to the promising Mexican economy. Then it took over the Wisconsin Central, giving improved connections between central Canada and the United States (previously, the WC had acquired the Algoma Central in Ontario, whose passenger service CN continued to operate).

In 2003, the CN acquired two more U.S. lines, the Bessemer & Lake Erie, and the Duluth, Missabe & Iron Range. These railroads had been built for iron-ore traffic in the Great Lakes region, but offered the CN improved connections into the United States. The same year, the CN bought BC Rail's shares from the British Columbia government. These acquisitions transformed the CN, and they were digested with little difficulty. Negotiations to merge with the BNSF, which would have created by far the biggest North American railroad company, were proceeding smoothly, but eventually the U.S. government refused consent.

The CN continued to be an innovatory railroad, and some of its initiatives were studied by other railroads worldwide. It decided to monitor the progress not only of freight cars or trains, but also shipments. This was an enormous boon for its clients, and led to a move toward instituting fixed and regular schedules for freight operations. That is, to organize all freight strictly to regular timetables, just as once passenger traffic had been regulated. Even support operations like car inspection were timetabled. The CN had already lengthened traction sections, obtaining more productivity from locomotives and their crews, and this timetabling regime resulted in further substantial economies as well as more attractive services. In 2006, the CN's operating ratio (cost as percentage of revenue) was only 61 percent, considerably better than that of the other big North American railroads.

Apart from services into the United States and to the Atlantic ports, freight in eastern Canada promised little further development, whereas in the West, it was expanding rapidly. Grain and mineral traffic, much of it for export via Vancouver, was very profitable, as were the container trains originating in Vancouver. Both railroads divested themselves of many of their lines in the East. Some of these were sold to private companies and became new railroads, but there was a Canadian innovation in the form of "internal short lines." These were operated in accordance with relaxed operating and labor conditions, just like short-line railroads, but continued to be owned by the CN or CP, although with a degree of independence. Meanwhile, the CP emphasized its reorientation by shifting its headquarters from Montreal to Calgary, and hiving off its eastern lines into its St. Lawrence & Hudson Railway. The Soo Line retained a degree of independence, but its Chicago–Kansas main line was put up for sale.

There was increasing cooperation between the CP and CN. In the mid-1990s, the former was hoping to sell its eastern lines to the CN, but the latter's privatization blocked this. There are many locations where the CP and CN have parallel, single-track main lines, as in the Fraser Valley of British Columbia, and economies are gained by sending eastbound trains of both companies over one track, and westbound over the other.

One of the joys of traveling through the magnificent scenery of Canada is by steam train. Tourist routes still run through the heart of the Canadian Rocky Mountains, past languid lakes, allowing passengers to experience what travel was like during the golden age of steam from the comfort of trains hauled by restored locomotives.

Primary Mexican Railroads

INCREASED TRADE WITH THE UNITED STATES AND CANADA, THE PRIVATIZATION OF THE STATE RAILROAD, AND SUBSTANTIAL FOREIGN CAPITAL INVESTMENT PUT MEXICAN RAILROADS ON A FIRM FOOTING AT THE BEGINNING OF THE 21ST CENTURY.

For most of the second half of the 20th century, Mexico's dominant railroad was the Mexican National Railways (Ferrocariles Nacionales de Mexico, or N de M), This had its antecedents in a network of U.S.-style, lines of 3ft (914mm) gauge laid in the 19th century and later, with one local exception, which was converted to standard gauge. It was the only railroad that could be said to cover virtually the whole country. Like other Mexican lines, it adhered to the Association of American Railroads technical standards, so there was through running of rolling stock into the United States and Canada without the need for transhipment.

N de M was heavily subsidized by the government; low-traffic lines were kept in operation, fares and tariffs were low, and labor productivity was abysmal. This last factor owed much to the lack of capital investment; the steam locomotive survived longer in Mexico than in the United States. Although General Motors and ALCO diesels were taking over in the 1960s, it was still possible to see postwar ALCO "Northern"-type steam locomotives hauling freight from Mexico City. While N de M was a clear failure as a business, as a service to the Mexican people, it had its merits. Thanks to low fares, local passenger trains were heavily used by poorer people, and low tariffs helped farmers and small businesses. Dismissing superfluous workers would only have created further unemployment, with its social and psychological consequences.

Of the other railroads, the Sud Pacifico had a long line up into the northwest, where it linked with its virtual owner, the U.S. Southern Pacific RR, which sold it to Mexico in 1951, after which it was known as the Ferrocaril del Pacifico. Another line in northern Mexico was the Chihuahua Pacifico, which also had links with U.S. railroads and came into Mexican ownership by stages. A private railroad that com-

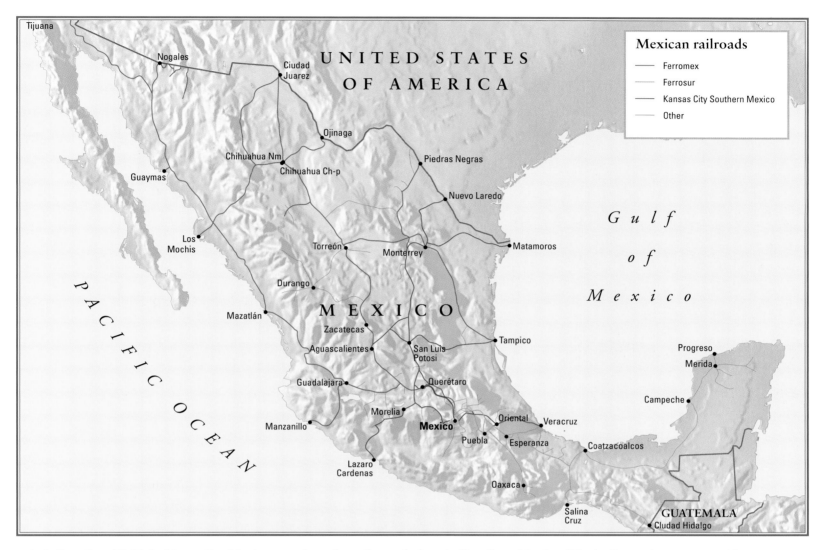

Mexican railroads

— Ferromex
— Ferrosur
— Kansas City Southern Mexico
— Other

peted directly with N de M was the Mexicano, whose heavily-graded main line from Mexico City to the port of Veracruz was partly electrified. It was bought by the Mexican government in 1946, and within a decade, it had been integrated into N de M. Its electrification has been abandoned.

In the South, the Yucatan was long isolated from other railroads until the Sureste line was built to the Yucatan capital of Merida. From Merida, the Ferrocaril Unidos de Yucatan operated a number of lines of 3ft (914mm) gauge that radiated into the region. In the Yucatan in the 1960s, it was possible to see not only the last operating examples of the traditional American 4-4-0 locomotive, but also the even more ancient disc-and-crossbar signals.

In the last decades of its life, N de M undertook a degree of modernization. A new line was built from Mexico City to Queretaro and was electrified at 25 kilovolts ac. Locomotives for this line were bought from General Electric in 1982, then stored to await completion of the line. There was a plan to electrify all the core routes, but beyond this initial line, little was achieved (and the new private owner of the Queretaro line has not made use of the electrification). The Union Pacific RR's Transportation Control System was adopted for the computerized monitoring of N de M operations, but its application was held back by the sudden devaluation of the peso in the mid-1990s. Meanwhile, the signing of the North American Free Trade Agreement in 1992 resulted in increased trade with the United States and Canada, boosting the introduction of regular cross-frontier intermodal freight services.

In recent years, Mexican railroads have benefited from foreign investment, most notably by U.S. companies. The routes of the main operators are shown here. The largest, Ferromex, has cross-border connections with the BNSF and Union Pacific.

The *Sierra Madre Express* train crosses Temoris Bridge through the Sierra Tarahumara, the region also known as the Copper Canyon, in Northern Mexico. This region only became accessible after a railroad line was completed from Los Mochis to Chihuahua in 1961. From the train can be seen jagged canyons, stunning waterfalls and beautiful flora and fauna.

The *Al Pacifico* train ran from the city of Chihuahua through Copper Canyon to Los Mochis, Mexico. Here it pulls up at the station in the small village of Creel, between 1985 and 1995.

In 1995, partly because of new thinking occasioned by the fall of the peso, it was decided to privatize the state railroad. One hoped-for result was the injection of much needed foreign capital into the system. The Mexican government would retain ownership of track and structures, and private operators would be offered 50-year concessions. The government would continue to be responsible for pensions and also for the expected redundancy payments. The accumulated debts would also be taken over by the government.

By the end of 1999, N de M (by then, known as FNM) had ceased to be a train operator, the last of its divisions having been sold off. In the late 1990s, almost all passenger services had been discontinued, reducing losses and thereby making the railroads more attractive to purchasers. The new owners did run some socially important passenger trains, but received subsidies for doing so.

The network was divided territorially. U.S. railroads were keen to buy into the properties, but needed to join with local buyers because foreign investors were not permitted to purchase a controlling interest at that time. Thus the largest of the new companies, Ferromex, with its 5,280 miles (8,500km) of route, is three-quarters owned by Mexican interests with the Union Pacific RR holding 26 percent. Ferromex links Mexico City with the North, and has cross-frontier connections with the Union Pacific and BNSF railroads. Its main business is long-distance freight, but it operates some state subsidized passenger services as well as a few tourist trains, of which the best known is the "Chepe" over a spectacular section of the old Chihuahua Pacifico line.

The second of the big companies, Transportación Ferroviaria Mexicana (TFM), extends for 2,640 miles (4,250km) and serves the Northeast, connecting with U.S. lines at Brownsville and Laredo. Originally, the Kansas City Southern RR had a 46 percent interest, but later it contrived to acquire a further 51 percent, making it the virtual owner. The modernization and upgrading of the 785-mile (1,263km) main line from Mexico City to Nuevo Laredo has been a priority, and by 2005, TFM was claiming to possess the youngest locomotive stock of any North American railroad.

Other regional lines include Ferrosur, which took over the lines of the former Sureste. It connects Mexico City with Veracruz and Puebla, but otherwise lacks solid traffic sources. Ferrosur attempted to merge with Ferromex in 2002, but the government withheld approval. Another U.S. company that succeeded in acquiring a controlling interest (in this case total control) is the Genessee & Wyoming, which now operates the Yucatan railroad as FCCM. It provides a link with the rest of Mexico and also continues to operate some of the light-traffic lines from Merida. With subsidies, it maintains passenger services on some lines.

The railroad network of Mexico City, including its major marshalling yard, is operated by a terminal railway (TFVM), in which Ferromex, Ferrosur, TFM, and the government each have a quarter-share. Minor companies include the Coahuila-Durango and the Istmo de Tehuantepec, which operate small lines that, for local reasons, do not form part of the bigger systems.

Amidst the hustle and bustle, wo trains wait at the rural Divisadero Station in Copper Canyon, Mexico.

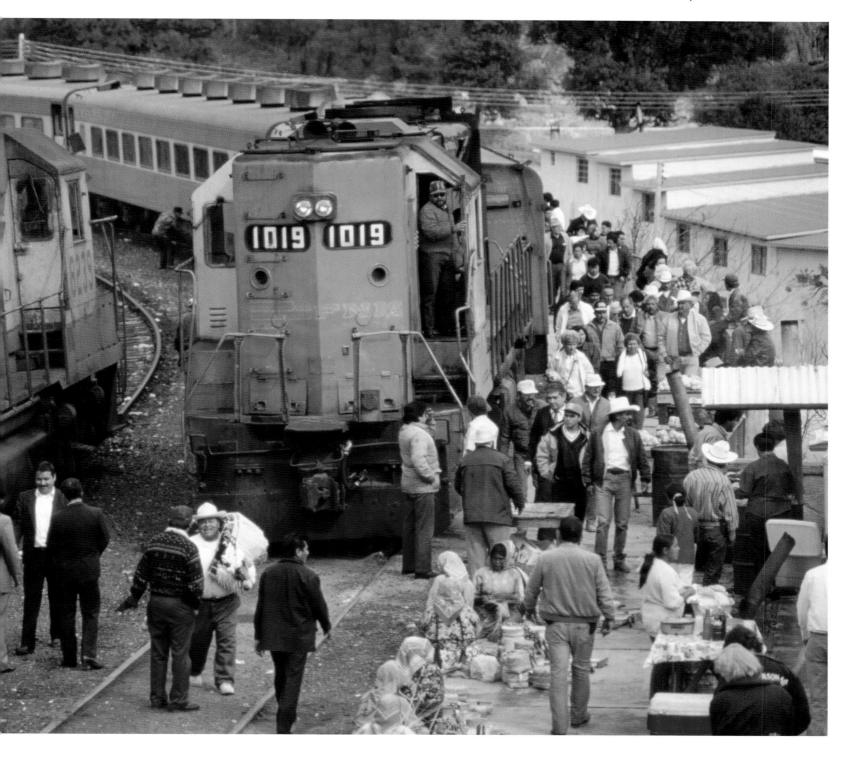

TROLLEYS AND LIGHT RAIL IN THE 21ST CENTURY

THE DESIRE TO CUT TRAFFIC CONGESTION AND, MORE RECENTLY, TO REDUCE POLLUTION FROM ROAD VEHICLES HAS LED TO THE CONSTRUCTION OF TROLLEY AND LIGHT RAIL SYSTEMS IN MANY U.S. CITIES. RESTORED VINTAGE SYSTEMS, MOREOVER, ARE SEEN AS POSITIVE TOURIST ATTRACTIONS.

The LYNX light rail, rapid transit service in Charlotte, North Carolina, ran state-of-the-art Siemens-built Avanto cars such as this, from 2007.

The surge of interest in light rail that occurred in the United States and Canada in the 1980s produced a number of useful systems, even though there had been setbacks when local authorities or popular votes had put an end to proposals, The main purpose of light rail transportation (LRT), which was to reduce the excessive use of automobiles, thereby easing congestion and cutting the expense of new highways, had usually been achieved. By 2000, the accent had broadened somewhat: increasingly, LRT was seen as a measure against pollution and also, partly because of this, was regarded as a positive aesthetic factor that could enhance the appeal of those cities that had such systems.

Technical developments began to make their appearance. One was the low-floor vehicle, which not only gave passengers access without a step, but also speeded up loading and unloading, increasing the productivity of vehicles. Traction control based on ac current had a similar impact as on main-line railroads and improved, among other things, the smoothness of ride. Modular design and the greater

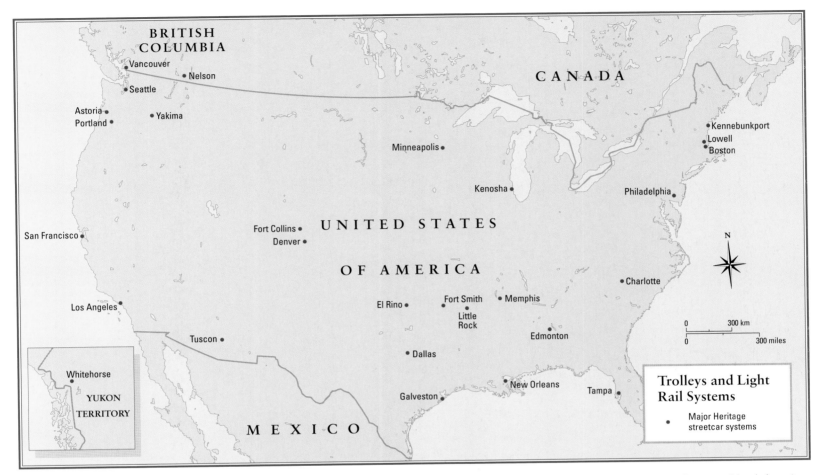

Trolleys and Light Rail Systems

• Major Heritage streetcar systems

use of composite materials simplified maintenance. By 2000, some companies were already experimenting with energy saving ideas; regenerative braking (where the vehicle's momentum is converted to electricity that is fed back into the system) was one of these.

Many of these improvements originated in Europe, where manufacturers supplied the American market, either directly or indirectly (assembly was required in the United States). The German Siemens company assembled light rail vehicles in Sacramento, and in 2006 was supplying Denver, Colorado, Charlotte, North Carolina, and Edmonton and Calgary in Canada. In the 1980s, the Canadian Bombardier company, which had acquired European builders, had been responsible for a high proportion of new cars delivered to the United States, and was continuing to supply the market. Japan also participated: Kinki Sharyo secured orders for, among others, the new Phoenix system, the San Jose system, and Seattle's Central Link system.

Although some systems used conventional cars, clearly developments of the trolleys of previous generations, others were different. These included lines that bore some of the characteristics of heavy rail, when disused railroad lines were made part of the system for example. The Los Angeles Sprinter Line, contracts for which were approved in 2004, was one of these and was planned to use two-car diesel formations, rather than the trolley-style concept with its overhead current collection. Siemens, which had supplied conventional LRT vehicles for Los Angeles' other lines, was the supplier, and trains similar to those used by German Railways heavy-rail services were chosen.

There were still a handful of locations where the old, conventional trolleys could be seen, but these were more in the nature of vintage exhibits with a certain tourist allure. San Francisco had kept its

Several cities in North America have retained their old streetcar systems. Today, however, they tend to act as tourist attractions rather than public transport.

celebrated cable cars, and also had a trolley line using vehicles that were painted in the liveries of defunct U.S. city trolley lines. New Orleans was equally well known among trolley enthusiasts, since its St. Charles line was served by vintage Perley Thomas cars. Those cars survived the 2005 hurricane; in its aftermath, they also ran on the Canal and Riverfront lines, where the modern cars had been put out of action.

Light rail was considered ideal for routes that carried 3–8,000 passengers per hour in each direction (for most U.S. cities, it was the peak flow that counted). Below this figure, buses were probably cheaper, while higher traffic might justify a subway or heavy-rail line. LRT, where it was not on city streets, could offer commercial speeds of around 12–18mph (20–30 km/h); the actual figure depended on the number and duration of stops.

In 2004, a dozen cities had new lines under construction, either completely new systems or additions to existing systems. These were Denver, Little Rock, Minneapolis, New Orleans, Phoenix, Portland, Sacramento, San Diego, San Francisco, San Jose, Seattle, and St. Louis. Others were digesting newly-built lines or refurbishing older ones.

Funding through the Federal Transit Administration helped the construction of new lines. Thus, of the original $1.4 billion estimated cost of the first 20-mile (33km) line in Phoenix, the FTA granted almost $6 million. Typically, projects were brought into being by a selected construction company on a design-and-build contract. Once built and accepted, another company would be selected to operate the line. In the case of Phoenix, for example, the five-year operating agreement was won by Alternate

The Hiawatha Line offered a fast, quiet light-rail service to 17 stations between downtown Minneapolis, and Mall of America, Bloomington, Minnesota. Bus routes were timed to connect with trains at Hiawatha Line stations, making it convenient for passengers to get to work, to shopping, or wherever they wanted to go by simply hopping on and off.

The TECO Line Streetcar System in Tampa, Florida, was opened in 2002 by the Hillsborough Area Regional Transportation Authority, and managed by Tampa Historic Streetcar, Inc. It was designed to connect downtown to the historic Ybor City district, and as of 2006, comprised 2.3 miles (3.7km) of single track, several passing sidings, and 12 stations.

Concepts Inc., which already operated the Houston system.

One of the most ambitious light rail developments was in Denver. A fast growing city, it was facing severe highway congestion, each household owning an average of 2.3 automobiles. Successive light rail projects were worked out as parts of an integrated scheme involving other forms of transport, notably buses and heavy rail. There was an exchange of information with private developers as well, so that, for example, housing, retail, and other developments could be coordinated with the opening of new stations. Where possible, such private developments would also include parking spaces for LRT passengers (park-and-ride shuttles based on those stations were also used so that passsngers could be drawn from more distant locations). By 2004, the so-called T-Rex (Transportation Expansion Project) lines were coming into service, extending the already existing LRT mileage. The key to the T-Rex plan was the reconstruction of two existing state highways that entered the city, while at the same time building light rail lines parallel with them. This involved some expensive and complex engineering when the junction of the two highways was reconstructed and the LRT route threaded through.

After the T-Rex plan, another, FasTracks, had been proposed, basically a commuter rail service radiating from Union Station, where LRT already had a terminal and where a bus station would also be built. The FasTracks scheme was approved by Denver voters, but turned down by the state governor and the state's transportation department; a measure, perhaps, of the public support for rail transportation that the LRT lines had generated. Increased sales taxes to finance the new lines seemed to arouse hardly a murmur.

INDEX

Figures shown in **bold** type signify maps. Figures in *italics* refer to photographs or illustrations.

ACKNOWLEDGMENTS

Jeremy Atherton: 352
Canadian Railway Musuem: 59
Corbis: 8 (George H.H. Huey); 9 bottom (Doug Wilson); 14 (Marilyn Angel Wynn/Nativestock); 17 (David Muench); 25, 27 bottom (Connie Ricca); 35, 63, 131, 167, 173, 258–259, 287, 307 (Bettmann); 53 (P.F. Goist); 82, 142–143 (Dave G. Houser); 98; 129, 182–183 (Lowell Georgia); 135 (Wolfgang Kaehler); 136–137 (Scott T. Smith); 210 (Minnesota Historical Society); 237 (Walter Bibikow/JAI); 264; 293, 295 (Underwood & Underwood); 304 (The Mariners' Museum); 327, 350 (Vince Streano); 333 (P. Magielsen/zefa); 357 (Jim Sugar); 362 (Randy Eli Grothe/ Dallas Morning News); 373 (Ursula Gahwiler/Robert Harding World Imagery); 374 (Gunter Marx Photography); 380–381 (Gerald French); 382 (Buddy Mays); 382–383 (Bob Krist); 386 (Layne Kennedy)
Dan Crow: 141 bottom
Edwards Railcar Company: 291 bottom
Robert A. Estremo: 324
GW Travel Limited: 302–303, 377
Mike Halterman: 387
Alan Harris: 251
Harvey Henkelman: 316 top, 319 center
Mike Hicks: 323
iStockphoto: 26 (John Graves); 27 top (Nhan Nguyen); 55 top (Randy Mayes); 70 bottom (Robert Young); 104 top (Sherry Sowell); 189 (Norman Reid); 211 (Rafael Ramirez); 220 (Vera Bogaerts); 240 (Matthew Mills)
Evan Jennings: 278 right, 291 top
Sean Lamb: 4, 138, 228 bottom, 244 top, 246, 247, 255, 294, 316 bottom, 318, 319 top, 321, 330, 348, 351
Library of Congress, Prints & Photographs Division: 6, 29 top, 30, 32, 33, 68, 69 top, 69 bottom, 77, 89, 91, 101, 104 bottom, 106, 108, 111, 112, 113, 114, 115, 118, 119, 120, 121, 122, 123, 124, 130, 134, 139, 151, 152, 159, 166 top, 169 bottom, 177, 179, 185, 198, 199 top, 208, 224, 225, 229, 231, 236, 263, 266 top, 266 bottom, 275, 276, 278 left, above left, 280, 282, 288, 289, 297, 298, 306, 308, 309, 310, 311, 339
J.B. Macelwane Archives, St. Louis University: 230
Maidenhead Cartographic Services: 223 (map)
Metropolitan Transportation Authority: 235
Mid-Continent Railway Historical Society, Inc: 272 (Bill Buhrmaster); 273 (Paul Swanson)
Milepost 92½: 221 (Colin Garratt); 299, 341, 358–359 (Gavin Morrison); 300–301; 355, 363 (Howard Ande)
National Aeronautics & Space Administration (NASA): 232
Robert T. Nordstrom II: 9 top, 245, 248–249, 343, 344–345, 365, 366–367, 370
North Carolina Collection Photographic Archives: 199 bottom
Photolibrary: 18 (Willard Clay); 64–65
Railroad Museum of Pennsylvania: 36
Dan Redlands: 161
Rochelle Railroad Park: 37 (Ross Frein)
Michael Rogers: 262
Jon Roma: 320
Ed Sanders: 158
Science & Society Picture Library: 39, 41
Smithsonian Institution Archives: 52
Stamford Historical Society: 274
Jon Stubley: 42
Ron Stuckey Collection of John Fuller: 70 top (George Witt)
Jon Sullivan: 178
L. Thomson: 338
www.trainweb.com: 296, 317, 319 bottom, 340 (Geno Dailey), 346, 349
Transit Toronto: 277